Memoirs of the Polish Baroque

The Writings of Jan Chryzostom Pasek,
A Squire of the Commonwealth of Poland and Lithuania

Published with the generous assistance of the
Alfred Jurzykowski Foundation

Memoirs of
The Polish Baroque

The Writings of
Jan Chryzostom Pasek,
A Squire of the Commonwealth
of Poland and Lithuania

Edited, translated, with an introduction and notes
by Catherine S. Leach

Foreword by Wiktor Weintraub

University of California Press
Berkeley • Los Angeles • London

The title in Polish is *Pamiętniki Jana Chryzostoma Paska*

University of California Press
Berkeley and Los Angeles, California

University of California Press, Ltd.
London, England

ISBN 0-520-02752-3
Library of Congress Catalog Card Number: 74-77731

To my parents and Lucille

Contents

APPENDIXES

Foreword

The Baroque was a rich period in Polish Literature. As yet, however, only two Polish Baroque writers have managed to catch the ear of the literary audience outside Poland. One of them was the Latin poet M. C. Sarbiewski, or Sarbievius, best known in England under his middle Christian name Casimir. His international fame evaporated when Latin ceased to be the language of educated Europeans, though Coleridge was a great admirer of his poetry.

The story of J. Ch. Pasek's *Memoirs* is different. They were not published in their entirety until 1836, and their appearance immediately became an event in Polish cultural life. No previously published work gave the public such an intimate insight into the mentality of the seventeenth-century Polish squiredom. Pasek's lively and often amusing stories delighted readers with their rich and racy colloquial language. So well did the *Memoirs* fit the Romantic idea of free narration — story-telling unhampered by literary conventions and careless of the niceties of a regular composition, writing in which one could feel the inflections of a living voice — that some people suspected the whole of being a clever literary forgery, another successful Romantic pastiche.

It was nothing of the sort. Pasek created this style partly out of his own artistic instinct, but mostly out of necessity. It was not that he lacked education, for he attended a Jesuit high school. But the training there, as in other Polish schools of the time, was to a large extent rhetorical. Mastery of the art of public speaking was more than the mark of an educated man; it was an attainment of considerable practical importance in that gentry democracy of his, with its frequent district dietines and constant courtroom feuding. Pasek, having mastered the tricks of that trade, was obviously and even naively proud of his mastery, and occasionally gave samples of his oratory. In small doses they are amusing and add a fine, period-piece flavor. In large doses they become hard to digest.

Rhetorical skills aside, Pasek's literary culture was meagre — fortunately so, one would like to say. When he had a story to tell — which was most of the time — he had no ready-made literary models to follow. He had to rely on his own *Lust zum fabulieren,* spinning out his tales as he used to tell them *viva voce,* in idiomatic Polish. In so doing, he produced an important landmark in the history of Polish prose. If Sienkiewicz managed dialogue so well in his historical trilogy, making it sound vivid, natural, and very much of the period (a feature hardly to be guessed at by readers of the heavy-handed and careless English translations of his novels), it is because he could follow in Pasek's footsteps. In our own time, we have a clear echo of Pasek's diction, part stylization and part parody, in Gombrowicz's *Transatlantic.*

This style poses a terrific challenge to any translator. Its seventeenth-century flavor should be conveyed accurately, but without suppressing Pasek's idiosyncrasies, his easy abandon and joyful spontaneity in the telling of a story. I suspect that the challenge has been met only once before in the French translation of 1922, by Paul Cazin. (There exist two German translations, one published shortly after the first Polish edition, the other fairly recently, but I am not in a position to judge their respective merits; certainly the fragments translated into Russian and Danish were presented for their interest as historical documents and not for their literary value.)

The present translation tries, like Cazin's, to do justice to the artistic value of the original. I had the opportunity of observing Ms. Leach grappling with multiple problems of the English rendering of the text, and I have learned to respect her work. Her success is to a large extent the result of her perseverance and meticulous attention to details, but in the end it is the product of her fine feeling for literary values and her ability to catch the nuances of the language. Thanks to this, her English version is not only an important historical document, skillfully annotated to present the reader with a clear view of the grandeur and decadence of the old gentry republic; it is also a highly readable and enjoyable literary work of no mean distinction.

Wiktor Weintraub

Preface

I would like to try to explain how I came to translate the *Memoirs.* My initial acquaintance with Pasek was made at the University of California, during a course of lectures on Polish culture, delivered in 1960 by Czesław Miłosz, the eminent Polish poet, essayist, and diplomat, who had just arrived in Berkeley from Paris to start a new career as Professor of Slavic Languages and Literatures. Miłosz transmitted to his students his own delighted enjoyment of Pasek's *Memoirs.* Later, in 1963, while living in Poland, I purchased Roman Pollak's new edition of the *Memoirs,* but the volume stood on the shelf until I was back in Berkeley completing my M.A. in "Slavic." At the time, the National Translation Center in Austin, Texas, was bestowing liberal fellowships on promising major translation projects, and Pasek won his share. Notice of my translation-in-progress appeared in *Delos,* No. 1, 1968. I had just completed the translation of Miłosz's autobiography, *Native Realm,* and had become intrigued by this literary genre, which is simultaneously both a search for form and a creation of order, a spiritual discipline and an elemental expression of the will-to-form to which men turn in times of change, times of chaos. Its inward, ego-centered focus is only needed when the outer structures of "the other" begin to crack and break up, when social, political, economic, and ideological values are called into question, when hierarchical structures are toppling. It is a form for which the men and women of our century feel a particular affinity, just as in the seventeenth century; in fact, so common is its appearance today that William Matthews (the author of several bibliographies of British, American, and Canadian autobiographies, and editor of the new unabridged multi-volume edition of Pepys' *Diaries*), speaking at a recent literary seminar in Berkeley, called the genre of autobiography a literary "vox populi." Our century, like the seventeenth — which in many respects can be regarded as the matrix of our own particular brand of civilization (mechanism-mercantilism- industrialism- centralism- ritualism) — has hurled souls through the violent turbulence of constant spatial, temporal, and spiritual changes. Perhaps, as with individuals, energy fields interact between centuries; memoirs, diaries, and autobiographies bridge the time-gap, create a community of sensibility, and enable us to react sympathetically to our predecessors undergoing similar stresses and struggles. To survive in an era of transformations, the individual is called upon to show resourcefulness, energy, initiative, and sometimes brutality. Pasek was such an individual, and his type flourishes on our continent and in our century.

For the initial, surface enjoyment of the *Memoirs*, I needed no rationale. I found its pages filled with whimsy, color, excitement, action, and humor.

Besides my personal motives, there were also literary and historical reasons for undertaking a translation. The reading public of the English-speaking world has made the acquaintance of novelist Henryk Sienkiewicz, but his authentic seventeenth-century inspiration, Pasek and his *Memoirs*, rings no bell. Because the Polish imagination has been and continues to be bewitched by Sienkiewicz's historical-adventure stories of seventeenth-century Poland — since their appearance in the 1880s every generation of school-children has devoured them as avidly as a Tarzan comic — the importance of understanding the source of the myth becomes obvious.

Another consideration: just as Old Russian literature has until recently been slighted by Western scholars, so much the more has the literature of Old Poland been ignored.

Then, too, in the West, there is a certain image of Poland, reinforced by Polish literature in translation, which is linked either to the pathos of tragedy stoically borne or to the absurd whimsy of metaphysical impossibility. Pasek and his *Memoirs*, by revealing the underside of these poses, can perhaps restore the balance.

Witold Gombrowicz (1904-1969), the eminent twentieth-century Polish writer, an exile in Argentina and then in France (where he died), having achieved no small recognition in Western Europe, once characterized Polish literature as "didactic, loyal, dutiful, anti-individual, and fearful." Pasek, at his best, escapes from this mold. In context, his art is just as outrageous as those Polish prose writers whom we admire today — Witkacy, Schultz, Gombrowicz.

Although they date from the end of the seventeenth century, Jan Chryzostom Pasek's entire *Memoirs* did not find their way into print until 1836. The 250 copies published by Count Edward Raczyński in Poznan proved to be not only an overcautious *tirage* but the literary event of the year. Appearing as they did at a time of great national distress, after the failed uprising of November 1830 and in the midst of the Romantic movement, Pasek's *Memoirs* sparked primal fires in the national temperament and offered some solace from the dismal present by resurrecting an authentic, colorful Old Poland from the twilight of incomplete knowledge as no contemporary work could have done. The figure of Pasek himself, the old yarn-spinning boaster, fulminating and gesticulating, came from an era of freedom which, even if somewhat tarnished, must have seemed truly "golden" to the sad and partitioned Poland of Chopin's time. The *Memoirs*, acclaimed with enthusiasm by writers both within Poland and in emigration, was called a poem, a romance, and Pasek became a national prototype. Soon, historical novelists, the most successful of whom was Sienkiewicz, were writing works based on the old veteran's vivid tales of peace and war in Old Poland, while poets like Adam Mickiewicz and Juliusz Słowacki, Poland's two great Romantic writers, were thoroughly captivated. Słowacki wrote a number of works, both verse and drama, under the direct inspiration of the *Memoirs;* and Mickiewicz (who in 1834 had himself written an idyllic novel in verse, *Pan Tadeusz*, about Old Poland) devoted two lectures of his Course on Slavic Literatures at the Collège de France in Paris to the *Memoirs*.

Just exactly when Jan Chryzostom Pasek decided to write down his *Memoirs* is a matter of conjecture. Most scholars believe he began writing them in 1691 after settling into the profitable estate of Ucieszkowa, given him by the king with a life-long lease after he had won his suit against the Margrave Myszkowski, which he was bringing to the king's attention in 1688, the year the *Memoirs* break off. That he began the writing toward the end of his life is supported by the many errors of date and time sequence, which were probably the distortions of memory and imagination. Pasek's consistent bending of events to flatter his own image, and that of his fellow cavaliers, no doubt arose after countless retellings, through which he was influenced by a desire to create an impression on his listeners, to raise himself in their eyes; direct effusions and didactic addresses to the reader suggest that he was recapturing and evaluating his most vivid memories. Even though the *Memoirs* are divided mechanically according to years, they can easily be rearranged more organically into chapters of anecdotes on given themes: the Danish expedition, the Siedlecki billeting, the Muscovite battles, the Grodno debates, the escorting of the Muscovite envoys, the Lithuanian adventures. But this is a structure grown from memory, not a faithful, day-to-day notation of events in sequence. Finally, the multitude of details testifies to the likelihood that Pasek told his anecdotes many times over during his lifetime; otherwise such details would have soon been forgotten.

Before the *Memoirs* were published in their entirety, two selections had appeared a decade earlier in journals.[1] After Raczyński's edition,

1. The first appeared in *Astrea* (1821) and was grouped along with fragments from several other sources under the title of "Extracts From Unprinted Old Manuscripts"; a second selection was published in *Pszczółka Krakowska* (1822) and con-

however, the *Memoirs* definitely stood out from other historical sources as a rare and artistically valuable specimen of seventeenth-century Polish prose. The more than thirty different editions which have seen the light of day since that time indicate that Pasek's significance has not declined. Perhaps only Sienkiewicz's historical trilogy of novels took some of the wind out of his sails by so successfully recreating the linguistic aura of the *Memoirs*, for Pasek's language above all secured him a lasting literary reputation among Polish readers.

Other European readers were not slow to recognize the extraordinary qualities of Pasek's story-telling. In 1838 the first German translation by G. A. Stenzel, based on Raczyński's edition, appeared in Breslau. Half a century later, the Danish historian S. Rożniecki published a partial version in Danish under the title *Polakkerne i Danmark* (Copenhagen, 1896) dealing with the Danish and Swedish campaigns. A partial Russian version had appeared in 1877 in *Russkaia Starina*. In our century, Paul Cazin's translation of the *Memoirs* into French was printed in Paris in 1923 as an abridged version with an excellent introduction. A new German translation by Gunther Wytrzens, also abbreviated, came out in 1967 under the title *Die Goldene Freiheit der Polen*.

At the time of the first edition, literary scholars tended to be critical to the point of disbelief. The *Memoirs* were taken by some historians of literature to be an artful nineteenth-century falsification. No doubt the notoriety of Macpherson's *Ossian* and the controversial Russian *Tale of Igor's Campaign* discovered in the late eighteenth century had made Polish academic circles wary of falling into a similar trap. Their skepticism is all the more understandable because the only manuscript of the *Memoirs* which has come to light is an eighteenth-century copy of the original. We have nothing in Pasek's own hand, which gives rise to several textual difficulties. But the problem of the authenticity of the *Memoirs* was happily solved in 1841 by a scholar who found a detail noted down in 1721 about an extraordinary otter that fished and tended cart and horse for her master, who was none other than Jan Chryzostom Pasek. Since then, other scholars have investigated and confirmed by their archival discoveries the historicity of *Pan* Pasek. Details concerning the later life of the diarist which do not figure at all in his *Memoirs* are especially interesting because they shed a new light on him. Far from being the pious, brave knight emphasized in the *Memoirs*, he can be seen as a squint-eyed bargainer, violent and querulous in his relationships with neighbors, and willing to stop at nothing, even murder itself, to maintain his advantage or revenge his

sisted of several anecdotes on social customs (the story of Pasek's three duels and of his revenge on his wife's relatives for insulting the Mazurians).

frustration. What also came to light were the number of mistakes, distortions, and exaggerations in the *Memoirs.*

Raczyński's edition was based on the manuscript — that is, on the early eighteenth-century copy that formed part of the Załuski collection, which was then housed in the Czarist Library in St. Petersburg (Polish Section IV, folio No. 104). It returned to Poland after the First World War and is now kept in the National Library (Plac Krasińskich) in Warsaw, No. 4501. To this date no public archive has yielded another copy. Until 1929, as a result of the inaccessibility of the manuscript, subsequent editors of the *Memoirs,* among whom Lachowicz and Węclewski should be singled out for conscientious work, had the handicap of not being able to use the manuscript copy; and Raczynski had edited the *Memoirs* in a somewhat cavalier fashion, Polonizing the Latin, correcting style and spelling, omitting verses and speeches. The one exception was Professor Gubrynowicz, who produced the first critical edition in Lwów (1898) based on the Petersburg manuscript. Professor A. Bruckner's 1924 edition which was based on Gubrynowicz's should be cited here for its Introduction, which argues that Pasek's *Memoirs* are an historical romance.

Not until 1929, however, did a definitive critical edition come forth which has been the basis for all subsequent modern editions. Jan Czubek, working from the eighteenth century copy, did the fundamental groundwork of establishing the text by reconstructing the portions distorted by copyists (the manuscript displays three different handwritings) or by material damage to the manuscript itself. For over a century it had been carelessly bound, the edges clumsily sliced so that all the marginal notes were halved. Czubek proceeded according to the principle that dialect forms probably corresponded to Pasek's own speech, whereas the odd spelling was most likely due to the copyist. The text that emerged was richer in folk forms than the "cleaned-up" version released by Count Raczyński. It was also Czubek who supplied the fullest information on Pasek's private life, from scrupulous research in the Kraków Government and Juridical Archives. Subsequent critical editions have compared the Brückner and Czubek editions with the best modern editions, which are Władysław Czapliński's (1952 and 1968) and Roman Pollak's (1963). Always, in cases of doubt, recourse was had to the manuscript copy. Pollak, who followed in Brückner's footsteps, supplied his edition with a valuable literary-historical Introduction, while Czapliński, a specialist in seventeenth- century history, polemicized with Pollak and in part submitted a new view, while adding many new notes to verify more of the historical, geographical, and biographical contents of the *Memoirs.* As Roznlecki had done before him, Czapliński carried out research in Denmark. He was able to confirm the veracity of practically all of the details in Pasek's account relating to his Danish sojourn. Not so accurate is the image Pasek presents of the Polish army as a model occupation force. Czapliński's 1952 edition brought an increase of scholarly interest in Pasek — to name a few names; J. Rytel, A. Sajkowski, and M. Kaczmarek. I myself am particularly indebted to the theories of Roman Pollak, Władysław Czapliński, and Jadwiga Rytel.

In general, historians and literary historians have not agreed on where the emphasis should be placed when evaluating Pasek's *Memoirs.* There are those scholars, usually literary-historians ironically, who deny significant historical value to the *Memoirs,* pointing out the flagrant distortion of the author's self-portrayal, the mistakes in dating battles or important events (even his own father's death is two years off), and other obvious lapses of memory. Historians, on the other hand, tend to be more respectful of the *Memoirs* as a source, accepting them in the main, but allowing for the author's obvious bias toward inflating the image of himself and the Polish soldier by emphasizing certain events and ignoring others of equal objective significance. For example, in 1657 Pasek lays stress on the bad end to which the Prince of Transylvania came, but says nothing of Rákóczi's devastation of Polish territory; he exaggerates the successes of Polish forces in Denmark, whereas Danish and German sources give a different picture. Yet Pasek never completely *invents* anything. (For example, the boy-bear who hurled a slobbery pear peel at Queen Ludwika Maria cropped up in a French nobleman's diary; and even the wounding of the French actors in the *theatrum* incident in 1664 has been verified.) He does exaggerate for effect (as in the joke about Rakóczi's craving for Polish garlic). On the other hand, the myriad details from all areas of Old Polish life are proving, one by one, entirely credible. They make the *Memoirs* an invaluable source of knowledge about daily life, army and civilian, in Old Poland; such a detailed picture of seventeenth-century culture in its everydayness is seldom met with in continental European autobiographical literature of the time. As for the accuracy of Pasek's accounts of events, Czapliński has compared them in detail and in outline with other Polish diarists' accounts of the same event and found Pasek's to be both more concise and more accurate. Finally, such respected Polish historians as L. Kubala, T. Korzon, W. Czermak, W. Majewski, and A. Kersten have quoted extensively, if selectively, from Pasek. But the minute episodes of day-to-day life so sharply observed and vividly expressed, with the same force and rapidity as they unfolded both within the diarist's actual experience and within the larger and tragic flow of history, constantly sensed in the *Memoirs* as an ominous background, also constitute an artistic accomplishment worthy of remembrance.

The present translation is based mainly on Władyslaw Czapłinski's scholarly edition of 1968 published in the distinguished "Biblioteka Narodowa" series of the Ossolinski National Publishing House. Czapliński based his revised edition on the Brückner (1928), Czubek (1929), and Pollak (1963) editions, resorting in cases of uncertainty to the manuscript itself. I myself consulted both Czubek and Pollak and frequently made use of their annotation. I also referred to the French and German versions (Cazin and Wytrzens).

I have made every effort to maintain a high standard of accuracy, steadfastly pursuing the *mot juste,* researching exhaustively (and exhaustingly!) in the two-volume dictionary (ed. H. Koneczna) devoted exclusively to Pasek, in classic and standard dictionaries of Old and Modern Polish (S. Linde, J. Karłowicz, W. Doroszewski), in encyclopedias dealing with Old Poland (Z. Gloger, A. Brückner), and in historical works on seventeenth-century Poland and Europe.

To render Pasek's seventeenth-century language, both colloquial and rhetorical, I have chosen to create a style that carries overtones of archaic speech structures yet on the whole retains a modern lexicon. It was not easy. Adam Mickiewicz, lecturing at the Collège de France in 1841 suggests why: "His style is classical. It has the freedom, grace, and lightness of French diaries, but it is wholly Slavic. . . He writes effortlessly, as if he were speaking; one cannot convey his style in French; it would be difficult to imitate him in Polish." Perhaps unruly English lends itself better to the task than French, which has been so carefully tended by the Academy. In any case, I sought to get as close as I could to a colloquial seventeenth-century English by immersing myself in many varied accounts, speeches, letters, sermons, and diaries of the epoch. To name but a few: Thomas Raymond, Sydnam Poyntz, Thomas Deloney, William Kemp, Samuel Pepys, Blaise de Monluc in seventeenth-century English translation, Thomas Dekker, John Donne, and many other more obscure works gleaned from the invaluable Camden Society series. Doubtless, too, my inner ear was listening to the lively cadences of my own Irish ancestors.

In creating a style, I kept in mind certain characteristics of the Baroque which also apply to Pasek. Baroque prose has been aptly described as inclining "toward the loose, the assymetrical, the disjointed, scoffing at strictions against dangling participles, shifts in points of view, even tense. But how much like the natural currents, eddies, confluences of animated talk! How true to the vivid, dramatic rhythms of talented narrators!"[2] Also integral to the Baroque style, and no less to the *Memoirs* is a good sprinkling of Latin, whether of isolated words, whole sentences, or quotations from Latin authors. For

2. Morris Croll, *Style, Rhetoric and Rhythm* (Princeton, 1966) p. 207-233.

Poles, the use of Latin was a sign of belonging to a ruling, cultured class. Only the nobility, as a rule, were schooled in Latin. I have, therefore, retained much of Pasek's Latin incrustations. Wherever the Latin might not be easily deciphered by a reader of average education, I have provided translations in footnotes. Where the Latin is not only difficult but carries no particular stylistic distinction, or where the passage seems too long to quote (such as the letter from Pasek's Danish lady-love), I have translated it in the text itself. Contemporary foreign speech or phrases have likewise been allowed to stand, it being typical for soldiers in that epoch to acquire a smattering of many languages from their contacts with foreign prisoners of war, mercenaries, or allies.

There are two sorts of omissions; both have been indicated in the text by bracketed notes. The first are "textual"; they correspond to the missing parts in the manuscript copy itself. The first fifty pages of the manuscript, as well as a few pages from the middle, are missing; there are also several blank pages. The *Memoirs* break off in 1688 in the middle of a sentence, leaving one-fourth of the page and the entire next page blank.

The second sort are "translator's" omissions, that is, those made by myself. Because Pasek's rhetorical effusions often weigh on the narrative like a rhinoceros, I have omitted very long and bulbous speeches, panegyrics, and invective if they offer nothing new in the way of information. Passages which are considered to have come from a hand other than Pasek's have also been left out. Nor have I translated Pasek's atrocious longer verses, notably the apostrophe to his horse with which the *Memoirs* begin. Shorter poems have been admitted because they do not hinder the narrative flow and even lend a pleasing variety. A long document of the Łęgonicki Treaty with the General Amnesty in 1666 has been omitted because Pasek had nothing to do with it and it entered the constitutions (*Volumina Legum*) of the Diet in a different form.

Occasional bracketed insertions have been made either to complete a name, supply a title, a date, or an explanatory note. Czubek's scholarly reconstructions have been translated without mention. Where the original runs for several pages without paragraphing, the present text has been paragraphed out of consideration for the reader.

Unless otherwise specified, the notes to this translation are Czapliński's and the translator's. Other bits of scholarly apparatus useful for a close reading of the *Memoirs* appear at the back of the book in order not to distract the reader from perceiving the artistic wholeness of the work or enjoying the excitement of the swift narrative.

Both endpapers carry specially designed maps to serve the reader as additional reference tools. The front endsheet bears a map of the physical area over which the action in the *Memoirs* ranges — from Denmark in the West to Muscovy in the east and from the shores of the Baltic Sea to the mouth of the Danube on the Black Sea. Included on this map are the countries, regions, rivers, seas, major towns, battle-sites, and fortresses that figure in the *Memoirs*. Modern political boundaries have been imposed upon this area for the sake of comparison. The map on the back endsheet represents the cumulative boundary changes of the Commonwealth of Poland and Lithuania from 1648 to 1686, the extent of the Cossack revolt (1648-1654), of Muscovite military activity (1654-1656), Sweden's boundaries after 1660, and many of the provincial localities mentioned in the later years of the *Memoirs*. In addition, two full-page maps in the text show Pasek's probable routes in both west and east.

At the end of the book are two appendixes containing additional material on the political and military history of the period covered by the *Memoirs*, a Glossary of Old Polish State and Provincial Offices. and a simplified Key to Polish Pronunciation for those unfamiliar with Slavic sounds or with their written representation.

All Polish personal and place names appear in Polish spelling unless there are widely used English equivalents. (In the Index of Proper Names English equivalents appear in parentheses.) Names or words in Western European languages have been left in the form Pasek or the copyist gave them, except for German, Danish, and Swedish place names for which there are common English equivalents. Russian personal and place names have been transliterated according to J. T. Shaw's System I; transliterations of Russian words as words, or of citations of bibliographical material follow System II, that is, the Library of Congress system without diacritical marks.

The Polish forms of address equivalent to "Sir" and "Madam" have been retained: *Pan* is used to address a gentleman, *Pani* a lady, and *Panna* a young unmarried lady.

C.S.L.

Acknowledgments

It is a special pleasure to thank those scholars in the Slavic field who, from the beginning, warmly supported me in this work and generously gave advice; in particular, I owe a great debt of gratitude to Wiktor Weintraub of Harvard University for his close reading and commenting upon the entire typescript — no small undertaking! Czesław Miłosz of the University of California at Berkeley also read most of the typescript and made a number of excellent suggestions for presenting certain extraordinarily complicated historical matters in the Introduction. Janusz Tazbir of the Institute of History of the Academy of Sciences in Warsaw gave wise counsel on scholarly procedure and research, a thorough reading to the notes, and was kind enough to share in conversation with me his great knowledge of and enthusiasm for the seventeenth-century Commonwealth of Poland and Lithuania. I appreciate the positive response and helpful remarks, both in conversations and correspondence, from David Welsh and John Mersereau of the University of Michigan, and from Jan Kott and Aleksander Gella of the State University of New York at Stony Brook, from Harry Willetts of St. Antony's and John Stoye of Magdalen College in Oxford and Norman Davies of the University of London's School of Slavonic Studies.

I would like to express my thanks to Andrzej Kamiński of the Institute on East Central Europe at Columbia University for reading the introductory material and sharing his expertise in this area of seventeenth-century Europe. His incisive comments led me to reconsider and clarify several passages in the Introduction.

Three institutions deserve mention for making the entire project possible: the Jurzykowski Foundation (New York) whose grant to the University of California Press to publish this translation is especially appreciated; the former National Translation Center at the University of Texas, Austin, which awarded me a translation fellowship in 1968; and the Institute of Literary Research (IBL) of the Academy of Sciences in Warsaw, which graciously covered the costs of reproducing the seventeenth-century etchings and drawings from Polish archives in Warsaw and Kraków for use as illustrations.

For their energetic assistance I am much obliged to the librarians and archivists at the University of Warsaw (Gabinet rycin), the Historical Museum of the City of Warsaw, the National Museum in Warsaw, and the Czartoryski Museum in Kraków.

I am indebted to Helen and John Sherman of the University of Washington in Seattle for the skillful cartography and to John Consiglio of Vancouver, B.C., who prepared the working maps to my exact specifications.

Hearty thanks are due to Maryse Ellis of Vancouver, whose typing wizardry not only overcame Polish hooks and slashes but created a distinctive manuscript page.

To Grant Barnes, Gene Tanke, and Sheila Levine of the University of California Press I present a Paskovian combat medal.

I cannot fail to acknowledge the incalculable debt to friends and "kin" in Poland who have steadfastly encouraged my work and made Polish culture a living reality to me.

Nor can I neglect to thank those of my friends in Canada who provided a conducive environment for this long and painstaking project and whose comments, reactions, suggestions have left their mark, for example, George Knox and George Rosenberg of the University of British Columbia's Fine Arts Department, who enlightened me on many of the fascinating controversies surrounding Rembrandt's *Polish Rider*.

Acknowledgment is made to the *Polish Review* for permission to reprint the fragment from the Year 1680 (the otter anecdote), which appeared in the Autumn 1971 issue; to Yale University Press for permission to use material from *Beginning Polish* by Alexander Schenker; to the Frick Museum for permission to reproduce Rembrandt's *Polish Rider;* to the Boston Museum of Fine Arts for permission to reproduce Ter Borch's *Cavalier in the Saddle;* to the University of Warsaw Library, the Museum of the City of Warsaw, the Czartoryski Museum in Krakow for permission to reproduce in this edition the seventeenth-century engravings, paintings, and drawings from their collections.

C.S.L.

Introduction

Liberty is a food that is
good to taste but hard to digest:
it sets well only on a
good strong stomach.
J. J. Rousseau

Because the *Memoirs* of Jan Chryzostom Pasek come to the English-speaking reader across vast distances of time and spirit, I have intended this introductory material to suggest not only an interpretation but also to serve as a modest briefing, drawing on the latest, as well as earlier, Polish research, for the reader's own journey back toward the time, the place, and the consciousness out of which the work grew. Pasek's autobiography is enjoyable on its own as a tale of adventure and useful as an historical source, and should anyone wish to travel first and read the map later, let him or her set to immediately; but for the reader who would prefer not to let the shape and sense of the *Memoirs* remain locked within the texture of history, I shall try here to capture some of its volatile substance, to describe the political, economic, social, and literary seedbed from which the historical person of the author, together with his literary image, emerged in the *Memoirs*.

The briefing will consist of two parts. The first will include general remarks about the land, the peoples, and the languages of the Commonwealth of Poland and Lithuania; then a sketch of the origins, formation, and structure of that amazing state; and, finally, an outline of the specific political, economic, social, military, and cultural features that distinguished the Commonwealth during Pasek's lifetime. The task of setting down in compressed form any satisfactory exposition of so complex, so diversified, and so unfamiliar an entity as the Commonwealth of Poland and Lithuania is a troublesome one, and the information presented here must necessarily leave many questions unanswered. In partial mitigation of this, a more detailed discussion of the army is offered in Appendix IV, and Appendix III provides an analysis of the important events of the period covered by the *Memoirs* in the light of the Commonwealth's international and domestic situation.

In the second part of the briefing, I shall introduce the literary side of the *Memoirs* by indicating the layers of fact and fiction in Pasek's self-portrait, situating the *Memoirs* in the context of Old Polish literature, and analyzing the structure of the work.

I.

Land, Peoples, Languages. Before 1648 the Commonwealth of Poland and Lithuania was the largest state in Europe after Muscovy. It occupied an area of about one million square kilometers, or nearly as much as present-day France and Spain combined. It stretched from the Baltic Sea in the north to the borders of the Ottoman Empire in the south, almost to the Black Sea; from the basin of the Warta and Noteć rivers in the west, it extended as far as the westerly tributaries of the Volga in the east.

In Pasek's time, the territory of Poland, called The Crown (Corona), consisted of the regions of Wielkopolska (Great Poland) and Małopolska (Little Poland); the Grand Duchy of Lithuania included, besides its ten provinces, Courland and Livonia.[1] Ducal Prussia, a Hohenzollern fief under Polish suzerainty, was released in 1657 to the Brandenburg Elector.

Before the calamitous wars of the mid-seventeenth century, population of the Commonwealth numbered about ten million. That figure, according to a cautious estimate, dropped to about seven million as a result of wars, raids, uprisings, pestilences, etc. during the second half of the century. The inhabitants of The Crown were predominantly Catholic; a fair number of the gentry had converted to Protestantism during the Reformation, but by the middle of the seventeenth century most had returned to Catholicism. As far back as the fourteenth century, Poles from The Crown had begun to migrate to the underpopulated areas of the Ukraine; the gentry kept up their Catholicism there, but the peasants quickly adopted the local rite of Orthodoxy. Many of the nobility of the Grand Duchy — the Lithuanians in the north (Samogitia and Aukštote) and the Orthodox Byelorussians in the Ukraine—had embraced Calvinism. But both groups were now being won over to the Catholic church. The not-so-long since pagan Lithuanian peasantry were mainly Catholics, and that interesting ecumenical venture the Uniate Church fought with Orthodoxy over the souls of the peasantry to the south. Even further south, the Cossacks, a fiercely independent military brotherhood, some of them runaway serfs and urban poor, had colonized the territory adjacent to the Tartar lands on the Dnieper River, popularly known as the Wild Plains. A sprinkling of Moslem Tartars had remained in Lithuania from the time of Grand

1. Wielkopolska contained twelve provinces: Poznań, Kalisz, Sieradź, Łęczyca, Brześć-Kujawski, Inowrocław, Płock, Rawa, Mazowsze, Chełmno, Malbork, Pomorze. Małopolska contained 11 provinces: Kraków, Sandomierz, Lublin, Bełz, Ruthenia, Podolia, Podlasie, Volhynia, Kiev, Bracław, and Czernichów (the last ceded to Russia in 1667). The ten provinces of the Grand Duchy were Wilno, Troki, Samogitia, Nowogródek, Brześć-Litewski, Mińsk, Smoleńsk (ceded to Russia in 1667), Połock, Witebsk, and Mścisław.

Duke Witold's struggle for domination of Eastern Europe in the fourteenth century; Lutheran Germans had settled in the west, mainly in Prussia and especially in the larger Baltic towns; Christian Armenians took up residence in the province of Ruthenia, primarily in Lwów and other urban centers. Jewish communities were scattered across the Commonwealth in larger and smaller towns and villages. Making up about five percent of the total population, the Jews were guaranteed personal freedom and trading rights by royal privilege and they maintained strictly separate, self-governing communities. Except for commercial activities, they kept to their own world and, on the whole, discouraged contact with the Christians around them. Nor did the Christian Poles see fit to integrate them; in larger towns, the Jewish community was usually assigned to certain streets, and Jews were unable to hold municipal offices. The Cossack Wars of 1648 cruelly decimated their numbers in the east, and in general the economic fate of the Jews, who were often blamed for the monetary crisis in the seventeenth century, paralleled that of the towns. Jewish rabbis of the period, however, were renowned for their piety and expert knowledge of the Talmud. The Armenians, like the Jews, resided in the Commonwealth as a legally autonomous group. Like the Jews, they were merchants and traders; but being Christians, they were allowed to mix with the town population as well as hold posts in municipal government. With time, they became thoroughly Polonized.

The Commonwealth was not only multicultural and multidenominational, but also multilingual. Since the linguistic tangle in these regions has yet to be straightened out, suffice it to say that Polish was the official language of The Crown as well as the language of culture, that is, of the ruling class; therefore, anyone with political and social ambitions quickly mastered it. But the legal documents of various groups of the population were written in five other languages: Byelorussian, Latin, German, Armenian, and Hebrew. Byelorussian was the official language of the Grand Duchy but it was understood by those who lived in The Crown. (Lithuanian was regarded as a language of the peasantry.) Towns were under German law and many of their inhabitants, especially in the Baltic towns, spoke German in everyday life. German was also associated with Lutheran Protestantism. Calvinists used mainly Polish and Latin. But for the majority of gentry, Latin, formerly the sole language of diplomacy, was still the language of erudition, of church, school, and some administrative offices. To speak and write it was the mark of a nobleman, although the wealthier townsmen were sometimes proficient in it. Its use among gentrymen, cultivated by the Jesuits, was meant to demonstrate their tie to the cultural tradition of Rome, their fidelity to the Catholic Church, and their superior social role. Armenians and Jews governed their autonomous communities in their own languages. The Armenians, however, were rapidly assimilated and began to use either Polish or Byelorussian exclusively. The Jews learned enough Polish or Byelorussian to conduct everyday business, but among themselves they spoke only Yiddish or Hebrew.

Other foreign languages were valued for their utility in diplomacy by the magnates of the Commonwealth, who maintained their own private legations in foreign countries. Veterans of the army's far-flung campaigns usually picked up a smattering of foreign speech in their dealings with local populations, prisoners of war, mercenaries, or allied armies. Hungary, for example, was much in vogue in the seventeenth century and Hungarians were often employed at magnate courts, either as attendants or as servants called Haiduks. (Poles often filled the same role dressing in Hungarian clothes.)

Origins, Formation, and Structure of Government. Two centuries ago, Rousseau mused: "As one reads the history of the government of Poland, it is hard to understand how a state so oddly constituted can have survived for so long. I see a body of great size: many of its members are already dead, and the remainder have no unity, so that their motions, well-nigh independent of each other, far from serving any common end, cancel one another out. It labors mightily without accomplishing anything; it is unable to offer the slightest resistance to anyone who seeks to impose his will upon it; it falls apart five or six times in each century; it is paralyzed the moment it tries to put forth any effort or to provide for one of its needs; and, despite all these things, it nevertheless lives and keeps itself strong."[2]

Poland and the Grand Duchy of Lithuania first joined hands in common cause against the Teutonic Knights who, having aggressively proselytized and colonized Prussia, were encroaching upon the Grand Duchy. In 1386 the two countries were connected by the marriage of the Lithuanian Grand Duke Jagiełło and the Polish Queen Jadwiga. In the sixteenth century, the threat of the expanding Muscovite state brought the two countries even closer together. The Union of Lublin (1569) made of the two countries a single political power under one sovereign elected jointly, one Diet, one monetary system, and one foreign policy. The Polish king acquired the additional title of Grand Duke of Lithuania, while Lithuania established central and administrative institutions very similar to The Crown's, that is, the two countries retained separate but similar treasuries, state offices, judicial systems, armies, and administrations.

2. From *The Government of Poland* by Jean-Jacques Rousseau; translated, with an introduction and notes, by Willmoore Kendall (Indianapolis and New York, Bobbs-Merrill, 1972), p. 2.

In 1596 the Union of Brześć, promoted by the Jesuits in an attempt to cut off the Orthodox Church in the Commonwealth from the sometimes pro-Turkish Constantinople patriarchy and from the newly established Muscovite patriarchy, brought the Grand Duchy's followers of Eastern Orthodoxy within the fold of the Roman Catholic Church. Only partially successful, the Union was accomplished by a policy of mutual concessions on the part of both Orthodox and Catholic hierarchies. The Orthodox side, in return for being able to retain its political influence and privileges, agreed to obey the Pope in Rome, while the Catholics allowed the Uniate Church, as it was now called, to retain its Eastern Slavic rite and liturgy, and permitted Uniate priests to marry. The majority of the Orthodox faithful, however, were opposed to the Union and with time the opposition grew sharper since the line between Catholic and Uniate was also a class line. The Byelorussian gentry tended to abandon their Orthodoxy in favor of either Catholicism or Protestantism, while the peasantry remained attached to Orthodoxy. Even though the Union had been designed to forestall attempts to foment political disunity in a religious context, stiff resistance in the countryside made its implementation problematical.

The government of the Commonwealth, known to its citizens as the *Respublica,* (or, as it was called in the constitution, the *Reipublica*) was the only large-size state in seventeenth-century Europe that could boast of an elected monarch. The king of Poland, who was also the Grand Duke of Lithuania, shared the legislative power with a two-chamber Diet.

The Polish parliamentary tradition had its beginnings in the thirteenth-and fourteenth-century district assemblies which were convoked by ecclesiastical and secular lords and which included the gentry. In the fifteenth century, the regional and provincial representatives of the gentry began to take an increasingly important part in the yearly sessions of the Royal Council. The sixteenth century saw the gentry establish their political ascendancy in a second house, called the Chamber of Deputies, which came to dominate the legislative process.

The Diet that Pasek knew was made up of the same two houses. The first was the Senate, deriving from the former Royal Council and appointed by the king, which consisted of all the bishops who were heads of a diocese and certain state dignitaries.[3] The second was the Chamber of Deputies, consisting of representatives of the gentry elected at local dietines. By the time Pasek was old enough to attend a Diet, there were about 150 senators and 170 deputies (48 of which were

3. The most important state offices are listed and briefly described in the Glossary of State and Provincial Offices.

Lithuanian). Gdańsk sent representatives to the Senate, and Kraków and Wilno sent representatives to the Chamber of Deputies, but townsmen and peasants had no vote in the Diet. The towns, having their own laws which afforded them protection from the central authority, preferred to ignore the Diet and to retain their autonomy rather than risk having to acknowledge gentry precedence and thus lose the benefit of their own corporate laws.

Before a Diet, the king convoked the local dietines whose responsibility it was to choose deputies, hear the business of the royal emissaries, and draw up a list of written "instructions" (like those Pasek helped to draw up in the year 1667). It was customary for senators to give speeches at the beginning of the Diet; the two chambers then separated to debate the legislation proposed by the king, exchanging delegates until the final session, which was held jointly. The debates were carried out without any rules of order except what the good sense and intelligence of the presiding Marshal decided. The outcome was the result of responsible compromise between majority and minority desires, and according to ancient custom it was acclaimed unanimously. As long as the gentry maintained ascendancy they legislated in their own interest, often to the detriment of other estates. The king, without the consent of both houses, could neither pass legislation nor carry out ennoblements. Royal power was further offset by the right of wealthy lords to maintain sizable private armies and private diplomatic legations. The gentry's success in winning for themselves political privileges that no other nobility in Europe possessed was due in part to the dual nature of the Commonwealth, since the nobility, having once struck a profitable bargain with Grand Duke Jagiełło of Lithuania, came to realize that the kingship was a lever for extracting privileges from candidates — at least if they were foreign, and especially if they were without the support of Lithuania.

This warrants an explanation. After the last of the Jagiellonian dynasty died in 1572, the practice began of electing a king by the entire gentry rank and file. The gentrymen, in electing Henri of Valois over Hapsburg and Russian candidates, understandably sought to safeguard their liberties from the Frenchman's autocratic aspirations by setting a price to the throne. The price Henri paid for his throne had far-reaching implications for the future of the Commonwealth. In signing the so-called Henrician Articles and the Pacta Conventa (by which he agreed to equip a certain number of troops at his own expense and replenish the treasury), Henri de Valois agreed in effect to gentry control of royal activity through the Diet, for he could raise neither money nor troops nor conduct an effective foreign policy without the ratification of the Diet. Afterwards a special Election Diet prepared for each new king a *pacta conventa* of essentially the same terms as the original. These privileges, added to those won earlier by the gentry from the Jagiellonian monarchs — namely, personal immunity from imprisonment before being sentenced, freedom of religion, and jurisdiction over its own class as well as over the peasants — formed the core of what the gentry called their "golden freedom."

What is more, if the king failed to carry out any of the conditions of the *pacta conventa,* the gentry were released from their oath of allegiance. For example, should the king die, or otherwise be unable or unwilling to perform his obligations, special dietines called "hooded dietines" were assembled by the Primate of the Polish Catholic Church (acting as regent) to organize a "confederacy" for the purpose of keeping the peace in the provinces and districts and of insuring the defense of the country from invasion.

A confederacy was organized like the Deputies' Chamber of the Diet; at the head stood a Marshal and his Deputy; representatives were chosen by the gentry. Unlike the diet, however, resolutions were passed by majority vote.

Confederacies were also formed to achieve a definite political aim. Sometimes they were directed against the king, sometimes they were organized by the king himself. During the Swedish invasion, part of the army capitulated. King Jan Kazimierz escaped to to Silesia, issuing a summons to resist. A confederacy was formed to repel the invader. Pasek describes with sadness the period of Lubomirski's confederacy, which brought tragic losses the country could ill afford. The union formed by the army in 1661 to demand back wages, and described in some detail in the *Memoirs,* was not a real confederacy. Although it was very similar to one and was often called by that name, it had neither the force nor the legal position of a true confederacy. Confederacies against the king won or lost depending on who possessed the greatest strength. Although part of the legal framework of the state, confederacies were a kind of desperado formation based on force rather than persuasion. They tested a government's support and could bring about civil war. At best they were a safety valve and a check on royal power.

Yet the gentry-elected kings were not puppets, since the basis of government was a social contract. On the contrary, most kings entertained ambitious plans of expansion to the east, and in the case of the Vasa dynasty consistently hoped for the Swedish throne as well. The king was supreme commander of the armed forces and only the king was able to make alliances. (However, in wartime the two grand hetmans, commanders of the Polish and Lithuanian armies, could treat directly with the enemy.) For winning adherents to his projects, the king had the power to confer offices, choose the members of the Senate, and bestow, lease, or sell crown properties. He also had the power (and always made use of it) to name bishops. Also within royal purview were matters related to the government of towns, the internal affairs of Jewish communities, as well as peasants and commoners residing on crown property. But no king who sought merely to strengthen his own authority could ever be popular with the gentry.

The political organism of the Commonwealth being primarily the product of over two and a half centuries of an evolving triangular relationship between king, magnates, and gentry, the state offices of the Commonwealth never developed into a centrally controlled administrative apparatus.[4] The whole concept of a centralized administration was alien to the citizens of the Commonwealth, for it went hand in hand with the abhorrent notion of an absolute ruler. The offices themselves retained their centuries-old medieval character; they were held for life unless the holder was found guilty under law.

Provincial officials were nominated for candidacy at special election dietines called by the governor *(wojewoda)* of a province and the king appointed the officials from among those candidates. Since local offices also carried life tenure, election dietines convened rarely. Access to higher offices was only for the wealthy; even to aspire to a castellanship one had to increase one's holdings considerably (which, as Pasek reminds us, was not easy). Most provincial offices were purely honorary. Specific functions were performed by the chamberlain and his deputy (judging property and boundary disputes), by the judges, deputy judges, recorders, and notaries in the provincial courts, and by the standard-bearer (in a general levy). The rest were honorary: cupbearer, master of the table, and so on.

The decline of the office of district supervisor *(starosta)* illustrates how diminished had become the power of the central authority. By the seventeenth century, the title of district supervisor had acquired the character of a provincial office, ranking just below chamberlain. In former days it had been an important state office combining a political with an economic function. In the Middle Ages, the district supervisor, as lord of a district castle *(gród)*, exercised judicial and police powers as the sole representative of the king in the provinces. He also administered crown estates, part of whose revenue (one-fifth) went to pay a permanent army employed to guard the borderlands. As the king's power waned, the district supervisor's judicial functions were superseded by the gentry-controlled Crown Tribunal and the Lithuanian Tribunal. However, the king still continued to confer the title as a reward for public service, when leasing, selling, or bestowing certain

4. See the Glossary of State and Provincial Offices.

crown properties. Only the district supervisor of Samogitia (in the Grand Duchy) remained a high office and gave its holder a seat in the senate. The office, however, did afford the quickest way to making a fortune.

The Commonwealth had no uniform codex of laws. Law consisted of the various resolutions of the Diets, the old Lithuanian Statutes, and custom. The so-called Crown Tribunal, established in 1578 as a gentry court of appeal, was composed of deputies elected annually at the local dietines. Because its verdicts were final, it pre-empted the royal judicial powers, giving the gentry control over their own estate. During an interregnum, the special hooded dietines, mentioned above, dispensed justice in extraordinary tribunals. Pasek notes their activity under the year 1668, the year Jan Kazimierz abdicated the throne.

Most gentry cases were judged in the first instance at the Castle Courts *(sądy grodzkie)* located in the castle towns (*miasta grodowe*) which had grown up at the site of the ancient royal strongholds, where traditionally the district supervisor (and lord of the district castle or *gród)* had acted as judge in gentry disputes and as custodian and defender of their legal records. Still connected to the gentry courts was the notarial chancery (known as the *sacrosanctum depositum)* where all the gentry's records were stored, from baptismal certificates to wills to resolutions of the local dietines. In charge of these archives were two officials, the notary and vice-notary.

Cases involving religious matters and cases between clerics were subject to canon law and dealt with in separate ecclesiastical tribunals. Towns, mostly under German law, had their own courts and their own statutes, as did Jewish and Armenian communities, although the king acted as the court of last resort. The peasants were judged by their masters.

The Commonwealth During Pasek's Lifetime. The Commonwealth of Pasek's day was still a government by and for landowners of noble birth. Land constituted the chief source of wealth; a coat-of-arms conferred the right to influence the destiny of the country. Among the privileged citizens of the *Respublica,* whoever controlled the land controlled the power, which meant that about 8 to 10 percent of the population ruled and enjoyed full political privileges. (In Pasek's native Mazovia, the gentry was somewhat more numerous.) As for social mobility, it was almost nonexistent, since townsmen, with some exceptions, could not under law acquire estate property. Here, an important factor in the position of women in Poland should be mentioned; namely, that the law of primogeniture never found its way into the constitution of the Commonwealth and women could inherit property. Marriage, therefore, to a certain limited degree, was a means of social advancement. Certainly, the landless Pasek benefited from his marital connection to the prosperous widow Łącka.

The basic distinction between the two Europes in the seventeenth century was exactly this: Western Europe had ceased to find its main resource in land. Absolute monarchs like Louis XIV in France had discovered the immense potency of money; they had allied themselves not with landowners but with the bourgeoisie, who had acquired enormous wealth in the course of large-scale explorations, trade, and finance during the previous two centuries.

Politically and ideologically (that is, in the realm of religious policy), many powerful states of seventeenth-century Western Europe had moved backward, in the sense of moving away from — instead of toward — ideals of individual human dignity and freedom as expressed in more broadly based structures of power. That regression to absolutism and Counter-Reformation was one of the factors which made it impossible for the Commonwealth to move forward economically or to avoid political petrification. The Union of Lublin in 1569 had signified a remarkable fact: that a government of responsible citizens was willing to extend its privileges to another group — equals by birth, to be sure, but alien in language, customs, and beliefs. Immense and sophisticated possibilities opened up for the Commonwealth as a multi-cultural, multi-denominational entity. Its natural line of development would have been a further extension of the privileges of its ruling class to more and more of the population, thence to a truly participatory system of government. But the Commonwealth did not fulfill the promise. It disintegrated from within, unable or unwilling to respond effectively to the processes of change that were transforming the structure of Western Europe.

No doubt the leisurely pace and comfort of a prosperous rural life were difficult to forego. The riches of both earth and forest could buy for the owners of country manors enough articles of luxury and convenience manufactured in the West or sold in the Far East to satisfy the craving for novelty and comfort. The century past had seen huge profits reaped in the Commonwealth from a rising demand in the West for raw materials and agricultural products. High demand was accompanied by soaring prices caused by the devaluation of gold and silver following the influx of precious metals from the New World.

Already then, certain of Western Europe's populations had begun the shift toward urban centers to engage in manufacturing, trade, and finance, and by the seventeenth century certain of its states such as England, France, the United Provinces, some Italian city-states, were being restructured by new technologies in the military and industrial sector and by absolute monarchies in the political sphere. The weakening of the feudal nobility who had ceased to profit from land cultivation signaled the rise of a moneyed middle estate willing to serve the throne in return for wealth and position. Although such ventures as joint stock companies for trading overseas marked the beginnings of capitalism, the control of economic activity was centralized; royal, nationwide governments took over the regulation of trade and commerce from local city governments and Western European monarchs were able to establish absolute rule with the moral and financial support of the commercial and capitalist classes.

In contrast to the burgeoning of new social and economic forms, in Western Europe, the Commonwealth plunged backward into a feudal type of economy which kept political and social forms static through the turbulence of wars and deep political unrest. Conservative economics went together with an indifference to technological progress, an attitude communicated by Jesuit educators during the Counter-Reformation; coupled with the gentry's preference for old manners and ways, it led to a rejection of the new scientific spirit.

And yet political anarchy together with the Polish traditions of freedom and tolerance saved the Commonwealth from such wild excesses of militant religious zeal as had occurred in the West during the Spanish Inquisition and the Thirty Years' War. The Commonwealth took no part in either the exploration or the colonization of the New World. Instead, the fertile stretches of its own vast territories in the east provided ample room for internal colonization. There was no need to join the slave trade when its own peasants could be coerced into serfdom. In place of piracy and privateering, the oppressed found an escape to freedom in the Cossack communities on the Wild Plains.

Although the development of Eastern and Western Europe radically diverged after the mighty gravitational shift toward the Atlantic, events in the one segment did not come to pass without repercussions in the other. And the fate of the Commonwealth in the seventeenth century bears witness to this complicated interrelationship. Major slippages were occurring in the power balances of Europe, and no change took place anywhere without effecting some alteration in the whole gravitational field.

What changes had come about in the Commonwealth by the time Jan Chryzostom was writing his *Memoirs*? If the previous century can be called the high point of gentry influence, the seventeenth century might well be characterized as the golden age of the high nobility. By mid-century, what the gentry called its "Golden Freedom" was slipping further from grasp with every passing year. It had been usurped by a small cluster of oligarchs; no other estate was functioning politically on a nationwide scale. The oligarchs exercised their influence at the local level by controlling the choice of deputies sent to the Diet. What appeared still to be the voice of gentry supremacy was no more than a mouthpiece for magnate dominance. This power shift had been accomplished within the legal framework through economic and political steps which enabled the great lords not only to control the election of deputies at local dietines but also to determine the content of the "instructions"which they carried to the Diet.

The local dietines, in turn, had imposed their authority upon the Diet through the so-called Report Dietines. The Report Dietines, usually called into session by the king or the governors, were held after the conclusion of a Diet so that the gentry could hear their deputy's account of the sessions and ratify the resolutions passed. The "hooded dietines" which exercised supreme authority during an interregnum also increased the importance of the local assemblies. In fact, dietines were convoked at the slightest excuse, independently of the king's or the governor's summons, in peace or in wartime. Report Dietines also elected deputies to the Treasury Tribunal. All important decisions on taxation and military recruitment were therefore left to local discretion. In addition, the provinces established separate treasuries and separate armies, which further diminished the military and financial capabilities of the central government. The drop in the revenues of the state treasury had fatal consequences for the country's defense, eloquently elaborated in Pasek's Grodno speeches.

During the seventeenth century, the principle of unanimity in the Diet fell victim to the intrigues of certain magnate factions. The former spirit of fairness and compromise was stifled by the inordinate use of the *liberum veto,* whereby if one resolution was voted down by one deputy, the whole body of resolutions already passed during the session was abrogated. Out of 44 Diets convened in the second half of the seventeenth century, 15 were broken up by a single *liberum veto* and two ended without enacting a single piece of legislation. Confederacies such as Lubomirski's in 1664-1665 clearly showed the disastrous drawback of the rule of unanimity; the all-or-nothing procedure stifled legitimate opposition and in the end yielded nothing.

Government by consent was becoming government by coercion, making a mockery of the very name of the *Respublica.* But the average gentryman bore mixed feelings of wariness and pride toward the Diet. Pasek himself considered the Diet an eye- opening experience: "You'll learn manners, you'll learn the law, you'll learn that which in school, as I live and breath, you were never taught," and he advises young persons to attend as many Diets as they can. Perhaps, as Rousseau imagined, the frequency of Diets and dietines was actually a great strength: "Frequent Diets, frequent renewal of mandates — these are the things that sustained your republic."[5]

As in the legislative so in the judicial process, the authority of both king and Diet was profoundly undermined in the second half of the seventeenth century. The Crown Tribunal had become a symbol of graft and corruption. Bribery determined most verdicts. It was common practice for the magnates, in order to win support for their political schemes, to buy judicial favors for their gentry "clients." To execute sentences, the courts sought assistance from magnates' troops, since the state was unable to afford the necessary manpower. And so, Justice, ardently pursued, but rarely dispensed with integrity, was literally in magnate hands.

Given such a state of anarchy, it is more useful, in discussing the structure of late seventeenth-century society, to speak in terms of pressure-groups rather than estates or classes. The king, for all practical purposes, had been deprived of effective power. He was regarded by the magnates as a pawn; among the gentry, if he cut the proper figure of courtesy, frankness, and conviviality, he was respected. Yet the gentry, not wanting to open the door to autocracy, did not trust him with control over their wealth or their social class. Even as protector of the country's interests and guardian of its territorial boundaries, the king was unable to assume full responsibility. There were too many battlefronts. More often than not, the defense of the boundaries was performed by the private armies of wealthy magnates who resided on the eastern frontiers. As dispenser of royal properties and bestower of high government offices, the king could still win adherents and exert some influence over the Commonwealth's affairs; in practice, this meant allying himself with one magnate faction or another. He could also seek outside assistance from more powerful foreign rulers. Jan Kazimierz and Jan III Sobieski availed themselves of all of these alternatives, yet their skillful diplomacy failed to bring about any consolidation of royal power.

After the wars in the middle of the seventeenth century and against a background of changing relationships to land, the economy, which had already begun to decline in the late sixteenth century, took a disastrous fall. This had important consequences not only for the nobility but for all social groups.

Highly differentiated in the seventeenth century, the relatively numerous nobility in the Commonwealth ran the spectrum from wealthy owners of a hundred or more villages to impoverished landless squires. One can speak of three broad divisions. First were the great nobles (magnates), extremely small in number, who owned vast estates

5. Rousseau, *The Government of Poland*, p. 31.

and hereditary demesnes; the most powerful of these were in the east, especially in the Ukraine. Second were the middle gentry, who owned at least one or two villages. Third were the very numerous petty gentry, who often owned only a plot of land which, like peasants, they tilled with their own hands, or, as became more and more common even among the middle gentry in the late seventeenth century, which they were compelled to sell or lease; by virtue of their coat-of-arms they retained all the privileges of the noble estate except the holding of provincial offices.

Throughout the sixteenth and into the seventeenth century, the gentry had striven to boost their production of wheat to supply an expanding foreign market; because the gentry resorted to a sort of plantation system of farming, the rise in yield occurred at the cost of the peasant. Over a number of years, law after law had been passed in the Diet, increasing the days of compulsory labor on the manorial farm, tying the peasant to the land, and giving the manor-lord exclusive personal jurisdiction over his own peasants. Often the peasants found themselves relegated to inferior plots, since any land temporarily deserted was taken over by the lord for estate cultivation. Ultimately, a peasant could choose to flee, refuse to work, or take up arms. However, only on royal estates (which furnished peasant recruits for the army) and in the Ukraine did the peasants resort to armed resistance.

In the Ukraine, the changeover to feudal serfdom had been much more abrupt, the gap between wealth and poverty was much larger than in Crown Poland. One Ukrainian magnate's annual income amounted to some 600,000 zloties; another magnate received 1000 beef cattle yearly as rent, and another received 1000 barrels of honey valued at 10,000 ducats. Fabulous sums these, if compared to the wage of a hired girl on a manor estate, which was about 40 groschen a year.[6] Also, the peasants of the Ukraine were united by a common adherence to the Orthodox faith, a common ideology, and a regional rather than nationwide consciousness.

The growth of huge fortunes in the Commonwealth after the Union of Lublin, owing to the inclusion of large latifundia in the east, was a major factor in the shift from gentry to magnate ascendancy. These latifundia were owned by a handful of Polonized magnate families such as the Radziwiłł, Pac, Sapieha, and Wiśniowiecki families, some of

6. In the seventeenth century monetary values were extremely unstable. A gold ducat could have been worth anywhere from 30 to 50 silver groschen; a zloty in the second half of the century no longer meant a goldpiece (the equivalent of a ducat) but a silver coin worth about half as much.

whom, either through marriage or royal favor, also acquired large estates in Crown Poland.

Another factor was war. The Cossack Wars, the Swedish Wars, the Muscovite and Turkish attacks devastated arable land and decimated livestock, causing crop yield to plummet. As a result, the petty gentry, and even some middle gentry, unable to maintain themselves on their land, sold or gave their land in pawn to magnates, or transformed their property into leaseholds; owners of large estates resorted to extensive farming; magnates and supervisors of crown estates reduced the amount of compulsory labor hours and replaced it with rents. Far from lightening the peasants' burden, this in effect forced the peasants to shoulder a good part of the costs of reconstruction, and on top of that they had to pay taxes on fields or cottages for the support of the army. Because these rents were fixed amounts, they worked extreme hardship on the peasants.

The pernicious effects of the plantation economy also touched the small towns. Trade was brought to a standstill since the peasants simply could not afford to buy the products of town craftsmen or traders. The towns were also affected by the monetary crisis which occurred in the mid-seventeenth century after the Swedish Wars, as a result of issuing nearly worthless coins to pay the army. Uprisings and army mutinies occurred in Russia and Turkey over the bad coin, and in Central Europe the devaluation of silver coins had been going on since the beginning of the century. Devaluation adversely affected trade within the Commonwealth, since the price of foreign goods fell below that of domestic goods. The successive wars wreaked great material damage on urban settlements and accelerated the process of decay already begun by the shift of trade routes to the Atlantic. Many townsmen, suffering from the decline in trade, enlisted in the army, especially in the dragoons. Large towns, however, like Gdańsk, Warsaw, Toruń, and Kazimierz-on-the-Vistula which were centers of the grain trade, remained active and prosperous despite customs and tariffs on imported and exported goods.

The crux of the struggle lay in the situation of the petty and middle gentry, who, growing poorer and poorer, were forced to seek "protection" from the wealthy. The petty gentry, who had to sell their land, were hardest hit. Although their coat of arms assured them of the right to vote in local dietines, they could not hold office. They found employment at magnates' courts, either in the administration of their estates or households, or in their private armies. Known popularly as "clients," they became the instruments through which the magnates controlled the central authority of the Commonwealth. Because the era was troubled with the evils of lawlessness — armed forays on the estates were common, as were rape, murder, robbery, and arson — most of the middle gentry, who were dependent on the magnates for loans, for patronage, and for security were also reduced to acquiescence. As the great lords extended their estates into latifundia, they became kinglets in their own territories while royal authority decreased in proportion. Suffering from the devastation of war, without the funds to reconstruct, the gentry had no other recourse but to support their protectors and creditors at local dietines or the Diet. Often, following their protector's instructions, they broke up sessions of the local dietine or Diet or the sittings of the Crown Tribunal. But the antagonism between gentry and magnates grew steadily more bitter. Pasek's Grodno speeches and the elections of 1669 give voice to this hostility.

Those gentry who, like Pasek, lived along the grain route, were still able to make a fair living; Pasek at least was able to provide a comfortable life for his family and retainers and dower four stepdaughters. Each harvest season, the gentry transported their grain on rafts or barges down the Vistula and its tributaries to Gdańsk to sell to prosperous merchants for export. Pasek, as one might have gathered even from his war anecdotes, did not lack a head for business — though commerce as such was considered an unseemly occupation for a nobleman and was even forbidden by law. This veteran of the Swedish and Muscovite wars did quite well apparently. In his favor were all the privileges of Golden Freedom: exemption from all taxes, from supplying peasants to the army, and from quartering soldiers. Yet to acquire and maintain a piece of land, Pasek endured the hardships of warfare and battled his way through social, political, and economic intricacies. Like many other petty gentrymen, the army served him as a vehicle of social mobility. Without the experience in the army, without the money and the booty he acquired, he might have ended his days as a "client," a landless gentryman; certainly he could not have written the same *Memoirs*.

As for the lower estates, the army offered a certain limited mobility, mainly the opportunity to acquire wealth through booty, or by distinguishing oneself on the battlefield; there was also the chance to move up through the ranks, and ultimately, for the very few, to win the crown of nobility and privilege. Minor officers in the Foreign Contingent were often veteran rankers — that is, peasants from crown estates, or poor commoners from the city fringes, or runaway serfs from gentry manors. The army offered the possibility to overcome a grinding poverty, to win one's freedom, or simply to participate in an exciting adventure.

In the latter half of the century, there were many ennoblements. It was the only sure way to become a member of the privileged class. One could buy a title by having a gentleman declare kinship, which was especially easy for the Hussars and Gentlemen of the Horse, but this was a more slippery path and subject to the coquettish goodwill of one's neighbors and friends. But whatever the path, it does appear that the Hussars, long assumed to have been mainly magnates and wealthier gentry, were, in fact, half-plebeian. The percentage was even greater in the medium and light cavalry. Non-noble professional horsemen, enriched by booty, and wealthy townsmen were sometimes among those who became Hussars or Gentlemen of the Horse.

Despite the slippages that had occurred on the economic, political, and social planes, the life-style of the Commonwealth remained in the mould of the gentry's making, the product of lively social intercourse. Not only frequent political assemblies brought the gentry together but also manor house revels where pleasures of table and cellar were enjoyed, often to excess, for several days or even weeks at a time. The intellectual level of manorial conviviality was often none too high and brawling was a common conclusion. Pasek himself had an obvious penchant for duelling, brawling, and tippling.

In the aesthetic sphere, although the level of culture had generally declined, much can be said for the originality of the style of the period. Known as the Sarmatian style, it crossed doctrinal lines, for Catholic as well as Protestant gentry displayed it. As a result of the wars with the Muscovites, Turks, and Tartars, the decorative arts and dress combined native with oriental elements. Take, for example, the *kontusz* and *żupan*. Both were essential parts of a nobleman's attire in Old Poland. The native *żupan* was an ankle-length, cassock-type gown, buttoned from neck to waist and worn under the *kontusz* (adapted from eastern garb), a coat of the same length, fitted at the waist, with long, split sleeves. The outfit was completed by a long, wide, ornate belt of gold cloth, a curved ornamental sword, and a fur cap. A gentryman's way of partially shaving the head, the ornamenting of armor, swords, harnesses, and so forth came from the Turks. The shape of certain church cupolas also came from the east. The hexagonal coffin-portraits of the gentry were unique to the Commonwealth. The eastern features of the Sarmatian Baroque style made it especially attractive to the Lithuanian, Byelorussian and Ukrainian gentry, to whom such motifs appeared familiar and accessible.

This is not to say that western influences were not felt. But they too were blended into a Sarmatian variant of the continental Baroque. The influences, of course, came mainly from Louis XIV's France, whose rays of cultural brilliance shone through the magnates' courts, where Polish practitioners of the elegant Baroque style found patronage.

From this quarter, the gentry learned a fondness for pompous façades and grand gestures; it seemed to fit the experience of an age of public spectacles, an age bombarded with blazing victories and shocking defeats, entertained with triumphal entries, coronations, and regal funerals, and familiar with drunkenness and feasting and poverty, death, and disease.

The particular culture of the Commonwealth during this period was labeled by art historians in the late nineteen-forties, first as "Sarmatism" and then as "Sarmatian Baroque." The term was meant to indicate that while the culture bears many features of the Baroque style as experienced everywhere in Europe — a preference for dynamic tensions, violent contrasts, accumulative detail, pomp and ceremony, exaggeration, and playfulness — its intellectual, social, and political content was a specific product of the Polish gentry, and that it possessed certain aesthetic contents found nowhere else in Europe. Foreign influences were usually formal; the contents always native. In other words, the concept of Sarmatism does not fully coincide with that of the Baroque, if the latter is taken to be only an aesthetic program.

Sarmatism was based on the concept of gentry superiority, bolstered in the seventeenth-century Commonwealth by historians and chroniclers who revived the myth of the ancient Sarmatians, the alleged conquerors of the local tribes in the Vistula region, who founded the ruling class from which the gentry of the Commonwealth was descended. Alone, the gentry constituted the "nation," a fellowship of equals between whom "brother" was a respectful form of mutual address. This explains Pasek's huff when, serving as escort for the Tzar's envoys to Warsaw, he is given a letter from Marshal Żeromski in which he finds himself addressed as "Friend," a title used for townsmen but never between members of the nobility. No other social group in the Commonwealth enjoyed the privileges of Golden Freedom. The fact that the eastern "boyars" in Lithuania and the Ukraine so rapidly adopted Polish culture after the Union of Lublin (even Muscovy began to imitate Polish cultural models) no doubt gave the Polish gentry that inflated sense of political and cultural superiority displayed with such relish and irony by the author of the *Memoirs* toward his charges from Muscovy. Between Muscovy and the Commonwealth lay an abyss of ignorance and distrust. Muscovite envoys were ridiculed for their boorishness, their customs, their bad taste. Instead of common Slavic origins, differences of tradition in religion, culture, and social values were emphasized.

The gentry's smugness degenerated into xenophobia at mid-century. Projecting their fears of royal tyranny into outright hatred of foreigners, the gentry began to see all foreigners, especially the

French, as conspirators against their Golden Freedom. There is a moment of pure psychodrama in the *Memoirs* when, in 1664. Pasek witnesses or takes part in a fracas during one of the French triumphal spectacles in Warsaw, dramatizing a military victory over Emperor Leopold. Some Polish gentry who were gathered around the *theatrum* pretend to become inflamed at the thought of capturing the Emperor and putting him in chains; they pull out their bows and arrows and manage to shoot down a few French actors, wounding some and sending them all scurrying for cover. In fairness, it must be said that many of the French who came to Poland revealed a complete ignorance of the real aims of the Polish Crown and the nobility.

Travel declined greatly in the latter half of the century and when the citizens of the *Respublica* did travel, it seldom brought them enlightenment. More interested in superficial curiosities than in understanding the governments and societies of other countries, the Sarmatian gentry remained complacently sure that they lived in the best of all possible worlds.

Sarmatism was a defensive culture, for the gentry's political effectiveness had been seriously undermined by magnate control of their financial affairs. Behind the screen of gentry equality stood a magnate oligarchy. The sentimental image of a fellowship of nobles did not stand the test of seventeenth-century reality, but it was compatible with the Baroque style, with its fondness for façade coupled with a disquieting dynamic of opposites, with its tendency to exaggerate, its taste for panegyric. And this style is as present in Pasek as it was in the political literature, the oratory, the poetry, and the drama of the era.

Responsibility for the shape and outlook of Sarmatism must lie to a large extent with the Jesuit schools where most of the gentry sent their children. Although other religious orders had their own schools, it was the Jesuit schools that set the tone and where the majority of the gentry formed their attitudes toward life. The Swedish Wars put an end to trips abroad for foreign schooling and the once high educational standards in Catholic schools declined markedly. The Arians had had to abandon their excellent schools in the climate of intolerance and war. Owing to the conservatism of the Counter-Reformation attitudes, new scientific theories were regarded as quasi-heretical and scholastic theology dominated the sciences. The schools imparted little technical or scientific knowledge but emphasized literary and oratorical skills, offering their pupils a smattering of history, mythology, arithmetic, and Latin grammar. Subtly, through pedagogical use of competitiveness, corporal punishment, ridicule, and encouragement of talebearing, they induced conformity in their pupils, taught them guile and a shallow piety based on ritualistic devotional practices. In the *Memoirs*

Pasek describes the eccentricities of a nobleman, the Castellan of Zakroczym, who illustrates the inadequacy of such a philosophy for satisfying more ardent souls. Both the royal court and the magnates were reluctant to subsidize scholarship, while the mass of gentry regarded education as a purely utilitarian endeavor, useful for providing the basic skills to manage their finances and to muster sufficient eloquence at local dietines and at the Diet. The result was intellectual uniformity: the gentry read the same authors, used the same quotes, held the same political and social convictions reinforced by group pressures at church, district dietine, and tavern.

From conformity it was not such a long way to intolerance, bigotry, and brutality in the name of law. The multitude of ills besetting the Commonwealth inevitably led to scapegoating by those smug representatives of the gentry who refused to check the decay within the structure they had created. The early half of the century witnessed outbreaks of violence against religious dissenters and non-Christians, against the Arians especially and the Jews. Although the atmosphere in the Commonwealth was still relatively permissive compared to the militant intolerance in England and Spain, for example, the Protestants, understandably, looked elsewhere for allies — to Protestant Sweden, Transylvania, and Ducal Prussia. Pasek provides an amusing story illustrating the Protestant hostility in Gdańsk to Sobieski's Viennese campaign, a tale that must have shocked and angered his Catholic listeners. With the spread of the Counter-Reformation, the intolerant mood grew more and more intense so that by 1658, the Arians found themselves accused of treason and banished by a decree of the Diet. In 1688, the Diet passed another resolution that made it a capital offense to abandon the Catholic faith.

The clergy, especially the episcopate (all heads of dioceses were senators), had gained an increasing political influence on domestic and foreign affairs as defenders of the Papacy and the Hapsburg Empire. Religious thought, however, stagnated. Theological compendiums were produced instead of the profound analyses of such basic doctrinal issues as Divine grace and free will that were absorbing Western European intellects; dissertations on morality and an emphasis on pious behavior submerged a true spirituality, which resurfaced in a fascination with the occult, with superstitions and omens. Numerous indications of this interest can be found in the *Memoirs* — references to astrology, natural phenomena seen as signs of supernatural activity, and an anecdote about an elfen wedding.

The gentry, in coming to accept the domination of the church and in assuming a Jesuit-inspired outlook, was in fact filling the vacuum left by the non-functioning of the state. The church succeeded where the king had failed in making of the chaotic existence of the seventeenth century an orderly affair by focusing the gentry's lives on religious holidays and life's natural events - births, marriages, deaths.

The image of Golden Freedom remained long embedded in gentry mentality, far outliving the historical realities. In the seventeenth century, it was fired by the common effort to repel external and internal enemies; later the fiction provided a calm center from which to view a world on the verge of collapse. In the eighteenth century, after legal and structural changes in government and economic life had occurred, Sarmatism simply faded into nostalgia.

In spite of the gushing panegyrics to Golden Freedom, the core of the nation, the gentry, was sliding toward political oblivion. Was the Sarmatian way of life worth preserving? Some aspects of it, no doubt. But because the gentry insisted on jealously retaining its privileges, preventing their extension to other social groups, it doomed the structure of the Commonwealth to atrophy and to the revenge of the lower orders. And yet, thanks to the written word, the painted image, the crafted artifact, that Sarmatian culture did not entirely slip away; thanks to the gentry's records and comments on both personal and public events of that era we can retrieve some of its eventfulness, some of its color. And Pasek, though hard-headed enough to see through much of what was ailing the Commonwealth, still gazed along a bias. He did not transcend the mentality of his milieu exept through his talent. Often his clashes with his fellow gentrymen were over trivia; at best, the hard-striving war veteran resented the softness, cowardliness, and apathy of many of his fellows. Had not the gentry and magnates at first capitulated to the Swedes, refusing to see their arrival in Wielkopolska as common aggression until the signs were all too unmistakable? Sarmatism was an ideological shield against the historical realities which contradicted it at every turn.

II.

Author vs. Hero. Although Pasek is representative of the Sarmatian Baroque, one should take care not to impose a "Pasek-model" on all of Polish gentry society for it was highly stratified. Since the first fifty pages of the *Memoirs* are missing, pages in which according to the conventions of seventeenth-century Polish memoir-writing the author's boyhood and youth would have been described, we know nothing of Pasek's early life except that he attended the Jesuit School in Rawa and subsequently joined the army. The year 1636 is given as an approximate date of birth. Pasek's birthplace may have been the village of Paski in the Sochaczew district of Mazovia.

His name probably derives from the Polish Christian name of Paweł (Paul), which has diminutive forms of Pach and Paszek. The latter, when pronounced in the Mazovian dialect, would sound like Pasek. After having been around a bit, Pasek began writing his full name as Jan Chryzostom "z Gosławic" Pasek. The addition of "z Gosławic" (from Gosławice) signified the possession of an estate. Since no other blood relative of Pasek's used this form, it is doubtful that it derives from an ancestral estate. In any case, the addition of one's hereditary estate to one's title was an old practice revived in the seventeenth century by the magnates, and many gentry followed suit.

It is probable that the author of the *Memoirs* issued from the numerous petty gentry of Mazovia. His father, Marcin, was a leaseholder in the Rawa district and it is likely that he worked his own land.

In the seventeenth century, Mazovia was (it still is) a poor and overpopulated region. For every square mile in Mazovia there were 20 gentry homesteads; in Małopolska, where Pasek eventually settled after his military service, the figure was as low as 1.3. The Mazovian soil is sandy and yields a poor harvest. The Rawa district where the Pasek family resided seems to have been the least populous, but the number of small leaseholds was still considerable.

Among their gentry bretheren in the rest of Crown Poland, the Mazovians had acquired a none-too-savory reputation. Tough conditions of survival had left their stamp on the regional character. The "typical" Mazovian possessed a cunning tongue (useful in constant, close neighborly contacts), a proneness to physical violence, and a careless disregard for the life and property of others; the most enterprising showed a hardy spirit of adventure which led them to seek their fortune in the Commonwealth or foreign armies, or at a magnate's court. Pasek was no exception.

Although his *Memoirs* relay the image of a jovial, boisterous, brave, chivalrous, and pious soldier, the Kraków law archives suggest certain other qualities. That he was capable of the same ruthless behaviour in civilian life as he exhibited on the battlefield should surprise none of us living in the twentieth century, nor, for that matter, any close reader of the *Memoirs*, who will remember the coarse glee which Pasek must have felt in shocking his listeners with tales of carnage and thirst for booty, a thirst which drove peasants to search men's bowels for gold coins, and officers to bargain over who would slit the throat of a wealthy Swede. Constant court cases cast a thin veil of legality over the rapaciousness of the average gentryman's struggle to survive, and when justice failed, as it often did in those chaotic times, one either paid for "protection" or took the law into one's own hands. Pasek staged many a raid on a tenant's or landlord's estate or resorted to other forms of physical revenge. For example, a neighbor's servant whom he caught bagging a hare on his property was made to eat the entire beast on the spot — raw.

Pasek's ruffianism irked his fellow gentrymen to such a point that the Tribunal finally sentenced him to perpetual banishment from the Commonwealth. But somehow he escaped from complying with the verdict. Even as his literary skills were out of the ordinary, the man himself was not everywhere so average as he has been made out to be. Unlike the rest of the gentry, Pasek refused to join the army confederacy; he always remained loyal to his commander, Czarniecki, and to the king — even if it was an interested loyalty. As a country squire, Pasek did not refuse King Jan III Sobieski his beloved otter, although the king's request pleased him as much as if "he'd been pulling a currycomb over my bare skin." (No doubt, the same old hope of a land grant or an office moved his spirit.) The archives tell us that Pasek won his case against the Margrave which he was discussing when the *Memoirs* break off in 1688. And (perhaps in return for the gift of the otter) Sobieski gave him a lifelong lease on the crown village of Ucieszkowa. Pasek prospered there until 1696 and would have remained if not for a violent animosity which grew up between him and a neighbor. He leased two more estates before his death, which occurred sometime within the first few years of the eighteenth century — an unusually long lifespan for that troubled time.

The incongruity between Pasek's inflated, self-styled image and the harsh facts unearthed by scholarly investigators in the early twenties of this century dismayed some Polish literary critics who were partial to the Sarmatian myth, who clung to notions of messianic heroism and self-sacrifice, virtues required of those who manned the ramparts of Christendom. But for today's reader those very discrepancies create a comic dimension; our age has enjoyed debunking heroes and hugely enjoys the spectacle of a confidence game, especially if the personality of the player is colorful or bizarre.

As a man functioning within a decaying structure, Pasek was bound to be infected by the corruption of civic apathy, and, in the interest of spirited self-survival, to have chosen the pursuit of wealth and property as a means to keep himself afloat in a chaotic sea of constant change. Czarniecki himself, the brilliant commander, lauded Pasek's ability to handle money. Pasek's fidelity to the king, despite the pious lip-service in the *Memoirs,* was doubtless an interested loyalty in part: he knew where the source of high office and land grants was, and he was convinced that knight-service was worthy of the highest recompense.

The image Pasek leaves with the reader can hardly be farther from the "Christ of Nations" image bestowed by the Romantics of the nineteenth century, reaching for pathos like a sweet narcotic. Pasek was often simply a brute, a rabblerouser, a greedy, small-minded squire; let us assume those negative qualities were the reflexes of survival in an overpopulated, feud-ridden, and materialistic environment, while the best and irrepressible qualities of the man burst out in independent imagination, a lively humor, a rare gift for story-telling. Let us also remind ourselves that certain positive values necessary for survival in Pasek's day have all but been forgotten in the anonymity of the technological society: the sacredness of kinship and of fraternal, knightly solidarity.

The Literary Context. Pasek's *Memoirs* crown a mass output of autobiographical writing in the seventeenth-century Polish Commonwealth. The extent to which such writing gained popularity at this time can be seen from the number of memoirs that have come down to us from the seventeenth century as compared to the preceding and following centuries: in the first half of the sixteenth century there were 5, in the second half 42; in the first half of the seventeenth there were 88, and in the second half 70; in the first half of the eighteenth, there were 55.

The violent disturbances of the times had much to do with the impulse to chronicle one's individual experience of extraordinary events. The more profound reasons for the phenomenon are complex and by no means contained within the boundaries of the Commonwealth. No doubt they can be sought in the humanist attitudes shaped in Renaissance Italy. Imbued with the spirit of scientific detachment and the conviction of individual worth, Renaissance humanists believed that the private as well as the public events of a man's life were significant enough to record in biographies and autobiographies. Unlike the chroniclers of Antiquity and the Middle Ages, who concerned themselves only with extraordinary individuals — the powerful or the saintly — because of their exemplary value, Benvenuto Cellini, Girolamo Cardano, Montaigne, Bacon, wrote in a fashion qualitatively different; they wrote of themselves as individuals emphasizing their own uniqueness.

It is also worth noting that Renaissance biographers enlarged the typology of biographies in prose by including men of learning. Once begun, the expansion of acceptable types could only continue, stimulated by the democratic and egalitarian corollaries of humanism, which found the greatest scope for political realization in seventeenth-century England, but also, in a very specific sense, in the Polish-Lithuanian Commonwealth.

Even more relevant to the Commonwealth was the mythology and literature of Greece and Rome, which was studied by gentry youth in the Jesuit schools, and the popularity of both Classical and "Modern" epic poetry; Piotr Kochanowski's excellent Polish translation of Tasso's *Jerusalem Delivered,* for example, was enjoyed by the gentry as a contemporary "campaign tale." Certainly a soldier of Pasek's bold and whimsical fantasy could hardly resist identifying with the heroes of antiquity.

Memoirs, both subjective and objective, proliferated in seventeenth-century England, but nowhere can one find a work such as Pasek's in the *res gestae* convention (giving the record of external events in the author's life) that can be called an important literary event. (Pepys' *Diary,* being a journal, belongs to a different category.) In France, on the contrary, Europe's dominant power, absolute monarchy in partnership with an increasingly wealthy merchant class had produced on the one hand a court-oriented culture, and on the other, a rapidly evolving urban culture which seemed not to favor the growth of autobiography. While giving his lectures on Pasek at the Collège de France in 1841, Mickiewicz observed that French memoirs of the sixteenth and seventeenth centuries tended to be "elitist." Even Blaise de Monluc's *Commentaires,* which purports to chronicle his rise from impoverished provincial to Marshal of France, has more to do with brilliant military strategy and tactical boldness, through which skills Monluc won both glory and court privilege, and less to do with ordinary human details. On the whole, French diaries tend to be either chronicles of aristocrats, deeply spiritual examinations of conscience, or salon-games of introspective analysis.

The truth of the matter was that despite the flowering of non-fictional prose in the sixteenth and seventeenth century, English and European narrative prose writers were developing a new synthesis of narrative techniques, namely, the novel, which left memoir-writing a marginal genre. Not so in the Commonwealth. Here, memoirs constituted one of the most vigorous spheres of written culture. The divergent socioeconomic patterns of East and West easily account for this circumstance. Seventeenth-century Muscovy, closer to Poland in economic structure though at odds in political development, also produced a significant autobiographical work, and though of a religious nature and practically unknown until the nineteenth-century, it is considered to have influenced the development of Russian literature.

The Life Written By Himself, by the rebel Archpriest Avvakum, marks the first time that colloquial, or at least what is thought to be colloquial, Russian was used for literary purposes. Like the conjecture that Pasek's *Memoirs* are more of a noting down of what were once spoken and countlessly retold anecdotes, it is probable that Avvakum developed his style from his own oral speech, from his spoken sermons; and like Pasek, who encrusted his speech with Latin — sometimes whole strings of Latin sentences — Avvakum embeds in his own flexible and vigorous Russian a formal liturgical language (Old Church Slavic). Both men witnessed the toppling of time-worn structures; in Avvakum's case it was the Russian Orthodox Church, in Pasek's, the political integrity of the Commonwealth.

But one cannot carry the similarities much farther. A vast chasm separated the realm of human experience and mentality which each represented. A full discussion of these autobiographies would be fascinating but would quickly reach book-size proportions.

If the type of narrative prose which distinguishes the realistic novel in the West has been shown conclusively to be tied to the rise of the egalitarian ethic of urban culture and the bourgeoisie, then the feudal structure of Old Polish society provided the conditions which favored the more anarchistic genre of memoir-writing. What is more, in Old Poland, memoirs served a social and political function.

Culture in the Commonwealth, like political power, was completely decentralized. The royal Court was simply one among many centers of cultural activity and was often not as imposing as some of the wealthier magnates' courts; the other centers were found at gentry manors and in the few prosperous towns like Kraków and Gdańsk. During the second half of the century, after the devastating Cossack and Swedish Wars, valuable literature circulated in manuscript form. Diaries and other written records, though not intended for publication, often served the purpose of a press and periodicals; chronicles, almanacs, military reports, travel accounts, speeches, polemics, panegyrics and satires, deputies' accounts and political journalism served the gentry's private needs for information at a time when momentous events were shaking the very foundations of the Commonwealth and printing presses were not operating.

Besides their informative function, memoirs served to perpetuate the myth of the gentry's cultural superiority and to pass on to posterity the Sarmatian model. The more slippery the gentry's hold on real power and the more mythical the nobility's "fraternal equality," the greater the need to represent the typical, in order to pass on the cultural pattern to succeeding generations. And since no records of lineage were kept, and no books of heraldry existed, memoirs enabled a man to confirm his belonging to a noble clan and to immortalize his personal contribution.

The Sarmatian myth provided the foundation for memoir-writing of epic scope: if the gentry was a superior fellowship, the actions and experiences of each of its representatives were worth commemorating.

And despite the domestic parochialism of such writings, they were social instruments of gentry solidarity and found a readership well beyond the immediate family.

Other types of diaries, memoirs, and autobiographies were commissioned or written by magnates to present a detailed account of an election Diet or a foreign court, or to justify their political actions. Memoirs and diaries of military campaigns were common. To the gentry they must have read like romances, for the century was filled with extraordinary victories and humiliating defeats. In the early part of the seventeenth century victorious Poles captured the Muscovite capital, which they held from 1609 until 1611, and in the latter part of the century, Sobieski's troops gloried in defeating the Turkish army at Vienna; in between, the Cossack upheavals and the Swedish "Deluge" engulfed the Commonwealth in complete disaster.

How much of the literary can be found in these writings? What structural and stylistic traditions did they establish?

Prose techniques had been evolving in Polish inconspicuously ever since the sixteenth century, which produced a considerable variety of narrative forms: exemplary lives, diaries of travel, military campaigns, and Diets, war and political correspondence, chronicles, personal journals, domestic memoranda or loose jottings on calendars, memoirs of various types, and translations of foreign romances and military tales. In the seventeenth century, poetry was still the only artistically respectable genre, hence diaries, chronicles, memoirs, and the like were not regarded as refined artistic production; for this very reason, they were practically the only narrative prose forms that admitted the free play of style and technique. Heterogeneous and uneven in style, half fact and half fantasy in content, one could find history, social events, household accounts, cooking recipes, medical remedies, letters, speeches, and Diet debates mingling on equal footing with prophecies, astrology, demons, tales of witchcraft, and outlandish customs.

The most primitive of such writings were albums of jottings on household details, family events; they included documents of personal and public nature, and random miscellany known poetically as *silvae rerum* (which can mean "forests of things" or "abundances of things"). Among these predecessors of memoir-writing — calendars, almanacs, *silvae rerum*, diaries, chronicles, biographies, letters — certain techniques became standard. It is in the context of these conventions that Pasek's achievement gains lustre.

Diaries and chronicles developed the practice of factual notation. Diaries were usually more objective, being a more or less accurate daily record of events or political conflicts in the Diet; yet diaries also were able to transmit the emotional and subjective quality of those conflicts or events. Long speeches, intricate debates, and descriptions of procedure were often interspersed with juicier passages conveying a speaker's fury or describing an outburst of violence. Chronicles, on the other hand, freely blended the real and the fantastic, treating them on a basis of equality. Generally, the chronicler tended to take a more synthetic approach to events and give more weight to an analysis of motive than the diarist who stuck to a faithful registration. Pasek combined these techniques. He mixed the personal with the public event, he joined accurate notation with a specific emotional tone, and mingled synthetic evaluations of events and motives with inserted documents.

Travel diaries created a taste for the exotic and developed descriptive skills. The *Memoirs* contain a multitude of all kinds of details concerning dress, customs, behavior, landscape, and so on. The battle scenes of the earlier years are depicted with a reporter's eye not only for the broad outlines of the action but especially for the vivid detail, the exciting incident, while the later years resemble the sparse notations of a gentry householder, describing property transactions, wheat sales, marriages, funerals, takings of the veil, and summaries of political and military events. Letters and whole speeches are inserted. And finally, direct quotes from the author and secondary figures are included as dialogue within the narrative sections. That Pasek was able to integrate all these conventions into his narrative sections sets his *Memoirs* apart from the others of this period. Pasek gave life to his account by constantly changing the pace, the tone, and the author-narrator's distancing; the resulting immediacy and emotional impact leave no doubt that the telling is the result of a highly developed narrative skill.

It would be useful to distinguish here the memoir from the diary or journal. While the two latter are concerned with registering the present, true memoirs are considered to be literary works of reminiscence about the past, based upon the author's direct or indirect experience. Regarded as a literary form, the seventeenth-century Old Polish memoir is more highly developed than the diary. It allows for greater freedom in selecting material and constructing the narrative and for more refinement in constructing a central figure, as I shall discuss below. It also presupposes a greater degree of self-consciousness and admits of greater self-deception; by the same token it opens the way for fictional treatment. Pasek — as we now know, thanks to the archives — consistently exaggerated the virtues of the central figure (his own), and this consistent distortion of the role of the main hero lends the *Memoirs* a distinctly fictional quality.

Most Old Polish diaries were structured by a linear time sequence —

day by day or year by year. Pasek follows the year-by-year convention, but he operates with infinitely greater freedom within what is obviously a mechanically applied structuring device, because the work falls naturally into definite topical sections: the Czarniecki years fighting Swedes and Muscovites, the Grodno debates, and the civilian years. Within particular years, Pasek tampers with the strict chronological structure by inserting flashbacks or glances forward. For example, describing the explosion at Kolding fortress in 1658, he recalls an earlier explosion in a different year at Sandomierz; after recounting the attempt to storm the ramparts of Friederichs-Odde, he speaks of the Poles' future success there; as he tells of how the army came to form a confederacy in 1661, he leaps ahead to mention the effects of the confederacy three years later. Moreover, Pasek frequently advances the narrative by means of free association. For example, from describing the pranks which his fellow cavaliers played on local churchgoers during the army's sojourn in Denmark, in an anecdote that apparently reached the ears of the Brandenburg Elector, he switches into a digression on politics.

In Old Poland, borderline genres such as diaries, memoirs, biography, speeches, sermons, political polemics, and anecdotes were creatively developing genres of artistic prose. There were no attempts at novels comparable to those being made in the West; at the most, translations or paraphrases were made of foreign chivalrous romances, campaign tales, and the like. Memoirs, a borderline genre, neither official nor unofficial, evolved into a serious artistic prose form. At this point, the development of Old Polish prose diverges from that of Western literatures. In the West, the memoir served as raw material for the novel, for example, Grimmelshausen's *Simplicissimus;* in the Commonwealth, memoir-writing itself developed creatively as a genre.

In memoirs (and diaries) there was room for amplifying the narrative with anecdotal threads and personal appreciations; the diarist could direct his attention to intimate details, historical or social realities, individual peculiarities. Pasek found the everyday details of his foreign sojourns exotic enough to relate to his gentry listeners — prices of meat, bedroom manners, the physical appearance of the people, topography, peculiarities of dress, social custom, cuisine, all that was *different* from Poland. He even spelled out his principle of selection. Recalling the Lachowicze fortress, he declines to describe its magnificence because it was situated in Poland where many could see it for themselves. Pasek's descriptive technique, however, is superior to other diarists' because the descriptions are fully integrated into the narrative.

Biographies traditionally manifested didactic and panegyric tendencies. In the seventeenth century, they commemorated magnates. These techniques also influenced autobiographical writing, and Pasek gave them a perverse twist by writing a panegyric to himself. Although he softens the bragadoccio by claiming to instruct young readers by his example, there is little idealism to be found in the *Memoirs*; Pasek is hardly a moral exemplum. Most of his advice concerns practical and mundane matters — the importance of a horse in battle, the disadvantages of marrying a widow with five daughters, and, most important of all, the equal right of all men to survival and to booty. Pasek aimed not at Virtue but at Success.

Because they made room for objective documents as well as subjective judgements, fact as well as fiction, prose as well as verse, the borderline genres — whether chronicle, diary, or memoir — paved the way for later forms of full-fledged fiction.

The achievement of Pasek's *Memoirs* is that it represents not only a culmination of the trends in Old Polish narrative prose but a surpassing of them. Considering only the literary elements, Pasek came close to producing a native epic in prose in the tradition of the old *chanson de geste*. As noted above, the epic in verse was widely practiced in seventeenth-century Poland; *Jerusalem Delivered* was a gentry favorite. Polish writers of verse epics like W. Potocki, W. Kochowski, or S. Twardowski approached their material with the same openness as diarists and chroniclers who combined both literary and documentary elements, ironic and moral elements, satirical and panegyrical elements. Obviously, in searching for literary elements in Old Polish prose writings it would be unfair to impose the same criteria used to analyze the fully developed narrative prose fiction of later date. But even if one measures Pasek's work against the structural and stylistic essentials of the epic, it does not fare too badly.

In the *Memoirs* we find a strong focus on a central hero (Pasek himself) and also on a civilization (the Sarmatian *Respublica*). The central hero, however, bears more resemblance to the roguish picaresque figures in early European novels than to the noble heroes of ancient epics and chivalrous tales. We find a narrative that moves swiftly and ranges over a very large field of activity. The rapid-fire pace owes much to the simplicity and variety of the style: short sentences (even non-sentences) spaced with longer ones, pithy dialogues, exclamations, glints of humor, here and there a short moral, proverbial sayings, the narrator's changing perspective. Like the early novelists, Pasek built his narrative out of episodes, which doubtless had much to do with the popularity of short ironical or satirical literary forms which tended to break up longer epic narratives into smaller anecdotal units.

The narrative also contains various types of digressions: addresses to the reader, poetic apostrophes, discussions of politics, and descriptions. The descriptions reveal a sharp attention to detail, an awareness of historical perspective (Pasek looks back on his own life and its connection to the fortunes of the *Respublica*), and an economy of style that puts Pasek in the forefront of Polish prose writers of any era. Often, the use of detail passes into poetic image — for example, the Danish forest resounding with the army's victorious *Te Deum,* the yellow bunting nesting outside Pasek's camp hut, or the birchwood hill streaming with blood. There are even hints of magic and the fantastic, as in the reference to the magician-inhabitants of the island of Fyn, and in the yarn about the Swedish house spirits *(spiritus familiares).*

Of course, the *Memoirs* is not an epic — not by a long shot — nor a romance, nor even a novel (though several critics have argued for this). It remains what Pasek intended it to be, and a little more. It is a memoir, but a unique memoir because it blends together so many elements: elements of the epic and the picaresque novel; elements of the chivalric romance (with its tales of brave Polish soldiers who defend gentrywomen, fulfill the royal trust, guard the king's honor, and court lovely foreign damsels); elements of the campaign tale (with its vivid battle scenes and camp settings); elements of the chronicle (with its discussion of motives, political affairs, speeches and documents, and evaluations of events); and elements of the diary (with its year-by-year notations and formulas) and the family album (with its collection of documents, letters, reports of profits from wheat sales, property dealings). And there is no question among scholars and critics today that Pasek's *Memoirs* occupies an exceptional position in Old Polish literature. No other prose work of the period has seen so many editions in Polish and in other languages. Over thirty different editions have appeared in Poland — complete, abridged, deluxe illustrated, scholarly, children's, and school editions. It has been fully translated into German and French; partial translations were made into Danish and Russian. At some time or other in his life, the average, educated Pole comes into contact with the *Memoirs.*

Structure. What gives the *Memoirs* a little more weight than that modest genre ordinarily exerts is the inner structure behind the *per annum* diary-chronicle façade. The scales are heavy on the side of the military episodes of the first five years. Between the army and the civilian years lies a clearly visible demarcation line marked by a definite change of tone. The lively momentum of the quasi-epic first section dealing with the expeditions against the Swedes and Muscovites contrasts with the slowing of pace at about the time of the confederacy in 1661, and a downright standstill during Pasek's Grodno imprisonment; the narrative never recovers its verve and buoyancy except momentarily in scattered anecdotes throughout the diary-like second section.

The basic structural design emerged out of the vicissitudes of both the private life of the author and the public affairs of the Commonwealth. At first, Pasek's successes and adventures coincide with the joyous upswing of the country's military fortunes; later, Pasek's capture, as a result of Mazepa's intriguing, his imprisonment in Grodno, followed by his debate with the senators, corresponds to the Commonwealth's embroilment in civil strife from which it never fully recovered, except momentarily during the Viennese campaign. So too, the last section with its flat, chronicle-like tone suits Pasek's less heroic existence as a gentleman wheat-grower at the side of an energetic and fairly prosperous widow and the declining health of the *Respublica*. The lot of an ageing gentryman who made his living from wheat farming was not easy in the second half of the seventeenth century, especially with four daughters to dower, and Pasek was unsuccessful in seeking a high office to compensate his army service.

The *Memoirs* contain three different structural and stylistic planes: the narrative ("epic"), the rhetorical, and the historical ("diary"). The unifying principle of organization is the autobiographical hero. Pasek performs a triple function as author, narrator, and main hero. As author, he constructs a story which, he maintains, is that of his own life. In fact, Pasek exceeds the bounds of his chosen convention for he makes use of third-person material, as when he relates campaigns, like the saving of Vienna, in which he did not partake; he acts as all-knowing narrator, presenting the feelings of secondary characters like the Muscovite generals in 1660, and he pokes his literary consciousness into the narrative whenever he oversteps the bounds of the memoir; for example, he cuts short a description of Denmark's geography and natural resources by declaring that he is not writing a history but the story of his own life. While using third-person material, Pasek will intrude to tell us that he is not entitled to say more because he was not there at the time. The sporadic author's commentary enlivens the narrative by changing the narrator's perspective from far to near, from first to third person and back again; although epic distance is lost, epic control remains, for monotony is avoided and transitions can be made smoothly. Sometimes the author's commentary is subtly integrated into the narrative, as in the story of Rákóczi's expedition to Poland for "garlic" in 1657. Pasek is able to turn the whole incident into an ironic parody by imparting to his voice a swaggering, sarcastic tone. Finally, as author, Pasek exercises selectivity when presenting the material from his own life. The principle is easily discerned: he uses whatever spreads a glow of heroism over Pasek and his fellow cavaliers in Czarniecki's division, and whatever excites the fancy of his listeners.

As narrator, Pasek propels events, recalls the past, projects future effects, and addresses the reader directly on a number of purportedly instructive subjects. (His asides are superficial and mundane, though often amusing.) Pasek's didacticism is a façade; to us, it reads like a parody of high moral purpose. Perhaps this was part of its appeal to his seventeenth-century audience as well, for the conformity and role-playing inculcated by Jesuit Schools could not have stood any test of credibility in that confusing, troubled, and disorderly era. Above all, he keeps his listeners in awe, admiration, and suspense. No doubt he shocked many. But the narrator's voice registers unevenly; it oscillates between a diarist's flat reporting of events, a poet's compression of events into brief, vivid narratives containing dialogue, description, and imagery, and a rhetorician's flamboyant distortion of events in speeches, sermons, debates, letters, and panegyrics. The multiple voices of Pasek-narrator echo the diversity and multiplicity of roles in which men of the Baroque era functioned.

As hero, Pasek plays out this variety of roles. He creates an inflated image of himself as warrior-hero throughout the multitude of episodes and anecdotes, betraying his egocentrism by exaggerating his own skill, strength, bravery, piety, and the numbers of his adversaries; in the Grodno debates he casts himself as orator-hero, triumphing over the malignant gossip of the courtier Mazepa. Pasek comes close to creating an epic figure out of himself in the early years, except that the figure is tinged by parody owing to his ignoble tastes for booty, violence, and status, and to what we know of his real character. When he exchanges the sword for the spoken word, Pasek as orator-hero emerges almost everywhere as an accomplished speaker and an impassioned and skillful debater, whether arguing with confederates, with senators, with Muscovite envoys, or with the king. And finally, Pasek as husbandman-hero would convince us of his feats as an enterprising and hardworking leaser of estates, growing, transporting, and selling his own wheat, as provident father and responsible husband (dowering four daughters) as well as respected citizen of the Kraków district. Should the reader catch inklings of Pasek's less than ideal attributes — his superficiality, short-temperedness, defensiveness, vengefulness, and cunning — they only add to his amusement at the posturings of this master yarn-spinner. As narrator-hero, Pasek never explains himself to us; ever the man of exploit and impulse, he brings himself to us in zoom-lens focus, wheeling through life with changing Fortune. There is the young Pasek in combat with the Swedes; as a witness to war's brutality (the plundering of Swedish corpses), he himself must have become brutalized; there is Pasek the smug cavalier laughing sardonically at the Rákóczi fiasco; and there is Pasek the brave, patriotic, and pious soldier from Mazovia marching off to aid the Danes; here he is at the storming of Kolding, now in wide-angle focus, a skillful, swashbuckling officer with a facetious streak of humor, and so on, up to the confederacy of 1661, his exploits and adventures unrolling kaleidoscopically.

Other figures who appear in the *Memoirs,* regardless of rank, are secondary; Pasek is central. This circumstance makes for the principle distortion which brings the work close to the sphere of fiction. King Jan Kazimierz, King Jan III Sobieski, and even the commander Czarniecki, only serve the narrator's anecdotal costruct of reality or as part of some background information in a report of the year's events. But the manner of presenting the secondary figures is the same, that is, they too are shown through action in the many tiny scenes that abound: the banquet with the Muscovite envoys, Mazepa's disgrace, Wolski the coward, Jasiński the duelling host, the eccentric castellan of Zakroczym, the Dutch admiral. They express themselves in terse dialogues, speeches, monologues. Most of all they enhance the narrative, adding the color of gestures, voices, movement, and tone. Another of Pasek's accomplishments in this area is the handling of crowds, especially in battle scenes, as a dynamic background of movement, color, and sound.

The centralness of *events* as unique, unforgettable, valuable units of men's lives is what impresses scholars of Old Polish diary-writing. And no wonder — public events were breaking in upon the private sphere with cataclysmic violence. Pasek upheld this tradition but also broke through it by changing the proportions: instead of treating historical events in chain-link fashion, Pasek used them for effect; the creation of miniature narratives that can stand on their own brought his memoirs close to the epic, close to fiction. Both main hero and secondary characters flash before us in momentous historical events as in a multitude of film frames animated by social detail, gestures, colloquialisms, clownish humor, emotional vigor. From the public event the narrator-hero cuts to a private event. For example, after describing Sobieski's victory at Vienna, he spins an anecdote about a few Gdańsk Protestants at an inn, who, expressing their disgust for the Catholic Sobieski thereby obliged Pasek to defend the honor of his sovereign and theirs. He may even insert a fantastic event such as the elfen wedding. At the same time there is no change of tone. The effect is to blur the line between the real and the fictional.

On the rhetorical plane, Pasek stays "in character" by showing off his education with properly elaborate pieces of writing or oratory for various occasions—whether it is a love-letter, a gift presentation, a deputy's speech, a funeral oration, or a formal invitation. Though he abandons his epic stance during the Grodno debates, Pasek proved himself to be as successful a duellist in words as he was with the sword. Against his senatorial accusers the orator-hero produces a political polemic that has almost Shakespearean breadth; his forthright stance and blunt counteraccusations give his speeches an emotional force which sets them apart from the bombastic but empty rhetoric of the day. Their style impresses us a great deal less than that of the narrative sections, but they are not without a strong effect. Here again, the style echoes the quality of the life that surrounded Pasek: magnate rivalries, court intrigue, foreign bribes, and splintered loyalties. The lack of a unifying political force was covered up in flamboyant oratory at district dietines.

The third structural plane of the *Memoirs* — diary-type jottings — can also be related to the state of the Commonwealth. The exhuberant tone maintained in the early narrative sections is not sustained in the last portion, despite the Viennese campaign stories (which were hearsay) and the lively anecdotes on the king's election, the Gołąb expedition, the Gdańsk incidents, the battle at Parkany, the Cossack ruse, and the otter episode. The flattening of the narrator's tone under the minutiae of domesticity, the unexalted news from the battlefronts, the unpromising political configurations, should not surprise us. Pasek was undoubtedly blessed with a fertile imagination, but even the wildest fantasy could not conceive life in the fatally weakened organism of the *Respublica.* Then, too, old age was overtaking the spirited campaigner.

The *Memoirs* stand within the Polish tradition of socially oriented literature. Certainly the old veteran of the Swedish and Muscovite wars must have revelled in the effect his stories made on his listeners, but the justification for writing them down was probably social, for their contents were entirely public, and Pasek betrays no great profundity of inner life. Yet in giving written expression to his life and his actions, he also gives voice to his selfhood — and they do not always coincide. But then, what did coincide in that age of contradictions, of change, of role-playing, of theater? Though one cannot call Pasek civic-minded, for his participation in political affairs was minimal and probably of an interested nature, he was deeply attached to his homeland and genuinely loyal to the king. Since the gentry citizenry in their complacent enjoyment of privilege had ceased really to govern, only the army brought a promise of political survival, and Pasek was keenly aware of it. But here too his hopes were dashed during the confederacy and the civil war. The need for reform was acute, for it was more and more

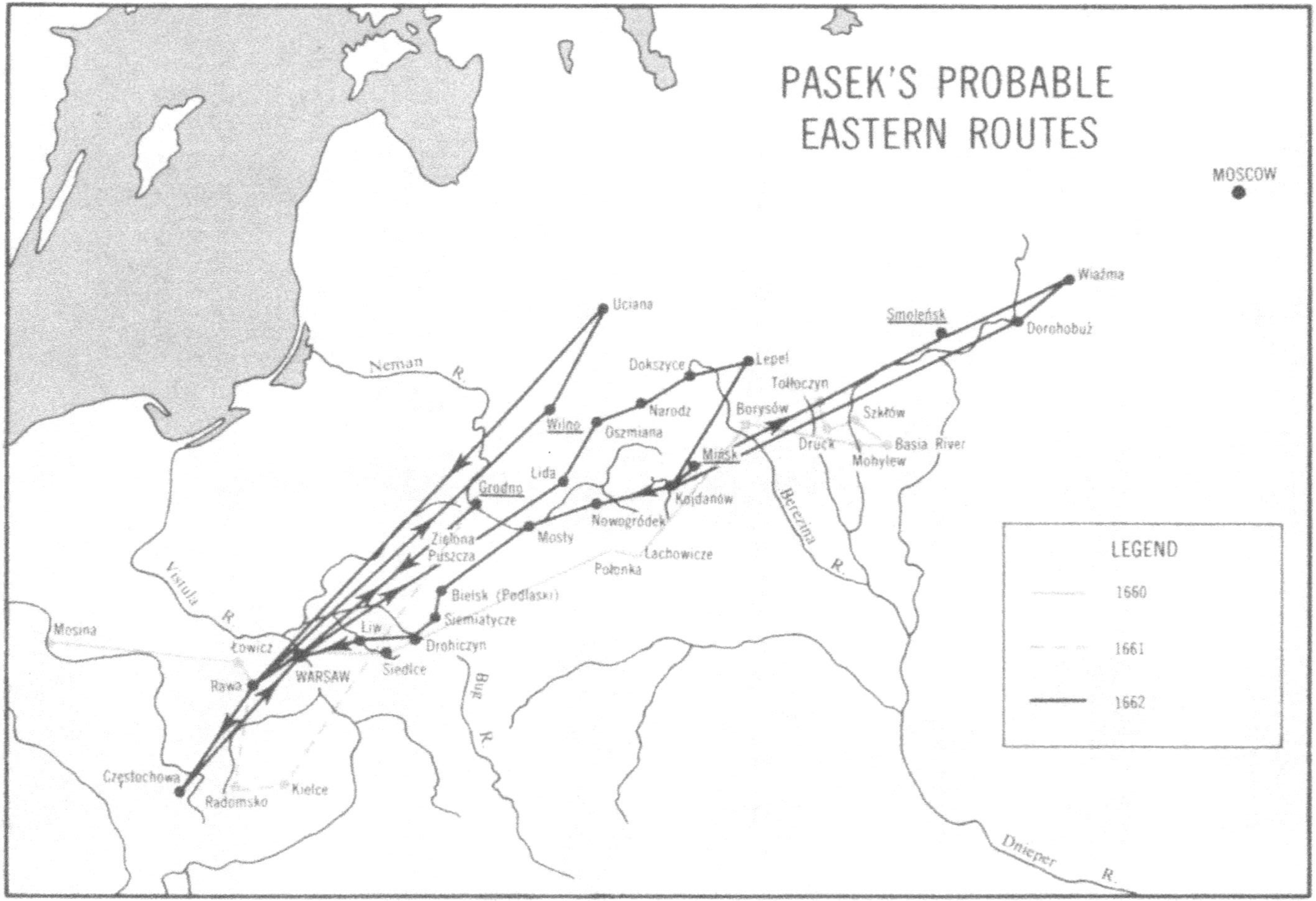

Pasek's Probable Eastern Routes

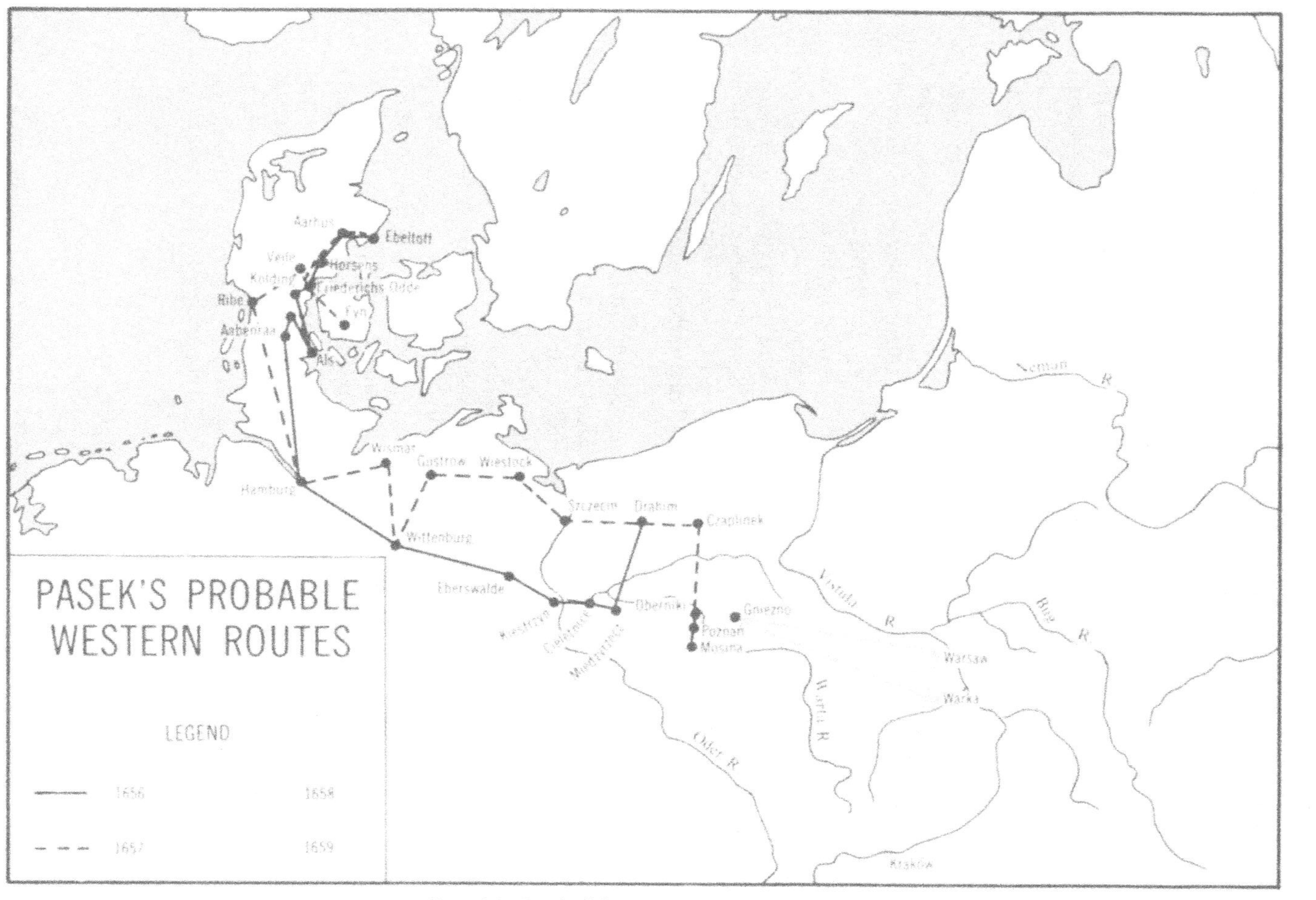

Pasek's Probable Western Routes

apparent that the weak fabric of the central government was incapable of holding back the pressures of aggressive neighbors rushing to fill the vacuum of power. Exemplary citizens were called for, not emblematic individualists. None came forth to lead the country out of its misery. Did Pasek view his own life as a worthwhile example? Both a soldier and a country squire, he was pre-eminently occupied with the business of living and earning. Perhaps, seeing the great disorder in the Commonwealth, having no sons to teach his truth, he was moved to set down his own life, as a model for the future young citizens of the Commonwealth.

There is also a definite impulse toward self-vindication: the magnification of his own person tells us this, as well as his various defensive attitudes. And there is certainly a constant sense of being insufficiently compensated, insufficiently recognized for his loyal service in the Swedish and Muscovite Wars. As a war veteran he feels himself to be somewhat superior to the non-combatant gentry. With typical baldness he says he would rather tend swine than lead a party of gentry fainthearts. But he seems to make no moral distinction between behavior in war and behavior in peacetime. His myriad lawsuits make it clear that he was as violent and pugnacious a gentleman wheat-farmer as he was a Gentleman of the Horse.

Raised in a district that was overpopulated and poor, where merely surviving tested your mettle, your endurance, and your cunning, Pasek came to the army equipped to endure in the raw conditions of seventeenth-century warfare. He found that the severe way of the army brought victory to those who took the initiative. Civilian life was really no different from war. One wins the regard of one's fellow men ultimately through physical superiority. Whatever the drawbacks to this simple soldier's ethic, it does testify to man's resilience, for it did enable Pasek and his fellows to stay alive and to prosper. Even when the last vestiges of order and justice break down, man can still keep body and soul together; the urge to glorify this act, to display the exploits of the living self, to boast of the cunning, the resourcefulness, should probably not be underestimated — because the sources of order lie within us. And out of the unquenchable fire of ourselves alive, new connections will be forged.

The Memoirs 

The Year of Our Lord 1656

[The first fifty pages of the manuscript are missing. The text began with Pasek's apostrophe to his horse, six stanzas of which remain; they have been omitted from this edition.]

The second battle of this year was near Gniezno[1] with the Swedes, with great injury to the Swedish army. Many of our Poles were still fighting on the side of the Swedish king [Charles Gustavus]; the Arians and the Lutherans had their own squadrons in which many Catholics served, some *per nexum sanguinis,*[2] others for the spoils and the adventure.

The third battle,[3] Warsaw being successfully retaken and the Swedish commander in chief, Wittenberg,[4] captured, came to a bad end owing to bad leadership; for we could have beaten the Swedish king before the Great Elector of Brandenburg [Frederick William] arrived with his own army of 16,000[5]; but when they joined forces, first our Tartar auxiliaries began to flee, then our army was driven from the field. Worthy soldiers perished, but so did Swedes.

The fourth, an exceedingly fortunate victory[6] at Warka, we with Czarniecki felling several thousand select Swedish troops, and filling the Pilica river to the brim with blood and Swedish corpses. From that time on, Swedish strength began to waver and markedly weakened.

The fifth battle, and nearly the last *inter viscera*[7] at Trzemeszno, when

1. Pasek must be writing long after the event, for he is very confused on his dates; this battle actually took place on May 7 and Czarniecki was defeated. Czapliński, p.4, note 7, and Paul Cazin, trans. and ed., *Les Mémoires de Jean-Chrysostome Pasek* (Paris: Societé d' édition "Les Belles Lettres") n.d., p. 45, note 2.
2. Because of blood ties.
3. Three-day battle near Warsaw on July 28-30, 1656.
4. The Swedish general was taken prisoner and imprisoned in Zamość fortress. Roman Pollak, ed., *Pamiętniki,* 2nd ed. (Warsaw: PIW, 1963), p. 427.
5. He brought barely 8,000.
6. April 7. Earlier than the Gniezno and Warsaw battles, although Pasek mentions it as the fourth. Pasek's vagueness about dates supports the supposition that he wrote his memoirs at the end of his life without using notes.
7. On home soil, that is, Poland.

with Czarniecki's division alone, having 2,000 Crimean Tartars with us, we wiped out 6,000 Swedes[8] who, being come together from various fortresses, were following their king to Prussia through Poland, acquiring plenty of wealth as they went; such was the slaughter that not one of that army was left, *nec nuntius cladis*[9] as they say, who could have carried the news of its loss; since anybody fleeing from the battlefield into forest or marsh died an even crueller death at the hands of the peasants; whoever was not ferreted out by the peasants had to walk out into a village or town: only to meet death after all, for there was not a Swede to be had. (And that battle was one mile from Rawa.[10] Among those who died there I know not whether a single one could be found who had not been disembowled, and for this reason: the peasants collecting booty on the battlefield stumbled upon one fat corpse with belly so brutally ripped open by a sword that his *intestina* had come out. The bowel being cut through, one of them espied a ducat; searching further, he found more: and so to rip open the others, finding in some places gold, in others muck. Even with those whom they found alive in the forests, first they searched for his money pouch; then, slashing his belly open with a knife, they took out his intestines, only when they found nothing, then: "Get on home, you thief of a galligaskins;[11] if you've no spoils, I'll spare your life."

The Swedes were routed in other places too, this year. But without being there, I would be hard put to write about it. For, throughout the wars I stuck close to that hide-whipper, Czarniecki, and lived through times of cruel hardship with him, times of joy too; for he was a leader on a par with your great warriors, and fortunate; *sufficit*[12] that over the entire period of my service in his division, I ran away but once only; while the times I rode in pursuit, I might reckon a thousand. To deal plainly, my entire service was *sub* Czarniecki's *regimine,*[13] and a very agreeable one.

8. The battle took place on August 25 or 28, 1656. Pasek has doubled the figure of Tartars and most historians agree that he exaggerates the Swedish numbers; the highest estimate is 5,000, and Czapliński gives 1,000 (Pollak, p. 427).
9. Not even a messenger of defeat.
10. The Old Polish mile measured about 5 kilometers and 564 meters, but the term was very vague, differing from region to region.
11. Trunk hose, a contemptuous name for Swedish soldiers who dressed in the German style, wearing puffy bloomers with tight-fitting hose.
12. Enough.
13. Under Czarniecki's leadership.

The Year of Our Lord 1657

We had the Hungarian war, for which new volunteers were recruited; and my relative Philip Piekarski being among those enlisting, I too joined up. That Hungarian brigand, the mad Rákóczy [György Rákóczi] had itchy skin — peace having made him restless — so he took a fancy to Polish garlic, which somebody, in jest, had bragged about for supposedly tasting better than Hungarian.

Just as Xerxes took up arms against Greece *ob caricas Atticas,*[1] so *Pan* Rákóczi, with similar fortune, upon recruitment of 40,000 Hungarians and Moldavians and *alterum tantum*[2] Cossacks, set out for Poland to get some garlic; they gave him the garlic all right and a taste of bitters too. For no sooner had he crossed the border, when Jerzy Lubomirski rode into his land, burning wherever he went and laying waste, leaving behind only bare earth and water. Finally, upon taking a large ransom from Rákóczi's mother, he went off to talk the son out of eating up all the garlic; at least he could leave some for propagation.

We of Czarniecki's division also served then as well as we could; and so glad was Rákóczi to eat his fill of garlic that he lost his entire army, himself falling into [our] hands; bargaining for his skin,[3] he consented to a million, having begged for his life like an arrested Jew, and was escorted to the border under guard in a very small retinue, himself and a few companions only; as security he left the Hungarian warrior-counts, the Katans,[4] who, at the start, drank wine and ate off Łańcut silver;[5] but when the ransom money failed to appear, drank water and chopped and carried wood to the kitchen; and in this misery ended their lives. The ransom being forfeited, Rákóczi himself — ever after

1. For some Attic fig trees.
2. Twice as many.
3. Rákóczi was surrounded by the Polish army on August 23, 1657, and pledged to pay 1,200,000 Polish zloties in ransom.
4. *Katan,* meaning soldier in Hungarian, is used by Pasek as a proper name for the two Hungarian magnates, Stefan Apaffi and Jerzy Gueröffi.
5. Łańcut was Lubomirski's estate.

without mirthful eye, hearing wherever he turned the laments and the curses of those sons, husbands, and brothers who had perished for him in the Polish war — fell into despair and died. So that's garlic for you!

On departing for that war, having bidden his mother farewell, he mounted his horse, but before her eyes, the horse collapsed under him. When his mother tried to talk him out of the war, saying this was a bad omen, he replied that the horse's legs were bad, not the omen. He mounted another; a bridge plank gave way, he fell once more from his horse: and again he said it was the plank that was bad. How often, after all, these auguries prove true.

The Year of Our Lord 1658

One army with the king [Jan Kazimierz] at Toruń, a second army in the Ukraine; meanwhile, we in *Pan* Czarniecki's division halted for three months at Drahim.[1] At the end of August[2] we set off for Denmark to aid the Danish king [Frederick III], who had created a diversion during the Swedish war in Poland. He did it, belike, not so much *ex commiseratione* for us belike; although *ab antiquo* this nation has been friendly toward the Polish people — early writings bearing testimony — as out of an *innatum odium* for the Swedes; seeing discord *in vicinitate,* he seized the occasion to avenge his injuries, the Swedish king being busy with the war in Poland. Taking his army, he invaded Sweden, putting to rout, to sword, and to death.[3] Gustavus, great and fortunate warrior that he was, upon his return from Poland, having secured several fortresses in Prussia, so mightily *oppressit* the Danes, that he not only regained his own possessions but seized control over nearly all of their country. The Dane, then, giving color to his cause, that he had acted precisely *per amorem gentis nostrae*[4] when he broke the treaties and mounted a war against the Swedes, asks the Poles for help, and asks the Emperor [Leopold I]. The Emperor made excuses: due to the pacts he had with Sweden he is unable to send reinforcements, also he had no army at the time, having permitted the Polish king to enlist all of it into his service.[5] Our king then sends Czarniecki with 6,000 of our army; on his own behalf, as it were, he sends General Montecuccoli with the Emperor's army. We were ordered to go there on horseback without the supply column. Meanwhile, Wilhelm, the Great Elector of Bran-

1. Pasek's memory fails him here; Czarniecki did not stay this long in Drahim. He received the order to march in Pelpin (Pomorze).
2. Actually it was September.
3. Pasek has confused two events: the Danish king did begin a war with Sweden, but in 1657. At this time he attacked Swedish possessions but was defeated by the Swedes and had to sue for peace in Roskilde in February 1658. In August, Charles Gustavus unexpectedly attacked Denmark.
4. Out of love for our people.
5. An inaccuracy. At this time the Emperor did not create any real difficulties.

denburg, taking the place of the Polish king, was commander-in-chief, so to speak, over all these armies.

We left our supply wagons then in Czaplinek, hoping to return to them at the most within half a year. There, as we were about to set forth, much debate went on among the men in our army. Many a man was uneasy about going across the sea where Polish feet had never trod, about going with an army of 6,000 against that enemy and into his own country, whose might we, with all our forces, were unable to withstand in our own homeland. Nor was it resolved that the Emperor's army should go with us. Fathers were writing to their sons, wives to their husbands not to go, though they forfeit both wages and retinue; everyone took us for lost. Yet my own father, though I was his only child, wrote and ordered me to have recourse to the Divine Name, not to be in the slightest upset, but to go bravely wherever my commander wills with both paternal and maternal blessing, and he warmly promised to beseech the Divine Majesty, assuring me that not a single hair will fall from my head unless God wills it.

When we got to Międzyrzecz and Cieletnice on the way to the border, many cavaliers and their retainers withdrew and went back to Poland, particularly the lads from Wielkopolska in the freshly recruited district squadrons, such as the Osiek district supervisor's regiment and the Podlasie governor's. Kozubski's entire squadron disbanded, except for himself, his standard-bearer, and one cavalier. The Governor of Sandomierz, Zamoyski, and his hussar squadron had stayed with us; but — to tell the truth — one after the other, the whole company ran off, leaving only six cavaliers and the deputy lieutenant in the squadron; they went with us anyway, and so trailed along with the army; we called them gypsies, because their retainers wore overcoats of thick red homespun. Other squadrons had two, three deserters each. These cowards so blighted the hearts of good fellows that many a one had a tussle with his thoughts. Crossing the border then, each made his vows to God according to his own mind. The whole army began to sing *O Gloriosa Domina!* in the Polish way. While the horses in all the regiments snorted so ferociously that our spirits rose, for we all took it *pro bono omine,*[6] as indeed it turned out.

We went forth, then, on the route from Międzyrecz. The army passed over a hill from which we could still see our Polish towns and the border. Many a man, upon looking back, thought to himself: "O my sweet homeland, shall I ever look upon thee again?" At first, being yet close to home, we were in the grip of melancholy, but as soon as we crossed the Oder, it lifted like a hand; and further on, Poland was even forgotten. The Prussians received us, then, quite courteously; they

6. As a good omen.

having sent their deputies to the Oder. Our first rations were given to us near Kiestrzyn, and so they were given wherever we went until we had passed through the Elector's country; and, it has to be admitted, in good order, because instructions had been given to register overnight lodgings throughout his entire country, and they had delivered the provisions to the lodging places. Since we were ordered to observe the German custom in our army, at each military display, while passing through towns, our command officers would ride at the head of their squadrons with swords drawn, while the cavaliers held upraised pistols and their retainers short muskets. Also, there was a penalty for any excesses: no longer death by sword or by gun, but, being tied to a horse by the legs, you were dragged in all your clothes round the camp review-ground, twice or three times, according to the decree; so it was for anyone caught in an excess. And at first it seemed a small thing; but it is a cruel torture, for not only your clothes but your flesh drops off; only bones are left.[7]

After that, the army set off for Nyböl[8], from there to Aabenraa; and from there we moved on to Haderslev[9] to set up winter quarters. Here the Governor encamped with only our royal regiment and a regiment of his dragoons; the remaining regiments, put up in Kolding,[10] Horsens, and other towns and villages. Though the army was to have gone deeper into the Danish kingdom, the Commandant thought to halt at the outermost edge for the winter, simply to eat up more Swedish bread than Danish. And so we did, all winter long; our scouts romped through their villages, avenging the wrongs done by those Swedes.

Plenty could be written about those scouts and what they did up there, having before their eyes the *recentem iniuriam*, committed in their homeland. From their expeditions they brought back a great quantity of divers viands, cattle enough, sheep; two Danish marks would buy an ox worth a silver thaler; they carted back a great abundance of raw honey; anywhere about the fields you saw spacious apiaries, all the bees in a straw box not in wooden hives; a surfeit of divers fish; bread aplenty; the wine was no good, but there were spicy Spanish wines and the meads were fine; wood was hard to come by; they burn earth [peat] chopped and dried, the pieces of which are so regular that oaken blocks could not be more shapely; stags, hares, roe deer in numbers beyond expectation and not at all skittish, since hunting them is not permitted

7. Contemporary accounts from Brandenburg generally confirm that the Polish army behaved in disciplinary fashion during this march.
8. The itinerary Czarniecki's division followed on its march is insufficiently known; in any case, the army went through Wriezen, Eberswalde, Templin, Feberlin, and Hamburg.
9. The Poles stopped here in November.
10. The castle at Kolding was a residence of Danish kings.

to everyone. No wolves there either and that is why the animals are not skittish, letting you ride up close to them and shoot. We had a singular way of hunting: upon sighting a herd of stags in the open meadows — for those beasts would come near the village like cattle — we would encircle them in the field on the open side and then, charging toward them on our horses and making a clamor, we would chase them down to the pits where people dug up the fuel — and those pits are very deep and wide — they would tumble on top of each other into the pits and from there had only to be dragged out and slaughtered. The wolves I spoke about: that there were none was so, because a law obliges everybody to a man, when a wolf is sighted, to leave the house and chase that wolf through town or village, harassing him, until they kill him or drown him or catch him; and so without skinning him, to string him up by a fat iron chain on a high gallows or tree, and let him hang there with everyone else until he turns to bone.[11] Not only do they refuse to let him perpetuate his species, but even to spend the night. Should he want to come in for venison, the only access is between the seas, the which is very narrow, for on one side there's the Baltic, on the other, *a septemtrione,*[12] the ocean laps the shores of this kingdom. From none of these sides can a wolf gain entrance unless he were to rent himself a little smack boat from the Lord Mayor in Gdańsk, and pay well for it. For this reason all sorts of animals abound there; though partridges do not for they are foolish: if startled by anything whatsoever they would fall into the sea and drown.

The people there are handsome too; fair are the women, even too fair of complexion; finely do they attire themselves; but town or country — all wear wooden clogs. In town when they walk over the paving stones, such a racket do they make that a body cannot hear what is said to him; ladies of a higher station though, wear the same sort of slippers as Polish women do. Yet in their affections they are not as reserved as our women. For though they show at first uncommon timidity, after but one visit and the speaking of a few heedless words, they fall passionately in love and are incapable of hiding it: father, mother, rich dowry, she is prepared to forsake all and ride off with her lover, be it to the ends of the earth.

Their beds are set into the wall like closets, and they pile them with plenty of bedclothes. They sleep naked as their mother bore them, nor do they see any shame in undressing and dressing in each other's

11. This information is accurate; according to an ordinance given in 1650 a massive wolf hunt was to take place in December in every region. Wolves would hang next to brigands. Rozniecki writes: "However, it happened then that they would hang a wild animal, too, as a punishment for it."

12. From the north.

presence, nor heed even a guest, but by candlelight they remove all their outer garments, and finally their underclothes too, hanging everything on wooden pegs; then, naked as ever they be, bolting the door and blowing out the candle, at last they crawl into that closet and go to sleep.[13] When we told them it was unsightly, in our country a wife would not do that in front of her husband, they said: "With us there's no disgrace, and no point being ashamed of one's own members that the Lord himself created." As for their sleeping nude, they say, "my shirt and other garments have enough of serving me during the day and covering me; by night at least one should preserve them, and besides, what need have I to take fleas and lice into my bed at night and give them leave to bite me, thereby keeping me from delicious sleep!" Our lads played various pranks on them, but they did not break their custom.

That diet of theirs is exceedingly droll, for rarely do they eat anything hot, but having cooked for the whole week various pots of food, they eat it cold, taking frequent mouthfuls even while they thresh — for their womenfolk thresh with flails like the men — scarce have they threshed one sheaf but they sit down in the straw, take some bread and, spreading it with the butter which always stands with it in a firkin, they eat it, then get up again to thresh, and so they work, by bites. When they kill an ox, a pig or a sheep, they waste not a single drop of blood, but draw it off into a vessel; they stir into it hulled barley or buckwheat, stuff the entrails of the beast with it and cook it in a pot; then on a huge platter they weave a garland of these entrails about the head of this same beast, and so at every meal it is placed on the table and eaten as a great delicacy. Even in gentry homes they do so; and they pestered me to death, offering it to me, until at last I said it does not befit Poles to eat it, for our dogs would turn against us, it being their dish. They do not have stoves in their houses, unless they be grand gentlemen, because the king takes a big tax from them; 100 thalers per year, so they said.[14] But they have broad hearths with as many chairs around them as people in the household; and so sitting they warm themselves. Or sometimes for better heating of the room there's a small channel, like a little trough, in the center of a room; it being filled with live coals, they puff on them from one end, causing them to glow and spread warmth.

The churches there are very beautiful, having been Catholic before; the service, too, is more beautiful than that of our Polish Calvinists because you see altars and pictures in the churches. We attended some sermons, since they had prepared them in Latin especially for us and invited us to hear them, and so circumspectly did they preach, without

13. The description of Danish customs and the built-in beds is true to fact.
14. An exaggeration.

pronouncing the slightest word *contra fidem,*[15] that you would say a Roman priest is preaching; and they were proud of this, telling us: we believe in the same thing you do, in vain do you call us apostates. But, as usual Father Piekarski flayed us for being present: many another attended in order to see the lovely damsels and their ways. During their German [Lutheran] service, they cover their eyes, the men with their hats, the women with their veils, and bowing, put their heads beneath the benches; at that time our boys would steal their books from them, their handkerchiefs, *etc.* Once, the preacher observed this, and so hard did he laugh that for laughing he could not finish his sermon. And we, watching that, had to laugh too. The Lutherans *stupebant*[16] that we are laughing, the preacher along with us. Afterward, he cited the example of the soldier who asked a hermit to pray for him: the hermit knelt down to pray, meanwhile the soldier snatched the little sheep who carried the hermit's bundle and fled. At the end of this story, *exclamavit: O devotionem supra devotiones! alter orat, alter furatur.*[17] From that time on, when the moment came to cover their heads, they first put away their books and handkerchiefs, but not without laughter did they do so, one glancing at the other. When I discoursed with them about what event they commemorated, covering their heads and shielding their eyes, since neither Christ nor the apostles ever did so, no one could reply; only one said that by this act they were remembering that the Jews had covered Christ's eyes and ordered him to prophesy. In answer to this I said: if you wish to commemorate fittingly *passionem Domini,* then someone should deal you all fisticuffs at the nape of the neck, while you cover up, for so it was done then; but no one would agree to this. In no time, the Brandenburg Elector knew about this church service and when the district supervisor of Kaniow was visiting him, he says: "For God's sake, My Lord, send warning to the Governor from me; he should forbid Polish gentlemen to frequent the churches, for surely great numbers of them will be converted to the Lutheran faith, because, from what I hear, so fiery is their devotion that the heat consumes the handkerchiefs of Danish damsels." The Governor had a mighty good laugh over that warning.

Prince Wilhelm [the Brandenburg Elector] conducted himself toward us with great courtesy, he tried on every occasion to please us, saluted us, dressed in the Polish fashion. When our army was passing through, however usual for one army to pass by the other, he would come out of his tent, or house if he stayed in town, and stand in front of it, holding his cap, until all our squadrons had gone by. Belike, he

15. Against the Faith.
16. Were stunned.
17. He exclaimed: O devotion of devotions! One prays, the other steals.

expected to be summoned to Poland after the death of [Jan] Kazimierz. As might nearly have come about, had his deputy [Johann Hoverbeck] not spoiled it all during the election; when a certain senator said: "Let His Excellency, the Prince, renounce Luther, and he shall be king in our country," his deputy, whose temper flared at those words, declared the Prince would not do so even for the Empire; the which Wilhelm held against his deputy, abashing him for speaking so *absolute* without consulting him.

There in Denmark, the Governor consorted often with him, as he was *in persona* of the Polish king and, as such, had authority over our army as well as the Emperor's, of which there were 14,000 with General Montecuccoli. The prince had 12,000 Prussians with him, but better people than the Emperor's, and we always preferred to go on an expedition with them, rather than with the Emperor's men; disagreeable it was to pitch camp near these people, for at once they despatched seamstresses to our camp. Curious, that in such a bountiful country, where we were supplied with plenty of everything, they had but to stop one week in a place, and already they were sending their wives over for charity. A woman would arrive, pretty, young, but thin, as if she had emerged from the heaviest siege, and at each shanty her speech was such: "Mr. Pole, kind Sir, gif us a little brot und ve vill zew your zhirts." So then, looking upon this wretched creature, we had to give alms; whoever also had to have his shirts sewn, she would oblige, and so for a week, even two weeks, she sewed. Linen was not hard to get because our reconnoitering detacahments brought back a great quantity, but as there was none to sew it — we having only one woman in the army, the trumpeter — for this reason, then, they were of some comfort. If, meanwhile, their husbands grew impatient waiting, they came looking for them from shanty to shanty; as soon as husband found wife, he tendered thanks for feeding her during that time and took her away with him. If she was still needed, the shirt being unfinished, well then, give the husbands some rusks and away he goes leaving her to stay a while longer, but he called on her from time to time. In this way, many a little monkey so improved after two weeks, that her husband did not even recognize her.

[Here a fragment of the text was omitted by the copyist. The text resumes with a description of the storming of Kolding. It should be noted that the taking of Als Island, which Pasek locates in the year 1659, actually took place in December 1658, before the storming of Kolding.]

Now, they consider how to dig trenches, how to chop through walls, but with what no one mentioned. And where were the axes? At last, the Sergeant-at-arms ordered the Wallachians [light cavalry] to ride to the villages within two or three miles around to get axes. Before it was light, they had piled up 500 axes. As soon as the clocks began striking four in the morning, the order to blow reveille was given, Czarniecki arose having hardly slept; he gave orders to divide up the axes between the horse and foot divisions and to sound the trumpet one hour after reveille so that all would be in readiness for the attack within an hour; each man was to protect himself from musket shots by carrying sheaves of straw in front of his chest; everyone was to charge to the foot of the walls together, hugging the wall as best he can, not to be struck from above, but able to shoot back. At daybreak, the army crept closer toward town; and I to the priest. [The Governor] says to me after: "Lieutenant Charlewski is volunteering to lead the foot. Why not let them go, Sir, but you stay." I reply: "Everyone heard you ask me to do this, Your Honor, and a body might think I had lost courage: I'll go."[18]

No sooner had we dismounted, when Paweł Kossowski and Łącki also dismount. There were five officers with the retainers from our squadron; but, as before, I was in command, having been put in charge before the old soldiers resolved to volunteer. Consigning ourselves, then, to God's keeping and His Blessed Mother's, each privately swearing his own vow and taking leave of his company as if for good, we stood apart from the Horse. The Jesuit Father Piekarski, exhorted us in this manner:

"Though every sacrifice be pleasing to God, if offered with a pure heart, in particular, he who bears his own blood to the battlefield for the honor of His Holy Majesty, this is the most pleasing *victima* of all. For what did He bless Abraham, that his tribe should inherit the whole earth? For this alone, that at a single divine command he was willing to consecrate the blood of his beloved Isaac. The affront to our Divine Lord inflicted by that nation [the Swedes] cries out to us, the Lord's holy places, profaned all over Poland, cry out to us, the blood of our brothers and our homeland devastated at Swedish hands cry out to us, and finally, the Mother of God, Our Blessed Lady, cries out in her immaculate name that this is a nation of blasphemers, that for these insults we should take up the sword wholeheartedly so that in our persons the world may yet see the undying spirit and the glory of our forefathers. Brave cavaliers, you together with Isaac, are bringing your own blood here in sacrifice to God; in His Divine Name I assure you that whomsoever God, being satisfied with the Intention alone, as with Isaac's, will conduct safely out of this battle he will be rewarded with fame and all the Lord's blessings; but should something happen to any of you, a drop of blood shed for His Most Holy Majesty and His Mother

18. Czarniecki had probably assigned Pasek to lead the soldiers during the assault, mention of which no doubt occurred in the missing fragment (Pollak, note 429).

will wash away every sin, even the most grievous, and without a doubt he will earn an eternal crown in heaven. Surrender yourselves to Him who is laid for you today, wretched, in mangers, who of His own will offers His blood for your salvation to God the Father. Offer up your deeds of today as a recompense for tomorrow's sacrifice, which we habitually celebrate at this time, welcoming the new guest — God made flesh and delivered unto the world. In Him I hope, whose Most Holy Name, Jesus, I speak and in the intercession of His Most Holy Mother to whom I cry: *Vindica honorem Filii Tui.* Intercede for us, O Mother, with your Son, that He may grant His blessing to this expedition and vouchsafe to lead successfully out of the heat of battle this worthy cavalry and to preserve it for the further defense of his Divine Majesty. For the road upon which we have embarked, I give you then, these leaders, deputies, guardians; and in this I place my firmest hope: that I shall welcome you back in good health all."

He said the act of contrition with us then, and all the additional prayers we say with those going off to their deaths by the sword. Stepping up closer to him I say: "My benefactor, I pray, give me a special blessing." From his horse, he clasped my head and blessed me; then, removing the relics he wore, he put them on me: "Go forth bravely, and fear not." Father Dąbrowski, also a Jesuit, goes riding round and preaching to the other regiments, weeping more than talking, for such was his weakness that although not a bad preacher, each time he began to talk he broke down and wept, not finishing his sermons, and making people laugh.

Meanwhile, the trumpeter, who had been sent to offer them our *parole* [promise to spare their lives if they surrender] returns. [But they:] "Do with us what your chivalrous spirit commands, and so shall we; being unafraid of you in Poland, so much the less are we afraid of you here." And then they began to fire; they made sport of us, seeing we had not a single cannon, only one infantry regiment, Piaseczyński's four squadrons and 300 select Cossacks, excellent ones.[19] They were saying of our cavalry that, being unaccustomed to storming fortresses, we will scatter at the first discharge; even the prisoners were saying so. Each soldier holds his sheaf of straw in front of him, while the cavaliers wore only coats of mail, some also had round shields [decorated oriental shields of interwoven staves].

Now Czarniecki arrives and says: "May God and His Holy Name protect you. Advance now, and when you have gotten across the moat, make haste and jump close to the wall, because at the foot of the wall there, they cannot do you as much harm." Since the clergy had told us to offer this up *in memoriam* of the morrow, it being the dawn of the day of Our Lord's Nativity that was breaking, I began NOW LET US

19. There were only 100 elite Cossacks in Czarniecki's division.

PRAISE THIS KING [a sixteenth-century Polish Christmas carol] with those who were in my charge. So did Paweł Wolski, who later became district supervisor of Lityń [a town in the Ukraine], but at this time was a cavalier in a royal company of Gentlemen of the Horse and in charge of the retainers of his own squadron, order his men to sing. And God so willed that not a single soul from these regiments perished, while those that did not sing were decimated.

When we got to the moat, those sheaves of straw began to feel mighty prickly. The retainers found them irksome to hold and began to hurl them into the moat; thus did many a man watching those in front of him, and they filled up that moat, making the crossing for those who came last far easier than it had been for us from the royal regiment who had gone first. For hard it was with those sheaves to climb up the snowy embankment; whoever did carry his out, however, was protected, and bullets were found in them which had not bored through even halfway. On coming out of the moat, I ordered my men to shout "Jesus! Mary!", albeit others were yelling "Hoo, hoo, hoo!", but I expected Jesus would assist me more than any Lord Hoo. Then we sprang toward the wall as fast as we could, here bullets flying like hailstones, there someone groaning, someone else striking the ground. I, then, with my band, happened to come upon a tremendous pillar, or rather a wall column, near which was a sort of window with a mighty thick iron grating; I gave orders to my men to start hacking away under that grille in shifts: one grows exhausted, the other takes over.

Meanwhile, above us, on the first floor was a similar window, also with a granting. Someone was shooting at us from that window but only with pistols, as he could in no wise use a longer gun and stick it through that grille unless to fire at those further away. I ordered fifteen muskets got ready, pointing upward, to open fire all together as soon as he thrusts his arm out. And so they did, and a pistol dropped to the ground. No more did they dare show their hands through that grating, instead they pushed stones out upon us, but from these it was easier to protect yourself than from bullets. In the meantime, my men are chopping around and around, as if it were that stove in Pinczow,[20] without knowing where they might strike Swedish hands. When the end of the grating is in sight, we rejoice, for here the hail no longer falls on us, would that we could get under a roof as speedily as possible, but having nothing with which to force the grate open we had to hack on.

20. According to Czubek's reconstruction of the text (only Pinowski appears in the manuscript copy), this passage refers to a famous bathhouse in Pińczów. It had a freestanding stove inside, which one could walk completely around. Czubek bases his supposition upon an anonymous work of the seventeenth century called *A View of the Pińczow Bath.*

When the hole was big enough for one, I order the soldiers to crawl through in single file. Wolski, being an eager fellow, wishing to be first everywhere, says: "I'll go." No sooner is he through, when a Swede grabs him by the head. He starts yelling. I take hold of his legs. Inside, they're inviting him to their side; outside, we're wrenching him back to ours: almost tore him apart. He shouts to us: "For God's sake, let go of me, you're pulling me in two!" I shout at my men: "Fire into the window!" They insert several short guns into the window and fired: the Swedes let go of Wolski immediately: then, one by one, we went in through that window.

There were about 150 of us there now. Meanwhile several units of musketeers arrive; apparently those who had escaped from the breach had told the story. They're about to enter the vault, when our men open fire into a crowd of them; six fell, the others retreated to the fortress yard. We make our way out of the vault safely and form ranks in the yard, more and more arriving by that same breach. The Swedes seeing us in the yard, began now to sound the trumpet and unfurl the white flag, signalling a plea for mercy; thereby reversing in a short time that habit of their swinish people who used to say: "we do not ask for quarter." Not until I have seen the enemy's total confusion, do I allow my men to quit ranks; nor does Wolski.

In the yard there's not a soul, everyone being stationed about, each watching at his post. Suddenly, on the stairs leading from the rooms of the commandant himself, we see the musketeers descending. Say I to my fellow cavaliers: "Well, well, we have guests!" Then we ordered the retainers to line up, not in a group, but in a half-moon,[21] because you are not so exposed in a line as in a group; and we gave orders to start slashing right after the first salvo. Out there, in the army, music blares, they're beating the drums — noise, din, shouting. The Swedes come out into the yard then, and at once fall into line; we advance toward them: we are just about to fire at each other. But meanwhile, out of the rooms by the gate, people are starting to flee; for now Lieutenant Tetwin had broken in with the dragoons. We spring at those in front of us. They fire. A few men on both sides fell; then we started slashing. Several fell on the stairs by which they came; our left wing immediately cut the others off from the stairs, while we were slashing away. Those escaping from Tetwin came to us as if they were brought on a leash; we mow them down with the rest. Whoever is alive among our knighthood scatters over the castle, there to plunder the rooms; whenever anyone is found about the corners he is seized and slain; the booty is carried out.

21. In a semicircle. This was a Turkish and Tartar formation.

And Tetwin comes in with the dragoons, thinking himself the first to enter the castle — droves of corpses lying about, only fifteen of our officers standing there, because the others have run off — and he crosses himself saying: "Who slew these people, when there are so few of you?" Wolski replied: "We did, but there will be some for you too; they're looking out of the towers." In that instant, a young shaver leads in a fat officer. I say: "Hand him over, I'll cut off his head." He asks: "Let me undress him first, he's got fine clothes and they'll get bloodied." The lad has just undressed him when Adamowski arrives, friend of Leszczyński, the Crown Carver, and says: "Brother, a fat neck he has for Your Honor's young hand, I'll behead him." There we are haggling over who is to kill him, and over there in the meantime, they've broken into a vault, where powder kegs were kept; other things having been carried off, they take the gunpowder in their caps or kerchiefs, or whatever else they had. A scoundrel of a dragoon came with a lighted wick, he, too, takes some powder: somehow a spark must have fallen into it. O Almighty God! When that blast rips the air, and those walls begin to crack, and the marble and alabaster to fly!

There was a tower at the very corner of the castle overlooking the sea; it had no roof on top, but the whole was covered with tin sheeting and was flat, like the floor of a room; there were gutters of golden brass for carrying off water, balustrades all around, and on the corners, statues, also of brass and very golden; in places, there were white marble figures too, that looked real, almost living. For, although I did not see them *in integro* close up, after the explosion we examined one, whole and untouched, which the powder had hurtled toward our side; it looked just like a living woman; and our men came riding to this wondrous mistress one telling the other that it was the commandant's Lady lying there, flung down by the powder-burst; and here was this monstrosity, arms outspread, in the shape of a human being, created, it seemed, out of handsome flesh; it was hard to tell without feeling the hard stone.

In that tower, or rather chamber, kings were entertained, suppers eaten, dances and other diversions engaged in, for it has a splendid prospect: practically all the provinces of Denmark are visible from it, and also a part of Sweden. To that tower, the commandant had fled, along with his attendants, and from there they were asking for quarter, though tardily; which they could have obtained, after all, but for the powder, which had ignited directly beneath that tower and lifted them on high; after all those floors exploded, such was the impact which seized them that up they flew, somersaulting amid clouds of smoke, so high that the eye could not catch sight of them beneath the clouds; only when the explosion had lost its force, could you see them better as they came back down and fell into the sea like frogs.[22] The poor souls wanted to escape from the Poles into heaven but they were not allowed in; St. Peter shut the gates at once and said: "You traitors! you are always saying the Communion of Saints is useless, that their intercession with God is unimportant and unnecessary. In Kraków's churches you wanted to stable your horses, terrorizing the Jesuits so that the poor souls had to pay you like pagans; now Czarniecki was offering peace and wanted to spare your life: you spurned him. Do you remember Sandomierz and the powder you treacherously planted in the castle for the Poles,[23] yet even there the Lord protected whomever He had to protect; a local gentleman, Mr. Bobola, along with his horse, was hurled by the explosion across the Vistula, and lived. And just now you were firing at us heavily, but not many Poles did you kill — and why? Because the angels guard them. But black demons guard you and just look how they serve you!" Dear God, how just are Your judgments!

The Swedes did our Poles an evil turn at Sandomierz, treacherously planting mines in the castle, but they built their own trap here. Not on purpose did our men act, a dozen of them being gobbled up in that accident. No one knew which of ours had perished, they only guessed, not finding them among either the living or the slain. This *spectaculum* both the Danish and Swedish kings saw;[24] all the armies of the Emperor and Brandenburg saw it, but they thought the Poles were performing some celebration *in laudem Dominicae Nativitatis.*[25] Radziejowski and Korycki, who were still with the Swedish king at the time,[26] told him that it must be something else; Poles have no such custom, only at Eastertide.

After this fortunate victory, having accomplished that work in but three hours, the Governor had Captain Wąsowicz with his men garrison the fortress immediately. We had a priest but no liturgical vestments. Just as we entered the forest, they were bringing the vestments to Father Piekarski, who had sent for them during the night. So the army stopped then; the stump of a felled oak tree was prepared for Mass, and there the celebration took place, a fire having been lit to warm the chalice on account of the icy cold. We sang *Te Deum Laudamus* till it

22. Pasek clearly exaggerates. It seems that only the interior was damaged.
23. In the spring of 1656, the Swedes blew up the castle at Sandomierz when they were forced to abandon it. Several hundred Poles were said to have perished.
24. An obvious exaggeration; both kings were in Zealand, at a distance too far to have seen it.
25. In honor of Christmas.
26. Later, Radziejowski was suspected by the Swedes of being in contact with the Poles; he was arrested and imprisoned in Sweden. Korycki, an experienced officer, remained quite long in the service of the Swedes and only in 1659 went over to the Polish side in Jutland.

resounded through the forest. I knelt to serve Father Piekarski at Mass; bloodstained as I am, I help the priest on with his vestments; the Governor even says: "Brother, at least wash your hands." The priest answers: "That does not spoil anything, God is not displeased by the blood shed in His Name."

Afterward, we met our camp orderlies carting provisions. Owing to our day-old hunger, anyone who found his man sat down to eat on the spot. The Governor rode about cheerfully, the occasion being nearly without precedent: to take such a fortress without cannon or infantry; he could have had both from the Elector who stood nearby, but he was proud and daring and did not want to bend, desiring the glory for himself alone. Trusting in God, he ran a risk and won.

The Year of Our Lord 1659

We began propitiously, please God, in Haderszlev where we celebrated Shrovetide, though not, of course, with as much merriment as in Poland. The island of Als[1] still stood in our path, and being at our rear, a great hindrance it was: the *praesidium* [garrison, of Swedes] there was large, they kidnapped our retainers on their watches, and seized our booty. The Brandenburg army passed by with both cannon and infantry, but, as before, either they did not want to attack, or did not dare; "crows won't pluck out crow's eyes" as they say. One day, the Governor with 300 horse rode off to reconnoiter, as if for a little exercise; without a word to anyone, he had the trumpet sound an alert and a call to horse for the following day.[2] This time we did not forget to think ahead, having ordered the retainers to take something *ad victum*[3] in the pouches, and so off we went. In a certain spot, we cut away the ice with axes, because the sea had not yet loosened it from the shore, even though it was not very cold and the weather was fine; on the other side, the dragoons did the same; and all flew on such wings that the *praesidarii* [the Swedes] were ignorant of it until we landed on the other side, for they were staying in the town and about the villages.

To swim it was about as far as from Warsaw to Praga,[4] but there was a place in the middle of the strait, about 200 feet of it, where a horse could touch bottom and take a rest. The Governor, after crossing himself, went into the water first alone, the regiments after him — there being but three, not the entire army — each man sticking his pistols in his collar and tying his munition pouch round his neck.

1. Als is an island cut off from the mainland by a narrow sound called Als-Sund. The island is about 33 kilometers long and 5 to 15 kilometers wide. Its capture took place in December 1658, before the taking of Kolding; Pasek's memory failed him.
2. An inaccuracy. Czarniecki was informed that the expedition was being prepared and was asked to participate. Some 6,000 soldiers from Brandenburg's army took part; Czarniecki brought only about 1,000 with him.
3. For food.
4. The sound was about 500 meters wide here. Praga is a suburb of Warsaw on the right bank of the Vistula River.

Reaching the middle, he stopped and ordered each squadron to rest, then move on. The horses had already been tried out in the water; any that swam poorly were placed between two good swimmers; they were not allowed to drown. Fortunately, it was a calm day, warm, not freezing; it had even started to thaw a bit, although, after this, winter took solid hold.

None of our squadrons had reached the shore yet when the Swedes dashed up.[5] They opened fire; the first squadron out of the water attacked the enemy immediately. The Swedes, seeing that, though just out of the water, our fusils had not gotten soaked but still fired and killed, took to their heels; on horseback we slashed our way through those coming to their aid and they vanished like smoke. The prisoners were saying: "we took you for devils, not men." The Danish king made request to have the local commander sent to him alive, for he had some great grievance against him; I know not what sort of welcome he got there.[6] Their task accomplished, the troops no sooner seized a warm house, but whoever could grab hold of someone, be it man or woman, straightaway tore the shirt off his back for a change of clothes. After ransacking the island — it was not large, only seven miles of it, a couple of towns, a few dozen villages — the Governor installed there a sensible Danish gentleman, a captain, with his new recruits. The ordinance being such that wherever we went in with the army, officers of the Danish king would call for recruits and these men were posted in the fortresses that came into our possession. The Governor, though, picked himself a hundred able Swedes and scattered them among the dragoons to make up for those who, here and there, had been forced to depart from the ranks; as they say, whenever wood is chopped, chips must fall. Afterward, the army returned to quarters, this time using boats to cross. As the last year had ended in glory with our conquest of Kolding, so the new one began quite favorably with our taking of the island of Als so *gloriose*.

The next several weeks passed quietly. Then we set off for Friederichs-Odde. A very powerful stronghold this; no town whatsoever there, only ramparts, excellently fortified from both land and sea. A wedge of the rampart extends into the water, so that a vessel sails up to the very wall; but from here they can halt the passage of ships and defend the fortress, be it against the entire fleet of Denmark. There — even though we knew it to be beyond our strength, but in spite of this

5. Pasek says nothing of the infantry which was transported by ship to the other coast. The cavalry was thrown on the opposite side with the aim of occupying the whole island more quickly. Part of the cavalry was also taken across in boats and the horses were pulled behind them.

6. An inaccuracy; the Danish king requested someone else.

tempted by the impossible — we tried our luck, making frequent sallies. The Swedes came out to us, too, giving battle near the fortress until they found it too rough, then back into their hole. Using only muzzle-loaders, they cruelly abused us; horses and men were hit daily, for the cannon balls reached everywhere. And yet the Lord silenced them — not at this time, but later in the spring — and in a curious way He delivered the fortress into Polish hands without great bloodshed.

And so we spent the winter in constant raids and skirmishes, battling the Swedes.

We set off, after that, for the Danish province of Jutland, and upon arrival there, the royal regiment stopped in Aarhus, which is a beautiful town. Since our squadron was assigned to a street without a place to put our horses and without an inch of anything from which to build stables — nor was there room to build them, the space between the waters being very narrow, as in Venice — we entreated the Governor to let us stay in the country. We stopped then in Herning, other regiments and squadrons being quartered roundabout in various towns and villages. According to regulation, we were to take 10 thalers a month per plowshare (what the plot of land is in our country, the plow is in theirs).[7] The first month we collected according to regulation, the second we took 20 thalers, the third, each one, after guessing a peasant's substance, took as much as he could, if the purse was a fat one. For a provisioning area, our squadron was assigned the small town of Ebeltoft, *cum attinentis*[8] and the villages belonging thereto, the which was situated at the very tip of the province between the Baltic Sea and the ocean, where going further by land was impossible. This province is properly known as Jutland while Hadersleben is situated in southern Jutland. Our squadron would have been very content to stay there, but we were not permitted *ex ratione*[9] that it was far away for the army to fish us out should we be taken by the enemy, and Copenhagen was but 10 miles away by sea, the crossing thereof being as easy for the enemy as a mile by land.

They despatch me there as deputy, chiefly owing to my Latin, as the peasants there can speak Latin, but seldom German, while no one speaks Polish, and the difference between the Jutlanders' speech and German is like that between Latvia or Samogitia and the Poles.[10] Though I felt a trifle squeamish riding about up there between two great seas, for it is at the very tip — glancing to this side and that: *ad*

7. Pasek is confusing things: in southern Denmark, where he stayed initially, a tax was levied on plows; in northern and central Denmark, taxes were levied on the land.
8. With dependencies.
9. For the reason.
10. Inaccuracies here: the peasants did not speak Latin; and the difference between Latvian or Lithuanian and Polish is greater than that between Danish and German.

meridiem[11] you have the Baltic, while to the north you might be looking at clouds, and whereas the one is water and the other is water, it is obvious that the one is different by nature from the other. I have observed that sometimes one looks blue, the other black; or sometimes one is the color of the sky and always the other is a different blue; or one is active, its billows playing wildly, while the other rests quietly; even when both are calm and you gaze at the place where they join, especially in the evening, you can tell them apart as *visibiliter* as if a borderline were there — it being a little, as I say, distasteful for me to ride around up there, yet having a perpetual appetite to see the world, I did not decline.

They gave me about fifteen retainers; I rode off then, stopping at Aarhus. There the Piekarski brothers say to me: "Have a good journey! Give our respects to King Gustavus, because you'll sooner be in Copenhagen than back with us." I, paying them no heed, set off. Even the Governor told me: "Up there, brother, is the larder I have managed to secure for myself. I am sending up my Lanckoroński, so be careful, both of you, not to go visiting Copenhagen."[12] The Governor chose the place because he had been told its folk were the most prosperous.

I got there at last, but Lanckoroński did not arrive until a week and a half after me; he was the Governor's personal attendant. I, on arriving there, as if I did not know Latin, showed my deputy's credentials. They ask me: "*Kann der deytsch?*"

I answer: "*Nix.*" They brought in someone who knew Italian; he asks me: "*Italiano pierla, franchezo?*"

"*Nix.*" The galligaskins nearly went wild with worry, being powerless to deal with me. No matter what they say, my only replay is: "*Geld.*"[13]

The ask me: "What will you have us give you to eat?"

So I, as before: "*Geld.*"

They ask: "What will you have to drink?" "*Geld.*"

But they speak to me most often in Latin, it being the *lingua usitata*[14] for Poles. A gentleman who lived near them — his estates and manor were immediately visible not far from Friederick [Friederichs-Odde] and who had served in the army and travelled variously is conducted to me, as if he might communicate with me. He says to me: *Ego saluto Dominationem vestram.*[15]

I say: "*Geld.*"

11. To the south.
12. The Swedes were beleaguering the city at the time.
13. Money.
14. Common usage.
15. I greet Your Lordship.

He says: *"Pierla franchezo?"*

"Geld."

He says: *"Pierla Italiano?"*

"Geld."

He tells them: "He understands no language." So sitting but a while longer, he left. The others are ransacking their brains, and a whole day there was of this. They were about to send for someone from the Brandenburg army to hire for discourse with me, and one fellow was already preparing to set out. Meanwhile, on the morning of the next day they brought me gifts, a live salmon, a large one, in a tub; a fattened ox and a domestic deer, also live; these they led to me on a rope and along with them, they brought 100 thalers in a cup. Knowing any language to be useless with me, they said in their *lingua nativa:* "We've brought you a gift." Finally, pointing to that cupful of thalers, I spoke to them: *"Iste est interpres meorum et vestrorum desideriorum."*[16] O how those Germans did jump for joy! How they began to guffaw, to hug me, how they tripped into town, saying "our *pan* has spoken," and then chased after the fellow gone for an interpreter; now at last to converse, now to discourse — the Fritzes had a drink too many on that joke. The morning after we got down to talking.

I showed them my official register, how many plows were listed for which village, and there was no squabbling, they could not deny anything, seeing that this was an official order and not my idea. They collected the money for the first month in two days. But now, whenever there was talk of thalers, they called them not thalers, but *interpretes,*[17] which money I had them carry off at once to the squadron, sending along with them three of my retainers. I wanted to go myself, but they implored me not to, as they were afraid the Brandenburg scouts would importune them, being only six miles away. And this indeed did occur from time to time, but not much harm was done, for though he snatched some animal or other, he let it go at once, seeing the garrison troops, and fled.[18]

Upon delivering the money there, they also told them about the interpreter, the which, later on, reached even the Governor's ears. So when I was in Aarhus afterward, he even says to Polanowski, Bratiansk district supervisor Działyński's lieutenant: 'Colonel! I have one cavalier in my army here who can speak any language, but *conditionaliter:*[19] you must first place in front of him an ample silver cup filled with thalers and he's ready to speak at once in whatever language is necessary."

16. Behold the interpreter of my wishes and yours.
17. Interpreters.
18. Pasek often switches, sometimes in the same sentence, from singular to plural, and vice-versa — a common feature of the Baroque style.
19. Under a certain condition.

Polanowski did not know the expression until the Governor explained it, and from that time on, thalers were called *interpretes* in the army, the Governor himself even did so, writing to his orderly, Lanckoroński, to this effect: "The treasurer counted that money you brought only after your departure, and he found over a dozen bad thalers. You can be sure they will fall to you, as you deserve; because it's an unsightly thing in a gentleman when he knows not how to deal with money. You have *Pan* Pasek nearby; he can teach you what a *bonus interpres*.[20] is.

For the second month the lieutenant wrote me that "all the squadrons here are collecting twenty thalers per plow, and you should too." The poor souls grumbled at this, saying it went against the agreement, but they paid up after all and delivered it.

For the third month they ordered me to collect more. But this I had no desire to undertake, for I saw how the war impoverished these people, though it was obvious they used to be prosperous. I was not inclined to vex them then, as they were good folk, only ravaged by the enemy. I wrote to the squadron: "Either content yourselves with the same as last month, that is, with 20 thalers a plow, or recall me from here, because I do not undertake to be the murderer of people who are allies, not enemies." It was resolved, then, to divide the plows among the cavaliers and let each one collect from his own peasant what he can. And so it came about; the retainers were sent around, each extracted what he could. Myself they ordered, as before, not to return, but to keep order among the retainers, lest they commit excesses; whoever then unearthed any money, rode off speedily and the peasant with him to deliver it with his own hands. Whereas I chose for myself those plows with which I had familiarity or which had entreated me themselves and made me bids.

Now I had a freer mind, I had every comfort *in victualibus,*[21] everything a man dreamed of: fine liquors, especially the meads, which the citizens themselves do not drink but, when fermented, they send by boat to other provinces; fish of every kind aplenty; two Leipzig coppers — which are worth four Polish groschen — and you sent a peasant out with his net, such a sack of fish he brought you, his back was bent under it. Bread they bake from peas, for they grow there in great abundance. Yet, even so, they kept me supplied with wheat or rye, specially forwarded to me from the gentry. In Lent they ate meals with meat, even the devout, and made anyone who did not feel ashamed. Fish being so plenteous there, I for my part, felt a scruple about eating meat, even the eels, which they cure in brine along with flitches in wooden troughs, I did not want to eat. There is a sufficiency of every kind of fish, talking

20. Good interpreter.
21. In the way of food.

as well as wailing,[22] except carp, of this there's a dearth, *etc.*

Divers amusements and pleasures I had there, seeing such things as in Poland are hard to see; but there's pleasure, too, in being out at sea for the catch; marvelous the kinds of fish and marvelous the sight. When they drag out a fearful quantity of them, those which appear best and most handsome to me are bad and not fit to eat, they cast them out on the sand for the dogs and birds; whereas others, good though they be to eat, are so ugly, it's unpleasant even to look at them. There is one fish so terrible that I used to see it painted on church walls only, flames issuing from its mouth, and I would say: "Even were I starving to death, I would not eat that fish!" Until I was in a gentle house, when, among other dishes (meat and fish are served at table without distinction), I began eating some fish, blasted good was its taste; and I fell to eating it so heartily I nearly finished off the whole platter myself. Quoth the squire: *"Hic est piscis, quem Sua Dominatio diabolum nominavit."*[23] I felt dreadful consternation, but saw that they too were eating it with great relish; and, secondly, I did not believe, so unlikely it seemed, that this fish having such an ugly body should be so full of flavour; however, after that, I never ate it again. The gentleman told me it can be had smoked for one ducat a pound; but I do not recall its name, it's a very strange one, as strange as itself: a head with eyeballs as terrible as a dragon's, jaws wide and flat like a monkey, on the head two crooked horns like a wild goat, but so sharp they prick like a needle; on the nape, a hook not much smaller than the horns, crooked toward the head, and the same, but growing smaller and smaller, all the way down the back right to the tail; the fish as a whole is round as a stump; skin exactly like the shagreen they use to sheathe sabres, and all over the skin, as on the back, are little hooks only smaller, like the talons of a hawk, and mighty sharp; only touch it and the blood spurts.[24] There are others, very marvelous ones, with wings like birds, or noses and heads like storks;[25] when one of them sticks its head out of a hole in the sack, there's many a man would swear he had a stork in the bag; and masses more could be written about these things.

We enjoyed divers amusements at sea, sitting out in a boat too. The water being calm, it was enough to stay still, without rowing, to look upon as many different creatures as one could wish for, divers fauna and marine animals, marvelous fish, especially in the place where the grasses used in making salt are, because so transparent is the sea in this spot that for 100 fathoms down you can see the tiniest fish or whatever

22. Perhaps he heard whales or porpoises.
23. This is the fish Your Lordship called the devil.
24. This is simply a description of the common ray fish, a Scandanavian delicacy in the seventeenth century.
25. The fish with a beak like a stork's is quite common in the western Baltic.

swims upon this grass, which *in profundo* shows up white as snow, and is why everything is visible upon that background. The grass they tear out with iron boathooks, dropping them down to the bottom on a long rope; and so to pull the grass up and drag it onto the shore, then fling it onto the bushes and, when dry, they heat it and make excellent salt from it. But not only does salt come from the grass, you can even find earth such that, when some dish needs salt, take a handful of soil, put it in a bowl and after washing it, pour the water into a pot, in half an hour very nice salt will settle on the bottom.[26]

As many curious and divers things as one could wish for are to be seen at the bottom of the sea. In one place there's pure sand; in another, grass and something like tiny trees; in one place stand rocks like columns of some sort, or edifices, and on those rocks sit some strange creatures. And if we wanted an exceedingly good view of these beasts — there was an abandoned castle by the sea, four great miles[27] from Ebeltoft, on an immense rock, called "Ryf van Anout"[28] — it was our habit to set out in the morning for that noble ruin and, securing our boat on the shore, to conceal ourselves without a sound among the ruins; onto those rocks would crawl enormous porpoises, sea lions and divers other animals to lie in the sun, sprawling on their mighty plump bellies. Having had enough of these wonders, we had but to toss a small pebble there and, in a twinkling, all disappeared into the water. The local residents said: even were you to shoot at one of them from a harquebus, it's a waste of ammunition, because it would fall with the shot into the sea; and though it die there, someone else will get it, for there's no knowing where the sea will toss it up.

I delighted, to be sure, in making sea excursions, but once I had a great scare, too, and this was the reason: I had a mind to go by sea to the Easter service at Aarhus where the Governor was stopping, not only because it was nearer by sea than by land, but also in order not to tire the horses. I would have been enroute on Holy Saturday, but the sea was acting up; when the storm let up at midnight, we set out, trusting to the sailors not to get lost. The night was pitch-dark; we were headed back the way we came, toward Zealand. I did not like it at once when, after a long time, we were still on our way, having gone but six miles. I asked, were we headed in the right direction? They say: "Travel at night is nothing new to us: sure it is we will not get lost." Only when we still do not arrive, after a long time, did they take alarm, realizing their mis-

26. Pasek is describing, rather inaccurately, the extraction of salt from sea water by boiling.
27. In seventeenth-century Poland there was a "flat" mile and a "great" mile. Measurements in general varied from region to region.
28. Anholt Reef near Anholt Island. Pasek has it perhaps confused with the reef near the island of Hjelm, which is situated not far from Ebeltoft.

take. Consulting among themselves, one with the other, they wanted to steer us into a better course, but got us into a worse. We kept on, till we were bone-weary, seeing naught but sky and water; then, as I had keen eyes, I was the first, and not they, to espy some buildings. "*Ecce in sinistris apparet forte civitas.*[29] They could not see it, they say: "*Deus avertat, ne nobis a sinistris appareat civitas; a dextris debet esse nostra civitas.*"[30] Coming closer, we see those are ships standing in the port of Nikopinus.[31] Then what dreadful alarm! We kept still until the town clock began to strike then, quietly, we moved off. But a sentry had already seen us, he calls out: "*Wer do?*"[32] We say nothing. A second time: "*Wer do?*" I say to our helmsman, "*Dicas, quia sumus piscatores.*"[33] And so he answered. The other asked: "From where?" He answered: "From the shore here." Then he starts to give us a tongue-lashing, wishing us ill: "You knaves! it's a holyday! it's Easter now!" Then did we rush off, on all six oars! heading toward land, not out to sea, lest they become suspicious.

Signs of dawn were now visible. Suddenly, behind us cannons went off; then it occurred to me that it was Matins, and I say: "*Ecce ibi videtis, quia ibi iest Aarhusen, ubi iaculantur.*"[34] — "*O, per Deum! non Aarhusen, sed Koppenhagen est, circa obsidionem iaculantur.*"[35] I tell him it's a Polish custom to fire cannon during the Matins *Resurrectionis Domini.*[36] Then they remembered that Aarhus was exactly there, and now, recognizing the shore and the port, they knew where they were. So placing ourselves in God's hands, we set to rowing so hard that rib was riding on rib, straight toward that cannonfire. We had not even covered a mile from those ships, dawn was about to break (and at sea a mile is as visible as a league by land), when they caught sight of us: if there aren't six boats slipping after us, and we, making a speedy escape! They chased us for two miles: but perceiving that the fugitive strives as ardently as the pursuer, and belike, having understood something at sea, they stopped, and went back.

We keep going, finally the captain speaks: "*Evasimus de manibus unius hostis, alter imminet ferocior, nempe tempestas. Orandum et laborandum.*"[37] O did we bend once again over the oars, did we pull! We are now well in sight of Aarhus, and the sea, bit by bit, was beginning to roil. Exceeding

29. Look, there's the city on the left.
30. God spare us, if the city is on the left, our city should be on the right.
31. No doubt Pasek is thinking of Nykøbing on Zealand; however, it is impossible for him to have actually sailed there, as it is about 100 kilometers from Aarhus along a straight line.
32. Who goes there.
33. Say that we are fishermen.
34. Look, that is Aarhus over there, where they are firing.
35. O God help us, that's not Aarhus, it's Copenhagen, where they're firing under siege.
36. Of the Lord's Resurrection.
37. We escaped from the hands of one enemy, now a second one threatens us, a mightier one, namely, a storm. We must pray and work.

fear, fervent prayer — ours as well as the Lutherans'. Almighty God deigned then to grant that the sea did not act up of a sudden, it first began to stir after a good clock's hour; so now we are slipping in closer and closer toward the town, the water is leaping higher and higher. It cheered us, too, that the wind was a trifle from the side, so that it helped us toward the land, not away from it, and the helmsman, too, performed very skillfully. They see us from the town; they're trying to see who it could be, coming from the enemy's side.

And now, how that water bestirred itself! how it tossed us about! Some are working the oars, others are bailing water out with their German caps, or whatever else anyone had, for there was only one container for bailing out water. Each time a wave broke, it covered us and the boat; no sooner does it recede and you cool down a bit, but you glance up, and another is already upon you, as if, once again, you had met a new adversary and your ultimate doom; one wave passes, another follows fast. The boat cracks as the waves break over it; the Lutherans cry out: *"Och, Herr Jesu Christ!"* invoking the Son only, but the Catholics call on both Son and Mother — thereby bearing out the sentence: *"Qui nescit orare, discedat in mare."*[38] This, having occurred to me just then, I had to cry out: "O God! do not let us perish; do You not see our desire in setting forth was to praise and serve You." Townspeople come running with the ropes usually thrown to the drowning, they shout, wave their arms: we don't hear a thing; our people shout, too, but they do not hear, for when the sea is rough, it roars like cannon-fire.

Meanwhile, we are now close to the quays. Everytime a wave carries us toward the jetty, a surge of water hurls us back out to sea; again a wave knocks us forward, and again hurls us back. At last, the men caught a rope, but just then a wave lashed the jetty and, as it struck, our helmsman fell out upon the quay, while all of us tumbled to one side in the boat, half-filled with water; there was a great deal of water in spite of our pouring it out ceaselessly. And so, crawling up the jetty like mice, we, who had come for Matins, did not even hear Mass, having arrived just before Vespers.

I went off to an inn, the innkeeper gave me a dry shirt; they made the room warm for me — heating up the coals in the middle of the room in the trough-like little trench according to their way there — and they hung up my clothes and those of my retainers. I am given something to eat, but do not want it, instead I had them put on a fair-sized pot of mead (the wines there being poor), I added cloves, ginger and drank it like that. On sobering up a bit, I even began to feel like eating. I sent to Father Piekarski, requesting a blest Easter egg, and ordering them to

38. He who knows not how to pray, let him not go to sea.

tell him of my situation. Then he sent me a little Easter lamb, some cakes and eggs. So I had my Easter feast and by now it was evening. Divers good friends came by, having heard about me, and I, in my shirt, sitting by the fire, am warming myself with that mead. And so at last they ask: "What have you done? How so?" I told them about my scare; then this one and another, having congratulated me on such good fortune, went their separate ways. And I lay down to sleep, because after such a dunking, one needs a good rest.

Arising the next morning — my clothes now dry — I went to the Commandant [Czarniecki] and, having replied to his inquiry concerning yesterday's ill-luck and our two scares — that is, from the Swedes and from the water — Czarniecki says:[39] "While it's quite true that the circumstances were not good, brother, you, Sir, now have one over the whole army, for you fight at sea, the army only on land. You, Sir, wanted to destroy the *regnum Sueticum*[40] by yourself, thereby taking from us the *honoris palmam*.[41] I answered: "If Christ Our Lord destroyed the *regnum* of our spiritual enemies on this day, then we ought to try and destroy the *regna* of our corporal enemies. And since, Sire, Your Honor, you yourself say that I make war in double wise, then I also make request for a double wage: one marine, the other terrestrial." And so jesting a while in this way, we went off to Mass. I also attended the services Monday and Tuesday. The others say to me: "Now will you prefer to travel 10 miles by land rather than by water?" [I answer] "I think yesterday's mishap should not cause me any uneasiness; He who saved me yesterday, will keep me safe tomorrow." So, notwithstanding, I did thus: after hearing Holy Mass on Wednesday, I got back into that gondola and off I went. But now I kept close to the shore, for there's no danger in travelling by sea, even in a small boat, as long as you are not far from shore, as long as you can escape, seeing some inclemency on the way. That is not what caused our mishap anyhow, it was losing our way at night.

After Low Sunday,[42] Czarniecki fell *periculose* ill. We all became exceedingly alarmed; divers physicians were brought in; the Elector sent his. A Dutch admiral sent one by ship, a very famous doctor, but I do not recall from which town. They were rescuing him by all manner of means. *Ex consilio generali*,[43] the medical men came upon the idea that music should be played to him *continue*. Quiet music was played then in the next room, on lutes, zithers, theorbos, and other such. And

39. The sentence construction here is typical of Pasek's Baroque syntax, which is a syntax of "sense" rather than "agreement."
40. Swedish kingdom.
41. Palm of honor, wreath of glory.
42. Low Sunday is the first Sunday after Easter; in 1659, it fell on April 20.
43. Conferring among themselves.

in this way, his health was restored, to the great joy of the army and with thanksgiving to God. The army remained in winter quarters until he had thoroughly convalesced; I was on that commission then, never idling, always making an effort to see that which I am unable to see in Poland. Yet it was ever needful to be on the alert; for as soon as the weather warmed up, the Swedes from Zealand and Fyn assaulted those shores more frequently than before.

Once, seven Dutch vessels[44] arrived at Ebeltoft and stopped in the port, thereby standing in the way of any Swedes using that route; they were also to convey us to Fyn. They stay a week, and more; since they were our allies and since the *princeps Auriacus* [Prince of Orange, William III] was a brother-in-law of the Prussian prince, his wife being William's sister,[45] and she being with him in this war, they too, now hobnobbed with us. When the admiral [Peter Bredal] came in to Ebeltoft from the ships for the church service, he introduced himself to us, and so modest was he, though he held a rank equal to our hetman, that he stopped in at our inn after church, inviting us to visit him also.

One Sunday, he asked me and Lanckoroński to his quarters. Although the port there is calm and quiet, it is inaccessible, for a large warship cannot come up to the quays, only perhaps those small merchant vessels, smack boats; so we had to be transported to the ship. We got into a boat and went out. No sooner had they served us food, but a sailor, the one watching from the tallest mast, yells out that two ships are approaching from Zealand. The sentinel comes and tells the commander about it in German, who then tells us in Latin, and immediately added: *"Isti duo nobis prandium non impedient."*[46] But he gave orders to look out for the colors, what kind they are, whether Swedish or some other, they being, as yet, hard to distinguish from afar. Again he [the sentinel] yells out that a second two are coming: right after, he says more of them are coming but still far away. They look through a spyglass. "What do you see?" The commander had his own spyglass brought: it was evident that either he had a better eye or that, as is usually the case, a gentleman's perspective[47] is always better, he descried at once from the foremost flags that they are Swedes, after which more and more of them come into view. When there were fifteen of them in sight,[48] he ordered his own ships to spread out somewhat more, as the port had room to hold them, but they were not to leave the

44. Pasek's mistake. There were five ships: two Danish, three Dutch.
45. Louisa Henrietta, wife of the Brandenburg Elector, was actually the sister of William III's father, that is, William II, who died in 1650.
46. Those two ships will not interrupt our dinner.
47. A play on words: Pasek uses "perspective" in its obsolete sense of optical instrument, or spyglass.
48. An exaggeration: there were seven ships under the command of Owen Cox.

port so that no one could *circumvenire* them, for though he would have bravely confronted them, despite their greater numbers, he sees that he had no men aboard his ships save those for sailing them, and scarcely any cannon or artillerists (he, as I said before, was to convey our army to Fyn and that is why the ships were despatched without soldiers, knowing that we had infantry.) The Swedes, having learned that there was scant strength aboard these ships, had come to take them. We found out that the Swedes had been told this from the Brandenburg army, there being no difficulty finding traitors everywhere.

When those first two ships are fairly close, the admiral says to us: "*Forsan abeundum est in civitatem?*"[49] I answer: "*Manebimus adhuc.*"[50] Lanckoroński says: "I will go; I have 15,000 in collected monies, lest in the turmoil someone should pounce upon it." Getting into a boat then, they took him to the quay; I remained. As they bear down upon our left wing, two of our ships sailed out toward them. When they fall upon each other with a mightly clash, both sides open fire so heavy that hand guns cannot open up heavier. They drive each other back at once, 10 furlongs at least, and begin tacking about, meanwhile loading the cannons: those two of ours went back to the port, then they tack about, waiting for the others to approach. Another two come up, stopping in line with the first two, having set their sails, and then a third pair, upon arriving, does as the second. In town they begin to ring the bells and to sound the drums of alarum; the populace pours out onto the jetty. Anyone with any nautical prowess whatsoever gets into a boat and goes out to the ships.

Meanwhile the Swedes are arming. When they had lined up, they advance in a body; they close in at less than a furlong's distance. Now do they begin to cannon each other so that the smoke darkened the air. One Swedish ship went astray, falling among the Dutch vessels like a moon among stars; and when fired upon from both sides as well as from the admiral's ship — enough said that its planks went flying; it went off to the side at once, just as a dog limps after having a leg broken. Again they close in, pounding from the cannon; now they move off a bit, only [to clash] again. The Swedes were bent on taking the Dutch rear, but in no way were they able to, since the Dutch kept to the port. So they fired at each other til evening; then, falling still, they parted. I got into a boat then, and went to the quay.

That night the Swedes took a merchant boat from the quay, and at break of day, they towed it into the wind, having rigged it properly for sailing, then raising the sails, they set it afire and loosed it among the

49. Perhaps you ought to return to town?
50. We shall stay.

Dutch ships; one ship immediately caught fire from it, because the thing is as flammable as sulphur. The Swedes move in at once after the fire, pounding brutally from the cannon. That was indeed a tragic *spectaculum*, you knew not whether to defend yourself from the fire or from the enemy! Here one had to flee the burning ship, there take heed not to get blown to pieces by the enemy, and here people are escaping from that flaming ship, snatching whatever they can, any plank, any piece of wood, and plunging with it into the sea. From town, whoever dares, rows out with boats to rescue the drowning, tossing out ropes for them to catch; while from both sides, the cannon roars. Just consider, with 80 and 100 guns on one ship, what the fire must have been like there![51] Terrible, indeed, is war on land, but far more terrible is war at sea, when masts go flying, sails drop into the sea, when a man's enemy is both man and the sea.

The cannonballs that missed the ships struck those people on the shore, who had left town. For if they would have routed the Dutch, the Swedes surely would have plundered the town. At the time, people still had everything in their houses, feeling safe with our army to defend them, but as soon as they saw the ships in flames, then did they hide their *pignora*[52] in the water.[53] For the securest depository they had was in the sea, not only for *comestibilia*[54] but also for *vestimenta*[55] and silver and money; *sufficit*[56] that he sinks it when he wishes and retrieves it when he wishes. And their way of doing it is such and their containers so fitted that nothing will spoil in them or get wet; also they submerge their things in places where the sea will not fling them away, such as bays, inlets, *etc.*

The sails on one Swedish ship had caught fire too, but they chopped down the masts immediately and tossed them into the sea. A second Swedish ship was so battered by cannon that it sank at once with all its people; few, if any, of them were rescued; they broke two masts off a third and the largest one on a fourth, the which must have caused them *mutilationem;*[57] also, the one ruined in yesterday's battle no longer helped, but kept at a distance. *Sufficit* that the Dutch would have taken them, if they had been stronger in numbers. By now, the Swedes saw that the mutilation and damage to themselves was greater than that which they had inflicted upon their enemy; they went at once into the crosswind, for the wind was no longer serving them as it had, and it was not calm for those who were returning.

51. Most ships of that time did not have this many cannon.
52. Valuables.
53. The practice of hiding valuables in the sea was quite common then in Denmark.
54. Comestibles.
55. Clothes.
56. Suffice it to say.
57. Damage.

The Dutch too, poor souls, patched up the holes in their ships, carried out their dead, buried them, and then recovered both their own and the Swedish weapons, as they themselves recounted when they came to us once at Friederichs-Odde.[58] For they possess *scientiam* and sea-divers whom they lower into the water, who walk on the very bottom and down there they install the *instrumenta* which can hoist anything up *ex profundo* and their sailors know how to swim exceedingly well so that *in necessitate* they can swim far. One woman from a Dutch ship, the one that burned down, swam more than three-quarters of a mile and she swam right to the jetty. When the Swedes were already gone, the Brandenburg infantry arrived, 3,000 of them; they were assigned to those ships where needed, the rest were sent back to the army.

The Swedes often used that stratagem *in pugna,*[59] especially when they find in a port *aemulos* who are *debilores*[60] than they. It was rumored afterward that they used the very same trick on them a second time; it had been some traitor from the Prussian army to give the Swedes the information. The commander of the Swedes at that time was Wrangiel.

Right after the departure of the Swedes, we went to the admiral with our condolences, but we found a cheerful man, regretting none of those damages; with them the loss of a ship is like firing a charge of ammunition. That he did not yield and that he caused harm to the enemy, he regarded as a victory for himself; me, he thanked for not leaving him the first day, although I was of no help to him there. And speaking about me in front of the Governor, he said that although a field soldier, I shrank not from a battle at sea. As for the sunken cannon, he said "they'll all be mine." So unlikely a thing this seemed when I thought of what a misery it was to have a cannon mired in the mud, how much worse in the sea! And I very much desired to see and be present at this retrieval; but they were waiting until the water warmed up, and I, in the meantime, was recalled from that place, as the army was at last setting off for camp.

As long as my leisure there lasted, never was it without conversation that was so agreeable I could not have found better among my kin in Poland. There were now various temptations not to go to camp; nonetheless, I decided to go, and I bade farewell to my good friends *cum regressum praecedentibus tot contestationibus et spe*[61] that we would

58. The battle at Ebeltoft ended in defeat for the Dutch fleet, which lost four of its five ships. Besides this, the Swedes burned the transport ships in the port.
59. In battle.
60. Enemies . . . weaker.
61. With so many assurances of friendship before my departure and the hope. . . .

have to come there with the army the next winter.[62] I rode off then to my squadron, having received a certificate of good behavior for the commissary, in which the *incolae*[63] beg the commissary to send none other than myself to them next winter. But my retainer, a certain Wolski, a squire from Brzeziny, remained and married a serf girl of that Danish gentleman, the daughter of a rich peasant, which step made them more hopeful that surely I, too, would return to them. But he did not keep his word either, for he deserted his wife and went off to Poland with Piaseczyński's regiment, claiming afterward that, asleep or awake, it was as if something kept calling into his ear: "You have forsaken God."

Once back with my squadron, we set off promptly on the fourth day for the camp that had been pitched between Friederichs-Odde and Ribe. Friederick is not a town, but an exceedingly strong fortress on the sea; while Ribe is the very beautiful town of the Ribe archdiocese,[64] once celebrated in the days of the Catholics. Beside Friederichs-Odde, the above-mentioned fortress on the sea, which faces Fyn, two other fortresses have corners on the sea, that is Helsingör [Elsinore] and Kronborg, which stand directly opposite each other;[65] and no one, be he with the most powerful fleet on earth, can pass through to the ocean *ex mari Baltico* without the permission of the Danish king and he is obliged to pay for it. *Fridericus Daniae rex* — which one I know not,[66] there being several Fredericks — admirably erected this Kronenborg by casting a frightful quantity of stones into the depths of the sea, out of which he built the foundation *in profundo;* and, finally, on top of this base, having raised it above that water and the tossing waves, he laid a foundation that has never crumbled under the sea's worst onslaughts. Everybody who navigates between these fortresses must bow and beg and pay the *vectigal constitutum* or rather *portorium.*[67] The local inhabitants boast of how once when Alexander Farnesius, *dux Parmensis,* was fighting *contra Belgas foederatos,*[68] five hundred Dutch ships were locked *in mari Baltico,* by order of the Danish king, so that all could be wiped out, no one being able to get away; but the allies, paying an enormous sum of money, ransomed them. Such is the advantage of

62. A discreet reference to Pasek's romantic experience described further on. The "friends" would be the Dyvarne family.
63. Local residents.
64. Pasek's error: it was only a bishopric.
65. Pasek is wrong. Helsingör is the town near which Kronborg (Hamlet's castle) is located on the island of Zealand. Opposite it on the Swedish peninsula lies Helsingborg. The castles in these two towns guarded the passage through the Sund.
66. It was Frederick II.
67. Established duty . . . port tax.
68. Alexander Farnese, the Duke of Parma, was sent to fight the United Provinces (1578-1592).

those straits in the Baltic, wherefrom the Danish king has an enormous revenue though there be no mines, *auri* or *argenti,*[69] in the country. In addition, he has provinces rich in game and fish, abundant in meads, one supplements the other, with whatever is needed. Greenland has so much fish that if people did not catch them, there would be no *fretum navigabile*[70] because of them, especially herring and cod, which they catch in January and leave outside in the wind and freezing weather until they're dry as wood. One thing is had in one province, another thing in another, and so none lacks for anything. But enough about these provinces and the nature of them, for I did not undertake to write a history, but to describe the *cursum*[71] of my life; I return, therefore, to the subject matter from which I have strayed.

Besides the order to get underway, an order was also issued to the effect that all the squadrons should arrive at the camp on the same day, and so we did, *cum aedificatione* of the foreign troops, for in one day our army poured into the camp as if out of a sleeve; whereas the Emperor's army took one week-and-a-half to assemble. Both armies then stood a mile from each other. General Montecuccoli resented the Governör because all the officers of the Danish king with their new recruits reported not to him but to the Governor wherefrom they took orders, having been so commanded by their king. During their first encounter, they quarrelled over this. The Governor said to him then: "There is no need for us to squabble here or to be angry over a grudge that the sword can settle between us. You are a soldier, I am a soldier, you are a general, I am a general: I'll give you satisfaction tomorrow." He sent Skoraszowski to him then, Crown Carver Leszczynski's lieutenant, challenging him to a duel in private,[72] lest the army become riled, but so polite was Montecucculi that he declined to ride out, only sending his officers with a treaty; and when the old man [Czarniecki] saw them he charged toward them like a thunderbolt supposing it to be the General riding out; but seeing someone else, he stopped and heard the delegates. The Elector, while this was transpiring, was three miles away from us with his own army, but when he saw Montecuccoli, he was to have said: "You did well by not riding because had you made trouble for Czarniecki, you would surely have had to do with me as well, since I am representing the Polish king here."

Three days later God punished Montecuccoli, for he was struck down by cannonfire; it was not a cannonball that hit him but a fragment of ship, blown out by the ball, that sliced both his calves. Besides, having eaten

69. Of gold or of silver.
70. Navigable strait.
71. Course.
72. The story of a duel between Czarniecki and Montecuccoli may be Pasek's invention. There were misunderstandings between the two, however.

bread for two winters and done nothing, he wanted to show off and prove himself on his own. He loaded his men into those Dutch ships, as well as other merchant ships which he had brought in, and sailed forth between Fyn and Friederichs-Odde; when the Swedes, from this side and from that, began to make him turn in circles, he returned in confusion and injured his calves. Evidently the Lord had ordained things so that the battle for this celebrated fortress, as well as that province up there might be waged not by a German rapier but by a Polish sabre; wanting, belike, to requite our people for the shame which He permitted them to suffer in their homeland from the Swedes.

From then on, the Governor had us harass them without respite, raiding, shooting, luring them from their bastion. And at first, they were foolish enough to let themselves be taken in; later, they refused and kept within the fortress. But now our men began entrenching themselves and by night were digging in so close that not only cannon, but musket shots could reach them; but as these trenches were imperfectly fortified, our army stood by all day to keep the Swedes from making expeditions to our earthworks and dislodging us. Only when night came at last, did they reinforce them; gabions were brought, earth and stones poured in, cannon transported, and all very quietly; for by day, it was difficult to do under the constant peppering from the Swedes. Friday, when they saw our fortified earthworks — at dawn the same day our dragoons under Lieutenant Tetwin approached so close they were within musket range — the Swedes lost heart, having been pried out of one corner tower. In the afternoon of that day, they attacked us, but our men withstood them forcefully. From the camp, our army charged full-tilt; they retreated, leaving behind several dozen corpses. That night, from Friday to Saturday, the Swedes piled onto ships, while on the side facing our camp they kept up shooting, shouting, and making a great clamor, and fled to Fyn, anticipating we would storm the fortress on Saturday morning.[73]

In the morning, we wonder at such quiet in our neighborhood, suddenly as our men were looking toward the fortress, people were unfolding banners on the ramparts and shouting: *"Vivat rex Daniae!"* Every one of our retainers who is quick runs out of the camp in search of spoils, but the Governor sent Męzynski, the Sergeant-at-arms, to order everyone out of the fortifications at that instant, under penalty of death, while Tetwin was to post a watch all around so that none should

73. Pasek's recollection is erroneous. These events took place the night of May 26—27, hence from Monday to Tuesday. It should be emphasized that the siege was not carried out by Poles alone, but also by the Austrians. Besides, the Swedes were defending themselves only in the Björsodde fortifications, in view of the destruction of the main fortifications. Thus the taking of Friederichs-Odde was not such a great triumph.

consider entering. Until the sergeant arrived, they plundered whatever they found; but there was not much of anything to take except for provant, and that very spot where they came and went carrying things was nearly over the place where the powder had been planted. After everyone had left the fortifications, the mines go off, but they caused not the slightest injury to any person, nor did they damage the fortifications or the buildings, nothing was touched, except for two oblong barn-like buildings which burned down — storehouses belike; other buildings remained whole. Now that is the work of a wise leader: to think ahead and to take precautions for the safety of the army; for unlikely it is that no harm would have been done there; another thing is that our men quickly understood that the enemy had escaped and rushed in immediately to take away whatever was there. Whereas the Swedes had supposed that their escape would go unnoticed until much later, which is why they set the explosive to go off so late.

In such manner, that fortress, which had gobbled up 20,000 people when the Swedes were taking it from the Danish king — as the commissaries themselves told it, 9,000 Swedes and 11,000 Danes perished[74] — returned to its owner and without casualty to our army. According to the commissaries, the ground there had soaked up human blood like water after a heavy rain. So the Swedes fled to Fyn from Friederichs-Odde and from death, thinking that it would not find them amid the seas; but in this they were disappointed, for in a short time, it sailed after them there too, about which I shall tell you by and by.

The Elector congratulated the Governor on this success, but there was envy in his eyes; the Germans being jealous that God had delivered up to us so renowned a fortress. The Swedes too were awfully vexed that the mine had missed the mark. Not until the third day, did the Governor install a *praesidium* of Danes and a Danish commandant, fearing lest there be still other mines. Those Dutch ships now stood at the fortress in the excellent port. Meanwhile they were conferring on what step to take in regard to Fyn, since so mighty a fortress as Friederichs-Odde had fallen into our hands; the which was a *socia* of Fyn, now turned *in aemulam.*[75] We remained in camp. But our old man [Czarniecki] was never idle, since there were some 200 boats; whenever he had a mind to it, the dragoons and select Cossack troops would embark and invade the Swedes on Fyn, sorely harassing them; the Cossacks, especially, performed astonishing deeds; 300 of them there were, selected for age and size; you would have said they were born from the same mother. The Swedes were kept busy on Fyn; there being

74. Pasek exaggerates. During the siege of Friederichs-Odde in November 1657 the Danes in reality numbered only 5,000.

75. Partner . . .into a rival.

14 miles of this province, they had to keep a steady look-out along the whole coast; never knowing where the enemy might land, particularly at night. In short, on all these occasions, whether raiding or storming, God manifestly gave us His blessing, for wherever we encountered the Swedes, we put them to rout. The Emperor's troops, on the other hand, the Swedes did not take seriously. During a raid they captured one cavalier, Myśliszowski, and sent him to the king at Copenhagen. The king, among other things, inquired of him: "What sort of army is it that Czarniecki has with him?" He said: The "one that normally marches in his division." The king asked: "Where were you when I was in Poland?" He said: "We were there, too, and we did battle with Your Majesty's army." "Why did you not fight then as well as you do now?" He answers: "Such, plainly, was God's will." The king: "Quite so; but I will tell you another reason; not every one would find his way home, should you happen to lose, and that is why you always try to win." The cavalier fell silent. The king asks him: "Why are you silent?" [He answers] "Because I know not what to say against the truth." But even the Swedish prisoners confessed that they see a complete shift in fortune.

As soon as the Swedish king learned of the taking of Friederichs-Odde, he began to treat with the Danish king for peace. And in the army he had the trumpets sounded to announce that whoever wished, was free to leave for Poland, being given official discharge and a contentment, *in gratiam* to Radziejowski. But few such turned up; although [thousands] of them were in the Swedish army, scarcely 150, all of them gentry, left with Radziejowski, among these were Kompanowski, Przeorowski, Kaznowski, and Rafal Jarzyna, son of Marcin the castellan of Sochaczew. Korycki remained, as did many Poles who *assueverunt*[76] there and did not expect their lot to be so comfortable in Poland upon their return. We being encamped for eight or more weeks near the Emperor's troops, made life utterly miserable for each other; they complain about us that "your patrols are stealing from us"; whereas we grumble at them, that their wives are eating up all the bread in our camp. We retreated three miles from them then, but as before the women found their way to us, only not as often. Meanwhile, communiqués arrive from our king, *denuntiando imminentia pericula*[77] to our country from Muscovy, and ordering us to be ready *ad regressum*[78] toward the border by the time the second missive arrives.[79]

76. Had grown accustomed (to it).
77. Informing (us) of the imminent dangers.
78. For a retreat.
79. Not quite accurate. The Polish armies initially were to be moved to the Szczecin coast, where it was hoped they could better be used against the Swedes.

As for me, an involvement of my affections is causing me great anguish. Frequent letters fly back and forth. At one moment the thought of staying occurs to me, at another, the thought that I ought not; again, that it cannot be otherwise and I must do so, for I feel sorrowful at having to cast aside so recent a happiness as this affect, the like of which is not easily come by. I wrestle with these thoughts as if with bears. While being of such a mind to stay, so jubilant did I feel; but when not of such a mind — there I was, distressed again, ruing the tender feelings of those people, as I beheld the picture of how I would fall *in censuram* for my ingratitude and deceit. Several men from my company took notice and they ask me: "What makes you at times thus absent-minded?" I told them that one cannot be the same all the time, but to no one in the world did I ever let my secret slip, and they would have known nothing, but for Lanckoroński blatting a little to our standard-bearer about my feelings. But though he was often with me even he did not know all there was to know; seeing but my inclination, he took my measure. Before long, my fellows of the Horse *investigarunt* a little these thoughts of mine and forthwith discouraged me from everything. Whereupon a courier arrives with a letter, they having found this out there, as the Polish army is nearing the border; the burden of this letter — all the other letters, of which there were plenty, having perished — was this:

Magnifice Domine[80]

What is dear to our heart, we readily adore in our soul, desire to affirm in our words, and yearn to see with our eyes. What esteem my worthy parent has conceived for the distinguished hero of a glorious nation and with what affection he honors him who is the companion of such a leader is proven by the very frequent mention of your name, My Lord, as well as the steadfast resolve, in which he persists, to love you not as an adopted son but as one of his own flesh and blood. If my father loves you, thereby does his daughter love you no less, for such a tender and ineradicable affection has taken root in her soul that were it possible to send in this letter her afflicted heart, all could read with ease, the clear and eternal proofs of her sincerity. I confess to you now what I have long concealed, that in my whole life I have never felt any attachment in my heart for any of the men, among the many seeking my hand, but for you, My Lord, and I am pleased to believe that this is God's will and the consequence of his decision. Should you, My Lord, cherish in your heart what you have confessed with your lips, then I shall call it happiness; but if your lips, in order to appease me, declared something quite different, it would be a dreadful sin against love of neighbor. Picture my love, which neither distance nor the modesty of my estate is capable of separating from you. It runs briskly through bullets, through cannon fire, through countless

80. The letter was composed entirely in Latin.

dangers; it hastens to visit the realm of Bellona without in the least fearing her adherents; it thinks of naught save how to slip within your camp, undaunted by the sounds of martial trumpets; it intends to go wherever fate may lead and the secret springs of the heart may call. God willing, may it escape vehement reproaches and may it enjoy the fulfillment of our troth. I offer you a faithful heart; receive it and rememember your word which awakened my hopes. My parent's house, thanks be to God, is distinguished enough and able to stand beside the most ancient families in the Polish Kingdom. There prosperity is no secret. My ways, though simple, you praised after all; if, therefore, they please you, do not be dissuaded. My Faith is no hindrance for I, too, believe in that person of the Holy Trinity who, by his Grace, inclines human hearts. My father's words, that my fortune cannot be taken out of the country, let them not stand in the way. The author of that law is my father; whereas you are its interpreter, you, My Lord, the plenary executive. Yours is to command, mine to obey. The honorable Ricaldus, Commissary General and a secretary of our kingdom, has furnished me with proofs of your sympathies toward me. To confirm my genuineness, I beseech God and my dearest sister, who surely will reveal my feelings clearly. For all my words, there are as many sighs; for all my memories, as many tears. Should someone ask me "why do you do it?" Enough to say: "Heart, answer for me." My heart is no longer my own, but yours; it has abandoned me, it accompanies you, abides in you. Do I speak the truth? Inquire. Counsel me what to do with my heart's rebellion. You can easily find a remedy for everything, should you wish to. If you forsake me, remember that divine wrath has always punished ingratitude. That, however, I do not wish for, I do not doubt your oaths, I only warn you, lest those outrages be repeated, which we condemn in people of previous centuries. It does not behoove me now to desire any more than your presence, My Lord, in my father's house, for your presence — so I believe — will turn all to the better. Come for one hour at least; I earnestly beseech you, ardently summon you, impatiently await you as the esteemed gentleman to whom I shall remain warmly attached my whole life.

Eleonora in Croes Dyvarne

After her signature, she put in a plea for my retainer who had got a wife there *me inscio:*[81] "*Dominus Wolski sperat hac occasione procumbere ad pedes Dominationi Suae una cum supplici nostrum omnium libello et deprecari gratiam Magnificentiae.*[82] Which letter I would not have believed myself, being phrased in a way most unlike a woman's mind, had I not known her *scientiam* and heard many a time her casual *discursus*. That letter now put my heart in chains. I resolved irrevocably to go there and wrote a letter promising to come. My letter was composed in words matching hers, phrase by phrase. I left three days later, without anyone

81. Without my knowledge.

82. Squire Wolski hopes to take this occasion to fall at your feet, with the humble supplications from all of us, to impore Your Honor's mercy.

knowing where I had gone or why. While enroute, I fell in with Piaseczyński's regiment, where Rylski, a relative of mine, was carrying the standard in the colonel's squadron. I disclosed my secret to him *in toto;* showed him the letters and accepted his *consilium*[83] as from one of my own family. He persuaded me *omnibus modis*[84] not to throw away this opportunity, declaring he would go with me himself. We spend a day drinking to this expedition, then another. The third day we set out; while enroute, news comes to us that several thousand Swedes have disembarked at Skanderborg,[85] through which place we had to pass in order to reach those people. Nevertheless, we ride on until Vejle but there we become alarmed. The Prussians are arming, they ask us where we are off to. We told them ; they convince us we would be unable to pass through, for the Swedes, since landing, have been repairing the old fortifications, desiring to establish themselves again in Jutland and gain some sort of *dominium*[86] in recompense for Friederichs-Odde, and the prince is getting ready to smoke them out." We listened to them, and so turned back.

We ride into camp, and here we find a sortie in the making. The Governor wants to set out, being *in procinctu*[87] for the road, when up runs an *oberstleutnant* from the Elector to discourage the army from this action, for, being the closer, he can cope sufficiently himself. The Governor replied: "With the old lady out of the cart, it's easier on the wheels. With this one battle, at least, let them make up for the good they've never done around here, except to eat bread aplenty." We encamped then; I, as before, intending to be on my way as soon as the Swedes are smoked out. The Prussians had not even set out before the instruction from the king to depart for Poland arrives.

Pondering these *impedimenta* I say to myself: Dear God, belike my design is not Your holy Will." And then Rylski comes in and asks: "What have all our plans come to?" I answered: "To naught, belike." Says he: "Just how I see it. We shall have to let well enough alone." And so discoursing, we took a drink or two, as Poles are wont. And this bit of tippling brought back all my tenderness, so that I was near to tint the liquor with my tears; afterward, we parted. The night did not bring drowsiness despite my being tipsy. And I drank even more, trying to get to sleep; but it was of no earthly use. So are the tender passions in

83. Advice.
84. By all means.
85. Skanderborg is a town to the northwest of Aarhus. As it is situated about 20 kilometers from the sea, the Swedes could not have disembarked here. The mistake may have arisen from the fact that it is on a lake and in Pasek's memory it remained a city on the water.
86. Hold.
87. All ready.

young people irksome. For me it was neither her wealth, nor her ineffable loveliness, joined as it was with an intelligence and learning uncommon to her estate, but the love which she conceived for me, a poor fellow, or to speak *in plurali,* which they conceived, for plainly both parents as well as house servants and serfs, just as she did, now looked upon me as their own son and master. Leaving this to the divine design and embracing the feet of the Infant Jesus whose picture I had with the Blessed Virgin, I applied it like a compress and forthwith a desire ensued to go to Poland and not remain there. Next morning the trumpets sounded the departure for three days hence; but it was delayed a week, as the Elector sent to us with a request to leave him at least a few detachments of horse, if only for our good name, if only to say that not all Poles had departed *ex regno Daniae.*

The decision then was to appoint Piaseczyński with 1,500 men. As soon as this order was given, my squire Rylski immediately changed his *consilium,* for what he had previously dissuaded me from doing — saying I should not remain — now *in contrarium* he was persuading me to do, *ex ratione* that he too was staying, pointing out that there will be many ways of getting there, many battles, and once there, we can decide *de ulterioribus,*[88] than be free to do whatever we will. Once again my mind was inclined to this plan. Father Piekarski learned of these designs. What storms of invective! "Do not do it! What are you after? Do you know where these things end? When you are seduced by the *ducedo* of luxury *et uses cohabitandi*[89] so that you never get around to leaving for Poland, when there follow *persuasiones continuae* and they land their catch, and you will be living here — a man is known by the company he keeps — you will become a Lutheran. Now this will be splendid: to choose a wife but lose your soul. Besides, what joy could such a good match here bring to your parents and relations, were they to hear about you only through the mails, but not to see you? Just so, as if you would have died and gone to heaven, a *regnum amplissimum,*[90] more bountiful than Miss Dywarna's *facultates.*[91] It's no comfort to hear that a kinsman is faring well 200 or 300 miles away, but it is when I have him close by. Do not do this! I beg you!" So it turned out, and well it did apparently, for Rylski perished soon after on Fyn. Who knows whether it might not have befallen me too there? For surely, remaining behind, I could not have missed that battle.

We set off then toward the border, after bidding farewell to those who were staying behind, I weeping as I glanced in the direction where they were expecting me for the winter. While they, learning that our

88. About what next.
89. Sweetness . . .and the habit of being together.
90. Most sumptuous kingdom.
91. Here, "riches."

army was off to Poland, despatched that same Wolski with a letter, having given orders, should he not find our army in camp, to pursue us even as far as Hamburg for further communication. They dressed the fellow in German clothes, but his speech was Mazovian, for he knows not how to utter more than *Gib Brut, gib Szpek, gib Haber!*[92] But they acted foolishly because had he rode in Polish garb, he scarce would have gone 15 miles from camp to overtake the army (I having compared the time in his telling); but after he passed through those areas, which the Swedes had once occupied — being now back where they came from, having retreated before the Elector, not wanting to try their luck — he came upon the Emperor's troops. They speak to him in German — nil; in Latin — nil; finally, they say: "You're some kind of spy: German clothes, but a tongue that fits them not." They took his horse, ripped out his letters, and reading them let him go back. So I did not hap to read those last attentions, whereof Wolski told me, having since returned home; an unlikely thing it would have been, not to have acted upon those letters, which were from her parents. The Emperor's men read those letters in Wolski's presence and afterward those who knew Polish asked him *de statu rerum,*[93] what it was about and why. When he told them, the prudent ones among them were indignant at his being held up and robbed, he being sent on an affair of such a nature. The fourth day they ordered him to pass freely from under guard; when he returned to his gentleman, the household filled with laments. They had hoped I would stay in Hamburg upon reading those letters, if he should catch up with me; from there some means of passage could be arranged. Curious it is — comparing my time with the time in Wolski's account — for exactly when all was going awry there, his being held up with the letters, his return bringing such grief, such a weight there was on my heart too, that I knew not whether I was dead or alive.

Jędrzej Zaręba did not leave my side for one moment, seeing that *alterationes*[94] upon my face. How, after all, the heart *praesentit!*[95] Plainly, it was not God's will, and so those things turned out as they did.

After we left Jutland, Kazimierz Piaseczyński, being an ambitious man and, in the art of war, nearly on a par with Czarniecki, made a valorous effort to stand up *pro gloria gentis*[96] so that those up there who *aemulantur*[97] with him could see that he was not eating bread for nothing. In order to leave behind a good name for both himself and Poland, Piaseczyński, having singled out a moment, the Swedes being

92. Give me some bread, some salt pork, some oats! (Pasek's orthography.)
93. About the state of affairs.
94. Affliction.
95. Has presentiments.
96. In defense of our people's glory.
97. Were in rivalry.

not so *diligenter*[98] in guarding Fyn's shores as before our army's departure, and seeing rather that they were preparing for action against the Emperor's troops and Brandenburg — took three regiments of foot from the Elector and detachments of horse and ferried an army across in ships. The Swedes strove mightily to prevent our men from landing, but as I said, their strength had been broken in the sundry fortified places along the coast; and before reinforcements could gather, those resisting our men could hold out no longer and so let ours land. Our cavalry charged, broke through, and put them to rout, then, coming to a halt, awaited the arrival of more guests. There were 12,000 Swedes in that place; as for the local inhabitants every man was a marksman, every man a soldier and, on top of it all, a magician.[99] So a mighty force descended upon a handful of men. As both sides clash in the very first charge, Colonel Piaseczyński, struck by a bullet in the breast, perished. Rylski, my kinsman, perished along with him together with several cavaliers and their retainers. Yet the rest of our troops who withstood the gunfire, took up the sword before the Swedes had time to reload. *Et interim* more Prussians crossed over in another spot; that is, in the place which the Swedes had just abandoned: now did they slash, stab, and shoot. The Swedes were laid low, towns and villages despoiled. Everyone received his full share, for the Poles avenged the blood of their colonel. And all the *incolae*[1] got a good drubbing, almost half of them perishing, as they were found armed and defended themselves like Swedes; since they now fully recognized the Swedish king as their lord, never expecting he would let them be torn from his grip.[2] But just as they had deserted their lord, so were they abandoned by their infernal protector in whom they trust utterly. When God must punish, even the devil gives way.

Throughout the kingdom of Sweden and sundry provinces of Denmark, there are spirits — they are called *spiritus familiares* — and they are treated like Turkish slaves; whatever is commanded, they must do.[3] When Rej[4] was a deputy in Sweden, his favorite coachman

98. Watchful.
99. Pasek ascribes satanic qualities to the inhabitants of Fyn, apparently because he mistook them for the Finns, who were then regarded as outstanding sorcerers.
1. Local residents.
2. Pasek is inaccurate here. The allied armies led by Danish Field Marshal Ernest Albrecht Eberstein crossed to Fyn on November 14. The Polish detachments crossed of November 15. Piaseczyński perished in the battle at Nyborg on November 24.
3. *Spiritus familiares* or house spirits can also mean "sympathetic" or "helpful" spirits. According to the Danish scholar Rożniecki, the Scandanavians believed in house ghosts *(nisser)*, which were kindly, helpful elves.
4. Whom Pasek has in mind is not known. It could be that he was confusing Rej with Andrzej Morsztyn, who was a deputy in Sweden in 1655.

fell ill so he left him behind at a certain nobleman's, thinking to pick him up on his way back to Poland. The sick man was lying in an empty room, and his fever having passed, he heard the playing of beautiful music. Thinking they are playing somewhere in the other rooms, he lies there; when suddenly out of a mousehole pops a wee little fellow dressed in German fashion, a second and a third follow him, and then ladies; the music gets closer and closer and now they all begin dancing about the room. The coachman's in a panic. Then they start coming out in pairs, going as far as the door, until finally the music emerged; and a young lady was led out in customary wedding attire, then they went out through the doors of his room, without laying a hand on him. He's nearly dying of fright. They sent a wee one back in to him then, who said: "Be not upset by what ye see here, for not a hair from your head will fall; we are house spirits. We're having a wedding; our brother is getting married. Now we are going to the ceremony and shall come back the same way, and you, too, shall take part." But the man, not having a mind to view that *spectaculum,* got up and put the door on the latch, so they would not return through there. Coming back then from the ceremony, they find the door shut. Once more the music is heard; *interim* they try the door — locked. One tiny fellow slipped through the crack under the door and before the coachman's eyes, making himself as tall as a man, shook a finger at him, and undoing the latch, opened the door; over the same path as before they all tread and disappeared into that mousehole.

An hour later or so, another little fellow came out of the hole carrying a plate with some wedding cake richly studded with glazed fruit and raisins and says to him: "The groom sends you this so that you, too, can enjoy the wedding dessert." He, thanking him, took it and with great trembling put it beside him. When the doctor who cared for his health and those who nursed him during his illness come in, they ask: "Who gave you this?" He told them the whole story. And they ask him: "Why don't you eat it then?" He says: "I'm afraid to." They tell him: "Don't be a simpleton, fear not, these things are good for you; these are our house spirits, our friends, go ahead and eat it!" But still the man is unwilling. Then, taking the wedding cake, they ate it in front of him, telling him that "we often get things from them to eat, it does us no harm."

They also employ these little people for sundry tasks and services. The Fynians rely very much on their backing, but I have yet to hear of any Pole nicking his sabre on one of their necks; but then, our men always seasoned their bullets and swords before battle by rubbing them with divers holy things.

Marching back to Poland along the same course as before, we got as far as Hamburg, where we saw the Augustinian monastery from which

Martin Luther fled into apostasy.[5] The Governor stopped there. I, being *curiosus* about it, went to inspect the monastery and the cells — all their beauty and their adornment. I was even in the cell where Luther lived, a few of us having said we were Lutherans, and so trusting us they guided us about all those *antiquitates* telling us forthwith what happened and how;and we sighing. If I remember well, they call that monastery Uraniburgum.[6] A marvellously beautiful structure it is, and in a place very convenient to defend; a mighty lake like a sea washed it on three sides, with access only from the fourth side, from a great plain. Each cell was so beautiful you could say it was a king's study; and there are five hundred or so of them. The windows in all of them are large, colored, and bright, as of old, some sections having pictures of divers saints, mostly of the Blessed Virgin, all *cum inscriptionibus,* and others are of glass white as crystal. The church itself is of such beauty and spendor that its equal in Poland I have never seen. The altars and pictures are ancient pieces, but their colors so lovely, all varnished and gilded, that you'll not see a speck of dust on any one of them, you would say it was but the third day since the monks were chased out. They say the revenue that comes to the monastery is large; but they also say there were four hundred monks.

All of those cells into which I glanced were full of women and children who had taken refuge there from the army, exceedingly frightened of being robbed; they feared us more on our return than on our arrival. But seeing that we do them no harm, although the Governor and several hundred men passed the night in the monastery, while the whole army camped in front, they were in gladder spirits the next morning; as the army started off they came out in front of the monastery, blessing us and thanking the Governor. From there we went toward the border, passing through Reineberk, Bersztede, Wismar, the Duchy of Meklemburg, Guszterow, [Güstrow] Tomaszow, Zuraw, [Zurow], Tobel, Wistock [Wittstosk], Brandenburg, Szczecin, to our own supply column in Czaplinek, *alias* Templeborg.[7] But it had fallen

5. This thoroughly bungled description of the monastery prevents us from locating it with any certainty. Czubek assumes it to be a monastery left from the Franciscans near Hamburg no longer existing in the twentieth century. In Czapliński's opinion, Pasek is thinking of the large monastery, Bordesholm in Schleswig, also situated on a lake, to the north of Neumünster. Czarniecki's armies stopped here on their way to Denmark in 1658. It is possible that Pasek visited it on the return journey. Why the mention of Luther? This monastery previously belonged to the Augustinian order, which the guide could have mentioned; Luther was a member of this order for some time. The monastery in Bordesholm was actually among the more wealthy.
6. Uraniburgum was the name of the observatory built by the astronomer Tycho de Brahe on the Swedish island of Hven.
7. Three place names seem to be distortions, by the author or the copyist: Bersztede,

to rack and ruin, for some soldiers had died; others had gone off to their homes; still others had gotten married; also the wagons had rotted, and no telling what had become of everything.

We walked over the border then, thanking God for allowing us to look upon our fatherland in good health and singing jubilantly to the honor and glory of His Almighty Name. Then the squadrons crossed separately. Our army was assigned to winter quarters in Wielkopolska and Warmia. At the same time, the army under Field Hetman Lubomirski was returning from Malbork [Marienburg].[8] When, during the march, various squadrons mingled together, no need to ask from which division a squadron came, for it was obvious at first glance: if they were thin, poor, barefoot, and horseless, they were Malborkites; but if they were on horseback, armed, and sufficiently clothed, they were from Denmark or, as they called us, Czarniecki-ites.[9]

As for those who, being afraid to go with us, had deserted us at the border, God punished them and they either perished or were ruined fighting here in Poland. Our squadron happened to be assigned to Oborniki and Mosina near Poznań. While marching there on that occasion, I contracted typhoid fever. This is how: They were bearing a sick cavalier on a stretcher, whom I had known since my youth and who was a good friend; I was still going to the schools in Rawa then, while he to the district chancery-office. (I was also a good friend of his brother's.) I took pity on him, not knowing what he was ill with and seeing he had lagged behind his squadron a mile or more. I invited him then to my lodgings to pass the night. A few days later I fell dangerously ill, my company was beginning to despair of my recovery, but they made great efforts to save me; and soon after I started to *convalescere.* Upon arrival in Poznań, I gave thanks to God for having brought me back to my former good health and also for deigning to preserve my health in a foreign land, where, through His Holiest Grace and His Most Immaculate Mother, not even a finger ached. Half of our squadron then stayed in Mosina, half in Obornki. I was quartered in lodgings on the market square, but both host and hostess were terrible rascalities. I went to stay then on Poznań Street at a weaver's, a serf of the village's owner and a decent man whose home offered me much

Tomaszów (perhaps Teterow, a town east of Güstrow) and Tobel (possibly Dabel). Given this material, any attempt to establish Czarniecki's itinerary runs into great difficulty. From his correspondence, we know that on September 20 he was in Wittenburg in Meklemburg and on September 29 was in Schwedt on the Oder.

8. In the course of 1659 Lubomirski had driven the last Swedish garrisons from the Prussian forts (Cazin, p. 105, note 1).

9. Other accounts (Kochowski and Walewski, for example) give a different picture of Czarniecki's troops. In short, they describe his returning soldiers as clothed in little but their glory (Cazin, p. 106, note 1).

comfort after my illness: as I would eat only small fowl, that man despatched everyone from his home to sundry places, trying thereby to have them at all times; and all these services he rendered with great gratitude. Henceforth, I came back speedily *ad perfectionem* of health, save that my hair had fallen out. And so I say: "God preserve me from another such malady in my lifetime!"

We ended the old year then — may God's name be praised — in Mosina in 1659.

The Year Of Our Lord 1660

Please God, we began in Mosina; stationed there for the entire winter we were, after such hard labors and so distant an expedition to the far side of the Baltic. But the dangers menacing us then from both Muscovy and the Cossacks did not even give us leave to indulge in a bit of peaceful Bacchic revelry in our quarters during Carnival Season.[1] Urgent summons are sent round,[2] not as an order this time, but as a plea, acknowledging that the army's due was rest and reward for its valor and its pains; the king made entreaty, for the love of God and country, not to feel wronged if the army is called upon to bestir itself during so severe a winter (for the Muscovites, having subjugated all of Lithuania were overrunning our fortresses in Podlasie and were now preparing to march on Warsaw), and promised recompense to our division at another opportunity. We set off then from winter quarters.

During all that time, from the moment Czarniecki was given a separate division, which made him a third hetman, so to speak, we never once chanced to spend a full winter in quarters, but were continually having to brush with the enemy. And, as before, our army was always in the best of shape. Thus does God bless a sincere desire to serve one's country. We set off then upon the road to Łowicz and to Warsaw, not in a beeline (as soldiers are commonly said to go), but *magnis itineribus.*[3] Everyone was astonished. They did not expect from us such willing obedience.

The soldiers called on the king, handsomely outfitted *in veste peregrina:*[4] a *żupan* of drilling, *kontusz* also of drilling, a jerkin made of cavalryman's vesting, German-style boots with high tops reaching nearly to the waist, the *kontusz* to the knee. From whence that short coat, wrongly called a Circassian coat, with the high boots and garters did come into being, for it was we who were forced *ex necessitate* to create this outfit, having worn our coats short in those countries on account of

1. Shrovetide in that year ended on February 10.
2. Royal summons called for troops to assemble in Podlasie.
3. In forced marches.
4. In foreign clothing.

the boot-tops, so long are they, and wide. It would have looked a fright if a long coat were to bounce upon those broad boots, both front and rear. No Polish boots were to be had either. The army having set off without the supply columns, each man went in those he had on his feet, and they could not be so durable as to serve throughout the whole period abroad until our return.

That costume came into style then; everyone forthwith had even the finest coats made short, and boots, though Polish, made with high tops, with garters which were studded with silver, gold, rubies, diamonds, whatever you could afford. And the coats were shortened to show off the garters, everyone together seizing upon this fashion, even shoemakers and tailors. For such is our way in Poland, if you turn your coat inside out, people will be saying it's stylish, and so that style has a great vogue until it reaches the common folk. What don't I remember of ever-changing fashions in coats, hats, boots, swords, caparisons, and in all dress, both military and civil, even hairstyles, gestures, manner of walk and greeting, Lord Almighty, I could not write all of it down on ten ox hides! The which is the *summa levitas*[5] of our nation, wherefrom stems great *depauperatio*.[6] Once having purchased it abroad, I could have had that outfit a lifetime, and my children would get it too; yet no sooner does a year go by, or even less, but it's out of style, it's not worn; so rip it apart, make it over, or give it to the rag-fair and order something else, for to show yourself in it anywhere but *inter domesticos parietes*,[7] straightaway, like sparrows at an owl, twit, twit; they'll point at you, say your clothes hark back to the Flood. Of ladies and their whims, I say nothing, for with that material I would fill this whole book.

The style that we brought back then *ex necessitate* from Denmark went into vogue with everyone then. When our soldiers came dressed in that fashion, Queen Ludwika [Marie Louise Gonzaga] in Warsaw and her ladies-in-waiting wondered in amazement and had them turn round and round, while they looked the lads over, enjoying themselves. So that even should a person have fine cloth, he would attire himself in motley drilling if he wanted to tease some favor out of the king.

They gave us our pay from the treasury at that time, but for two quarters [of the year] only; the which I, receiving, set off directly from Łowicz for my parents', three miles beyond Rawa, in Bieliny. I, having arrived safely and surely in good circumstance, they welcomed me with such boundless weeping that for an hour they would not be comforted. I brought home with me various curios, particularly *nummismata*,[8] whereupon you will never look here in Poland. For my lady, we being

5. Greatest silliness.
6. Impoverishment.
7. Within the walls of one's own home.
8. Coins.

partial to each other, *panna* Teresa Krosnowska, the Rawa cupbearer's daughter, I brought a gift of linden-wood shoes; in Poznań I bought a singular little casket especially for them, made of ebony, inlaid with mother-of-pearl, and lined with crimson damask. And so I presented it as a great rarity *cum facunda oratione*[9] by my fellow cavalier and neighbor, *Pan* Franciszek Ołtarzowski, who, before showing what was inside the casket, first explained quite pleasingly how the gift he is presenting has never been seen in Poland until now. Whereupon they, taking measure from the handsome little casket, were expecting to see there something expensive and marvelous.

He spoke then to this effect (though I'm not like to recall all of it): "Love, My Esteemed Lady, is a volunteer in the human body, which, accepting no commands from any of the senses, is his own master and able to awaken a liking in himself for whatever he wishes. Let him cross the high Alps, let him swim across swift river-currents, let him tarry in the bottomless depths of the unfathomable ocean, he yet has his goal, toward which, with gracious eye, he directs his heart, toward which, though far away, he was wont to apply his kindly designs. Not having neglected such ways as would testify to his devotion, His Honor, *Pan* Pasek, brother gentleman and fellow cavalier, pondered long over what sort of gift to serve you with, My Lady, from those travels so distant from the borders of his native country. For it is nothing unusual to bring you something from far lands whereof the value and price cause people to commend it highly but which have familiarity in Poland; nor is it the fashion to bring from other countries what can be got even in Poland; but a curio such as, up to this time, Poland has never seen is unique. Let bold Jason flaunt his golden fleece for which he braved Colchis, seeking therein his own profit; let Hippomenes win the friendship of fair Atlanta by throwing a golden apple; still those presents cannot match this one.[10] And why? Because there was nothing rare about them, being made but of gold. Whereas I, on behalf of my brother, can make the boast that the gift I am presenting is so unusual that surely, neither in the king's nor in the emperor's treasury will the like be found; whose equal not even that famed and worldly woman of fashion, Cleopatra, enjoyed or possessed in her wardrobe. The which, even you yourself, My Lady, will readily admit, upon viewing this uncommon item. Through me, this gentleman thereby entreats you, My Esteemed Lady, to enjoy and graciously deign to accept this gift."

9. With a fine speech.
10. The mythological hero Jason, from Thessaly, made an expedition to Colchis in the Caucasus seeking the golden fleece. Atlanta, a mythological heroine who was unsurpassed in racing, killed with a spear the rivals who overtook her; in a race with her, Hippomenes kept throwing down golden apples, which Atlanta picked up along the way, thus letting herself be outrun.

They, taking measure of this testimonial, understood that inside the casket is a priceless gem; yet upon seeing the wooden shoes, they were as gracious as before. To view them, nearly everybody from thereabouts came round, neighbors as well as kin.

Having celebrated Carnival in good company then, among good neighbors, particularly with Mikołaj Krosnowski, the Rawa cupbearer — he at my parents', we in turn at his home — I went off to my squadron, though without much willing it. But what was to be done when such was the strictness in our division at that time that Lord preserve any cavalier from absenting himself for long from his squadron, or from failing to lead his squadron either to its station or back to camp, or worse, to miss a battle; straight off a trial, a punishment, they'd quote the regulations, and he would not be an officer, who did not have them at his fingertips. I overtook my squadron then, the men were nearly piled on top of each other, squadron crowded upon squadron. As we marched into Podlasie then, Muscovy, who with Trubetskoy and Słoński was making inroads around Siemiatycze and Brześć [Litewski], withdrew toward Mścibów. An order came from the king then, for the Governor to position the army during Easter week on the gentry's estates here along the edge of Podlasie and to live by the generosity of whoever might offer an invitation, as neither crown nor clerical lands any longer sufficed, having been devastated by the enemy and the Lithuanian army; also, the armies of the Hetman's divisions were pitched far away.[11] Warsaw, nevertheless, had to be protected along this side no matter how; and our army was to be ready to set off right after Easter.

We chanced to get the little town of Siedlce, belonging to his lordship the castellan of Zakroczym [Tomasz Olędzki na Chłędowie], for our respite, with three gentry parishes, all poor, for our provisioning. I was then delegated, along with *Pan* Wawrzyniec Rudzieński, who was to be our standard-bearer later, to assign billets and divide up these meager supplies. Off we went. They received us in a friendly manner *nemine reclamante,*[12] for Lithuania had inflicted such a stern discipline upon the *nobilitatem* in these parts that they had nearly turned into peasants. We stopped there on the fourth Sunday in Lent, first paying our respects to her ladyship, the castellan's wife, as she lived nearby just outside of town [Siedlce] on an estate named Strzała. Her husband resided elsewhere, some distance away; they lived apart, as he suffered from lunacy now and then; besides the Siedlce estate was her own, she being the heiress of the house of Wodynski. Riding off to see her, we

11. Hetmans Lubomirski and Potocki were then in the south in Volhynia, where they were keeping the Cossacks supported by Muscovy in check (Cazin, p. 114, note 1).

12. Without resisting.

were saying: "They'll be trying to protect themselves from quartering us *ratione iuris bonorum terrestrium,*[13] but then we told them the reason of our visit, showing them our written orders, and not the slightest opposition was there, indeed, they showed every gratitude, offered us food and drink, gave us leave to quarter troops.

Returning to town, right away the next morning we inspected the lodgings. The townsmen, having read the orders, knew which parishes were assigned to provision us. The gentry there, on learning of it, came two from each village to welcome the deputies, in the name of the rest of their brothers, fifty or sixty houses being in one village; and they brought with them oats, breads, oils, *etc.,* though no one told them to, asking for our regard and kind treatment of themselves. Here and there, one requests a good master for his village, expecting us to treat them as does Lithuania. Tuesday we assigned quarters; Wednesday we went off to the villages, riding about until Friday, still we did not finish our rounds, though the villages are crowded close together, but there are as many as thirty farms to a parish.

We returned to town then, issuing orders for each village to send two men with the tax receipts so that we could learn which village has more, which less, of cultivated lands.[14] Straight the next morning they stood before us, but as our squadron was about to arrive, we were obliged to leave them in order to lead it in, so they had to wait for us. On Passion Sunday, after morning Mass, we sat down with those receipts, reckoning with them till evening. This fellow and that is asking for a good master, one promises a goose in requital, one a capon, another a lamb for the holidays. We told each one singly and in secret: "that we've appointed the best and the least obtrusive of cavaliers"; so the fellow thanked us, promising a bounty. And they did not leave until we wrote the orders and handed them out to the cavaliers. And so true to their word were they, that whatever they promised *nomine* their village was delivered in Holy Week. They remembered us deputies too, so even had we taken no bonus for ourselves, we would have been well off and could have fed plenty of others besides. While delivering the provisions, they were accompanied by thirty or forty squires. The cavaliers, *per respectum* for their gentry brethern and also because they were provisioning us, though not obliged, made them to sit down and offered them something to drink. Sometimes they drank more than they brought, but *in recompensam* for being entertained, they delivered more without being asked. To the skies they lauded us then, saying that *Pan* Czarniecki's soldiers are angels, the Lithuanians devils. And none

13. By reason of the law for landed estates.
14. The tax collector, who collected the taxes levied by the Diet, distributed receipts; the soldiers demand to see them in order to assess the wealth of the villages.

of those who had implored us in private for a good man, could catch a single misdeed. It was, after all, a tolerable provisioning district or (as we spoke of it) respite.

I took the village of Strzała for myself, where the castellan's wife resided on her estate; she herself requested me. And I was very content with it, the lady being so decent; not only did she have me provided with food and fodder, but bade me to live there until my squadron departed. Besides, the village is just outside of Siedlce and my retinue and the horses were given whatever they might need. As for myself, I ate and drank in the manor house amid such high-flown frolics,[15] I thought I was in heaven.

She was a most upright woman, though full of kindness and jolly; one daughter she had, the only heiress, the girl later married Oleśnicki,[16] the Sandomierz chamberlain's son. On each holy day, she invited me there, bade me ask the cavaliers from my company, saying I should invite them to my own lodgings, for cards and dancing. For she had her own music, and a dozen or so ladies-in-waiting from excellent families, with good dowries, only one daughter, the heiress to several hundred thousand, to whom Stefan Czarniecki[17] then began to pay court — at the time he was district supervisor of Kaniów. He took part in that contest on the advice of the Governor, his uncle; who, from camp, fitted him richly for the courtship with a group of gallant soldiers, but luck wasn't with him; apparently it was not God's will. Later, I was told why he was not to her liking: seems he made too many jests and menacing grimaces; the same year she married Oleśnicki, the Sandomierz chamberlain's son.

My sojourn there passed like one day, so comfortable an existence it was; another like it I had not throughout the whole period of my service; for they loaded me and my wagons with such delicacies, the which you'll not find in camp, but only in homes where people eat them, and they carted things to me even in Kozierady as long as we were encamped there, it being only six miles away. Enough said that not even a mother could have shown more kindness.

The husband of that upright gentlewoman was the castellan of Zakroczym, a decent person he was, an old soldier, tested and true, save

15. There are several variants of this passage. Cazin translates it as "in joyous company." Czapliński suggests it is "merrymaking" not "company". The ambiguity has to do with the word "konwersacyja," which ordinarily means "talk" but here means "merrymaking." The *Słownik Języka Paska* suggests that in the context, the meaning may be "company." Wytrzens used the German *Konversation.* The adjective *arcyszumny* is equally ambiguous: it can mean "boisterous, uproarious, bombastic, high-sounding, grandiloquent, or sumptuous."

16. Her name was Joanna; she married Stanisław Olesnicki.

17. Stefan Stanisław, nephew of the Governor.

for being touched in his head, and that's why they lived apart from each other, having borne only one daughter. He ruled over his estates, she over hers; and each kept a separate court and staff of servants. When sound, he was a man of such valour, that all feared him. Once he trounced Karol Potocki's squadron in the first encounter, they at their full strength, himself riding out with ten cavaliers and explaining to them "not in my village, lest you'll be saying I'm confident in a crowd; but I'll wait for you in the open field," and so he did. When both sides had assembled, he challenged the lieutenant who rode out of the squadron. "To sword!" The castellan charged, smote him hard twice, and the man fell from his horse. Whereupon the entire squadron attacked him; he stood his ground then, and with his own suite set about subduing them: he sliced them to bits, slaughtered them, took their standard and drum, and sent it to the hetman.

He committed none of the evil deeds madmen do, only made himself into some mighty pious sort. Sewed onto his cap a little crucifix, neither glanced at anyone, nor bowed, passing through a room or the church; only lifting that cap with both hands so that he had the cross before his gaze, he would fix his eyes on it; his page walked at his side, carrying a sword. And he never laughed. His servants told how they had been serving him for a dozen years and had never seen him laughing. He visited his wife, but never desired to stay the night; dinner and supper eaten, he rode four miles off to spend the night at home. He spoke cleverly, too, sometimes — sometimes foolishly.

Once he came to his wife's for dinner; there was a company of four of us at the table. His lordship's arrival being announced, I say: "My Lady, do we go out to welcome him?" She says: "There's no need of that as he thinks himself unworthy." He entered the room then with that gravity and piety, holding his cap with the crucifix in front of his eyes; straight to her ladyship he went, kneeling down while she, like a bishop, laid her hands on his head, such being their custom, and he remained kneeling until she had done this. Sitting next to her ladyship was our comrade-in-arms, Kościuszkiewicz, a very gallant cavalier though elderly, a Volhynian, a very dignified personage, robust, tall, beard to his belt. And his lordship, on rising, says to this Kościuszkiewicz: "Hail! Lord Hetman!" The cavalier replies: "Hail! Lord King!" and they shook hands. Then he asks: "Is His Lordship *Pan* Pasek here?" — I speak up: "At your service, My Lord." He shook my hand, too, and I his, and he says: "I guessed at once it was Your Lordship, they told me you were young." And further: "I came here to thank Your Lordship, for being my wife's protector." And his page is holding that sword for him just at his elbow. I answer: "Such an honor as Her Ladyship's protector, I do not usurp for myself, but rather of all your subjects lying within this provisioning district." Then he says: "So you must, so God has ordained from heaven." Says Kościuszkiewicz: "Will my Esteemed Lord Castellan, as our host, deign to be seated, and command us to do the same, for the dishes grow cold." "Agreed, My Lord Governor, I, too have not yet eaten." After shaking hands with that company sitting next to Kościuszkiewicz, the which he had not yet welcomed, he went off toward the door. We move aside, we ask him to take a higher seat. His wife says: "Your trouble is to no avail, for he'll not do it by any means, and he'll ride off; such is his way." He took a seat then, lower than his wife's attendants and ours. He ate and drank well, at each glass, going first to his wife for permission, kneeling down for her to clasp his head. At times his discourse was to the point, at times pointless, and the sword right beside him with the boy, whereon I kept a sharp eye, a madman after all, being a touchy matter.

Dinner over, he says: "My Esteemed Lady and Honorable Benefactress, why so cheerless here? Have you no musicians?" She replies: "I do, My Lord, but they haven't the means wherewith to buy strings." Says he: "Call them over, Brzeski," and he reaches into the pocket of the boy holding the sword, and gives them three gold ducats; they came then and played. Dancing started up and whenever they bowed to him, he made the sign of the cross over them with that little crucifix and kept on drinking. As soon as he became tipsy, not a word more to anyone, but taking his leave, he knelt before his wife, then was off. She began to weep then for sorrow, that having such a husband was, for all that, as good as having none at all, when he conducts himself so unlike other men. Before he went off, one of our cavaliers, *Pan* Łącki, a Lithuanian, said to him: "Why does Your Lordship not partake of our good cheer in your own home?" He, striking his sword with two fingers, replies: "I've grown used to dancing with this maiden alone; were I to dance with her in battle array, it might make things unpleasant for someone." After that they left him alone and no longer invited him to dance. It was said that even at home, being in his cups, he has music played, and he performs various fencing maneuvers, now thrusting, now parrying, on and on, till he drops from weariness. An expert fencer he was, so they say.

Sojourning then in Siedlce, two of our cavaliers died on us, *Pan* Jan Rubieszowski and *Pan* Jan Wojnowski, old soldiers. *Mirabile* it is that these two people lived in such closeness that if things went well for the one, so they did for the other, and if badly, so for the one as well as the other. Both were Mazurians, both of them old, both soldiers, both named Jan, both were married and next to each other on the squadron roll, both equally mettlesome.

At Chojnice, when the Swedes attacked us in the night[18] both of

18. Chojnice is a town in Pomorze near Gdańsk. The battle took place January 1, 1657.

them were hacked, pierced with rapiers, and left on the field for dead; both recovered together from these grave injuries and both thanked the king for their funerals. The king, seeing how grave were their wounds after the battle, had ordered 600 zloties given to them, declaring it was for a funeral not a cure. Upon thanking the king then, they came away with 1,000 zloties each and continued the war, being with us in Denmark; and having a sort of pact with each other to share their fortunes both good and bad, both fell ill together in Siedlce and died the same day. When the time came to pay them a last homage, Jan Domaszowski, our lieutenant, arranged such a funeral for them in the church at Siedlce, a senator could not have had a more elegant, *in praesentia* of the local nobility and the soldiers, as well as many of the clergy. At the wish of the lieutenant and our company, I was bade, being also a Jan, to welcome the guests to the funeral repast. I set about this then, without having time to prepare a proper speech — those quarters of mine being a hindrance to me, for I was constantly summoned either to cards or chess or sometimes checkers — but I did put forth an effort not to make a mockery, knowing what a great number of people would be there; I also knew that *Pan* Gumowski, the cupbearer, a great orator, was to speak for the guests and *Pan* Wolborski, District Supervisor Rokitnicki's lieutenant, to offer condolences from the army.

When I finished, *Pan* Gumowski, the cupbearer, delivered his speech very *facunde,* very *erudite,* [19] but mixing the meaning *et connexiones,*[20] and anyone who knew a thing or two noticed this, especially the clergy; he skillfully got himself out of it later, complaining that I took several arguments that were part of his speech, so then he had to discard the ones that people heard in mine. He set forth how an architect is embarrassed if someone takes the wood already trimmed and planed for making a framework. Everybody understood the circumstance, and so it often happens, one orator taking the material of another. *Pan* Wolborski gave the funeral speech on behalf of the army. Those Arcadians[21] then being laid to rest, a relative of *Pan* Rubieszowski's, *Pan* Wąsowicz, came for his retinue; while *Pan* Wojnowski's retinue and wages were sent to his wife.

Orders came then to set off, the squadrons to assemble at Kozierady; news of Muscovy being that they were already rallying. We arrived at Kozierady three weeks before Pentecost.[22] The army hale and fit, save

19. Eloquently, eruditely. [Pasek's lengthy funeral oration has been omitted.]
20. And the logical connections.
21. "Arcadians" is an allusion to Virgil's *Eclogues* (VII,4), the two dead men having a common age and fate.
22. Pentecost fell that year on May 16; therefore, it was around the 25th of April. Czarniecki, as his correspondence reveals, was residing in Międzyrzecz in April and at the beginning of May he arrived in Kozierady.

that it was — as the Lutherans say —*pusillus grex,*[23] for there were but 6,000 of us in *Pan* Czarniecki's division.[24]

A thing to marvel at when they built me an arbor of birch boughs in front of the tent: the selfsame day a yellow bunting began to make a nest for herself at the very door to my tent, in the branches of that arbor. Fearlessly, she bore things to her nest amid a crowd of people; and having built it, sat upon her eggs and hatched them. There was a deal table on trestles in the arbor; at that table we ate, drank, played cards, sometimes fired shots, shouted, but the bird kept on sitting, unafraid of a thing, though she was right in the corner where the table was; when she felt like eating, she picked at the oats in front of my charger. Finally, she saw her fledglings come forth, she brought them up, and sent them on their way. Everybody said it was a sign of some glorious good fortune. Well, good fortune there was indeed, but it was the bird's who calmly hatched her eggs, it was not mine; for such troubles overtook me, I thought I would never get clear of them, and even with great loss to my earthly goods. Those troubles and losses beginning near Kozierady did not desert me for the whole year.

Two cavaliers from Czarniecki's squadron, the Nuczynskis, were drinking with their cousin, *Pan* Marcyjan Jasiński, a cavalier from our squadron; *Pan* Jasiński had also invited me to that feast. Would that it had never been! Having drunk sore too much, one of the Nuczyńskis began to provoke me greatly. I, being as drunk as they, say to Jasiński: "*Pan* Marcyjan, better you had not asked me here, when they provoke a quarrel and sprinkle mead on it." And I left the arbor, wishing to elude the devil, yet saying, "Whoever has a dispute with me, let him tell me tomorrow, not in his cups." I'm half-way to my tent, when Nuczyński overtook me: "Fight it out with me!" I replied: "You'd not take me for much of a sluggard, brother, but the obstacles are two: one, we're in camp;[25] two, I don't have my sword, as I went to my fellow officer's for a social gathering, not a battle. But if there be no other way, then tomorrow morning, and outside the camp not inside." I'm off to my shelter then, his groom is restraining him, holding him back. He gave the lad a punch in the face, tore out of his grip, came after me. I had to go out to him, after getting my sword. He's taking swipes at me and saying: "You'll die." While I'm saying: "God decides that." On the second or third thrust, I struck his fingers and I say: "So you see, you've gotten what you asked for." I thought he would content himself with that. He, being drunk, either did not feel it, or perhaps wanting vengeance, attacks me again, brandishes his sword once, twice, blood

23. A tiny flock.
24. According to Calvin's teaching, only a tiny flock of people will get to heaven.
25. According to the military regulations, dueling was forbidden.

now spattering upon his face. When I slice across his pulse, he collapsed. By then the revelers had been told; they thought he'd gone to the privy. The younger brother flies over, starts slicing thick and fast. God looked down on my innocence. We clash: both his hand and sword dropped. The cavaliers rushed out, but it was already over. Then Jasiński, the host of that carouse, comes and says to me: "O traitor! You've smitten my brothers on me! You'll have to deal with me now!" I say: "They got what they asked for." He began to call for swords, being without his, and to lead me off by the arm. The cavaliers are arguing with him: "You're the host; you ought to have stepped in and straightened the matter out. Do not commit this deed." By no means will he let himself be talked out of it, he leads me onward. Meanwhile, the lad brought him his sword. To be plain, I was afraid of him; several weeks ago, in front of the squadron, he slashed one of our company, Kossowski, to pieces. I wrench my arm away from him then, stand alone, and say: "What are you blaming me for? Hold off!" The cavaliers are holding him. When he lunges at Drozdowski, they let him go: "Be off, before you're killed."

There was a little, narrow river which we used to have to cross, narrow planks being placed over it. "There now, tear off toward that forest; we'll see who'll lay whom low, so that he'll not be coming back to camp any more." He shoves me ahead onto those planks: "Go in front, you! No sooner do I step upon the plank, but he slices from behind at my head, ,but theVenetian velvet was excellent and the Lord preserved me, it didn't cut through, save in one place the velvet gave way a little, and beneath was only a red welt as from a whip lash. Yet it befuddled me enough, so that I fell off the plank into the water. I pulled out of that place, fearing he might try to do better, and I make for the other side, saying: "Lord, thou seest my innocence." I come out of the water, he, too, had crossed the planks. I say: "You strike on the sly, you son-of-an-infidel!" He moves toward me: "I'll strike you right here now."

And here they all come out of their tents in the camp, they're all watching, the squadrons being encamped all along that little river. So mightily he smote then that I felt my own sword shudder in my hand; I withstood the first encounter. We clash a dozen times; neither side gaining the upper hand. I say: "Enough of this, *Pan* Marcyjan." He says: "You son-of-a-so-and-so, you've not done a thing to me and you've had enough." No sooner did he speak that reproach, but the Lord so deigned, that I cut across his cheek with the very tip of my sword, and leapt away from him. Now does he strike out at me even more; when I wound him in the head, he loses his footing. Then, taking my sword in both hands, I began striking him with the flat side, forcing him to the ground. Now do the cavaliers from ours and other regiments rush over, saying: "Hold! Kill him not!" Before they came running up, I thrashed him about 50 times with the flat of my sword in requital for that traitorous blow on the head from behind.

Such an ill-fated day was it that some fifteen duels were fought in divers squadrons. As for myself, the Lord obviously took me into his protection that day, if, having dueled with three men, he kept me from harm. No valor of mine was the cause, simply the Lord's regard to my innocence. Many other such lessons do I recall, wherein the one who provokes a quarrel always loses. Whoever will fall heir to this book of mine, I admonish and exhort to model himself on my example and the examples of many like me, never to make light of the most trifling instance, so that — even though a man be tried and tested — trusting of his own powers and mettle, never should he provoke a duel and go to it in arrogance; for let him know that he's easy prey. But if in all humility he should defend his honor from injury, calling on God to aid him, he will always win. This is my experience and many others'. Every time I gave provocation, I was always defeated; everytime someone provoked me, I was always victorious. So then, as a conciliatory gesture, I gave 1,200 zloties for the wounds and pain they suffered — as it is a *practicatum axioma* that "the loser weeps" — and separately for whatever the surgeon took. Jasiński got nothing for his mug; they also sentenced him severely: "for your being the host, doing nothing to reconcile your guests, or preventing them from fighting, and even challenging a man yourself to a duel, you will give 600 zloties to the Observants in Brześć and stand through three Masses on a holy day, wearing your armor and holding your sabre."

Then Skrzetuski[26] was sent off to make a surprise attack with a company assigned under orders — two cavaliers from each squadron; for there were already reports that Muscovy had assembled her troops and was moving closer. The raiding force set out then, and it encountered Słonski's squadron. The Muscovite squadron, though numerous and well-equipped, was captured. Making their way back our men feared pursuit; all night they marched. When day dawned, they had come to a village; putting their horses to pasture in the meadows, and themselves being weary, they made haste to sleep, having set a good watch round the Muscovites.

Now, close by on the river, was a gentry manor; a few of the soldiers rode over, wanting to get a meal for themselves. There they were about to pillage something, when they caught it — uproar, shooting. Our men were alarmed, thinking the Muscovites have taken to horse, but

26. Mikołaj Skrzetuski (a lieutenant for the Osiek district supervisor, Adam Uriel Czarnkowski) came out near the Russian armies around the middle of May.

they soon found out what it was. Lukasz Wolski,[27] a cavalier from Rawa with the Crown Carver, startled from his sleep, no sooner mounted on his horse but he charged straight into the river, and swam to the opposite side; he being both sleep-drunk and faint-hearted — for he was such as do not reckon with their own mettle, he joins the army when he would as like be raising chickens and chasing the kite away from his chicks — without looking round at what was going on, he plunged through the forest and arrived two days before the expedition, causing sore panic in the army.

We made haste then to run to the Governor and Wolski came to give his account. The Governor asks him: "What happened there?" To our still greater regret, that fellow tells how they captured about 300 Muscovites, how they took the whole squadron with everything, how they had great spoils, and then came the pursuers who, finding them asleep, attacked them and put them to the sword; the rest drowned in the river beside which they were grazing their horses. The Governor asks: "And Skrzetuski — was he taken alive?" He says that with his own eyes he saw how a Muscovite shot him, then cut his head off, "for I stood a long time, after swimming across the river, and I saw that no one got away with his life." I could hold out no longer and I say: "And why didn't they kill you?" The Governor shook his head at me: "Leave him alone!" But he himself asks him: "How did you get away?" He replies: "Since I wasn't sleeping, but holding onto my horse, and I hit out on the instant across the river; they fired several dozen shots at my back, but the Lord preserved me." Czarniecki asks: "What could the strength of that detachment have been?"He says: "No detachment that, Your Honor, but the entire might of Khovansky, for I saw nearly the whole army; it covered the fields like a great cloud, other divisions were streaming over the hills. And I chanced upon a gentleman fleeing, who also said that Khovansky was advancing with his whole force."

The Governor is vexed, but shows not a sign of it, he says: "The Lord is on our side! No matter, Sergeant, let the trumpet be sounded for the horses to be led in at once." They sound the trumpet then; the camp is abustle with comings and goings: our horses being several miles away from the camp, nearly every squadron's drove apart from the other's. Now did each nose droop, thinking: "The first ill-luck." They're asking Wolski, each about his own officer, and he tells how each perished; to be short, the camp was full of panic, grief, and confusion.

We went off to our squadrons, each to set his things in order; they're flying in all haste to the droves, some on horseback, some on foot. I

27. Łukasz Wolski was the son of the Lord Steward of Rawa and a cavalier in the squadron of Wacław Leszczyński, the Crown Carver. Another Polish diarist, Łoś, described him as a "brave person, a youth of some experience."

arrive and there my little attendant is saddling my steed. I ask: "And what do you think you're doing?" He answers: "Going for the horses." When I go at him with a cudgel: "Infidel! My life is dearer than all the horses in the world! Are there not three soldiers with the horses? Others will take their own, and they'll bring mine along, but I keep this horse tethered to the stake here in case of need. Should anyone attack, would you take this one away from me?" After putting my things in order, I went to the Governor again. On my way, I pass the bazaar and there is Wolski already at the Armenian's, weighing some booty, some silver spoons. I say to him:*Pan* Lukasz, did not our Jaworski escape too? He's ever a cautious one, you know, and he's on a good mount." Then he says: "You'll sooner glimpse your own ear, as see *Pan* Jaworski." I say: "For God's sake, *Pan* Łukasz, were you not mistaken or did you not get cut off from the party somehow, for I know you, you're a windbag from way back." He began once more to assert that which he had at first and, unburdening himself, he even became angry. I let him alone; I'm going to the tents, when here's Father Piekarski: "Stay," he says, "it's an evil day, brother." I say: "Remember, brother, there's but half the truth in that Wolski story, for I know his nature, he's prone to inventing things."

At that moment the Governor comes out of his tent, he's twisting his beard; that was a sure sign of vexation or anger. Approaching Father Piekarski, he says: "What are you speaking of?" The priest tells my words. To me: "So he has this weakness?" I say that such is his nature; his father, who is the tax collector in Rawa, has the same; even in the schools we used to call him "General *Nugator*."[28] The Governor taps himself upon his velvet headgear and says: "And I'm exactly of the same mind; for if a pursuit party did overtake them, unlikely it is that it so encircled them that all should have perished. Nor is it like to have been the entire force of Muscovy, for the reports I have say they're preparing for tomorrow's storming of Lachowicze with all their might, ladders and other instruments being just now transported to them, for they had lost all that during their earlier stormings." Straight after that he had Wolski summoned; and no sooner was this done but someone says to Wolski: "Brother, you weren't mistaken? It's a hanging matter to sow panic in the army." He says, "I'll wager my life, my neck, if something proves otherwise."

So the whole army since morning is *inter spem et metum* [29] its spirits as if nipped in the bud. The nearby droves are being led into camp, the other men are missing their droves, looking out for them. The squadrons organize themselves for the expedition until the day drew toward

28. Prevaricator.
29. Between hope and dread.

the close. The sun is setting when suddenly, someone is seen coming from the other direction, and I say: "Well, we've got some news now." They didn't recognize him, for he's on a captured Tartar horse, and wearing a Muscovite kalpak trimmed with fur and pearls. He gallops across the camp reviewing grounds, passing the squadrons, shouting: "Good news! Good news!" They rush out to him, asking whether the news is good or bad. He told them as he passed Polanowski. Now are they all outdoing one another in speedy pursuit of him, right to the Governor, in front of whom he tells the matter itself: "Tomorrow, God willing, our leader will greet you with a more multitudinous group than that wherewith he was sent out, and at your feet he will cast an enemy standard. We have only one hurt to regret: we lost and excellent knight in the battle, a cavalier of the Crown Carver's." Says the Governor: "God be praised! That cavalier you've not lost yet; you'll lose him tomorrow. Run and get that son-of-a-bitch." The Carver stands there, his lieutenant, Skoraszowski, too, as red as if his cheeks had been pinched. *Pan* Wolski they put in irons.

And thus the occasion was merry and agreeable *ex ratione duplici:*[30] first, that God had so favored us in this initial battle; second, that we now saw alive those for whom we had grieved and, above all, some hope now gladdened our hearts. As for Wolski, they wanted absolutely to chop off his head. None of us from Rawa even went to visit him, we were ashamed of him. He made request to us to plead on his behalf; no one wanted to become implicated. Only Father Piekarski and Skoraszowski, his squadron lieutenant, these two saw that he was spared; he was not tried but was ordered to start riding forthwith, leave the army, and never to say he had ever served in Czarniecki's division.

So then, the detachment, arriving safely the day after the cavalier it had sent, entered the camp in triumph, bearing the enemy standard unfurled and driving a mass of prisoners before it, all bound together, nearly as numerous as the detachment itself. When they present the prisoners, a great multitude gathered at the Commandant's. I too was there. The ceremony being over, I'm standing near the tent with Rafał Jarzyna, also from Rawa, and here the Governor says: "I thought that all of you from Rawa were good soldiers; but I see they are also fools." I speak up: "But you find them only in the Wolski family." And two Wolski kin are standing there, decent men: Paweł, who was later the district supervisor of Lityń, and another, whom they called "Castiron." That Wolski from the royal squadron began to bristle until the Governor says: "He is speaking of the Wolskis from Mazovia, but you are from Ruthenia; and there are others — the Romans, whereof Ovid

30. For a two-fold reason.

wrote *saevit atrox Volscus.*[31] So, plainly the Italian and Ruthenian Wolskis are good soldiers, being called *atroces,* while the Wolskis from Rawa are fools; side not with them. But from this day hence, I'll own *Pan* Pasek is a good judge of human nature, since he saw through all of Wolski's untruth." Our discoursing then ended in jests. A few prisoners were sent to the king.

News being come then from Sapieha, the Lithuanian hetman, that his army was as well equipped for combat as possible, we set out forthwith upon the route toward Mścibów. And Khovansky, the Muscovite hetman, marched toward us with all his forces — 40,000 strong they were — having left a few men at Lachowicze to watch the camp and of course the fortress they were so long in capturing, in order not to cease the assault, not to give a *respirium.*[32] For he promised himself he would take it immediately upon his return from the campaign, after putting us to rout. And there he came, just like a wolf into a herd of sheep, for so he was given to do in Lithuania, always marching to meet them as if toward certain victory. To greet us then, he sent Nashchokin, the second hetman, several miles ahead with an elite force of 5,000.

On the vigil of Saints Peter and Paul, they met our advance guard, the which, as it was not so strong as the Muscovite expeditionary force, sent to the army with word of the enemy being now face to face with them. And at that moment Muscovy charged them headlong. Until our squadrons and volunteers arrived, the advance guard was in a terrible plight; nevertheless, they mightily withstood the fire. There were already a few corpses on each side, and no sooner have we arrived, but half of Muscovy veers toward us; while the other half finishes the battle with our advance guard. A mighty blow they deal us then, wanting with their first charge to throw us into confusion. Yet we held up, though a dozen or so fell from their horses. When they see there's strong resistance here too, they did not appear so sprightly in the second clash.

At that moment, out of a grove of pine saplings come the 200 horse of Tuczyński's squadron and Antonowicz's Tartars; and once out, they break into a trot. Muscovy discomfited. We attack. And at once we're into their ranks, we've broken their lines. Now did we take up our swords, rarely firing now, but slash we did. The last of them took flight. We gave chase, overtook, and licked them. At that moment, the sun went down; our army arrived too, and we pitched camp right on that battleground. We held on to our horses throughout the night, placing two regiments on guard about the field. The Lithuanians also stopped next to us; there were 9,000 of them with their grand hetman Paweł Sapieha; their field hetman Gosiewski (also under-treasurer at that

31. Not from Ovid, but from Virgil's *Aeneid,* IX, 420: "Fierce Wolski rages."
32. Respite.

time) had been imprisoned in Moscow, put away by the same Khovansky.[33] This fate Khovansky anticipated for us too, even while sending Nashchokin ahead on that expedition, he charged him to "try and get me Czarniecki and Połubiński alive, so Gosiewski will have someone to keep him company."

Against the Muscovites' 40,000 we had only 15,000 with the Lithuanians.[34] Very small a fraction it was; nonetheless, a hope did comfort us; what is more, the corpses were falling with their heads toward Muscovy, the which soldiers always take as a sign of victory, if the corpses fall with heads toward the enemy. So then, that night we had something to eat, having ordered hardtack brought along in our satchels and in the wagons; we had grog too, in those metal ammunition boxes of the sort then used. A nip or two of that and your head spun round a bit, so that before long you felt like sleeping. Many a fellow, upon lying down in the grass, is fast asleep. Serving with us was one Kaczewski from Radom, a great rogue, and he says: "*Pan* Jan, why should we put a fist under our heads? Let's use this Muscovite for a pillow instead!" And lying there nearby was a stout Muscovite who had been shot. I say then: "Fine, I'll keep you company." So, laying down our heads, he against one side, I against the other, we fell asleep, having wound the reins of our horses round our hands; we slept thus for about three hours. But toward daybreak, something belched inside him, so that both of us sprang up; belike a soul still lurked therein. No sooner had it grown a little light, but a muted trumpet was softly sounding the order to mount. Our army set forth, with God as our aid, in order to gain an early start at this play. On the march, everyone performed his own devotions — songs, hours;[35] our chaplains, riding on horseback, heard confessions. Everyone was making himself as ready as he could for death.

Being come half a mile from Połonka, the army stopped to draw up in battle ranks, Czarniecki arraying his forces, Sapieha his.[36] The right flank with the royal regiment was given to Woyniłowicz, the left flank, artillery and infantry, to Połubiński. We marched on then in battle

33. Wincenty Gosiewski was actually captured by Dolgoruky. In Polish this is a play on words: "put away" *(schowany)* sounds like the name Khovansky (spelled Chowański in Polish). According to Pollak (p. 435), Gosiewski was imprisoned in 1658 and returned to Poland in 1662. After his return, he presided over the Wilno commission, which was negotiating with the army over the soldiers' unpaid wages. Bought over by the Queen's French faction, he supported the candidacy of Condé. He was killed in November 1662.

34. According to the Muscovite prisoners, Khovansky had 24,000 men. Today historians estimate his forces at 11,000 soldiers, and the combined Polish-Lithuanian forces at 8,000.

35. Hours were chanted devotions to Mary, very popular in Old Poland.

36. The battle took place June 28, 1660.

array, coming to a halt in view of the enemy, as our leaders desired the enemy to cross the river and come out to us; being unable to lure them out, we were ordered to keep advancing. Then about 6,000 foot came across toward us; three of our regiments advanced forthwith, shooting at them from this side; we drove them back across the river. From the other side, they began to pound us then with the cannon and our men were struck down. Standing next to me, one cavalier's horse caught a bullet in the head; and there it was flying out the tail; the cavalier jumped higher than three arms' lengths out of his saddle but was unharmed.

Over where our left flank and main bòdy were crossing then, they were having an arduous time; while we on the right flank had, for five furlongs or more, such boggy ground that in places a horse would sink up to the saddle ornaments and in other places walk on the surface, only those tangled weeds gave way like eiderdown. Nearly half the men were on foot, leading their horses. Here we're pulling ourselves out of that swamp and over there on the left flank a mighty battle is already raging. Just opposite our right flank at the crossing was a manorial farm, stockaded; Muscovy, anticipating we would try our luck there, had garrisoned within several hundred foot with four small cannons. They concealed themselves until we were struggling out of that marshland onto solid ground; only then did the Muscovite infantry move out. Now do they give fire, now do they scorch us from the cannons, balls fly like hail, felling many of our men; others are shot down by musket-fire. Nevertheless, we charged them at full tilt, knowing we had to unless all were to perish, should we turn our backs. And now, having jostled blindly into the fire, we mingled with them like wheat and chaff, for there was little else to do.

Then did a fierce massacre take place in that crush, the worst were the battleaxes. Yet a quarter of an hour did not go by, from the moment we tangled with them, before we had slain them all, so that not a single one escaped, we being in the open field; there were 100 corpses it was said. Our men also suffered, some were killed, some wounded; my bay was shot in the chest under me, smashed in the head with a battleaxe, another time in the knee. I would have used him still, if not for that knee-wound. Such luck I had with horses in the army, that I can't recall ever selling one, after having paid dear for him; every one of them was either injured, or died, or was killed; this ill-luck drove me from the army. For I would be a soldier now, and would have been all this time, except that my father no longer had the means wherewith to buy horses, and I, too, was disgusted by this ill-luck; many a time I'd shed tears over it. I changed mounts then, switching to my gray horse, having bid my retainer who was riding it, to wander back on foot across the river; but he soon overtook me, riding a captured horse, a better one than that upon which I was seated.

We're putting that infantry to the sword, and here Trubetskoy, under order, is hastening to their aid with ten squadrons of Duma boyars[37] and 3,000 regular horse. We stood then with our backs to that infantry and our faces to the new enemy. They attack as if they would devour us; we sustained it, for we had to. Seeing they want to press us into that bog, we fight like devils. The mercenary cavalry opened heavy fire on us, whereas our men fired but seldom, having already used up their charges on the infantry; besides, we lacked the time to reload. Thus, I always say that a loaded musket is most useful while advancing on the enemy; but once armies are locked in combat, reloading can but seldom be accomplished — the sabre's the main thing here. Only sabres are effective when it's man against man, this one against that, that one against this; so warm then did we make it for those mercenaries that they did not load their muskets. And as before, things did not go so harshly for us, though they had attacked us, firing.

We struggled, then, like two wrestlers fighting, now one, now the other being forced to bend. Trubetskoy, like a top, whirls about on a gray Kalmuck horse. Corpses pile up; by now as many as six of their banners were lying on the ground, a cavalier of the Dobrzyn district supervisor's squadron dealt Trubetskoy such a blow on the head that his kalpak fell off; two Muscovites at once seized him by the arms and led him off. Now did these Muscovite gentlemen scurry to their ranks; we in pursuit, slashing away at them, drove them right into the center of their army. Half of them perished then on that battleground.

And here in that welter, our *corpus*[38] comes into play. Nor are the Lithuanians idle on the left flank; yet Muscovy, esteeming them lightly, does not direct its best troops against them but against us. Several fresh regiments of theirs turned around then and went the other way. The Governor, seeing our squadrons at the enemy's rear, sent to Sapieha: "For God's sake, charge Muscovy with your entire force and break in upon them, or we'll lose the royal regiment."

But now Muscovy is in disarray, they twist and turn like someone who feels unwell sitting at table. Dread you could see all over them. Nor were those who had turned to march on us any longer fighting with mettle. They rush upon us, then again away from us; mightily now, our *corpus* assails them. The hussars charged, we assaulting them from behind. Now we even had a moment to load our muskets. And suddenly Muscovy turned tail. Their entire army was fleeing past us; now

37. Belonging to the Duma, the tsar's Senatorial Council.
38. Main body.

then, to fight! take your pick of whomever you please, here's a fine one, there's one still finer!

A yellow-bearded patriarch, a fierce fellow rushed at me. I bar his way, he aims his pistol at me, a golden sword hangs from his shoulder-strap. I thought, his pistol is empty, he's using it to terrorize me; I make bold to slash at him: he fired. At the same time, I struck him with a powerful slice on the shoulder. I perceive that his shot has not touched me: after him! I ran him down; again I charged him, for though on a good horse he made off with some difficulty; whether owing to the injury, or to languor. I sliced him across the forehead and he cried out, "*Pozhalui!*"[39] He hands over his sword to me and drops from his horse. No sooner do I take up his sword, but there, fleeing on a buff Tartar horse in glittering caparison is a young upstart wearing a *żupan* of parrot-green satin and a powder case on a silver chain. I slip after him and run him down. There he was, a young boy, fair; holding a cross studded with jewels in his hand and sobbing: "*Pozhalui dlya Krista Spasa, dlya perechistoi Bokharoditse, dlya Mikuli Tsudotwortsa!*"[40] I felt sorry for him, and I saw a great throng of Muscovites running at me from this side and that side; I was fearful lest they surround me. Not wanting to tarry there with him, yet loathe also to kill him, recalling his fervent plea, I only took his cross out of his hand and struck him on the back with the flat of my sword: "*Utikai do materi dichchi synu!*"[41] Then does that lad run, hands in the air, he's gone in a wink.

It was difficult to take anyone alive *in illo fervore,*[42] while the entire fleeing army poured over us: either you would hold on to your prisoner, or defend yourself, or load your musket. The cross I took from him was a very handsome one; about 20 ducats' worth of jewels. And I hadn't even lingered about that young pup for as long as a single prayer. I run back to long-beard, but he's already lying naked and a cavalier is leading away his horse. I say to him: "Twas I toppled the enemy from his horse, and you're taking it? Give it here, otherwise I'll unload this charge on you, the which I'd prepared for the enemy." And the Wallachian cavalier did not protest much, having seen the Muscovite shoot at me, and me knock him off his horse. He handed that splendid horse back to me then, which was not a Muscovite horse, but one of those chesnut-bays, stalwart creatures, from the Ukraine. A pity it was to discard him; and not a single retainer around, not a soul to take him, but at last I chanced upon an acquaintance's retainer: "Take this

39. Mercy!
40. Have mercy for the love of Christ Our Savior, for the Immaculate Mother of God, for Nicholas the Miracleworker!
41. Run away to your mother, you son-of-the-devil!
42. In the fervor of the moment.

horse from me, and I'll give you ten thalers if you bring him out for me; or if, meeting up with one of my retainers, you hand the horse over to him." He took it then, and I made off, whither the Muscovites and our men were fiercely engaged.

Now, we were slaughtering them like sheep. Had I had but one retainer with me then, he could have had his choice of the handsomest steeds, for the superior officers were being cut down, and whatever was elegant was on horseback. What can you do if your rascal of an attendant is most alert when his master is at the bottle, but nowhere to be seen when in battle! Nor is it very much in style for a cavalier to be holding the reins of a second horse; if there is no one around to hand it to, then he who values his dignity will prefer not to take it at all. But seeing other cavaliers leading whatever they have by the reins, I, too, when that massacre was over, took a beautiful Wallachian horse with a black stripe; he had a slight cut near the ear, but it had not harmed him at all. No sooner do we ride out of that throng, but my lad runs up; I gave him the horse, bidding him to keep watch over it. The scoundrel had tied all sorts of rubbish to his saddle — cavalryman's leathers — for his mount; but had he been with me, he would have tied to his saddle satins, velvets, and caparisons and could have taken away good horses.

I caught sight then of our squadron's banner. I dash over to it, but there were not even six men around it; other standards, too, were without escort. Everyone was chasing about in all haste; slashing, axing, pursuing. And I say to our standard-bearer: "The Lord has repaid me for my bay and given me another in his stead, a very handsome one too, but I handed him over to somebody else's man; I don't know if I'll get him back." The standard-bearer asks: "And whose is that tawny one?" I replied that it was mine too.

Muscovy's left flank and *corpus* had markedly dwindled and now her right flank, which was skirmishing with our left flank, begins to flee. Once again, so dense was the swarm; enough said: you chase one here, and another is already standing with his sword over your neck; you finish slashing one, another takes off like a hare toward the hounds. You needed a head on a pivot to look before and behind yourself, for if, recklessly, you dallied too long around one, those fugitives, as they passed, would slash our men from behind.

A Muscovite standard-bearer is fleeing, a robust fellow; he had wrapped the standard around himself; I ride into his path, aim my pistol. "*Pozhalui!*" He yielded up his standard. I lead him along; he's praying fiercely, hands folded. I think: "This one I'll bring out alive," when about 400 Muscovites, a large pack of them, are just ready to fall upon me. My standard-bearer began to hang back too, even though I had disarmed him. Seeing that not only would I not bring him out, but would perish myself, I ran him through with the tip of my sword, he fell; and I, with the standard, sprang out of their way. The Lithuanians come riding upon them; while others from the sides are already waiting for them ahead.

I hurling down that magnificent, golden banner, dash after them then; for I was ever sorry to miss a battle if there was someone to fight. We slash them to bits, but a second pack, just as large or even larger, follows; no sooner are these routed, when another appears — enough said that we fought till our arms dropped; as those who happed to escape could not do so but by passing our squadrons, the which, at the outset, had been at their rear. That massacre stretched for three miles. Some of us withdraw then, while others yet give chase. I being sore distressed, not having taken any live hostages, console myself with the horses, especially the bay, which was an exceedingly handsome beast, though I was not sure if it would suit me.

Suddenly, out of the forest come a dozen or so Muscovites who had concealed themselves in a small grove; we had stirred them up like a herd of roe deer. One fellow, his garments of silk, his kalpak embroidered and costly, makes off on a superb horse, richly caparisoned in glittering hussar style. Whoever is quick races toward him from this side and that, I'm nearest. Thinking it to be Khovansky himself, I call out: "Stay! Fear not! Your life will be spared." He began to rein in his horse, glances sidelong at me: I looked untrustworthy, being in a gray *kontusz;* he distrusting me, thinks me someone's retainer, some poverty-stricken yeoman, the which sort are most feared; they say you never find generosity in such people (as he himself related later). But in the distance he saw a cavalier, one of ours, save that he was wearing red — a crimson, threadbare *kontusz* — and was astride such a nag that should he chase the Muscovite till judgment day he would never overtake him; he supposed that this was a person of note and he rode straight to him. One of the cavaliers racing alongside shot at him, missed; and the Muscovite rode on like a blindman to the other. He became confused, twists around on his mare; at last seeing he'll not evade me, he yields up his sword, his pistols of ebony incrusted with silver, and cries out, "*Pozhalui!*" I took him alive.

Khovansky himself got away, twice slashed in the head while fleeing; whereas their infantry was hardly touched, except for those few hundred killed near the crossing, and all had remained alive; there were 18,000 of them. They went to the birch grove nearby and made an abatis. We surrounded them then with artillery and infantry, that birch grove being sparse. We opened fire from the cannon, balls were flying from all sides, and after we had weakened them with cannonades, then did we assail them from all sides and made mincemeat of them. Hard it was to look upon so much human blood as there was in that throng, the soldiers being packed close together and so to perish corpse upon corpse; the blood poured down from there in streams — as the birchwood was on a hill — just like water after a heavy rain.

We ride off then to our squadrons; there my retainer had received my captured bay. But no sooner had he taken it from the other attendant, when it was shot in the shoulder; I had to sell him to another nobleman for 10 zloties and he was worth at least 800 or 1000. The prisoners recognized that horse and said it had been ridden by Zhmiyov, a governor and brother-in-law of the field hetman, Nashchokin.

We herded them in like cattle. The grand hetman, Khovansky, twice wounded, escaped. Shcherbaty, another hetman, lost his life (there being several hetmans in the Muscovite army). Governors, princes, *duma* boyars perished in great numbers. No more than 4,000 horse got away with Khovansky, and there had been 46,000 in that army as the muster-master general himself said, who had been captured by Kaczewski; 60 cannon were left behind, and so many Don flintlocks, various muskets, and battleaxes that even the peasants were taking them.

At that time our deputies[43] were treating in Minsk with the Muscovites. Czarniecki, fearing lest Khovansky carry them off with him as he fled, sent forth on an all-night journey to their defense twelve good squadrons, ours among them. Command was given to Paweł Borzęcki. So then, after these heavy labors, without dismounting from our horses, we traveled to that town by night. We arrived there utterly numb from weariness. Our leader says: "Gentlemen, we need an informant to tell us what's going on in the town. May I have volunteers to ride to the outskirts and seize any man that's chanced upon." No one says a word, they plainly don't want to go. When he sees there are no volunteers, he says: "At least will you have the kindness to grant about 15 horse to keep me company, and those of you remaining, be alert, should fighting start up." Two from his own squadron rode out, no more. I, remembering his kindness at Kozierady in my misfortune, rode out and, seeing me, 20 horse from our squadron also rode out.

We came to one hut on the outskirts: no one there; to a second: the fire's going, a sign that a meal was being cooked, but there's not a soul around. Taking a light, we search every corner: nothing. We're just walking out of the hut when a woman coughed in the pigsty. They

43. Hieronim Wierzbowski, the governor of Sieradź; Stanisław Sarbiewski, governor of Mazovia; Jerzy Hlebowicz, district supervisor of Samogitia; Krzysztof Zawisza, marshal of the Grand Duchy of Lithuania; and Cyprian Brzostowski, the referendary of the Grand Duchy.

found three women then. With us was a cavalier who knew how to express himself in that speech of theirs. [The woman says] "*Kash su ster?*[44] He asks, "*Ne mash tu Lakhov?*" The woman answers: "*Ospane nimash, ale trvokha velikaia. Pribezhalo tut chetyri korakvi nashykh panov prewodnykh; tot chas zabrali nashykh komisarov i pobezheli, znati shchto khdes chuvaiut Charniestskovo.*" [The cavalier says:] "*Chi poberemo ikh?*" The woman: "*Oi, poberite, panunka; pre Bokh zhyvi, postinaite dichchikh synov.*"[45] He bids the woman then to take him to our deputies' abode. The woman with great willingness, in her night shirt only, runs and shows us the deputies' quarters.

The squadrons halt then in the town square. The deputies took alarm, hearing from the guard that the town was filled with soldiers. Our commander orders Charlewski to inquire in Muscovite speech who is posted here and about the Muscovite delegates: more fear. The infantrymen, standing with the caravan on the town square, had already retreated into their lodgings; a group of us dismounted then along with the commander. Charlewski says in Russian to a servant: "Tell the delegates they must get up and all assemble together." The servant went into the hut and soon a light showed inside. This was the quarters of the Samogitian district supervisor, Hlebowicz, the chief deputy and an eminent senator. Next door was the governor of Sieradz, Wierzbowski; in the third, the governor of Mazovia, Sarbiewski. Meanwhile, we walked over to the horses, until the deputies had come together; then the head servant appears and says: "Their Lordships request you to enter." Several other servants had come out behind him with large tapers.

We, wearing sundry kalpaks, enter then and the deputies, *consternati*, took a step from the table toward the door. Forthwith, the Mazovian governor recognized Lieutenant Borzęcki, his son-in-law; he shouts: "Just and Merciful God! They're our men! They're ours!" Borzecki then speaks a few eloquent words, bringing greetings from our leader and announcing our fortunate victory. The Samogitian district supervisor, as chief deputy, replied eloquently but with such tears of joy that he was unable to finish. Now they all rush upon us, hugging us, embracing us, giving thanks to God for such a blessing! They inquire about the conduct of the war. Borzęcki is telling them when a cavalier exclaims: "Say no more, Sir, until they give us something to eat!" Now do the servants, the chefs of all the delegates, spring to light the stoves,

44. "What can I do for you, sir?" — probably a garbled version of *kakzhe; su* is an abbreviated form of *sudar; ster* is an old polite formula.

45. "Are there no Poles here?" "None, Sir, but there is great alarm. Four of our escort-squadrons came through here; they took our deputies and galloped off, which means Czarniecki is lurking about somewhere." "Should we capture them?" "Oi, do capture them, Sir, for God's sake, kill those sons-of-the-devil."

to bake, to boil; we meanwhile to drink some vodkas, meads, wines. All our men have dismounted from their horses. So then, amid that boundless rejoicing we told them about the battle and the victory; they told us how they suspected as much when the Muscovite deputies fled, about how they feared being carried off, about how we had made them anxious, thinking that "Khovansky has sent for us"; about how they were to have signed the treaties the next day, about how the Muscovites reviled them. As for me, though I had heartily wanted to sleep, that desire left me, listening to these discourses and looking upon this sincere joy. The day dawned then; and bidding them farewell, we rode out of town, stopping on the meadows just beyond to let the horses graze and give them a rest. The deputies, too, made ready to depart and they set off soon after us.

From there we went to Lachowicze and found our army in the former Muscovite camp. To be sure, they had left quarters for our squadrons, assigning sentries to watch that no one plundered them, but the guards themselves ransacked the best of what we had. Much could be written about the fortress at Lachowicze, so handsome is it, but since many are well-acquainted with it, not being in a foreign land, there is little reason to describe it; to be short, there's not another like it in all of Poland. This is Sapieha's demesne. About 30,000 Muscovites perished there in the assaults.

Then came the feast of the Visitation of the Virgin Mary [July 2]. Every soldier who was quick assembled for Mass; each rendered his thanks to God for the favors bestowed on him in that battle. The noblemen in that fortress, and noblewomen, all attired themselves in marvelous finery, one more beautiful than the other; another so magnificently adorned herself with gold and jewels she could scarcely move. Small wonder Muscovy contended vehemently for that stronghold. And it could not have held out a month more, provisions being low. Two advantages were gained then from the army's haste: rescue of the fortress and the breaking off of the treaties, all owing to the courage of Czarniecki. For Sapieha had been procrastinating, waiting until the army was equipped with some sort of lances and such, at which Czarniecki said: "Soon even lances won't help us; in Lithuania it's easy to get poles from the hops fields. In the name of God, if you don't set forth with your army, I'll do so with mine."

And so he did, our army setting out then from Kozierady. Out of shame Sapieha had to join us. And so the poor wretches set to work whittling poles, painting them motley-colored or white, like the canes beggars make, and hanging upon them banderoles of linen; spearheads were brought from the towns as many as were needed; and so all looked as fit and handsome as before. That speed in giving battle yielded us a third advantage: our leaders now had intelligence that

Dolgoruky was on his way to Khovansky's aid with a mighty army. And we did not expect reinforcements save from the Lord himself. Should those forces join, it would be impossible to break them, or if possible, then with great hurt and loss of men; hard enough it was to break each of them alone, especially Dolgoruky, about which I shall write below.

On account of the wise counsel of a good commander those two armies, which could have attempted even the Turkish Sultan, failed to come together; the harmful treaties were torn up, and all those fortresses in Lithuania fallen into Muscovite hands, but two, were liberated from the enemy; Sheremetev's armies contending with our hetmans lost heart, the which contributed markedly to our victory at Cudnów.[46] Only Lachowicze had not fallen, but all other towns had been subjugated and the entire Grand Duchy of Lithuania.

Czarniecki, riding then into Lachowicze on the feast day of the Blessed Virgin, was hailed in a procession by the monks, by the gentrymen and women, and by whomsoever had been in that heavy siege, crying out: "Welcome unvanquished leader! Welcome unvanquished warrior! Welcome providential defender!"Some, especially among the women, even cried out: "Our Savior!" Czarniecki muffled his ears in his cap, not wanting to hear this flattery. Whereas Sapieha, who rode in after him, received not half the cheering, only a plain greeting, even though it was his own *domicilium*. The knighthood from ours and from the Lithuanian army dismounted in force and went into the church. Now to sing *Te Deum laudamus!* Now to celebrate the triumph! They fired the cannons till the earth shook; and then a splendid Mass, sermons, felicitations, and thanks to God for His blessings; there was rejoicing throughout mingled with tears; magnates from all over the Grand Duchy of Lithuania having removed to that fortress.

For everyone it was an exceedingly joyful victory *ex ratione* that after so many misfortunes, it brought the first good fortune to our fatherland, Muscovy having so firmly seized the upper hand until then that wherever they discovered our army, they would march toward us as if toward certain victory, ready for captives with stocks and irons, the which we found in their camp at Lachowicze; but the stocks and irons turned out to be quite as useful to us for putting them in fetters. Sapieha hauled into Lachowicze a great quantity of ordnance seized in the battle — fine pieces, all of brass; not an iron piece did he see. Some 20 of them Czarniecki sent to Tykocin,[47] adding to his own gunnery two captured cannon of exceeding long range.

46. Rewera Potocki and Jerzy Lubomirski subdued Vasily Sheremetev, the Muscovite commander, at Cudnow. The Muscovite army, surrounded by the Polish armies, capitulated on November 1, 1660.

47. Czarniecki was district supervisor of Tykocin; he had received the estate in recompense for his military services.

When the trumpets sounded for the delivering up of prisoners, all of them wept for exceeding dread of Czarniecki. I had turned mine over at once before riding to Minsk for the envoys; but the others who had not been handed over straightaway were crying and begging our men not to deliver them up. The muster-master general, whom I mentioned above, the one who tried to escape from me, says to me: "Since your custom is to hand prisoners over to the deputy hetman and you cannot keep me by your side, then take this course: forego your wages and your property, come with me to the capital; I'll give you 50,000, I'll give you my daughter, and all I possess." And this wretched soldier even began to think it over; meanwhile we were ordered to deliver the prisoners and I had to hand him over. The Governor heard of his promise to pay me 50,000. Seizing upon this at once, they reckoned his price at so much and would have none other. When he refused to give so much, saying in his own defense that "I promised it to awaken his greed so he would let me go; but such a huge sum I had not, nor can I have," they would not hear of it. They had the gentleman scribe put in irons and assigned him along with the other prisoners to the wheelbarrows on the ramparts of Tykocin; he had to promise, then pay.

For his prisoners, the Governor acquired around two million, there being none of ours to take in exchange for them, as hardly any of the prisoners in Moscow were from our division. Sapieha, on the other hand, released all of his prisoners, there being many noblemen, noblewomen, and soldiers from the Grand Duchy in captivity. When Field Hetman Gosiewski himself was ransomed, a great multitude of Muscovite captives departed; such is the ordinary thing — a hetman's head is a costly one. And yet, that head, ransomed from Moscow at such a price, needlessly perished when those beet-eaters[48] killed him like tyrants; though he was innocent those traitors, being drunk, killed a fortunate warrior, good commander, and most worthy senator, about which I shall write below.

Having stopped then for three days in the former Muscovite camp at Lachowicze amid such bounties, such abundances of every foodstuff, we set out for Borysów, a not negligible fortress on the Berezyna river. There we halted, expecting to take it *non vi, sed formidine.*[49] We stood there for two months;[50] but seeing they had no mind to surrender voluntarily and knowing what armed might was being readied for us, the Governor thought it better to withdraw from that fortress, and withdraw he did. Not to remain idle, we marched to great Mohilev in Byelorussia, the which is a fortress both large and strong on the Dnieper itself.

48. An abusive epithet for Lithuanians, for whom beets were a staple food.
49. Not by force but by fear.
50. Łos's diary gives the time as two weeks.

The district supervisor of Bratiansk, Dział, lured by the promises of Hetman and Marshal Jerzy Lubomirski, sent an order to his squadron to leave our division *sub praetextu*[51] of having to transform it into a hussar squadron. The Governor was sorely perturbed, not so much because he regretted losing the squadron, though an excellent one, but because of Polanowski, whose counsel he very often heeded. He tried *omnibus modis*[52] to talk them out of it, begged them not to do it; he could not. Since his pleas were vain, he had to let them go, but he did so with a curse, the consequence of his extreme regret, and at the moment of farewell he pronounced these words: "May you all die there, together with your commander, in the first battle!" And so it came to pass. They arrived in Cudnow and the next morning the squadron commander perished,[53] twenty cavaliers were killed, and about forty retainers. Commonly a change of place also brings a change of *fortuna*. Polanowski himself came within a hairsbreadth of death.

Not wanting to await the enemy near such a large and populous stronghold, the Governor, seeing that *melius est praevenire, quam praeveniri*,[54] set out with the army then on the route to Kryczów toward *Pan* Dolgoruky, so that he might see we had no thought to shrink from him. Perceiving this, the enemy at once blunted his advance; he who had been proceeding *magnis itineribus*,[55] no longer did so — for every three miles covered, he rested three days.

Just as once a certain grand gentleman challenged me to a duel, indicating through responsible persons that he was determined to kill me. So I, without waiting for that uncertain hour, preferred to choose it myself, the speedier to be rid of the thought rather than fear it longer. I rode into his courtyard and despatched a boy to announce that "my master, whom your Lordship has declared he will kill, not wishing your Lordship any ado in seeking him all over the face of the earth, and before he grows any thinner, has come and hereby gives notice of his presence." That gentleman did not kill me; he restrained himself and apologized. In the same way, *Pan* Dolgoruky had been impatient to see us, sending word round to all the fortresses to bar our way should we try to flee, but as soon as we started to march on him, his spirit flagged.

Our army made a halt then in a field about an eighth of a mile from the Basia river. Still we did not fully believe how powerful was the enemy; we took captives, roasted their sides a little; they tell us Dolgoruky has a fighting army of 70,000. Only then do we believe. And we

51. Under the pretext.
52. By every means.
53. Adam Działynski was actually killed at Cudnów.
54. It's better to anticipate than be anticipated.
55. In forced marches.

prepared ourselves carefully for that greeting, beseeching the Lord to assist us.

I have forgotten to write that while encamped at Mohilev, I found myself in a plight similar to the one in Kozierady. This is the way it came about: Gorzkowski, a cavalier in Lord Chamberlain Branicki's squadron, brought a suit against me in the military tribunal for the murder of his brother whom I had struck with my battleaxe for the reason aforesaid *in anno* 1657,[56] during a halt in the Radom district after the Hungarian war; both of us were serving with *Pan* Bykowski. Gorzkowski demanded I answer for this deed *ex carceribus.*[57] But the Governor pronounced officially that soldiers, especially good ones, were not to be fettered, marching into such a terrible conflict, and if any were fettered, they should now be released, and when taking anyone to jail, two should be let out, if possible. I was obliged only to swear I would respond to the summons of the tribunal.[58] When I made my oath, then, they gave me leave to go *ad locum facti,*[59] Czarniecki adding this: "If you're guilty, God will punish you in the battle for which we're preparing ourselves; if you're not guilty, you will come out alive and for me that will be a proof of your innocence."

Whereupon that foe of mine returned to Poland to evade the battle. As he was leaving, I went to the Governor declaring that before the battle I would not go to any inquest, but would allow myself to be judged by him from whatever evidence Gorzkowski brings back. This was very gratifying for the Governor and in front of several cavaliers he said: "Trust in God to lift you out of this distress in return for your valor in preferring to go into battle with us and your adversary may be ambushed and killed there in the bush." I went off then, and was in every battle, living and fighting under that oath. Everytime the Governor saw me he would say: "Who's that there? *Pan* Sworn? It's clear you're not guilty, if I see you alive still, after such heavy firing."

Pan Dolgoruky being now encamped but two miles from us, the time had come for a *consilium bellicum.*[60] Some advised letting him cross over to our side of the river; they gave their reasons and Hetman Sapieha took their side. Others said we should cross over and Czarniecki and Połubiński took this side. We stand there several days: the enemy does not come toward us; why, we know not. Captives were taken and quizzed: they don't know either. That Dolgoruky should fear us, no

56. There is no mention of it under this year. Either Pasek forgot that he did not write about this affair, or this section of the *Memoirs* has been lost.
57. From jail.
58. The law allowed the gentry, in case of a crime, to swear to appear in court when summoned, but meanwhile to remain at liberty.
59. To the scene of the deed.
60. War council.

one was like to believe, he having such a huge force; but what was the secret all about? At last Czarniecki ferreted it out of some local nobleman: Zolotarenko is coming with 40,000 Dnieper Cossacks. Again: council. It was resolved then that better *praevenire, quam praeveniri.*[61] We made the crossing then; though the water only came up to our saddle skirts, they were of a mind to place a bridge on it, being *in accessu*[62] very muddy on both sides and the bottom very quaggy. But *res non patiebatur moram*[63] — the woods being far from that place; each made the crossing then, thinking to himself that should you, God forbid, not hold up, better to beat your way straight into the enemy's battle ranks rather than ford that river again.

The army was arrayed then as it had been against Khovansky; only now the hussar squadrons, of which there were nine, were divided, each into three troops; behind each troop a squadron of Gentlemen of the Horse. So resplendent was our army then, that there appeared to be 6,000 hussars. We form battle ranks; our squadron once again with Woyniłowicz on the right flank. All camp attendants, both from ours and the Lithuanian army were ordered to stand in battle ranks under standards, an officer for every standard having been assigned as captain. There were also a few squadrons of volunteers commanded by Muraszko. The camp retainers were added to the volunteers and arrayed behind the mountain far from our army. They were ordered not to appear until the ranks began to come together and close inwards. Those attendants now gave our small force an even more splendid appearance; looking upon them, one would have thought it was another army; Lithuania, especially, keeps a great many of these victualers.[64] Altogether there were several thousand assembled.

Making up with mettle for what we lacked in strength, we having not even one quarter of our enemy's might, the commanders sent to Dolgoruky to give battle "for we came here to fight not to loll about." Our envoys found him already marching toward us in battle ranks; on returning they described the size of the Muscovite army and how it was advancing with moving forts, the whole army being engirded. Those moving fortresses are built on a frame like a turnstile in the shape of the stockaded wooden siege towers we call 'garlics" and often use at corner bastions with our fieldworks; that is, hollow logs are laced together in a cross and fastened at the ends with iron clasps. They are carried by foot soldiers in front of the battle ranks; as the army goes into battle, they place them on the ground and stick their muskets through them;

61. To anticipate than be anticipated.
62. At the approach.
63. There was no time for delay.
64. One of the chief functions of these attendants was to procure food and fodder for the cavaliers and their horses.

there's no way to charge these things, no way to break in upon the enemy, for the horses would be speared. Being behind those things, it's as if an army were behind a fortress, whence the name: moving forts.[65]

No sooner had Czarniecki heard about this stratagem, but he ordered earthworks thrown up forthwith in front of the ranks, small in size but close together. Both infantry and retainers threw themselves into the task at once, carrying earth away in whatever they had, cap or coat tails, as the army did not have many spades in its weaponry. Within an hour or so, the bulwarks were up, the infantry and small cannon brought, all very speedily. Our battle ranks did not have to advance beyond the fortifications, they were to fight from there *defensive,* moving forward by regiments and taking *refugium* behind the earthworks if the fighting was burdensome. But things turned out differently, for not only did we abandon our fortifications, but we broke up their moving forts, whereof I shall write below.[66]

Orders were given then for volunteers to gallop up to the enemy's ranks. Between us was a wood, not a wide one, but long and sparse, through which the armies could not see each other. We dashed toward that forest then; the enemy too, seeing us, sent their volunteers, the army following behind. Ours halted at those earthworks as if rooted to the spot. Still on the other side of the thicket, about an eighth of a mile from our ranks, we began to engage each other; this one running after that one, that one after this one; now we were even chasing each other into the wood.

Among the volunteers was a lad who knew how to pick a quarrel with them and gall them. So that whenever they would cry out: "Tsar! Tsar!" the lad, galloping right up to them, would call out loudly: "Your Tsar is a so-and-so!" Or he would show his backside: "Your Tsar can kiss me here!" Now would Muscovy race after him, several dozen or more coming to the fore. But the lad rode a nimble Tartar horse; he escaped, having led them far from their ranks; then we, galloping toward them from both sides, slashed and hacked our way through them and took prisoners. Enough said that thanks to this lad we sent the Governor about thirty captives from that initial skirmish. Over and over again he would dash up to their lines shouting something else about the Tsar; Muscovy was infuriated — to them there's greater offense in a slight to the tsar's name than to God's — they rushed after

65. *Hulajgorod* in Polish. This was a mobile wooden siege tower, used in the seventeenth century by the Muscovite army on the battlefield; it resembled the wooden towers used by the Poles in sieges. Perhaps the pickets of the stockading reminded the Poles of garlic cloves, hence their nickname for them. In seventeenth-century English texts, the term "sow" is used for a similar contraption. The word *hulajgorod,* according to Bruckner, has a Russian etymology: *gulyat'* (to walk); the *h* is the Ukrainian variant of Russian *g.*

66. The battle on the river Basia took place around October 1660.

the boy again and again, giving frantic chase. Right into the wood they pursued him, determined to lay hold of him, for they had surely to skin him for such pranks as he played on them. We chased after them.

I went after one and by a jot missed being a piece of spoils myself. I had carelessly guided my horse toward some brush of the sort one often sees, new growth covering up what had been chopped down; my horse, wanting to jump over a stump — I had a small, greyish horse, very fleet and nimble; I used to ride him into battle often, fitted with two small bridles in case the bit broke, so that one pair of reins was in my hand, the other tied to the saddlebow — somehow caught his leg in those reins which were hanging down, for that traitor of a lackey had left them a bit too long. The horse made as if to limp; I thought he had been shot, when another old long-beard is dashing toward me. The one whom I had been pursuing also turned round, upon seeing what had befallen me. The bearded fellow attacks me; I empty my musket straight into his chest, he fell from his horse. The other one, a young fellow, is after my neck; plainly he wanted to carry me off alive (for they had not yet captured a single prisoner, only killed a few of our men); or, perhaps, he had not wherewith to shoot at me, as both his pistols turned out to be empty. With my left hand I grabbed him by the arm that held his sword, exactly at the moment he clutched me by the neck, and so engaged, we dragged one another along like two hawks.

Further on, another Muscovite on a white-dappled Tartar horse is slashing away; the young fellow calls to him: "*Khfedor, Khfedor, sudi!*"[67] But Khfedor was busy preserving his own skin, for two of our cavaliers were overtaking him. Seeing me, the cavaliers gave up their pursuit of the other and rushed over. The Muscovite calls out: "*Puskai, ta poidu do didka.*"[68] I now no longer wanted to let him go; but had he invited me a minute before, I would surely have let him, and gladly; he would not have had to ask me twice. They seized him then, and cut through those extra reins of mine. The bearded one who lay on the ground being yet alive, my fellow cavalier pierced him with the tip of his sword. He wanted to dismount and rifle his pockets; there was no chance of that now for our battle ranks were entering this same brush, volunteers were swarming through it like ants. I walloped our prisoner's horse with the flat of my sword and we dashed off to our men; but as before to carry off a captive was a hardship. Jakubowski then smote him in the neck; down he went. And off we galloped to our battalion, while the Muscovites having come out of the brush, stood like a field of blooming poppies.

67. "Feodor, Feodor, over here."

68. "Let go, and I'll go away." (Pasek's approximations of Russian speech are extremely garbled.)

Both armies now see each other. The skirmishers were called off the field. The Governor rides into the regiments; going round to them all, exhorting, entreating: "Gentlemen, remember that to this battle as in sacrifice, we bring our life and blood in the name of God."

Both formations stood quietly then for about two hours, neither provoking the other; once again a skirmisher was ordered to attract attention and lure them into the field. They moved away from the wood then, and into the field so that we were within cannon range of each other. Meanwhile, out of those moving forts, [the enemy] brought Prince Cherkasky with an army of about twelve thousand, so they said. I changed horses. We stand in battle array. Suddenly, we see Prince Cherkasky heading straight for our right wing; the Governor rushes over to us and says to Woynilowicz: "Well, old soldier, start us off successfully in the name of the Lord." Riding by our regiment he says: "Hold up under the onslaught, I entreat you." They're creeping toward us then, very slowly. As soon as Prince Cherkasky is near enough, the Governor says: "And now to work: Call upon the Divine Name to assist you!" The squadrons begin to move slowly, our commanders riding in front, their forearms bared.[69] And now, there being no more than two furlongs between our armies, they charge toward us, and we toward them. So close did they lead us, that one could have seized the other by the chest. The Governor then, having led us into their very battle ranks, withdrew to the side and the two armies engaged. The fray lasted a good quarter of an hour, neither side yielding an inch of ground to the other. Sapieha, seeing us in difficulty, being few, sent 1500 good soldiers from the left wing. These came toward the Muscovites from the side, attacking in such a mighty charge that the detachments instantly tangled.

Now was there heavy fignting with corpses enough. Muscovy recoils; here, we're pressing through; more corpses fall. Muscovy in retreat. Their infantry now let fly with a mighty heavy volley from their firearms, but by the grace of God we held out as before without much loss in our men *ex ratione* that we rode up very close to the cannon and the balls passed over our heads. A dozen or so of our men perished as before, but all whose horses were shot down under them escaped alive. They killed Woyniłowicz's horse under him and many were those who went deaf; being too near the mighty boom and roar of the cannon caused their hearing to be damaged; my own head buzzed like a public-house for more than three months.

We marched back then, having taken six enemy standards and markedly thinned out the Muscovites themselves, dealing out divers

69. A custom observed by commanders when leading their men into attack. (Pollak, p. 437.)

specialities of our own to those who got away. A foreign cavalry captain whom we took prisoner told us later how Dolgoruky was quick to scold Prince Cherkasky for letting himself be driven from the field. To which the prince replied without deliberating: "It won't be long before I'll see you in such straits, if you're going to withstand them the way you have taught me. Those are hornets over there! Not people, hornets!" We stood then a long time, only cannon-fire coming from their side. Our commanders again sent word to Dolgoruky that it was getting toward evening and we had come there to fight not to loiter. He answered thus: "Whoever has his death put off, let him not begrudge it; whatever is to befall you, will not pass from you. Though evening is at hand, the army I have is such as can subdue you in an hour, and mete out to anyone his due, without needing a whole day for it." After such an insolent reply, he forthwith ordered the regiments to be led out to the field from those moving forts, leaving inside a part of the infantry with the cannon, and mixing some field pieces and foot soldiers among the horse. He was expecting to overwhelm us at one blow, relying on the great size of his army.

An order was sent to Muraszko to lead out our volunteers and camp attendants from behind the mountain within view of the enemy. Very speedily do they move into view then, like freshly arriving reinforcements come to our aid; they ride at a good trot toward our left wing, coming to a halt a slight distance from the Lithuanian army. Muraszko bustles about with his horsetail,[70] runs to and fro with his mace, drawing up his troops like a newly appointed hetman with a fresh army; all this was accomplished with such flourishes that our spirits lifted as we watched those lackeys.

Muscovy presumed that new reinforcements had come; and the shouting they heard in our camp they thought to be a cheer for the newly arrived reinforcements. By now they had led their entire horse out of the moving fortresses and half the foot; our cavalry also came forward, leaving those fieldworks at their rear. They batter us from the cannon; terrible arrows the size of wagon tongues keep falling among our ranks, sometimes they fell in front of us; they had arrowheads like cleavers; we wonder what sort of bows they must have, whether some giant might be shooting from a huge bow, or what? We didn't know they were Astrakhan Tartars; one tip of their huge bows rests on the ground, the other sticks up above their heads.

Between our leaders it was decided that Sapieha was to attack first, he himself making this request; but as Muscovy was suiting its own designs and not ours, it charged our right wing first; we then, being

70. A kind of ensign consisting of a horse's tail tied to a shaft, used by Tartars, Turks, and the Zaporozhe Cossacks.

first, had to fight. The Governor rides by, saying: "Gentlemen, I see the enemy has taken a fancy to you; fear not, the *corpus*[71] will be seconding you."

We engage then in bloody combat. Their ranks are fearsomely dense, several of them to one of ours; but even so we do not let ourselves be smashed, we stand firm. Men who have been shot fall from their horses, the wounded are taken to the rear. That mixed foot and horse of theirs did us much harm; for no sooner do we push the enemy back, but we fall among those traitors; like getting a punch in the mug it was. On our left wing, Lithuania is giving a beating immeasurably better than the one Khovansky got. Their spirits had fallen so low then, but now they took fresh heart. Those lackeys of ours with the volunteers fell upon the enemy's lines so boldly, a Tartar could scarcely do better — indeed, all were possessed of a fierce ardor, nor could it have been otherwise, with such tremendous power facing you. Never in the course of my entire service, both before and after that battle, did I see Poles fight the way our army fought then. People were saying: "If the Poles always fought so ardently, the whole world would be under their sway." Muscovy depended on the size of the army, while our men trusted in God and in their own mettle; one man taking example from the other, ours and the Lithuanian army vied so with each other that greater rivalry you're not likely to see. And, in truth, everyone has to confess that in battle array the Muscovite armies, especially those boyar squadrons, are formidable as no other people are. With their beards, they look the picture of *maiestas;* seeing them, it's as if you were setting upon the venerable fathers of the church.

The Governor, having ridden off and given orders to the hussars concerning the attack, also sent to Sapieha to advance at once, for the sun was setting. He rushed back to us (Would that more such commanders be born! Happy the mother who bears such sons!): "Now, Gentlemen, whoever holds God and virtue dear, follow me!" We attack with a mighty clamor and a massacre ensued, we being unable to break through; not letting them to do so; we put up a strong resistance *ex ratione* that it was *gloriosius occumbere in opere* than *in fuga.*[72] Plainly, the hand of God was protecting us, if, having pitted ourselves against such immense might, God gave us both victory and few losses in men. Never shall I forget this and I'll tell it ten times over, for I consider it a great wonder: when 3,000 Muscovites let fly all together at those four squadrons of ours, which had galloped too far in pursuit of the enemy and had been driven aside and nearly led into the lines of fire, as usual only one cavalier and four retainers perished, and my horse was shot down.

71. Main body, middle divisions.

72. More glorious to perish in combat than in flight.

How true the saying: "Man pulls the trigger, but the Good Lord carries the bullet"; for at least half of us ought to have dropped from our horses under such fire. The hussars then charged with lances as into a wall; some lances splintered, others held. According to the order, anyone whose lance shattered was to take up the sabre. But God help anyone who hurled down his lance without wetting it in enemy blood, unless he pick it up again.

Here is how one troop from Czarniecki's squadron behaved, and a squadron of Gentlemen of the Horse behind it, I don't recall whose, for the weaker squadrons were arrayed behind the hussar squadrons. They encountered a weak spot in the wall — some who were anxious about their bellies. The wall stepped aside and our men bored like a drill through the enemy's lines, nearly without a single broken lance; they came straight to that place which served as the gateway between those moving forts, through which the battle ranks were led out onto the plain. Only one cavalier they lost, as they beat their way through, and one horse. Upon taking up their position at that gateway, they turned and with their standard faced the enemy's rear lines. Word reached the Governor that his ensign had been sighted at the rear of the enemy's ranks. Fearful lest they be overwhelmed there, Muscovy, too, being not a little disturbed, the Governor ordered the rest of his troops to give charge and he himself dashed ahead of us, urgently wielding his sword, shooting, endangering himself, not like a hetman but like a common soldier.

Now was Muscovy thrown into confusion; now did they take to their heels! Now cut! Now slash! Whenever a Muscovite squadron races toward that gateway hoping to escape behind the moving fortresses, those hussars, who had pierced through the enemy ranks, present their lances: the Muscovites were turned aside. A huge number of them pressed about those movable bastions then, wanting their men to give fire and repulse our hussars, but their men could not shoot without doing even greater harm to their own. Nor were they firing from the cannon anymore, it being to no avail amid the tangled armies. At that moment we charge into them, shooting, slashing; the moving fortresses were difficult to demolish in a hurry, being strongly fastened together with iron clasps. The Muscovites make for those moving forts, which we call "garlics" in Polish; our men slash away without cease. Vast numbers of the enemy were laid low there, corpse falling upon corpse in a heap. Those corpses piled up into something like a bulwark or embankment, higher even than the moving stockades. And so, what they devised for the enemy, they themselves succumbed to. *Qui facit foveam, incidit in eam,*[73] but not a single soldier of ours perished on

73. He who digs a pit, will himself fall into it.

account of this contraption in which they had placed their greatest hope. So does God often ordain that he who sets the trap for others falls into it himself, *etc.*

Nearly that entire cavalry detachment of theirs perished then, very few escaping. Many governors, princes, *duma* boyars, officials of the tsar were killed; for we were not taking anyone alive, there being no time to dally with such a vast enemy force. For taking the enemy alive means to do nothing else, but if, meanwhile, by the grace of God, you can kill several in one spot, why tarry with one? I myself happed to slay some personage of distinction, and afterward, taking his measure I noticed he was attired as if for a wedding, but there was no chance to take even his kalpak on which was a slew of pearls and a diamond clasp, it being impossible in the heat of battle; you're mounted and ten others are beating their way to it on foot.

Our infantry had the most spoils, for they followed right after us, snatching everything up. They found great quantities of money, for, having been a levy in mass, there were eminent boyars. All the Muscovite foot which had been led out onto the field perished; the remainder would have been killed as well, had not nightfall prevented it. They, meanwhile, made off into the forest and the night saved them. We gathered up several wagonloads of banners, a mighty lot of heavy cannons, even a few captives; and, finally, several hundred foot were chosen for Sapieha and for Czarniecki. But no prominent personages; three colonels only, a few captains of horse, some boyars too, and several dozen Germans and Englishmen. Dolgoruky and those who escaped, were saved by the dark; for had there been more light, they all would have gone to their deaths.[74]

Zolotarenko [a Cossack colonel] was only three miles away with his Cossacks during the battle. A reconnaissance party of his, so they pretended, was there watching the battle; seeing Dolgoruky's defeat, at once they turned tail. Ukases — they're called "orders" in Polish — were sent from Moscow to Zolotarenko to join forces immediately with Chmielnicki, the which he made haste, *magnis itineribus,* to do. I know not whether he was of any help there, for at about this time our hetmans put Sheremetev *gloriosissime* to rout so that *nec nuntius cladis*[75] survived. Some fell on the place, others were captured by the Tartars *a partibus nostris,*[76] who took Sheremetev himself as payment for having helped us to fight the Muscovites. A great and glorious victory that was, but I shall not write about it, for I was not there; I'll write about only

74. In reality, although the Polish armies caused grave losses to their adversary, this battle did not end in a decisive victory for the Poles.
75. Not even a messenger of defeat.
76. On our side.

those battles in which I myself took part, for such is my endeavor: to describe *statum vitae meae, non statum Reipublicae,* in order to *reducere in memoriam* each of my *actiones*, having once seen them *in scripto, in quantum* my memory may not retain everything.[77] But this battle, too, must have had God's blessing, if, from so vast an army (in which it was said there were 70,000 besides the Cossacks) not even one was to have escaped. Almighty God took pity upon the Poles and snatched our suffering country *ex faucibus*[78] of a cruel enemy who would have pounced upon her had not the Lord granted us victory; wherefore may His Most Holy Name be praised!

Nonetheless, after the battle on the river Basia, the Ruthenian Governor [Czarniecki] sent off powerful detachments to those places where there was talk of the Cossacks, he intending to greet them upon a signal from the detachments. But the Cossacks had already slipped away; seeing Dolgoruky's reception they had no mind to wait around for the like. To anticipate the enemy, not to let him build up his strength: this is the shrewdness of a good commander. For if the Cossack troops had joined forces with Muscovy, what they would have done to that small handful of our army! Instead, Muscovy took a whipping, the Cossacks fled, and those Astrakhan Kalmuks, whom we had feared, perished; our regiments who had had to fight them said that the Kalmuks lacked prowess; indeed, they whirled their whips a bit at the start, but took wing even faster than Muscovy, and never did I hear anyone to complain of a wound from their weapons. Thus God is good and, when He wills, bestows His blessings, giving right counsel to commanders, courage and daring to knights, whereof we clearly experienced in those battles with Muscovy, when victory seemed impossible, having such a slight army.

Our detachment, on its way back to the army from the Dnieper, passed through Mohilev, having been so instructed. In Mohilev, where (as I said above) people had shouted, had hooted at our army as we passed through, threatening us with Dolgoruky, menacing us with fetters and imprisonment in the Muscovite capital, this time, not a mouth gaped open, nor did they shoot at our men. How terrible is the *nomen victoris;*[79] how God does transform human vanity and self-importance!

We thought then that after such hard labors we, being covered with both our own and the enemy's blood, would have a respite; but repeated and unchanging intelligence comes to us, that Khovansky, having forgotten his earlier drubbing, had, in accordance with a ukase

77. To describe the affairs of my own life, not of the Commonwealth, in order to recall each of my deeds having once seen them in writing, inasmuch as my memory . . . .

78. Out of the jaws.

79. Name of the victor.

from the Tsar, put together a good army of 12,000 from the remaining *duma* boyars and the Tsar's court officials, that he had crossed the Dnieper at Smolensk and was advancing toward us from the Polish side of the Dnieper, resolved to perish himself; he had declared to the Tsar that he would charge us in the initial battle and that he would not let us cross the Dnieper before Dolgoruky had strengthened his forces and come to do battle with us. But even this design of his failed, for it's hard to catch the cautious fox asleep.

No sooner had Czarniecki heard of this undertaking, but, quick as a fox, he marched his army *magnis itineribus* back to the Dnieper. We crossed it then at Szkłów as well as we could, some taking the horses across, others sailing with the boats and ferries; the cold being already severe, the poor horses balked and many a one bared its teeth. We made a halt then at Szkłów. Lithuania in the open field, a quarter of a mile from us; we at the very Dnieper, on an islet in the middle. Sapieha at once sent off Colonel Kmicic, a good soldier, on reconnaissance with 3,000 good men, to Czereja where Khovansky had pitched camp, building as if for the whole winter and entrenching it; he, intending to winter in the field.

The day after the departure of the reconnaissance party, Czarniecki — likely inspired *spiritu prophetico*[80]— ordered the trumpets sounded for the army to mount horse within two hours, taking along supplies. And so it was done. Having sounded the muted trumpets, quietly as could be, and without saying a word to Sapieha, we set off. Through forests we go then, in all haste; not knowing why or where. But Khovansky had done the same; he took a special detachment, wanting to surprise us while we were divided in two, crossing the river. He encountered Kmicic then at Druck, or rather struck him from the rear, having already passed him by, while on another route. (A townsman from Druck whom Muscovy captured somewhere on the road told about the Lithuanians). When they attacked each other there, the Lithuanians, poor souls, fought hard to be sure; being unable to hold out, they were broken in upon; now did things go badly for them, now did the others begin to beat them, seize them, tie them up. Czarniecki had sent several squadrons on ahead; as soon as they came to the ford at Druck, or rather Odruck — for the town is known by both names — our men halted at the river, and the river Drucz [Druć] had bridges, but these the Muscovites had torn down; hearing gunfire and the sounds of a battle, they sent word to the Governor. The army forthwith set off at a gallop. Only now did we guess Czarniecki's purpose.

We come to the ford at Druck, a bad one: the river though not wide, was deep and fast and had two arms; you had to swim twice, for about

80. With a prophetic spirit.

half a furlong and its high banks were as steep as a stove wall. The Muscovites, those simpletons, having pulled down the bridges, supposed they were safe. And by now they knew that our army was as far as Szkłów and that there would be no aid for the Lithuanians; therefore, this ford, which they could have properly defended, was not watched.

Says the Governor: "Gentlemen, *res non patitur moram,*[81] there's no time for building bridges. You can hear the firing and you hear Muscovite voices; that means their men are beating ours, not ours theirs. We've swum through sea water: and we must do it here; now beseech God for help, and follow me! Pistols and ammunition boxes into your collars!" Czarniecki then dashes forward alone off the bank; the horse drifted downstream at once, the river being very deep. He swam across then, and stands on the opposite bank; one after the other, the squadrons swim over quietly, for they were no more than fifteen furlongs from the spot where the fighting was going on; but the Muscovites, being on the other side of the forest, could not see us. Standing on the shore, Czarniecki keeps calling out: "In ranks, gentlemen, in ranks." The which was unlikely, for every horse does not swim at the same speed: one pushes himself more, the other less. Our first cavalier to go, Drozdowski, had a horse which he did not know well, it swam somehow curiously on its side; as soon as it did so, the water at once carried him off his mount; he began to drown, having let go of his horse. I grasped him by one arm, another cavalier took him by the other, and so we held him afloat between us. No sooner had we brought him ashore, but the Governor says: "You are fortunate, brother; there are some big fish around here, a pike might have gobbled you up together with all your armor" (he was nettling the lad about his small build).

When we had crossed the second arm [of the river], Czarniecki ordered the royal regiment to charge into battle forthwith; he himself remained to direct the others across. We galloped off. The Muscovites were dumbfounded: "Where did they come from?" Their army has not kept ranks: some are dawdling about in groups, some are tying up Lithuanians, others are floundering about a pond, dragging out from the reeds those who had fled the field; few of our men were being killed, for Muscovy wanted to take as many hostages as possible to exchange for her own men. There, the Lithuanians, poor souls, had escaped from the rout into a very large pond, densely overgrown with reeds, just outside the town. The enemy, thinking we are some scouting party come to assist, attack us; they see us dripping wet yet our guns giving fire. Well, into the fray! They see more and more of us pouring out as if from a sleeve; their spirits sink lower and lower; but ours,

81. There's no time for delay.

contra[82] lift ever higher, for Czarniecki had each squadron rush after us immediately upon crossing. The Lithuanians were tied up like sheep in bunches of several captives. Kmicic, their colonel, escaped from a hut somewhere as soon as the guard left him alone; he races into our midst, his hands bound behind his back, crying out: "Help me, for God's sake!" Someone cut him free then. At the same time, the enemy captured a retainer from our army and they ask him: "What sort of party is this?" He says: "No party this, it's Czarniecki with his army."

Ferocious carnage, corpses falling everywhere. Those who were routed begin stirring about the pond, then ducking down; now, for every Muscovite that had dragged off a Lithuanian, there was the Lithuanian tugging the Muscovite by his beard. So does fortune change by and by: for one hour she favored the Muscovites, now she left them in the lurch. When they understood from their captive that this was no party of scouts but an army, they see they're in bad straits: here they're up against a wall; while over there, ever more squadrons rush out of the forest, as if they're dancing a reel. The enemy command begins to flee, the army scatters. But they weren't long in their flight, for they had utterly exhausted their horses battling the Lithuanians and trying to head them off but missing them and having to turn back; and thirdly, those mighty fat horses of theirs kept coming to a standstill on splay legs along the way.

We descended then, slaughtering them over four great miles. Whoever did not lose his life within the first mile, did so within the second or third; you overtook him, his horse was standing under him like a cow; or dismounted, he was kneeling with hands folded: cut his throat! then — be off after the others! The enemy was slain within those four miles; beyond that there were no further corpses. Even so, very few of them got back to their camp, as the peasants and other captives whom we discovered there told us; no sooner had these rogues perceived how things were going, but they ransacked the huts and now they were acting the grand gentlemen.

We came then to their camp at Tołłoczyn, seven miles from the spot where the battle had taken place, wherein we found all their provisions and supply wagons, even horses aplenty. For the fugitives had no-chance to seize their things with us riding right on their necks; and those people, such as the wagon drivers, who had remained behind in camp had had scarcely time enough to jump on a horse and escape, so that the belongings of the dead had not yet been taken by anyone. There were a few cattle, the which we considered a great novelty; whoever happed to get an ox or a heifer had no need to go inviting guests, for they came of themselves, even from three regiments away,

82. On the contrary.

upon discovering a fresh piece of meat being cooked. Meat was very hard to get near the Muscovite border, much of the cattle having already been requisitioned, and the rest — whoever still had any — taken deep into the woods and kept there both winter and summer. So we were starved for meat after living for several months off garden vegetables alone, mostly on baked beets out of which we had concocted many specialities, such as baked *pierogi* — you mashed the cooked vegetable, put it on the dough, folded it like an ordinary *pieróg* and into the oven with it; ground hempseed was then spread over the top; a great specialty this.[83]

We stopped in their camp then; quarters were assigned as in any town. Lithuania was not allowed in, upon arriving four days after us, but we did allot them victuals. We found stables with floors even, ready for use, there being plenty of autumn mud already; decent buildings they were, for the Muscovites build their camps solidly. Our wagon-trains arrived after we did, along with the Lithuanian army. Sapieha then pitched camp apart from us, about a mile or so distant. Inclement weather descended upon us, the snows came; Lithuania's horses began to weaken and they went to quarter their men in the villages roundabout. We remained in the camp as long as we had something to eat for ourselves and the horses, a few of which we had lost due to the recent fighting and the rainy autumn, and that swimming through the cold river water; nevertheless, that battle more than recompensed us for them, there being horses enough here — very good Astrakhan horses from the steppes, besides Tarter and divers Ruthenian horses.

Gentlemen soldiers of the present era, who often lose their horses, could follow the example of our soldier's life. I tell them that they've never seen greater hardships than we; *et consequenter* such loss in horses have never had; even so, our army of horse never turned into foot. With us, losing a horse was no worse than letting a crawfish slip out of a basket, for each man knew that the Lord could give another in hand-to-hand fighting with the enemy. So, if the enemy takes your horse you try for two of his, since you are no less a man than himself, no less a soldier than himself, and his skin is no more made of armor than yours.

83. A *pieróg* is a triangular-shaped piece of thinly rolled dough (similar to Chinese won-ton), made to enclose stuffing of various kinds; it is folded over and usually dropped into boiling water to cook. Variations exist and are popular all over Eastern Euorpe. For an interesting discussion of the cultivation and uses of hemp *(cannabis sativa)*, see *Encyclopedia Brittanica*, eleventh or fourteenth editions.

The Year Of Our Lord 1661

With God's grace I began at home. In which year the Lord tried his servant by curious circumstances, alternating the *vicissitudinem* of Fortune 'twixt good and ill; nevertheless all turned out for the best. Whereof below.

After the feast of Epiphany, I went to the Radom district for that inquest but Gorzkowski had carried out his own there,[1] in what manner I know not; he set out for our camp with it, arriving, it appears, within a week after my own departure from the army. The governor said to him: "My good sir, all this time you've been dallying with inkwells and penning black calumnies, conducting your inquisition, while *Pan* Pasek has been here with us writing in blood. Now Your Honor is pressing a suit *contra absentem;* impossible! for he, too, would like to save himself, but has only just left for the place from whence Your Honor is come. Better both of you had gone together to the inquest, rather than forego so many splendid battles. You, Sir, reek more of the chancery office than of war. Better Your Honor either have done with this annoyance, for if he's come out alive from such fire as I myself saw him in, then it's a sign he's not guilty of your brother's blood; surely you recall, Sir, how I put him to such a test: 'If you come out of this battle alive, then I'll reckon on your innocence.' As soon as he returns from his own inquest, I'll give you a decision; but if Your Honor has understood anything, better not to make a fuss. He does not deny striking your brother; but he desires to prove that it was not the cause of your brother's passing from this world. Or, since it happened so long ago and outside my discretion, take it to court, it being a matter between two gentlemen." Some earful the Governor gave him then; not only did Gorzkowski let his cause rest, but, after the quarter was up, he left the army.

Arriving in the Radom district, I found out that the people most needful for my inquest were no longer living, notably, the couple in whose home that quarrel had taken place; there was but the priest who had administered the last rites. Directly after saying Mass, he wanted to give me a *testimonium* to the effect that Gorzkowski in his last confession

1. This inquest is mentioned in 1660.

did not hold me guilty, but the priest wanted me to see to it that he was given a permission from the bishop. I also hoped to obtain testimony from my fellow cavaliers who had remained under *Pan* Piekarski's ensign. Also there was *Pan* Jan Olszowski and *Pan* Jędrzej Zaręba who were then serving with me under the standard of the castellan of Lublin.[2] I came away then without a thing in the Radom district, but intending to see about the permit from the bishop. Arriving home after that, I learned that my adversary had left the army, taken a wife, and settled down on his property. I supposed that he would desist; I made no further endeavors to gather evidence. I used even to run into him in Studzianna [a village in the Kielce region] at the home of *Pan* Starołęcki, castellan of Żarnów, while *Pan* Michal Łabiszowski, a cavalier in Prince Dymitr [Wiśniowiecki's] squadron, was courting that gentleman's niece, *Panna* Przyłuska.

Pan Gorzkowski made no mention of anything then, but he refused to shake my hand as we were greeting the company, wherefore the gentlemen who were come with us, especially the Petrykowski and Radziątkowski brothers, relations of mine, and others, wanted to seek satisfaction on my behalf; they were about to pull out their sabers, but the host intervened; I too told them to stay; let him content himself with refusing his hand. So they let it pass, only the judge from Rawa, Jan Relski, said to him: "My good fellow, you take up the cudgels because your brother was struck with a battleaxe, but you yourself should be caned for being such a *boor.*" Well, he lasted out those days of courting there, but he kept away from us, for he was afraid; we, better than 100 horse, all throwing him menacing looks for that refusal of his hand; nor did he do any dancing, not even once. When several people spoke with him about what more he is thinking of doing, he said he prefers the civil courts, seeing favoritism in the military. On which account I was very glad and no longer tried to collect evidence; but he didn't start the civil suit either, belike he felt he couldn't prove anything. Off I went to the army. The Governor, seeing me, says: "Back with the inquest?" I answer: "That I am." "It's not likely," he says, "that you'll both settle the matter here, if one arrives as the other leaves." I told him then that Gorzkowski was going to take it to the civil courts.

Soon after this, the army set about forming a union.[3] Incessant embassies and letters came from Hetman Potocki's division, inviting us *ad societatem*, proposing *communem iniuriam et commune bonum.*[4] Our

2. Stanisław Widlica Domaszewski, district supervisor of Łuków and from 1663 castellan of Lublin, commanded a squadron of Gentlemen of the Horse.
3. From here on, the terms "confederacy" and "union" are used synonymously, although strictly speaking they are not the same. (See the Introduction.)
4. To join their association . . . common weal and common woe.

division opposed it, seeing therein great *detrimentum* to our country. The Muscovites had lost hope, having now no means of resistance, and were intending to surrender and beg for mercy; the Wolski sort were removing their wealth to some place beyond Biańe Jeziora.[5] To be plain, such a man was rare in our army who sincerely sighed for a confederacy. But the hetman's faction finally convinced us at least to confer with them. I announced to my lieutenant that he would have to look for a cavalier to replace me; whereupon the Governor hearing this, had Mężyński, his lieutenant, deal with me about enlisting in his own squadron. It was resolved then and we shook hands on it.

The army left Kobryń then and joined the hetman's troops, but not all the squadrons did so; for the royal squadrons, Czarniecki's own, and others, such as his son-in-law's and the Kaniów district supervisor's, did not wish to join.[6] At the general assembly then, there was a great stir *pro et contra,* the hetman's army blowing the bagpipes for confederacy, they having a fierce mind to it. Whereas our men were of two minds, for sweet was the lure of gain, yet a pity at this stage to slip from discipline, having the opportunity to expand our borders. Some regretted coming near the general assembly, others were saying it was absolutely necessary, since *quot capita, tot sensus,*[7] not all of us being birds of the same feather. We finally had to let them have their way, but under the following *conditionibus:* first, that the marshal of the confederacy be chosen from our army; second, that having obtained good provisions and duly raised the pay of our retinues, we be on our way at once, not under the command of the hetmans but under our own marshal; third, that we leave behind *deputatos administratores*[8] on the crown estates and properties, who would oversee the *bona regali*[9] and collect the revenues for the cause of the army; and finally, that we not dissolve the confederacy until the army has been rendered satisfaction *in toto.*

Ad primum,[10] the leader of the confederacy could not be from our army *per rationem* that their army was twice as large. *Conclusum* then to choose the marshal from theirs, the deputy marshal from ours. Świderski[11] was chosen marshal then, the army perceiving him to be a

5. "The Wolski sort" harks back to the episode with Łukasz Wolski in 1660; here Pasek has made Wolski's name synonymous with men of little valor. Biańe Jeziora (Beloe Ozero) is a town on the lake of the same name, about 400 kilometers to the east of what is today Leningrad.
6. Wacław Leszczyński was Czarniecki's son-in-law; Stefan Stanisław Czarniecki, the Governor's nephew, was the Kaniów district supervisor.
7. Two heads are better than one.
8. Delegated administrators.
9. Crown estates.
10. As to the first condition.
11. Samuel Świderski, Prince Konstanty Wiśniowiecki's lieutenant; according to Łoś, he was a "terrible drunkard."

simple and sincere man; as deputy they elected Borzęcki, an erudite man, of grandiloquent manner, lieutenant of a squadron of Gentlemen of the Horse for Franciszek Myszkowski, the Margrave of Pińczów. Half the counselors were from our army, half from theirs. *Ad secundam illationem*[12] our army made clear it was our firmest resolve to eat our bread while performing our duty, not lolling about the manors. They heard us announce *plenis buccis*[13] that on this point we will not yield, even if we have to take up arms to defend it, should the justice of our cause not prevail. *Rationes e contra*[14] also were put forth: that the confederacy would be no threat at all were we to go back to work; having us still to defend it, the Commonwealth will take no heed of us nor settle our back wages, etc. The deputy most strongly supported this and the marshal concurred, but he dared not speak openly *propter offensam*[15] his party. Karkoszka, a cavalier I know not from whose squadron, speaks up: "These are the useless conjectures of a few; if there is to be a union, let there be one. But let there be none and we'll never see our back wages. They'll turn us into dragoons. As I say, a conjecture of but a few lordships; the rest are silent, which means they think as we do." The deputy glances at the colonels, the lieutenants, he says: "Gentlemen, how much of this is true?" They answer: "Let us confer with our companies." The assembly was put off then *ad cras.*[16]

The following day, all of our men in their separate squadron assemblies agreed *unanimi voce* not to abandon our position. At the general assembly, the lieutenants were ordered to declare their stand on behalf of each man in their squadron; those wishing to voice their own declaration did so *ore proprio* while those lacking facility with words conveyed the resolution *per deputatos.*[17] Our Krzywiecki, though a fine soldier and surely a man of dashing good looks, but not an orator, especially *in facie publica,*[18] instructed me to make the statement; he ordered all of our cavaliers to attend the general assembly, he himself staying behind, urgently answering letters. Since neither the royal squadrons were there, nor the Governor's, nor those of his son-in-law, Crown Carver Leszczynski, the very first declaration came from the squadron of which Borzęcki was lieutenant; a cavalier, Kraszowski, delivered it. The next declaration was our squadron's, wherein I had still to serve a quarter of a year, though I had given the Governor my

12. As for the second proposal.
13. Without mincing words.
14. Arguments against that.
15. In order not to offend.
16. Until the next day.
17. Through their own lips . . . through deputies.
18. At a public meeting.

word. Our cavaliers and the rest of the squadrons having clustered around in great numbers, I make this speech:

I know not how any man could call himself a son of this fatherland, who could wholly forget its public interests for the sake of his own private ones. Prodigal the world calls such sons, who trade their entire substance for one fleeting moment of comfort, thereby losing at one stroke the patrimony whereby they might have benefitted and whereof enjoyed *per portiones*[19] with their heirs. We have a grievance against the Commonwealth for reneging so long on our pay. But when I consider that it is our own Commonwealth, not the Hungarian, not the German, but our own Polish mother we complain against, then we should conduct ourselves as with a mother; for every mother, if ever she should lack for bread, ordinarily makes amends to her children for a missed breakfast with a good dinner; she does not allow them to grow very weak from hunger. If, on the other hand, her wanton children were all to ransack the larder, belike she'd not only not recompense their missed breakfast, but the wherewithal to provide them further would have disappeared..... [There follow two blank pages in the manuscript.] Delay is harmful. The enemy will build up his strength if we allow him a truce. God will grow angry and should His grace and that Divine Hand which did battle for us go against us, then we'll not get the enemy's land and will lose our own. These things are obvious, gentlemen; it is obvious that up to now we have had God's protection. We'll not read in the chronicles how myriads so mighty fell beneath Polish swords, despite our army being so meager.

Let us consider how this deceitful people plundered three-quarters of our fatherland with fire and the sword.[20] Let us consider how many outrages against God they committed in His churches. Let us consider how much of a hindrance they were during the Swedish war. Let us show them that we too are capable of finding our food abroad in the country which robbed us of so much of it. Finally, let us rid ourselves of the proverbial chiding from our neighbors: "Threatening war, never waging it, is all the Pole ever does." Greater glory and a better advantage will be ours, for God will bless our cause *in ulteriori tractu*[21] and our brothers, though they have hard hearts, must respect our staunchness. And once being come into a country of plenty, perhaps God will think up better nourishment for us than upon our own native soil.

In delivering then this declaration in the name of our entire company, I serve fair warning that whosoever is displeased by *pia vota nostra,*[22] neither will his (I know not what title to give them) please us, nor anyone in our division, if I may say so, we knowing all about one another, and I solemnly

19. Bit by bit.
20. *With Fire and the Sword (Ogniem i mieczem)* is the title of one of Sienkiewicz's trilogy of novels on seventeenth-century Poland.
21. In the long run.
22. Our good intentions.

swear before heaven and earth that if, on account of anyone's obstinacy, our fatherland were to come to harm, it is not thus we desire to show our filial love.

They listened very quietly while I was speaking; no sooner had I finished but a great hubbub commenced. One was saying this, another that; a third, "No other way"; still others, "He's wrong, nothing will come of it." A few bibbers, all clamoring at once, blurt out: " 'Tis no wonder the Czarniecki-ites are having scruples; over in their division they've got all Jesuit chaplains. And it's they who stuff 'em with scruples." But the others shouting them down, they fell silent. Borzęcki though, listened to my speech with pleasure and showed it plainly, perceiving that all the glory of whatever would turn out well would attach to his *reputationi,* he being a man of action and a good soldier. And the marshal was of the same opinion, only he showed it not, lest he seem to give assent. As soon as the commotion subsided, the remaining squadrons declared their positions, one after the other. When the royal regiment had finished, other regiments, even those squadrons who had opposed us, and there were six of them, after whispering together, gave up their previous plan and like us, declared themselves in favor of setting forth on a campaign, after having enjoyed some repose and made themselves ready.

The hetman's men, seeing our perseverance, did not want to annoy us, seeing they'll not break our resolve; they saw that to put us off would do their cause no good, if Czarniecki had troops that were *totissimus* for the king. *Conclusum:* everyone consented to this plan. The assembly's deliberations were called to a close then, a promise being made to come to a decision, God willing, after we were in quarters.

The following day, quarters were assigned; the Kleck castle to the marshal and deputy for headquarters. The senior officers took a cunningly rigorous oath of allegiance to the army and the army in turn to the officers; some put off their oath (as did I) until the next assembly.

The regiments went off separately then, each to his own post. Three thousand of the army were sent after the other squadrons then, nine of which were from our division, in order to *compellere* them to join the confederacy; that is all they were needing, too — to be forced, *per regulam*[23] of politics; they being regiments of the Crown and the Commandant, they needed the cover of being compelled. So it came about then that they joined the confederacy. They went about seizing crown lands, dividing them among the army.[24] Having ensconced themselves

23. According to the rules.

24. Pasek mentions three different categories of Crown lands confiscated by the army: properties leased by the king to the gentry *(starostwa niegrodowe)*; property granted

in their billets, no sooner did they get a taste of luxury, of carouses, but that pious intention fell into oblivion. If anyone mentioned it, he was shouted down at once; they grumping at the king and the Commonwealth, for "threatening us so, for importuning us, promising to reprimand us, and why should we jump at their beck and call?" The Commonwealth also tended somnolently to itself, and so everything came to pass just as I, simple fellow though I was, had said; the confederacy lasting into its third year, Muscovy reinforced her positions; once entered upon negotiations, she saw her own strength and took account of our discord; bolder now were the Muscovites, from whom not only could we not take something, or get back our own, but we had to pay them right fair damages for that which we had won from them in battle; about which I shall write at more length below. So, as a rule, God withholds his blessings from those who know not how to use what is given to them; as they say, *Vincere et victoria uti non idem est.*[25]

We had won such notable victories over the enemy and, with God's special protection, freed Ukrainian, Lithuanian, and Byelorussian lands, sowing their fields with corpses — Muscovite and Cossack corpses, that is — and drenching in blood that land for which Muscovy, thirsting to possess, had waged war; we had liberated our conquered fortresses, some by storm, others by treaty, and quelled that immense fire. But then we, [instead of] hastening to the Muscovite capital with our triumphant army and forcing the enemy, who were stunned now and nearly exhausted, to recognize our victorious hand and receive the *iugum servitutis*[26] (the Muscovites were all talking of it, would have had to submit out of the fear which the Lord had visited upon them, had even fled the capital to Beloe Ozero,[27] which I, being in Muscovy learned about later, as I shall write further on) — [instead] we, the army, entered into a confederacy, not so much on account of our pay being withheld as the conspiring of certain factions to promote their intrigues under the cover of our unpaid wages, by keeping the army in a confederacy. And Muscovy's tsar spared no tinder to kindle that blaze, for the rubles fell thick and fast. This circumstance gave rise to that confederacy: someone wanted to *piscari in turbido,* seeing the king *sine successore* and the line of the glorious Jagiełło family dying out.[28]

The Commonwealth truly was in debt to the army; notwithstanding, the army could have held out as before, accepting more on credit from

as security or in return for services *(tenuty)*; and properties whose revenues were destined solely for the upkeep of the royal court *(ekonomije)*.

25. To win and to profit from the victory are not the same.
26. Yoke of servitude.
27. See note 5, this chapter.
28. Fish in troubled waters . . . without a successor.

the Commonwealth; it was not so poor, especially we of Czarniecki's division who had come from Denmark rich and mounted; surely we lost nothing in the battles with Muscovy either, rather we gained. The army could have gotten by without wages and without setting up a confederacy; but in doing so, the army should have been won over there and then, only with kindness, not harshly, the which when it did happen later, was already too late; having savored wantonness, the stag already felt his antlers, and 60,000 swords were as if plucked from the throat of a dove.[29]

Having taken up quarters then in Kielce, at the first assembly they raised the issue of swearing in those who had not yet taken an oath *super fidelitatem* to the officers, *et non revelationem*[30] of secrets, and of not resigning before general amnesty was granted, at which some of the squadrons murmured, having the fear of God in mind, especially those who had no great appetite for the confederacy; yet, little by little, they were forced to consent, some out of fear of punishment, others being captivated by sweet luxury and good victuals. Whereas I, *inter incudem et malleum,*[31] with no less pay owing to me than they, and no less deserving than they of a prosperous existence, desired to be in the union, having already been appointed to the secretary's office, but by no means did I want to bind myself with an oath, and so long as I could, I *subterfugiebam,*[32] having always been by nature wary of such swearing. At the fourth assembly, when the lieutenants were delivering up the lists of men in their companies who had sworn, they begin to press me seriously to take the oath without further delay. I address the assembly then; I'm just about to begin my discourse, when the deputy marshal interrupts; he informs the army he will take it upon himself to *flectere* me *persuasionibus;*[33] I shall do it at his intervention, I shall swear by the agreed formula. And he speaks to me without showing fear that I spoke bluntly or squirmed out of the oath; those in their cups would have got into a scuffle with me. I, having taken a bit of cheer in good company, too, it might have easily happened.

The *sessio* being over, Borzęcki disputes in all manner of ways with me, *proponendo utilitatem* to the whole division and *emolumentum*[34] to the entire Commonwealth of having the office of secretary in our hands, since we who were come into the union *magis inviti, quam invitati*[35] shall

29. The sense of this saying seems to be still unclear to Polish scholars.
30. Of loyalty . . .and of no disclosure.
31. Between hammer and anvil.
32. Wriggled out (of it).
33. To incline (me) through persuasion.
34. Setting forth the usefulness . . . and the advantage.
35. More reluctant than invited.

dominate in the councils, also *proponendo fructum*[36] for improving our condition from that office, even telling me that the office can bring revenue to more than one entire squadron, and *proponendo* that if more of us who wish the fatherland well, who, having had our bread, desire to set out upon a military action, enter into the leadership of those councils, then the speedier shall our design bear fruit; and should we succeed, and the army does go forth under our leadership on a campaign, the world will know of both my name and yours. But none of these delicious promises, splendid as they were, whetted my appetite, when I recalled the oath: so deeply was that scruple lodged in my head. Borzęcki, infuriated, blurted out these words: "You don't want to do it at my kind bidding; well you'll see at tomorrow's council that a few hundred maces will be more persuasive when they show up. And I won't be there this time, since my friendship means so little to you."

The next day Borzęcki did not go to the assembly, nor was I eager to rush there; but they sent for me and I had to go. The subject of the oaths being broached, whoever had still not performed it, should absolutely do so now. First, Chochoł took the oath, then several other cavaliers; at that moment the deputy arrives; being ill, he had excused himself. But he took pity on me, after all, lest I get into bad straits, for he was very fond of me. So I, being ordered to take the oath, speak thus: "Since it is not a commandment of the Lord to require each and every cavalier to perform the oath at the general assembly, he can as well make it before his own officer at the special assembly as here." They answered me: "No, you can't, it's here isn't it, that you want to accept that honor which the army intends to give." I wanted to ask if I might think it over until tomorrow, but something seemed to whisper to me: say now whatever you have to say, and plainly. To be honest, my heart was not in that confederacy at all, nor in those promises; why, I do not know. I began to speak to them then in these words:

> Worthy Gentlemen! From the beginning of my service, while bearing with unflinching gaze the enemy's onslaughts, bearing all military labors *hilari fronte*,[37] suffering the *vicissitudines* of battle with a brave heart and losing therein my wretched substance, never was I seen behind the battle-ranks but where I had to be, with the standard, mother mine. Boldly am I able to say: whoever knows this to be not so, *proice lapidem!*[38] For which reasons, I feel myself to be on an equal plane [with] other deserving sons of this land. The which, if it be so, then he who does his work like everyone else, should receive his pay like everyone else; I, having the same claims on the Commonwealth as does every one of you worthy gentlemen, do thereby feel

36. Setting forth the advantage.
37. With cheerful countenance.
38. Let him cast (the first) stone.

able to speak boldly here of my well-earned soldier's wage and as boldly reach for a portion of winter pay and rations,[39] for I'm not sitting down to that bread just now as it's taken from the oven, but I've long been fighting for it with sharp steel. It is not for bread then that I ask; having earned it with my blood, I deserve it as much as anyone else. But I ask that having labored *non abiurando,* I be permitted to eat my bread *non adiurando.*[40] That you worthy gentlemen, and especially our elder bretheren, have chosen the advantageous moment to wrest our wages is a *gloriosum opus,* for which thanks are due and should always be due. And that you estimable gentlemen, *stabiliendo ulteriorem cursum* of our affairs, particularly *in casu saevientis fortunae*[41] (not knowing what is to come) by barring further battles, have thought out such a binding oath, I do not condemn, but I have thereof an innate loathing, and at the outset in the first assembly I declared to you that I intended not to swear; for just as sometimes even an Arab snaffle will not curb a tough-mouthed horse, so too whomever inbred decency will not deter, neither will the likes of such binding oaths keep in hand. And surely greater is the outrage to the Divine Majesty if, having sworn before God, we break our word of honor. I wonder whether Catiline did not regret making certain that *conscios facti obstruixerat iuramento;*[42] I wonder how it aided Hannibal though he vowed *solenniter super Romanorum perniciem,*[43] if the heavens had devised a different casting of the dice for him than he had promised himself. Consider what solace was there for Xerxes in binding Demaratus, the Spartan, by an oath of loyalty if the exile, being more sympathetic to his own country — though it was ungrateful — sent there *per ceram erasam*[44] all the secrets of the enemy that was advancing on his homeland; later he instigated Xerxes' brutal murder by his own uncle, Artaban.[45] Even more instances could I enumerate of those whom virtue and decency restrained rather than an enforced oath. And so I say now, I fail to see the good of such an oath as you worthy gentlemen are requiring of me: if it is to bind me lest I resign from the confederacy, then it is *contra rationem* that I, having never been a deserter from camp even during our wretchedest days when food was scarce and fighting heavy, should now withdraw from the army, when fighting is nil, the eating plentiful, the drinking sweet; but even if I should resign, I'm no colonel; officers and regiments would not follow me, out of the tens of thousands in the army little harm would be caused by my person; if, however, the reason is that Your Lordships wish to install me as *cancellariatus,*[46] then I am prepared to be obedient to the will of Your

39. Winter pay and rations were extracted by the army from clerical and royal estates during the winter respite.
40. And never forsworn . . .without having sworn.
41. Establishing the eventual course (of our affairs, particularly) should fortune turn against us.
42. Those aware of the deed be bound by oath.
43. Solemnly that the Romans would perish.
44. By scraping off the wax.
45. Artaban was the captain of Xerxes' bodyguards, not his uncle, as Pasek would have it.
46. Secretary.

> Gracious Lordships and to serve *pro posse meo cum conditione*[47] that I need not take an oath, for neither this, nor any office, nor the largest revenues, can ever bring me to that. If this is possible, Your Gracious Lordships, then I am entreating you. I promise to observe more strictly than anyone under oath all these circumstances to which the army is swearing, pledging my life and blood, the which shall always be in Your Lordship's hands. But if my plea goes unheard and I am unable to deserve the trust, then I no longer wish to partake in the council meetings, nor desire to know any secrets, but I shall not forego my bread, since he who has well earned it can well consume it without being certified under oath.

A goodly clamor arose *pro et contra* according to each one's inclination toward me, especially from Pukarzowski, then a cavalier with the district supervisor of Krasnostaw [Szczęsny Potocki], who heartily wished for himself that post offered to me; he was indeed up for it, but as one among six. He spoke out then in the name of all: "It would be better for him who does not wish to march in line with us to leave us; whoever's not with us is against us." I replied that "you've misunderstood my words; though I'm not grabbing for this novelty, the cause being hurtful and pernicious, my bread I do want and do not scorn, having better as well as longer merited it than you, Sir."

That very day I went to bid farewell to the marshal. He asked whither I was off to. I said: "To my squadron to fetch my retinue, and since here in the confederacy I am not worthy of my hard-earned bread, my home soil will yet feed me, thanks to my father's kindness. The deputy, though a great friend of mine, wished neither to see me nor to say goodbye, being both angry and grieved. What I had disclosed to my trusted friends, though, got back to them: that no sooner I am home and the horses rested, but I'd ride to Czereja to my squadron leader in Byelorussia who was then routing Khovansky, the Muscovite hetman, for the fourth time.[48] No sooner are they acquainted with my design, but send at once to my squadron causing it to refuse my release from the troop, the which had to happen, since the marshal's cossack[49] arrived at my squadron before I did. By this circumstance, they hoped to deflect me from my plan, but even that was impossible; after several days of leave-taking spent with my squadron, passing the time in good company, I rode off without another word but that I was going home, leaving behind my retinue of soldiers and taking only the servants.

My father praised my plan exceedingly, giving thanks and blessing me for having so acted. My mother, too, though I was her only son, was of such a character as never to dissuade me from the largest, most

47. To the best of my ability under the condition.
48. Pasek means Czarniecki; he won a victory on November 4.
49. A lackey dressed in Cossack style.

dangerous of battles, firmly believing that no evil can befall a man except God will it.

Having gotten myself some clothes at home, I left there on the feast of St. Martin [November 11], my horses well fed and having bought a few more; for, by the grace of God, I still had the Danish money, and my father put in some too. On my way, I encountered one of our hussar squadrons in Łysobyki, Kossakowski in the lieutenancy; they were going to enter the confederacy *post multas deliberationes.*[50] Many of my kinsmen being there, I had to pass several days with them, but did not make known my intention saying only that I was going to my uncle, *Pan* Kazimierz Gorzewski, in Targonie near Tykocin; he was commandant (of the garrison) at Tykocin. This they readily believed, knowing he was my uncle; had I revealed my plan they could have tried to discourage me, especially my cousin, Stanisław Trzemeski, who was deputy lieutenant.

After taking my leave of them, I descended on a village near Zielona Puszcza[51] for the first Mass of Advent [November 27]; also there was his lordship *Pan* Stanisławski, the Warsaw cupbearer and royal courtier; seeing me in church, though he did not know me, yet being a decent fellow, he began heartily to entreat me to visit him and take my ease or at least to dine with him. When I, making excuses, told him forthrightly where I was headed and under what circumstances I had withdrawn from the confederacy, all the more did he implore me, wishing to show me his gratitude for being *pars regalis*[52] and promising to write to the Court, so that I would there be shown every manner of appreciation. There being no other way but to accept, I stopped by his estate where such hospitality greeted both me and my servants that it seemed to us we were in paradise; even my hunting dog was seated at table on a silken pillow, food served to him on silver dishes straight from the platters.

While I was there, Mazepa, groom of the royal chamber, arrived.[53] An ennobled Cossack he was, on his way from Warsaw to the king, then in Grodno.[54] During my visit there the talk touched on matters of state; from this he, imputing some dignity to my person, got the idea that I could not be riding into Lithuania and Byelorussia without a hidden

50. After many council sessions.
51. Zielona Puszcza is the old name for the forest between Grodno and Białowieża; today it is a national park near Białystok.
52. On the king's side.
53. Jan Mazepa (c. 1644-1709), a Cossack who for some time was groom of the chamber for King Jan Kazimierz; from 1687 he was hetman of the Cossacks in the Ukraine. He was a figure that kindled the imaginations of both Slav and non-Slav alike. Among those whom he inspired were Pushkin, Słowacki, Voltaire, and Byron.
54. The king was then meeting with the senate in Grodno on the Niemen River.

reason. I rode on slowly then, while Mazepa rushed to the king *magnis itineribus* and, wanting to curry favor, he told them that a confederate cavalier of the Ruthenian Governor's squadron was coming; he pretends to be passing through to his squadron leader in Byelorussia, but under the circumstances it looks unlikely.

[Nine pages of the manuscript are missing here. They doubtless contained the following details: the king, mistakenly informed by Mazepa, sent an armed detachment to arrest Pasek and hand him over to Grodno. On the way, a detachment of Lithuanian confederates, having learned that the royal detachment had a captive confederate in tow, attacked the royal troops in an unsuccessful attempt to free Pasek. This made things even worse for Pasek. Taken to Grodno by the king's soldiers, Pasek stood before the senators and made a speech in his own defense, only the end of which has survived. The fragment which follows is this final portion of his defense.]

> . . . to the deserving, for scarcely one tenth do I see *in manibus bene meritorum.*[55] I have wasted already half of my father's substance — wherewith the whole army is acquainted as well as my commander; more than once have I shed blood copiously for my country; I would have consented to find my name closing the list of *bene meritorum,*[56] but neither I nor many others more deserving than myself happed to taste that recompense. Yet many are those whom I see as have shed their blood by opening a vein with a French lancet,[57] or by having been carelessly shaven by their barber; and they without earning it now press hardest toward the purse of the *bene meritorum,* they, doing so first in order to feed themselves, then to become lords from it, then to oppress the *bene meritos* and those who are poorer; they set off brawls in the Diets and regional dietines and scorn those more deserving than they. What good are such men to the Commonwealth or to His Majesty? Good but to obstruct the Diet and regional dietines with their private concerns, promoting their own interests, stealing time from civic affairs with superfluous luxuries and banquets, having torn the bread from the mouths of the deserving, using it for factions, intrigues, for graft and the furtherance of their own interests; they grope blindly toward the treasury of the Commonwealth like a kitten for its milk. But no sooner does fortune frown or the slightest *adversitas* appear, no sooner does the mild west wind cease to favor them, the north wind begin to blow harshly, but like geese to warm climes do they flee, forgetting the cares of their fatherland, and let themselves be skinned like gypsies in foreign towns. *Domi leones, foris vulpeculae.*[58] A recent proof we have: the Swedish war; when *saevire Fortuna et cuncta miscere*

55. In the hands of those who deserve (it).
56. Men of merit.
57. Pasek is referring to the gentry's custom of yearly blood-letting for the purpose of "drawing out humors."
58. Lions at home, vixens abroad.

coepit,[59] when our neighbors bore down nearly all at once with all their might upon us, and to resist such a heavy onslaught from the enemy we needed not handfuls of terrified soldiers to aid us but so many *centimanos Cottos.*[60] Were there many men of zeal to be found who would uphold their fallen land *in necessitate* with counsel and substance? Did many subjects rally to the side of their king? Seeing him *omni spe et consilio destitutum,*[61] each went his own way, they all fled save for a few who put themselves either at the king's disposal or at the army's, and a very few good and decent senators and lords; the army, dashing from place to place within the country was like a wild boar, snapping back at cruel mastiffs.[62] Not until God looked graciously upon us and the country had shaken off some of its misery, did our gentlemen zealots burn to defend their fatherland. *Sero molunt deorum molae;*[63] only then did some teeth appear as if from a mousehole looking for bread, although there were no hands from a Trojan horse to defend us. Let these parasites get ready to meet their downfall, perhaps soon, at the hands of the army; to a valiant steed 'tis painful if a blackguard of an ass eats up the food in his trough.

I know very well that this *captivatio* befell me *ex consilio,*[64] but the world will judge whether that *consilium* is salutary for his Majesty and for the country. If this befell me on account of the virtue and love I've shown toward my country, *innocuus lapidor;*[65] if it befell me as an envoy, then it is both *contra iura gentium, contra regulam iustitiae,* since *quidquid non discutiter, iustitia non putatur.*[66] For whichever of these two motives, at first it is clear to him who sins that he has acted well, *vel peccantibus virtutis species prima iucunda est.*[67] But consider the conclusion. Out of 60,000 soldiers, I alone have acted thus, not out of any necessity, neither on account of any misdeed, but simply out of love of country; I spurn rest and those comforts which the lowliest cavalier can now enjoy, I'm riding off to war; heedless of the severities of a nasty winter, I ride off on a campaign; I'm on my way to the fighting, to

59. Fortune began to rage and everything to grow confused.
60. Giants with a hundred hands.
61. Deprived of all hope and counsel.
62. Pasek here is thinking of the five squadrons that in 1655 did not surrender along with the rest of the army to the Swedes "and for this reason not only were they not given quarters for the winter but throughout the entire winter both Swedes and Polish gentry . . . persecuted them" (Łoś, 10). Who knows if Pasek may not have served in these squadrons.
63. The mills of the gods grind slowly (Greek proverb). The Poles used to say: "God is not hasty, but He's just." Pasek, however, seems to have applied the saying differently: God granted success late, and that is when the magnates made their appearance.
64. Imprisonment . . .on the recommendation of the (senatorial) council.
65. An innocent man is being stoned.
66. Contrary to the law of nations and contrary to the principles of justice, since whatever has not been thoroughly debated cannot be regarded as just.
67. Since old style virtue is agreeable even to sinners.

where blood is sweet cordial. For this step my father praised me; all those attached to my home and everyone wishing the country well praised me, all but vowing that my country would recompense me with gratitude.

Well, I see my recompense has begun, as I'm ambushed on a public road in the middle of a forest, robbed, taken prisoner, and brought here, like that African captive to Rome, in triumph.[68] O, such a mighty victory that one should be subdued by the many, that the many should wreak fury and shower abuse upon one man! Where you have 60,000 sabres glistening before your eyes, there you should show your prowess, not here to one man! The army will know how to protest the insult it suffered in my person. For though not a confederate, I am a soldier as much deserving as they of recompense; though I'm not an envoy, yet this dishonorable deed was committed as if I were, therefore, *intentio pro facto.*[69] When most of the army was across the sea, no one made sport of Jaskulski's confederacy;[70] all the strength being in one bunch can help and hurt. *In quorum manibus arma sunt, in eorum potestate est conservare et perdere Rempublicam.*[71] I shall return to the army and I'll be able to tell them what sort of gratitude they may expect for their bloody services; I'll know how to seek redress from everyone who did such dishonor to me and, through my person, to the whole army. And now, before heaven and earth, I protest this injustice and I sincerely regret everything that I accomplished for my fatherland. *Cum vitia prosunt, peccat qui recte facit.*[72]

No sooner had I stopped speaking, but some of the senators began to raise objections and each one of them I had to counter. First, the Lithuanian vice-chancellor, Naruszewicz, spoke to this effect:

When I come to consider the content of this speech, I perceive the argument *accusat* more than *excusat;* you repudiate the confederacy, Sir, declaring you are not an envoy, yet speak on behalf of the confederacy, taking the part of the army as would any official envoy, and even more. I who would not sin by suspecting as much, did not think of it until the end of your speech, considering that for such a design one needs no credentials; all that can be expressed on paper, can fit into the head. A second reason makes its being so a great likelihood, that some rogues from the Lithuanian army assailed the king's soldiers; it is plain they were acquainted of it. A third, that you speak to us so arrogantly, that you distrust us senators and insult his Majesty, the king, wherefore alone you are *hostis patriae et reus criminis laesae maiestatis.*[73]

68. Yugurtha, king of Numidia, waged war against Rome in the second century B.C.; he was defeated and died in prison (Pollak, 439).
69. The intention (is taken) for the deed.
70. In 1659, Marian Jaskulski's confederacy was appeased by an advance on the wages.
71. Whoever holds the arms can save or doom the Commonwealth.
72. When vice brings gain, he sins who acts decently.
73. An enemy of the fatherland and guilty of the crime of lese majesty.

And he spoke at greater length, but it's difficult to express word for word another's words and sentiments. To which I reply thus:

The great senator's remarks are just and, I should say, sound genuine, for I, belike, sitting in his place would not have judged his lordship otherwise in the same circumstances. For his consideration, I put forth this argument. As to the first, I have my father to thank for not sending me out to tend heifers at an early age; besides, there is a *practicatum axioma* that *necessitas acuit ingenium.*[74] As to the second: not I should give account of myself, but those who wanted to collar me without either knowing or seeing me; belike they did so believing that I was what they took me for, namely an envoy. But that Your Lordship should call them rogues; until now I knew not that in so worthy a nation as the Grand Duchy of Lithuania were to be found rogues, for you'll find none in our army. Against the third remark, I say this: a wise man must take his own person as the measure of each thing. If Your Lordship, whose decency is manifest, were pronounced a traitor to the Commonwealth, if Your Lordship, in manifest innocence, were to be seized on a public road, having been by no law persuaded, incarcerated, and clothed in the garb of treason, I beseech Your Lordship to deign to teach me in what spirit he would accept such an outrage. If Your Lordship should tell me it would have been a grave affront to a noble heart, then it is a *consequentia* that for me it is the same, who by birth and by breeding can measure up to any good man. If this distresses me, it does not shame me, for I know my innocence. *Maximum solatium est vacare culpa.*[75] But even if I were guilty, shame would be of no help to a good man, though I cry my eyes out, if he is outraged in his honor and reputation by a wicked man. It should never shame an innocent man, even though somebody transgress law and justice for he does so at his own expense, he cannot take away a good man's courage. *Bonus animus in re mala dimidium est mali*[76] — so wise men say. As for the charge of *laesae majestatis,* even Catonian censure will do me no harm; someone else can succumb, sooner than I, an ordinary man. For it is not to his Majesty's person that I direct my words: no one will read into my heart any intent to criticize his gracious Majesty's reign; this is a singular cruelty — if I may say so — but adds to the indignity I've suffered. Inasmuchas it comes from an excess of malice, guilty is he who has accused, not he who punishes me. I speak to those who have done this to me, who sat in council, who imprisoned me here. What I said before, I say again — *nescit vox missa reverti.*[77] I shall know how to seek redress from everyone who is my equal by birth. I have the regional dietines, I have the tribunals, I have the general assembly; *utraque civis,*[78] for I am both a gentleman and a soldier; my own words I can never deny. *Hoc mihi pietas, hoc pia lingua odit.*[79]

74. Tested truth (that) necessity sharpens the mind.
75. The greatest consolation is not to feel guilty (Cicero, *Ad Familiares,* 7, 5).
76. A good thought in misfortune cuts the evil in half.
77. What has been said cannot be unsaid (Horace, *De arte poetica,* 390).
78. I am doubly a citizen.
79. Honest lips blench before what I consider virtue.

Next to speak, as I remember, is the governor of Troki, [Mikołaj Stefan] Pac, in words to this effect:

> In truth, it must be painful when any hurt befalls someone; in which straits, should he speak more heatedly, not his the blame, but the one who brings him to this impatience. For sorrow they say, is not cautious. If then, committed in innocence, I do not much hold it against him; but if this gentleman is guilty, and so arrogantly preaches, then his sin is no longer single, but double, wherein are reflected as in a mirror both the crime of lese majesty and the discredit to our senatorial dignity. And so, in view of those remarks of his lordship the vice-chancellor, a senator and brother, I do judge him guilty rather than innocent.

And immediately he turns to me with this apostrophe:

> You menace us, Sir, with the army, you threaten us with vengeance of some sort, you vow to go back to the confederacy. But are you certain you will depart from this place alive? Have you asked yourself whether you shall be allowed to leave with your head? Does such behavior not deserve death? We ourselves shall see to it and will be pressing his Majesty the king not to release you willy-nilly for insults such as these, inflicted by a person neither so esteemed nor so deserving, as indeed his years indicate.

And he talked on rather lengthily. [Then I replied:]

> Your Lordship admitted that it is a painful thing for an innocent man to suffer so great a slander; Your Lordship also admitted that whatever sorrow the heart feels, the tongue as its natural *interpres* must declare to the world. And yet, Your Lordship adds *afflicto afflictionem.* With Holy Scripture I must ask: "If I speak the truth, wherefore dost thou chastize me?" Your Lordship threatens me with death — this is the universal law of all the living. *Quisquis ad vitam editur, ad mortem destinatur.*[80] These are age-old threats wherewith Your Lordship terrorizes me, and I wonder but they won't penetrate to your study more swiftly than to my hut, and you won't be more terrified behind your golden bed-curtain than I on my wretched soldier's pad. Whoever serves in war is a scoffer at death for he goes in search of her, not she him. I, though of youthful age, have sought death by the Dnieper, the Dniester, the Oder, and the Elbe, and at the ocean and the Baltic Sea. And My Lord, My Most Gracious Lord, would as soon belike, never meet up with her. As for myself, I care not, knowing such is the *sequentia* in this life: *exilium, luctus, dolor, tributa sunt ista vivendi.*[81] If we must die, then let us die well; and a better death there is none, belike, than that to which a man goes in innocence for virtue and love of country. If it be an *actus meritorius* to die for one's country, then it be so for a country's sons to die by the hands of their fathers; but where the profit in view of such an end? Perseus — so they write — wanting to serve his country, *occidit anguem, e cuius collo guttae cadentes*

80. Whoever comes into the world is bound to die.
81. Exile, lament, pain are inseparable from life.

innumeros genuere colubros.[82] No one will use my innocent blood to quench that fire kindled, I know not but to the downfall of the country, by someone's wicked counsels. God, the army, and my poor clan will take up the cudgels for my innocence; there will be no lack of kin, for long have I been a gentleman. Here my head will lie and along with my teeth will remain some sort of memory of my name. No novelty that. Persons of eminent name have found themselves in similar straits. *Ita semper illustribus viris animo vivere longe antiquius fuit quam corpore.*[83] My innocence then bids me neither to fear all these terrors nor to lose hope. *Aegrotus quamdiu animam habet, spem habet.*[84] God's mercy is greater than the madness of the whole world. *Dei proprium est protegere, quos dignos indicat.*[85] That my person lacks gravity, as Your Lordship, My Gracious Lord, calls it, what is there to do? Neither my years nor my present rank require such gravity as to swell up and sit in a [senatorial] chair like a spider. Sometimes the level of even these heights is base. He who is cautious will not even tread on an old hoop; he who is wise ought not to slight even the paltriest of men. *Nemo est contemnendus, in quo aliqua virtutis significatio apparet.*[86]

Again Pac speaks:

Quot verba, tot minaciae, or rather, I'll say, *tot scommata.*[87] He who listens may well perceive that it does not befit an accused man to argue thus, to exasperate so insultingly his Majesty the king and the senate, to brag no less needlessly of his services to the country, reciting expeditions, places, rivers, oceans; if it was so, I know not. We too, after all, have been at sea and across the sea, but make no mention of it. (He pronounced some maxim here but I don't remember it, though it was appropriate for his criticism). Better to do nothing for one's country and cast it not in our teeth; but no matter how much good is done for one's country, one bad deed *annihilat* all those services, if he who exalts his country one time drags it down the next, if he shows himself its son one time, a stepson the next, if, having done wrong, he yet flatters himself and insults the estates of our Commonwealth; but for such boldness we have the tower and the sword.

To which I give the following reply:

It's one thing to be accused, another to be guilty; I see myself accused but do not feel guilty, and therefore I defend my innocence. My innocence fights for me. I am hoping to God no one fishes in these troubled waters. I

82. Killed the serpent out of whose neck and the drops of blood flowing therefrom grew countless multitudes of serpents. (Actually, Perseus killed the snake-haired Gorgon, not a serpent; and the idea that he did so to serve his country is Pasek's invention.)
83. Illustrious men have lived longer in spirit than in body.
84. As long as soul and body are together, a sick man does not lose hope.
85. It is an attribute of God's that he shields those whom he deems worthy.
86. One should scorn no one in whom the mark of virtue is to be found.
87. As many threats as words . . . as jeers.

do not twit you with my services to the country, I only mention them so that they may be placed in the balance, should I deserve a recompense other than the present one. Should anyone have doubts about my services, the *cicatrices adverso pectore*[88] will bear witness to whether or not they are genuine; there are as many of my comrades-in-arms as having been there to see them will give testimony. For him who sat at home in domestic comfort, eating oysters, snails, and truffles, to have seen them would have been a hardship. Whether anyone was or was not at sea or across the sea, I do not wish to dispute; indeed, *facile credo* for *indicat vestis, quales intrinsicus estis.*[89] But the nature of *peregrinationis* is different; it is one thing to learn *pierla italiano? pierla franciezo?*[90] It's another to learn "Who goes there? Give the password!" It's one thing to learn ballets, capers, dances, listening to a graceful melody, placing one's feet according to the notes; it's another to listen to the sound of a martial band; one thing to pour sweet cordials, another to spill blood. I feel I have always done *what I could for my country;* so I can safely call myself a son, not a stepson. More likely, I'd sooner uncover stepfathers *inter patres patriae, quorum machinationes* have enfeebled the Commonwealth and brought it to the extremity of destitution, *quorum iniuriis* her fame sank *in profundissimo Democriti puteo,*[91] whereas the army through its courage and manliness brought it out of so intolerable a labyrinth and restored its glory. We need to seek no further than the Swedish War for proof — how much harm, how much havoc was wreaked upon the country! And who paved the way for the Swedish War? *Mala consilia ordinis intermedii*[92] and the unfair verdict on Radziejowski, wherein unfair I shall not explain, as I speak to those who are familiar with that affair.[93] If make war you must, then start it on a solid ground, in order that the end confound not the beginning, in order not to regret what we have begun, whereof the Swedish War is a manifest example. It can be recalled how difficult it was to forsake domestic bliss, our harvests, our estates, to scour the corners of foreign countries; *e converso,* how pleasant, though our purse was ruined, to return to our properties and greet our *Lares.*[94] Who made it possible? Certainly not the one who stayed abroad and asked how goes it in Poland. Who then? God *per instrumenta* of His commands, through the courageous toil of our army, through the labor and vigilance of our

88. Wounds on my chest.
89. I have no trouble believing it (for) the clothes indicate what you are inside.
90. Pasek's garbling of "do you speak Italian? French?"
91. Among the fathers of the contry whose machinations . . .through whose injurious deeds (her fame sank) into the deepest well of Democritus. (The Greek philosopher Democritus asserted that the earth is hollow inside.)
92. The evil counsels of the intermediate estate (because it was supposed to mediate between the king and the nobility).
93. Hieronym Radziejowski, vice-chancellor of the Crown Treasury, had been condemned by a verdict of the marshal of the Diet to banishment and infamy for an armed assault committed in the king's presence. See page 356, Appendix III, and the Index of Proper Names.
94. Roman gods of the hearth.

good leaders, or, to speak *in singulari, unus homo nobis cunctando restituit rem.*[95]

But with the confederacy, or to speak more diplomatically, with the present association, how to proceed? I shall see whether he who formed it will as swiftly dissolve it. A *nodus Gordius* it is; two fingers had no trouble tying it, but soon even teeth will not undo it; whoever tied this knot is guilty before God and country. Once a pious monarch called out to his careless administrator: '*Vare, legiones redde!*[96] Our Commonwealth should beware of such Varuses. Stand to account for the Swedish War which you kindled with your private and ruinous battles counter to God and the law; make amends for the blasphemies committed by those apostate Swedes in God's holy places; return the towns that were burned to the ground, the mansions, the castles; requite the gentry for the oppression it suffered and the fortunes it lost; restore the blood so lavishly spilled in combat and give back to the country all its sons who perished; remove that indelible shame from his Majesty the king and our entire people. I speak to those here present: *redde*, give back to our wretched people the bread which our bloody work has taken from their mouths and nearly drained of their last drop of blood; restore to God His holy praise; retrieve Smolensk, Kiev, Nowogród Siewierski [occupied by Muscovy in 1654], the Dnieper region and beyond. For whomever planted the seed of confederacy, a new hell should be devised, new and uncommon tortures; for him summon the sharp sword and cruel hand of the executioner. Meanwhile, before the confederacy will have disbanded, the enemy will grow strong, and fortune may take a different turn; then the enemy will haggle out of us what we should get from him, such being the way with us; after putting an enemy to rout — we're given to paying him damages.

I speak then to the stepfathers of our country — let this be clear — not to its fathers, not to upstanding senators. Let him whom the shoe fits take offense if he wish; never have I been a stepson, only a son to this country, my mother, nor could I be should I wish it; my innate love would not permit me, being of ancient Polish stock, *ex nativo sanguine,* not a foreigner with a title from abroad. So save your threats of tower and sword for those good counselors; I do not fear them, *etsi caelum ruet, impavidum ferient ruinae.*[97]

Before I even finished my speech some had tried to speak up; but toward the end when I said: let him whom the shoe fits take offense (a hackneyed saying, familiar to all), I might as well have put them to sleep, so hushed were they all. But the king — as they told me — who was listening behind the curtains, had a mighty good laugh and said: "What a stout fellow, he's a blunt one, he's telling them the truth. For

95. In the singular, one man rescued our country through delay. (The words of Quintus Ennius concerning Fabius Kunktator; Cicero, *De senectute,* IV. Jotted in the margin of the manuscript is the name "Czarniecki".)

96. Varus, give me back my legions.

97. Though sky may fall, and ruins cover the intrepid man. (An inexact quote from Horace, *Carmina,* III, 3,7.)

that very virtue alone, I'd not have him brought low, though he be indeed an envoy." Not until later was I told this.

After the hush and those glances cast about, Jewłaszewski, the governor of Brześć Litewski, speaks up; his words and argument were long, but their sense was this:

> Heavy indeed is the blow to our senatorial estate when we are called stepfathers, idlers, parasites, and finally even traitors. Whether there be anyone to deserve it I know not. As for me though I feel no guilt in all this, since I am a senator, pain me it must. If we meet with such affrontery from one cavalier, we can expect the like from others. It behooves his Majesty to stand up against his and our insult. After all, the army is our servant and we are the heads of this Commonwealth, a condemnation is absolutely necessary.

He spoke on in this vein lengthily and splendidly, but I'm not like to recall the whole of his speech. I had anticipated reproaches such as these, realizing from the way things were going that speeches of this sort were bound to occur, and I prepared appropriate arguments against them; the Lord suggested the other arguments which came to me *ex occasione*. I make my answer to this point then:

> If it is distressing for him, who deems himself not guilty, to see only a slight allusion directed at others who are, let him take from that the measure of how intolerable it must be for one who, never having earned the ingratitude of his country but who, on the contrary, deserves every sort of *gratitudo* in requital, and who, while entirely innocent, yet suffers such slander, insult, and abuse as I shall long remember. Your Lordship talks of "one cavalier," scarce adding "and an insignificant one," but Your Lordship may recall how you yourself were a cavalier before becoming senator and should not scoff now at those who are poorer. *Sacerdos de una missa.*[98]

He was infuriated, begins to speak in a rush: "Do you think thus to slip round us, one after the other? I'll hurt your reputation if I wish, you remember it, hurt it exceedingly," etc. I speak again:

> That each man's friendship is advantageous to me I know; but so is mine for each man. But let none try me with such tricks, rather would I forever renounce his support. That this slur cast unfairly upon my innocence will damage my reputation I expect not, nor these words of truth I have uttered on this spot. *Ei sane non multum poterit obesse fortuna, qui sibi firmius in virtute, quam in casu, praesidium collocavit.*[99]

With this maxim I ended.

His Lordship, the senator, was angered most of all by two things: first

98. A priest only good for saying Mass. (A priest who makes his living only from saying Mass; hence, a poor one, a simpleton.)
99. Fortune is unable to do much harm to him who provides himself with a defense; he who is virtuous is stronger than blind fate (Cicero, *Ad Herennium* IV, 19, 13).

by my allusion, *sacerdos de una missa,* he not possessing enormous wealth, one village only (yet with 300 plows to till it); second, for that "cavalier". Deliberately, I was hinting at whatever I could think up for whomever — so did I rely on my innocence as on an army 100,000 strong; but they turned it around to the bad side, saying I wanted to slip out of the blame *sub specie* of innocence.

Then in came Father Ujejski, bishop of Kiev, who, during the Troki governor's speech, had gone out into the chamber where, behind the curtains, the royal couple was listening to that discourse; taking the floor, he spoke to this effect:

> That whereof we have no experience we cannot understand so perfectly as he whose own person has been tried. In my own life, I also suffered one slander that I, being innocent, am unable to forget, the bitterness having even to this day stuck in my heart and belike till death shall not vanish from my memory. I'm disposed to believe in this instance — and I would go so far as to put my name to it — that the accused here is innocent; taking into account all the particulars, I see education and upbringing proper to a gentleman's son, and having already observed here *in parte* his modest and civil manners, as well as his youth and stanchness, I think it safe to conclude he has been unjustly libelled. And if so, then it must pain him; and if painful, one need not, *consequenter* hold it very much against him, that out of grief he must say a great deal. Though I owe the dignity of this senator's seat to Providence and his gracious Majesty the king, I have ever been sympathetic to the whole army — *omnis mercenarius sua dignus mercede;*[1] that the army should remind us of its services should surprise no one, for it is of absolute necessity to pay them back — but this I do say: would that they had yet put forth their purpose for one last time, not entering into a confederacy, the which most certainly will bring down great calamity upon our country — *utinam sim falsus vates!*[2] And would that His Royal Highness and the Commonwealth could hear those wrongs from the mouth of the soldier standing *prae oculis,*[3] so that they not resort so speedily *ad violentia media,* not act so *inhumaniter*[4] toward his Majesty the king, our gracious lord, seizing his curriers on the roads, inspecting their documents, having no respect for the lands which are the support of his Majesty's court. I speak openly, I cannot countenance such action; for which reason his Highness, our Gracious Lord, must needs exercise particular vigilance over their scheming. Out of which circumstance, someone, seizing the opportunity, passed on intelligence to the king as to how you, Sir, were to have been an envoy not only to the Lithuanian conspiracy, then disputing what further action to pursue in their undertaking, but also to that part of the army which remains in the service of his Majesty and the Commonwealth under the command of the

1. Every hireling is worthy of his hire.
2. Would that I were a false prophet!
3. Before our eyes.
4. To violent means, (not act so) inhumanely.

Ruthenian governor in order to lure them into confederacy, thereby depriving the king of *omni praesidio et custodia corporis.*[5] The which, if it were so, would indeed give the king cause to take offense; but if it is not true (as I myself think) then such a misunderstanding as befell Your Honor was due to human guile and must be ascribed to the *infelicitati temporis.*[6] You need not be unquiet thereby, that this occurrence will cause you hurt or ill-fame; indeed, since you inform us that, having withdrawn from the confederacy, you are on your way to those soldiers well-disposed to his Majesty and the country, the king will find this pleasing and, mindful of your services, will requite them with every sort of gratitude. One should never judge a thing too finally; as they say: *nihil adeo malum est, quin boni mixturam habeat.*[7] I assure you that what has happened will not damage Your Honor's reputation, but on the contrary, give you goodly access to every kind of regard from his Majesty and the Commonwealth. Difficult are the paths, sometimes, to great glory in the world, but if it is of a more durable kind than that sent by the propitious westwinds, what doth it matter? I can find many more such men whose virtue, *per ardua,*[8] left a memorial to the world. *Hectorem quis nosset, felix si Troia fuisset?*[9]

But now, as time itself must part us, kindly retire to your lodgings, Sir, to await his Majesty's further behest.

He spoke at great length, choosing his words well: I have written out only the *essentiam* of the matter. The bishop's words of solace at the end were plainly not to the senators' liking, they taking them to be *ex mente*[10] of the king; I, too, suspected this, since the bishop had come from the king's chamber.

I gave then this answer to his words:

God be praised that *inter tot moderni collegii sinistras opiniones,*[11] I have heard at least one judgment for the honesty and *pro innocentia* of a poor nobleman and soldier. But they say *facilius est consolari afflictum quam sustinere;*[12] usually the one who suffers, suffers on. I humbly thank the great bishop and distinguished senator of our country. And yet, *vulnera dum sanas, dolor est medicina doloris.*[13] That little word "if" is a sign of doubt; that no one takes me completely for what I feel myself to be causes pain. But what am I to do? *Iugulatur virtus;*[14] only this consoles me, that virtue oppressed is more

5. All defense and his personal bodyguard.
6. Infelicities of the times.
7. There is nothing so evil it is not mixed with a bit of good.
8. Through hardships.
9. Who would have heard of Hector, if Troy had been fortunate? (Ovid, *Tristia,* IV, 3, 75.)
10. According to the mind.
11. Among so many bad opinions in this present gathering.
12. It's easier to console the afflicted than to raise them up.
13. When you heal wounds, pain is the medicine of suffering (Cato, *Disticha,* IV,40).
14. Virtue is oppressed.

> praiseworthy. If I am falsely accused through someone's deception, Fido can also bark at a wayside Christ Tormented in his shrine; I share Seneca's view myself: *Ille enim magnus et nobilis est, qui more magnae ferae* [*scit*] *latratus canum securus exaudire.*[15] Show me proof, I shall submit. But meanwhile, regarding myself no traitor to his Majesty or to the country, if I'm worthy *videre faciem domini,*[16] I beseech Your Grace for this favor.

Says the bishop: "Your Honor, you will certainly have an audience with the king, but not today."

They dispersed then; I too went out, only to find no one around but the ordinary watch by the door! Those others were no longer there, only my servants. I ask then: "And where are my gentlemen *custodes?*[17] I'm told all of them left about an hour ago. I supposed that they went to my quarters and I say: "And an envoy could not escape now if he wished?" The officer, Karpieński, who was on watch outside the king's chamber, replies: "He could have done so long ago belike, had he but the will." I went off then; arriving at the inn: no one there, no gun on the pegs — and plenty of them in the hallway there were — my usual meal from the royal kitchen is on the table. The innkeeper came over to me, offered his congratulations for the Lord having comforted me at last. I ask him where they've gone to? He tells me they came from the palace, took their belongings away, recalled those who were posted here, then helter-skelter off they dashed, cursing Mazepa. I sat down to eat then, inviting the innkeeper to keep me company; Father Gostkowski having been forbidden to visit me; they saying he brought me all the news he learned from the courtiers. Having drunk one bottle of wine and — it being excellent — a second, I went to bed.

Before daybreak, I wake up hearing some kind of rustling round the walls. I call to my boy: "Orłowski, take a look out, will you, and see what all that commotion is in the entranceway." He goes out into the passage, and the head-groom, who slept out with the horses, tells him that the same men who had been here at first, were come again. When he told me that, I wondered what was going on: were they — as children do a sparrow they've tied by a thread, if it attempts to escape, they pull it back with the thread — trying me, or what? Mighty awful weather outside, snow. Back and forth they tread, stomping. They heard my tongue wagging and began to shout: "Hallo, Your Honor, let us into the hallway, we'll freeze out here." I pretended I was asleep, and my servants called out from the hallway: "Don't wake the master! And so till daylight they stood out there, stomping about in the snow. In the morning, I bade the innkeeper to open only an hour or so after it was light. When they came into the hall, I ask them: "In the name of what,

15. Great and noble is he who like a large animal listens quietly to the barking of dogs.
16. To look upon the countenance of my lord (the king).
17. Custodians.

do you come and go from here?" They say: "We ourselves know not what they are about with us or with Your Honor. When Your Honor was at the palace, they ordered us forthwith to betake ourselves and all our things from this post, so that the cavalier will return to the inn and find none of you around. After midnight they sent us round again to watch you as best we could."

I imagined that what had happened was this: the king, judging me innocent, was to have sent me off in the morning; but the senators kept filling his ears with talk of my holding some dignity, of my offending his Majesty, swearing to it and willing to sell their souls to the devil if I was none other than an envoy. Again, the king had let himself be persuaded, and again had sent the guard. Tyzenhausz, too, the Uświat district supervisor, my great adversary, had held forth, saying: "Your Highness will see those words of mine come true; this man, though young, carries an old head on his shoulders."

The bishop of Kiev comes to visit me, urging me to put not my life in danger, but to rely on the king's favor, telling me that

> mail has come which reveals the army sent you as an envoy, and it will be best for you if, of your own accord, you confess all; there will be favors, you will advance, the king forthwith will count you among his attendants, there will be a good estate, a title. What can the army's favor bring you? The king already sympathizes with you, hearing your speeches; he already sees in you a worthy subject, he will make use of you; he already knows your constancy; he praises you for keeping your word to the army *inter tot infractus,*[18] for refusing to expose their secrets, which in any man is praiseworthy; gentlemen welcome such people, avail themselves of their services, and confide in them. As soon as you permit yourself to be inclined by my persuasion, I shall take you upon my priestly conscience, not a hair shall fall from your head; indeed, reputation, royal favor, and dignities of every sort will be yours. If you are concerned about an oath whereby you are mutually bound to each other *super non revelationem,*[19] I absolve you from that. For the king has no other mind but to render unto them, as they rendered to him. The king's letters destined for Vienna and France were intercepted; they, reading confidential matters, inspecting a fine gentleman, captiously questioning him as though he were some traitor. There was nothing in the letter *contra Rempublicam,* nor against the army; but being from the king, this should not have occurred; this it is he deplores.

These and such like he proposes to me, I keep silent, I listen: and I feel both angry and amused at the thought of what curious things God visited upon me; they wanting absolutely to talk me into that whereof they had need, I having nothing to do with it. It crossed my mind then how the guard, after having been removed, was restored at midnight; I construed how the mail which the bishop mentioned must have come

18. In the midst of so many ups and downs.
19. Not to reveal any secrets.

exactly at that time, and this envoy's mission was described therein, but surely my own person could not have been mentioned, for I know on what business I ride, and whither I go, unless it were done by an *inimicus homo,*[20] in return for my not wishing to be part of the confederacy, to make trouble for me. I put my intention itself in God's hands, and make reply in these words:

> Had his lordship, the Uświat district supervisor, come to me about this, together with his lordship, the son of the governor of Smolensk, as they were given to visiting me at first, I would know how to answer their lordships, for a layman can also sometimes address another layman *per parabolas;*[21] but being Your Grace, a great and distinguished senator, as well as my great benefactor whose favor and sympathy I have experienced, I must proceed kindly, though the matter be painful.
>
> Let the One God, creator of heaven and earth, creator of Your Grace and my unworthy self, bear testimony as the protector of *innocentiae,* when my own virtue and honesty cannot do so for me; and let him who has needlessly disturbed Your Lordships accuse the one responsible for this opinion of me. I would not need these oaths, but time as the *omnium malorum medicus*[22] will reveal my innocence; it will come to the surface like oil. Were I such an *idiota* as not to know what a defense a pure conscience is for every man, I would have bowed, I would have looked for expedients; and not once but once times ten, I would have escaped; but in my innocence I know that no lies will hurt me. At the first hearing I said that a dog can bark at the Lord's Agony. Neither menace nor persuasion can lead my spirit astray. Neither will the sun turn into an oil cake for the asking; nor truth be made into untruth. God sees that I shall not yield one inch under threat even though, being yet innocent, something were to befall me here; I'll neither beg nor be afraid, obedient to the poet's wise advice:
>
> *Nescia mens fraudum inculpataeque integra vitae,*
> *Scommata nullius, nullius arma timet.*
> *Omnia contemnit ventis velut ovia rupes,*
> *Mendacesque sonos unius assis habet.*[23]
>
> Let the unvirtuous take pleasure in thrashing out the honesty of the virtuous. And let him who expects with true reality to satisfy, entertain awhile his ardent hope, unless that hope should lead him into a reckless adventure. It is for me to follow with unflinching heart that wise, old-fashioned sentiment:
>
> *qui sapis, ad vitam sapias; gere conscia recti*
> *Pectora nec strepitu commoveare levi.*[24]

20. Person inimical (to me).
21. In parables.
22. The healer of ills.
23. A man devoid of disloyalty, unblemished and pure/ fears no one's scorn nor attack/ cares for nothing, like a rock exposed to the gales/ and to lying voices harkens not.
24. If you are wise, then show wisdom in your life/ keep your conscience pure and tremble not at every rustle.

As there was none before, so is there now no reason to suspect me; all the particulars free me of guilt and I say this: as you, Your Grace, leave the sacrifice of the Mass, believing your soul holy, so do I now swear by God's name that I am innocent of this slander. These broadsides shall not embarrass me; nor shall all these clouds obscure my vision, nor will threats frighten me, for I am not guilty. As openly do I justify myself to you, Your Grace, as if *sub sigillo confessionis;*[25] I could not do otherwise nor could I justify myself more frankly to his Majesty the king, my gracious lord — should I be worthy of it — than I have before you, Your Grace, who are — I say it *sine fuco adulationis*[26] — worthy of this; and most humbly beseech Your Grace not to reveal how I wield so openly the name of God. Let them understand me as they wish, until the manifest reality itself displaces this opinion.

[He answered:]

Now I believe fully that you are *innocuus* and, though I intended to defend you before the king, *omnibus persuasionibus,*[27] I shall keep silent, as Your Honor is confident, for I see that greater honor and glory will be yours if your innocence with irrefutable argument be cleared; *et interim,* Sir, you may be of good cheer and I shall not fret over you.

He went off then, gave I know not what account there, and sent me food from his larder; I was even better off than before, food being brought to me now from both his and the king's kitchen.

They summon me to his Majesty the king. The Lithuanian vice-chancellor speaks: "That favor which Your Honor desires of his Majesty the King, Our Gracious Lord, assuredly will be granted Your Honor, as his royal Highness does not refuse to give ear to your defense." Having seen that there was no great press about the king, only the bishop of Kiev, the vice-chancellor of Lithuania, Sielski, the castellan of Gniezno, and few courtiers, I speak then to the king:

Your Gracious Majesty, My Gracious King and Lord! It is well-known not only to me, an ordinary man, but to every condition and to every state within the Commonwealth as remains subject to Your Majesty, My Gracious Lord, that Your Royal Highness's innate kindness, which we acknowledge, will not permit any need to go unheard; for which I thank you with a humble subject's heart. This much I know: that I would have been free of this slander long since could I have but obtained this favor from Your Highness, therefore nothing remains but to fall at your feet, Sire, and humbly to entreat you if I might be so fortunate as to remove this garb of guilt, the which I must tell you, has been *in superlativo publicissime*[28] cut out for me, and to remove it in the presence of a larger company of their lordships, the senators residing near Your Majesty, than I see here, since it was they had

25. Under the seal of Confession.
26. Without any trace of flattery.
27. By every means of persuasion.
28. With the utmost publicity.

judged me guilty, and nearly all Poland discusses it as if this slander were true. I therefore humbly beg of Your Majesty, My Gracious Lord, this favor and your regard for my honor.

They began then to whisper among themselves, they see night is already come; before all the senators residing in divers parts of the town could have assembled, much time would have passed. The king himself speaks up: "And so we shall; but time has grown short, until tomorrow then, in the morning." I bowed then and went out with Father Piekarski.[29] The king, having detained Tyszkiewicz inside, we waited for him in another chamber. Upon entering, he says to me: "I hold you an honest man now, conducting yourself the way you did, making it clear you did not want to set forth your defense before a small company of senators; I am grateful to you for that courage." They made merry with some wine from the royal cellar; I drinking only a few, nor were they pressing me on account of tomorrow. Then off we went to bed.

The next morning, after hearing Mass at the Jesuit Church, we went to the palace, but there waited about two hours before the senators assembled. Finally, I was sent for; I perceive all the senators there now, and sundry other wealthy lords, the king's attendants, divers persons of quality and whoever wished was there, for access was not forbidden. Then the vice-chancellor says: I expect now things are going well enough to your liking, Sir, that His Majesty the King, Our Gracious Lord, having summoned to his side all those senators who are able to appear, permits Your Honor an audience in their presence. I began thus:

[Pasek's defense follows. It is an even more flowery and lengthy reiteration of the previous arguments outlining his modesty, his loyalty as a soldier of his country, his fears of losing the war owing to petty political rivalries, bad councils, and foreign intrigues; he concludes by pleading that the circumstances of his arrest prove his innocence. The whole speech is well-stuffed with Latinisms, quotes from both classical and Christian sources, indiscriminately mixed.]

When I was telling how they threatened me with death by the sword, the king turned and said to the royal chamberlain [Teodor Denhof] "whoever said that is a cur." Agreeable it was to hear that; I now expected a happy expedition. All clustered round the throne, talking with the king, saying what I know not; but I saw the king shrug with annoyance, and pulling out from his pocket the speech I had made before the confederates' general assembly, he thrust it upon the Troki

29. Father Adrian Piekarski, who appears in 1659 as the chaplain and Pasek's uncle, is now royal preacher and the author of several minor historical works.

governor. They read it for themselves. Then the chamberlain began to speak:

> Of old they used to say misfortunes stalk man, not the earth; a man would not be human were he to float in good fortune always, never to experience adversity. And Scripture itself clearly bears this out; great is the worth and respect of a man in heaven if he has been visited by exasperating difficulties. God himself confirms it with his own words: "*Quem amo, castigo.*[30] The which not only must the Christian endure with grateful heart, but even the pagans appreciate. Philip, the great Macedonian king, upon receiving news of the great victory his generals had won for him, after utterly routing the army of the enemy, upon hearing that the Dardanian kingdom had surrendered swearing eternal obedience and that a son, Alexander, had been born to him with signs of a future of greatness in the world, cried out in a loud voice:[31] *O dii, mediocre aliquod infortunium tot tantisque meis felicitatibus apponatis, oro!*[32] Plainly, he had observed that unhappiness usually followed great good fortune, but God was accustomed to look with a merciful eye upon man after misfortune and tribulations. So too in the present circumstance, whatever happened, was according to God's will; His Majesty the King, Our Gracious Lord, should not be blamed, he wishing to safeguard at least his own person, by keeping that handful of the army serving with the Ruthenian governor. As you, Your Honor, were represented to him, so he had to believe of you, not knowing your uprightness and your kind deeds which have now come to light. Your inborn honor and your honest deeds have not been nor can they be damaged; indeed having been made public, they will bring you even greater glory than if unspoken; consider: nothing is so bad it cannot be turned to good use. *Hectorem quis nosset felix si Troia fuisset?* Nor would a diamond hidden within stony ground be so dear, if not polished by the skilled hand of man. Nor gold be so alluring, so pleasing to the human eye, if the intensity of hot flames were not to purify it. Virtue would be unknown to the world, if divers *adversitates* were not to try it. Your Honor has suffered no discredit or injury on account of this circumstance, on the contrary, you are recompensed with a good name, favor, regard and the gratitude of the Commonwealth and His Majesty the King, Our Gracious Lord.

As soon as he finished, I went to the king, made a low bow; and the king clasped my head saying, "Forgive us, these traitors are doing a mighty bit of intriguing, thus we, too, misjudge decent men on account of wicked ones, especially hearing such slander and circumstantial evidence. But he who deceived us has already been requited for

30. He whom I love I chastize.
31. The Dardanians were a people inhabiting Moesia (Serbia today). Philip, on conquering Potidaea, received three favorable pieces of news: the subduing of the Dardanians, the birth of his son Alexander, and the victory of his horses in the Olympic games (Plutarch, *Life of Alexander,* III, 20.)
32. O gods, I beseech you; add some small annoyance to such great and good fortune.

his thoughtlessness; he has lost our favor and can never regain it." He rose from his seat then and went into his chamber. Some went with him, others turned toward me. They began to chide me: "How you rebuked us, nettled us! But we are not surprised now, having proof of your virtue; you had to act thus, being innocent, but now let us forgive one another mutually."

So *verba pro verbis*[33] until a royal courtier comes and says: "It is the king's will that Your Honor stay awhile here." I think to myself: have they dreamed up some new thing about me? Not a quarter of an hour had passed before he comes to bid me enter the chamber. I went in. A lengthier discussion ensued on the dealings of the confederacy and an inquiry into other particulars. And again: "Forgive us, forgive us, we shall remember this always." At every bow I made, he clasped my head, and with his own hands he gave me 500 ducats, asking me: "Whither now?" I said: "Whither I had set out to go, to my commander in Byelorussia. Says he: "Not to the confederacy?" I answer: "My Gracious Lord! What we express in a moment of passion, sensible reflection will not allow us to commit!" The king says: "Well and good! The man who does a good deed for his country will never be tossed over the fence. So you'll carry an official document and letters to His Honor the Governor."

Turning to Father Piekarski, he says: Rejoice for your kin and chase that worry with a good quaff." *Interim* they were preparing the king's table; we left then. We arrive at my lodging; they've brought us a splendid meal from the royal kitchen, sparkling wine, the same he drank himself. *Bonae voluntatis*[34] we were. A barrel of mead was also sent to the inn for my servants, along with raw foodstuffs, oats for the horses, etc.

And so, by the grace of Our Dear Lord I ended the year in somewhat more favorable circumstances, having discovered that a man need never despair, though fortune frown, for God disposeth both man and his fortune: making him to be downcast when he wishes, consoling him when it is His Holy Will.

Let it be a lesson to all who will read this; as even those people learned who considered my good luck to be running out, never to rise again.

33. Words of honor were exchanged.
34. Of good cheer.

The Year of Our Lord 1662

God willing, I began happily in Grodno. The king forthwith set off to Warsaw; and he ordered me to ride after him, my despatch being *non in toto* prepared. There, finally, I was given an open letter to cities and towns, so that they might provide me with food *quantum satis,*[1] and confidential letters to the Governor [Czarniecki]. In addition, they handed over to me some dragoons to lead to camp; they had been in the Governor's charge in Mścibów and chastized for raising cain there, an alarm being given after some uproar wherein a dozen or so were slain, and eighteen men with their sergeant-major had come to the king asking for a letter of safe-conduct. The king said, "I am despatching thither a cavalier; travel then under his command and obey him in everything, since you're so wanton that towns cry for help on account of you." They were given then a thaler apiece and, causing me to be summoned, the king handed them over, ordering me to command them as if I were their own officer and to punish *excessivos.* They travelled then under that letter of mine, the which I still have; it read to this effect:

> We hereby make it known to one and all who should be informed, namely, our nobility, our faithful district supervisors, the tenants and stewards of our crown lands, as well as village heads, mayors and town councillors, that we are despatching to the army on certain of our interests our loyal and beloved Jan Pasek, who will be serving in Byelorussia *in opere belli*[2] as a cavalier in the squadron of His Honor, the Governor of Ruthenia, [with some men] whom he is conducting *in disciplina militari* to camp where, for the time being, he will leave them. We command therefore that food *ad sufficientiam* be supplied to the aforesaid cavalier as well as to the soldiers in his charge and we desire that anyone who opposes our royal will be punished accordingly. For greater credence we have hereon had our seal pressed, and we sign in our own hand.
>
> Given in Nowydwór [the royal estate near Grodno] on December XXVII

1. As much as I needed.
2. On a military expedition.

of the year MDCLXI, of the year XII of our reign as king of Poland and Sweden.

(Locum Sigilli)[3]
KING JAN KAZIMIERZ

Moreover, the two letters wherein I am commended to the Governor, these I have in the original still, having got them back from the Governor's secretary after he'd read them, but they were not written at the same time for the dates do not agree. [The first reads:]

JAN KAZIMIERZ by the grace of God King of Poland, Grand Duke of Lithuania, Ruthenia, Prussia, Mazovia, Livonia, Kiev, Volhynia, Samogitia, Smolensk, Czernichów, and the hereditary king of the Swedes, the Goths, and the Vandals.

Sir, Our Dearly Beloved!

We, owing to false testimony, did hold the bearer of this letter under suspicion of riding from the Polish army, now in confederacy, to the army of the Grand Duchy of Lithuania, but he having irrefutably proven that he was heading directly to Your Excellency, so much the more desirous are we to despatch him to Your Excellency, commending him to your favor, as a man many times tried in knightly combat and our steadfast adherent in these current painful circumstances. The Cossack despatched by Your Excellency as well as the nobleman Wolski, who returned a few days ago from His Excellency the Khan [Aadil Girey], we are detaining until the conclusion of the *consilium generale* commencing in Bielsk [Bielsk Podlaski] *quinta die Ianuarii futuri.*[4] Whatever is resolved there you will be sufficiently informed by us and by his Grace, our reverend father, the crown chancellor [Mikołaj Prażmowski]; concerning further matters, there will be reliable intelligence through the nobleman Wolski or a faithful Cossack. Until then, may the Lord God grant Your Excellency health and *felices rerum successus.*[5]

Given in Nowydwór on December XXVII of the year MDCLXI, the year XII of our reign as king of Poland and Sweden.

KING JAN KAZIMIERZ

I know not why two letters were written then, instead of one — the latter one a trifle more candid, only with a different date — though they handed them to me together. But I suppose they did not trust me straight off; then, belike, on the word of Father Piekarski, reconsidering, they trusted me absolutely and wrote of more confidential matters.

The king then in a second letter writes thus:

JAN KAZIMIERZ by the grace of God King of Poland, Grand Duke of

3. Place for the seal.
4. General assembly . . . on January 5 of the coming year.
5. A happy outcome to affairs.

Lithuania, Ruthenia, Prussia, Mazovia, Livonia, Kiev, Volhynia, Samogitia, Smolensk, Czernichów, and the hereditary king of the Swedes, the Goths, and the Vandals.

Sir, Our Dearly Beloved!

Upon reconsidering how reprehensible it would be for Your Excellency not to know now what the nobleman Wolski accomplished with His Excellency the Khan, we have managed *per litteras brevibus denuntiare.*[6] As Wolski declared to me, he found great willingness to meet our demands, especially on the part of His Excellency the Khan and both sultans,[7] they promising to raise an army of 60,000 Tartars by early spring. *Ad minimum* we shall have 12,000 Prussians; joining to these whatever other forces we can acquire, we shall be able with God's help to form a fit army; if the confederates do not come to their senses, we'll get along without those rebels. *In consilio generali* we shall not neglect to deliberate *de nervo belli*[8] in order to arrive at the Diet with a ready proposal that the business not interfere with other matters. More on other matters through the nobleman Wolski. And now once more we commend *Pan* Pasek to Your Excellency that he may enjoy the respect of his squadron leader and commander as a man whose notable courage and manliness are known to Your Excellency from all previous battles. And we, having been told, are now also well acquainted with his *actiones;* he could not have done more for country or Crown, especially in the present situation; how he stood *pro aequitate*[9] at the confederate general assemblies is also now known to us. That his *probitas*[10] not be rewarded is unthinkable, unless God were to take our life! It is right, therefore, that others should also know what kind of gratitude to show those who are on the right side. To conclude, we wish Your Excellency good health and *felices successus.*

Given in Nowydwór January II of the Year of Our Lord 1662, and the year XIII of our reign as king of Poland and Sweden.

KING JAN KAZIMIERZ

He addressed the letter thus: "To His Lordship Stefan Czarniecki, Governor of Ruthenia, and District Supervisor of Piotrków, Kowel, etc., Our Dearly Beloved."

I, taking the letters and bidding farewell to the king, once more he clasped my head saying: "Forgive us now, be at the Diet with the Governor and come to see us; we shall be sure to keep you in mind."

I ordered those men to set out forthwith by way of Lida, and to travel in a straight line, so that I could overtake them in one day, though I should leave a week after them. I sent my servants with them and my horses, of which I had no need, while I myself, with two other atten-

6. To inform you briefly by letter.
7. Sultan was the title given to sons of the Khan.
8. About the financing of the war (money was called *nervus rerum*).
9. For the right.
10. Steadfastness.

dants, went back to *Pan* Tyszkiewicz's, having given him my word. Upon arrival, I was received as a welcome guest; much feasting we did, carousing. A week I was there. After the week, I want to be on my way; they don't let me go. So that those dragoons might hear of my whereabouts, my host despatched his cossack through whom I gave orders for them to pass beyond Białystok, there slowing the pace until I overtake them, and to leave word of themselves for me in Lida and Ośmiana. Another week did I stay there amid that amiable talk, those mutual compliments, they promising divers *promotiones,*[11] offering me their niece *Panna* Rudominówna, an heiress with a substance worth more than 100,000, save that she had only just entered her ninth year. With assurances of undying friendship, with curses upon him who should not keep his word, we went our separate ways. Those speeches of mine, however, that I'd delivered in his presence, not only to the senators but also to the king, he'd caused me to repeat, copy for him, and leave; even my speech at the confederate assembly he copied down with his own hand from Father Piekarski and put it away, relishing it greatly, though it was nothing so extreme, and he said: "Even were you to have no more substance than what is in your head, for me that substance is large enough to give my niece."

I set off then, having taken my leave *cum plenitudine* of sincere and unalterable sentiments of cordiality, riding off only to go back again and again, as good friends are given to do. I come to Ośmiana but neither my men do I find nor any intelligence of them. I surmised that they were moving ahead at a turtle's pace, being overly mindful of my order. Three days after I'd come, the sergeant-major at last arrived with two others, as if to assign quarters; having spotted them from afar, I had the gate half-closed so they would not know I was there. They stopped at the mayor's; bawled at him rudely, saying there were 100 horse in the squadron; they show him the royal letter, the one given to me, where it was written "we are placing some men in his charge," but how many is not specified. The townsmen are willing to oblige, for they had been hearing for a week now that these men were drifting about the countryside; they let them have 70 zloties, a barrel of beer, some bread, meat, etc.

I bid the innkeeper to watch them and to give me a sign when they count the money. They loaded all the food now onto the sleighs as fast as their legs could carry them, for the soldiers were to travel on out of town, the sergeant-major being ashamed of his soldiers. Here are the townsmen heaping the money, while at the other end of the table he's writing me the message he was supposed to leave with the mayor — and suddenly there am I in the doorway. Seeing me, off went the cap. The

11. Advancements and backing.

townsmen look up, they're astonished, they're seeing me in town now for the third day: what's the meaning of this? I ask then: "What's this money they're counting?" He answers: "The honorable townsmen kindly offered it to us for shoeing our horses." The townsmen say nothing, but they think: a nasty kindness is it that's got by holding a club over someone's neck. I ask the mayor: "What did you agree on?" Says he: "70 zloties, a barrel of beer, some bread, some mead; there it is already in the sleighs." Only then do I say: "the food is ours, the money yours — put it away for yourselves. There's neither bare ice nor frozen mud now; the horses won't cripple themselves, for the snow is up to the saddle flaps, it's a soft road, no need for horseshoes." The townsmen go for the money, into their sacks with it; and that put the rogue's nose out of joint. The townsmen, the same who took no cognizance of me before, nor brought me so much as a bundle of hay, I not having asked for it, were now my humble servants — dashing in carrying divers things, piling them up. But I wanted none of it; having fed my horses, I set off, but they had also of their own accord put a six-pot keg of spirits into my sleigh.

I set forth with them then, slowly, feeding the horses well. Everywhere, in villages, in towns, they gave us food and drink, but money — Lord preserve us! — nowhere did I cause the men to take it. All the way to Lepel then, we prospered unfailingly; even were each of us to have ten bellies, we'd have had food enough and drink. Complaints I had only from their officer for not allowing money to be taken; with that letter, he said, I could have taken several thousand before reaching the camp, and he urged me to do so, pointing out the profit, but I did not permit it, for my reputation was at stake. Anyway, those scoundrels devised their own means for getting money: the provisions they obtained in one place, they sold off in another.

Once we're riding through a great wilderness, and we come upon a village in the forest, where we hear shouting and tumult. A widow was living on the manor, her name I don't recall. Riding nearer, we see the manor's being looted, the noblewoman walking about, wringing her hands. Here they are, strapping hog's carcasses, flitches, a few valuables onto their horses, leading out the cattle from the barn on ropes. I took it for the execution of some court verdict; I don't meddle, I pass the gates; besides, I intended to stop in that village, it being near nightfall. But the woman, no sooner having caught sight of me, rushes out: "Have mercy on me, Your Honor, they're robbing me, a poor orphan; worse than the Muscovites they are, worse than the enemy." I ask: "Who are these people?" She said: "*Pan* Muraszko's men." I then return to her courtyard and say: "Gentlemen, have you no fear of the Lord? Do you attack a gentry manor?" "What's it to you, Sir?" I say: "I'm a gentleman!" To her then I say: "My Lady, have your people take it back." They: "You won't get it back." The lady ordered her peasants to retrieve it: they to sword and to musket; we the same — and we're at each other! Cleared them out of the courtyard we did; this one and that got a bit of a licking; one only had his horse killed under him when a dragoon amongst them fired. And one only of our men had a horse struck on the side, nothing grave. All of their booty they abandoned; the peasants seized a few of their horses, which I, however, caused to be driven after them. The lady began then mightily to thank me, saying: "Blessed are Czarniecki's men, accursed Sapieha's!" We spent the night all of us in one inn in that village, for I knew the others were within two miles; with villains, the important thing is that they not desire revenge. And at that time we were as pleasing to the confederates as a hedgehog to a dog wanting to eat him yet not daring to take a bite. Several had got some rightful gashes; I then assumed they would give a thought to vengeance, and so they did.

The widow, poor woman, sent us what she had in the house — spirits, beer. The dragoons were bibbing then, and I with the sergeant-major, there being drink in the sleighs. The second cock crowed, we set the watches. No sooner done but there they come, 300 horse. The watch sighted them from afar against the snow, banged on the window: "Get up, Your Honors, we have guests." They move in closer, he calls out: "*Werdo?*"[12] They answer: "You'll get *werdo* soon enough, you son of the devil!" The dragoons had no gunpowder; I gave them some, ordering them to load their muskets forthwith. Then they'd no bullets, but I, having a few, packed them into my own piece and what I could, I handed out to the others. As they approach then, our watch calls out: "Advance no further, or I'll open fire!" The sergeant-major went out, he asks: "What do you want?" "We'd be complainin' about yesterday's fracas, wherein some of our men got trounced. Who's the elder here?" Said the sergeant-major: "I'm the elder, for I'm 45 years of age already, the others are all younger." " 'Tis a jest," they answer "but who's in charge? He told them then I was inside. They say: "Let us in to see him." Says he: "We'll let you in, only not all together; that's not the way you go riding to complain." "Let ten horse go in." He answered: "Let it be twenty."

Fifteen horse came then; pistols in their belts, some in holsters. No sooner did they start to ride in but I had some men stand at the gates, others on alert at the doorway, their horses already saddled. They enter the room: "Hail." "Hail." A soldier questions me then: "His honor the Colonel inquires what men are these, whither do they go, whence are they come, and wherefore did they rob and slash up the soldiers of his regiment?" I ask: "First, let me know which gentleman is

12. Who goes there?

your colonel?" Said he: "His Honor, *Pan* Muraszko;" and the others are huffing and puffing, gnashing their teeth, pulling their moustaches, biting them. And here were 300 horse closing in on the hut, shouting: "Halt, you royalists: we'll soon have you tied up like sheep."

I reply then: "Being a responsible soldier *in servitio* of the Commonwealth and listed on the army's payroll,[13] I am not obliged to explain to you, Colonel, Your Honor, wither I go or whence I come; but since I am not ashamed of my actions before the whole world, neither need I be before a beggar living on alms; and so, for this reason, I'm not of a mind to *denegare*[14] to inform my interrogator whither I am going; "Your Lordships being the excellent soldiers whom I saw fighting alongside us in previous battles, so much the more willing am I to do so."

As I'd uttered one word in Latin *denegare,* one of them spoke up: "Not in Latin with us, Your Honor, for you're dealing with plain soldiers here." I answer: "I see that you are a plain soldier; but I speak plainly to the plain and to the crooked as it pleases me." Meanwhile, I say to the sergeant-major: "Give me the letter you have on you." He pulls it from his pocket; I give it to the man, he reads it and then asks: "Why did you assault our patrol and slash up some of our fellows?" I answer: "Because in our country it's not the style to go robbing gentry houses, especially while lying in winter quarters; seeing which committed we thought the Muscovites were carrying on. And now, having made my report, I will require the same from you: may I know what is your business with the Commonwealth, or rather what is your claim; being volunteers, due no wages, yet you entered the confederacy and now you're raiding and looting gentry manors; and another thing, why do you attack me in a night raid, belike wanting to steal something?" Says the same senior officer: "You had it coming to you."

I perceive our humility is getting us nowhere and we'll have to deal with iron; as I was holding a club in my hands, I straightaway dealt a forceful blow to his chest: he fell under the bench. On the very same instant, two of them fired pistol shots at the sergeant-major and myself. They shot a hole in the sergeant-major's gown, but the Lord kept me safe, belike on account of my bending down to pick up my pistol, it having fallen out of my belt when I struck that soldier. Now did we go at

13. Volunteers (such as Muraszko's men) did not receive pay and were not registered. J. Cedrowski in his *Diary* mentions Colonel Muraszko under the year 1657 as a leader of a detachment of peasants who made life miserable for the gentry. It is highly likely that Pasek met up with this same Muraszko. This would account for his contemptuous attitude toward the colonel and his readiness to defend gentry property. The fact that Muraszko's soldiers did not understand Latin also lends credence to the supposition.
14. Refuse.

them! Half of them remained in the room, half rushed into the passage. We dealt it to those in the room, the dragoons give it to the others in the passage. One of our dragoons had a fearful Muscovite battle-axe; with that axe he was making mincemeat of those fleeing from the room. No sooner had that pack outside heard the shooting in the room, but they charged headlong toward the hut; both sides open fire, ours held fast at the gates. Only three of our dragoons were firing: two of their men fell from their horses and one of ours was shot in the neck. We meanwhile, having subdued those inside, locked them into the room; those in the passage, having got a sound whacking, were slipping stealthily along the fence away from our mounted dragoons; and that troop of theirs, withdrawing about a furlong, begins to clamor: "Out here! Into the field now! Into the field!" I shout back: "Just wait: we'll be up to that too."

Re-entering the room I had those fellows tied up, turned them over to the innkeeper along with our two sleighs, warning: "Hands off, peasant, it'll be your neck if we miss any of this; we have the royal treasury on these sleighs, for I'm carrying money to the army." Those men are praying, lamenting: "God's punished us; they sent us to tie someone up and we got roped in ourselves." I step out into the courtyard. What to do: ride out to them or not? Some urge me to do it, others, most of all my kinsman, Chlebowski, dissuade me, since "there's a great mob of them, we'll never hold out." And the sergeant-major says: "We're looking to see if the lady whose property we defended from those looters will send us aid, or she'll order her peasants to do something; nothing in sight so far."

We were about to drive them back defensively from that hut, when what do we see, but they are gathering up sheaves, setting them ablaze, and just as they're ready to hurl them onto the hut I call out: "Brave cavaliers, trouble yourselves not; you'll see us out there forthwith; do not bring others to harm on our account." It's getting light now; our dragoons, having gathered up their belongings, mounted the good horses and left their more wretched ones in the yard, loaded their muskets with whatever they could: pebbles, horseshoe nails, there being no bullets; a few helped themselves to what charges they could find in our prisoner's pouches. The fellow who had been shot lay by the gate groaning and writhing; a certain Jankowski, one of our dragoons, had fired horseshoe nails into his knee; the other who'd been shot down at the same time was carried off by that mob.

I call out then: "Bother, gentlemen, get along with you, forbear!" "Oh no you don't, you so and so. You'll not fool us and slip away from here, we'll smoke you out like a badger from 'is burrow." Says the sergeant-major: "Attack us, and first we'll slit the throats of everyone tied up here." They answer: "We've already reckoned with that loss, but you'll not resurrect either, you son of an infidel!" And straightaway they scoot up to the hut with the blazing sheaves: "Come out of there, you sons of infidels, for simple folk are going to suffer on your account." I answer: "Directly, my kind sirs, directly."

We march out in step then, as a troop of twenty-some men, counting our servants; I giving orders for the rear line to turn round instantly and face the enemy, should they surround us, with their backs to the front rank, also not to shoot but when I or the sergeant-major shall order it, and then only in twos and threes; he being in charge of the rear line, I of the first. The sergeant-major is astride a frothing roan, an Astrakhan horse captured from them; it whirls about under him like a top; his own he'd handed over to a dragoon. We have firearms enough, taken from those prisoners.

Well, we'd not even moved a furlong away from that hut, when, of a sudden, they slipped away from us, and so it turned out as I had said: they began to come up on us in a semicircle in order to take our rear. When they drew close to us, I called out to my men: "*Alt!*" The rear line faced about. They, the same instant, give a battlecry *hostiliter,*[15] charge us, letting fly with dense fire from their pistols and short muskets, they close in, our lines clash; I open fire from both my pistols at once, for I had a third in my belt and a hunting-piece on me;[16] and next, my dragoons, three or four at a time, fire from their muskets at my signal. The fellow who had closed with me, clutched his saddlebow, clearly he'd been shot; a dragoon thrusting himself forward, slashed his neck with a sabre, and he fell (they say he was a coddled young scion of an eminent Lithuanian family, one Szemet; his father being furious with him for serving with the volunteers), one of my dragoons from the front rank was also on the ground, his horse shot dead beneath him. On the instant I saw him getting up — single file! They recoil a little, then once again — at us! That Jankowski fellow had a musket with a cruel barrel, now it spits out those horseshoe nails; once more he spattered; many a fellow is groaning. Got a few of them in the rear lines too.

Seeing they cannot break us asunder, they yell: "Return our men to us, and the devil piss on you!" The sergeant-major replies: "What good are they to you if they've no heads?" A third time they charge, but now they shoot from a distance, without closing in. We're just as pleased; my men advancing, fire in pairs, the rest load; little by little the others give way. We drove them to the vegetable patches bristling with fences;

15. In enemy fashion.

16. In Polish, the word hunting-piece denotes a type of firearm used to hunt wild boar.

crack! they went down, we too close in, they fled on, one fence broken down, on to the next! And there was a forest just beyond those patches; over the fences and into that forest they flew, leaving their horses behind. Our gain in the end; I did not order a pursuit, but a few were caught on the fences; some were wounded and two killed. Three of my dragoons were also wounded, my lad and I were grazed in the left thigh, I not feeling it, 'til after it was all over; six of our horses were wounded, however, two killed, but we still had enough in that spot wherefrom to choose. Later, that lady's confounded steward came crawling around with one of those wee muskets for shooting does; he gave me a bladder of gunpowder and bullets for the road.

I then had the three officers taken from among our bound prisoners and the soldiers flogged, that they should remember Czarniecki's men; the dragoons stripped them and drove them naked into the forest in severe snow to follow the others. I then, upon choosing the forty best horses, set off with the three captives. So many saddles and firearms did we collect that our sleighs sagged under the weight. The rest of the horses with those of ours we'd left behind as a token of friendship to replace better ones taken, I handed over to the steward and the peasants; those roaming about the vegetable patches (very few of those men having got away on horseback), I had the steward take as well, so that no one else should take those horses on our account.

I set forward then and did not make a halt until Żodziszki. Having seized such a flood of horses — every other dragoon was leading three — I decided we should give them back to Muraszko's men for, though hostile to us, they were not the enemy. The sergeant-major is telling me not to give them back; I, that it is a question of my reputation, it could not be otherwise. It was resolved then, the dragoons would pick out the best for themselves and hand over their own to make up the number; my own servants took two, theirs went into the drove. There was no castle town then, we would have had to turn back to Ośmiana; so we handed them over in Narocz, after inscribing our complaint in the municipal register that some scoundrels had waylaid us, wanting to rout us, and here we introduce three of them. They begged and they swore that no one would seek redress; they took it upon themselves to testify in the books, as if voluntarily giving evidence that it was so, that they had attacked us, wanted to rob us, tie us up, the which *oris confessionem* with the town seal and with the notarization of the mayor and the whole government I took, leaving them there with that drove of horses, having watered our farewell and returned their own horses to them as they had entreated. Even after that, we had horses from which to pick and choose. But the sergeant-major held on to his roan, later selling it to Captain Gorzkowski for 340 zloties, which was but very little; it was said to have been captured from Muscovy.

I set forth then by way of Dokszyce, Dolcze, and so on, toward Lepel, where the Governor was encamped. I proceeded slowly after passing two weeks at Tyszkiewicz's, while the king despatched Father Piekarski to the Governor to inform him of what Wolski had accomplished, Wolski once more having been sent to the Khan. The priest overtook me and reached the Governor's before I did. Says the Governor, upon reading the king's letter, wherein he wrote that "as we mentioned in our last letter sent through *Pan* Pasek": "But I've not laid eyes on *Pan* Pasek." The priest takes fright: "Oh Lord! He set out so long ago, the king put him in charge of such and such men." Once more they felt uneasy about me; again the suspicion: "so the traitor did go off to the confederacy, resenting what befell him. They'll have something to read in the confederacy, especially what the king penned with his own hand. How shall I ever show my face to the king?" And the priest could not sleep.

The very next day, no sooner have they risen from the dinner table but the Governor, standing with Matczyński, Mężyński, Niezabitowski,[17] says: "Pshaw, he's not done that, for he'd already set out to come here to me, voluntarily spurning the confederacy; they're but having a fine time, grazing their horses, travelling slowly, [given] food [enough] everywhere with that royal letter." And there I am at the door. What rejoicing then: "He's here!" The Governor looks around. "*O desiderabilis!*"[18] — he grasped me by the shoulders — "your good uncle [Father Piekarski] would have died of worry had you not come today; I thank you for lending such luster to the Commonwealth and to me who inclines to you favorably. And we shall show our gratitude. One cavalier who stands by me is dearer than a whole squadron. But where are your men?" I said: "they're here." He stepped outside and, noticing the horses: "But what's this? Where did you round up such fine horses?" First off, I said that I'd run across Khovansky, we clashed in the field, were victorious, and seized booty; and then I told him the truth as it really happened. At first, he thought these things unlikely; but I having shown him those *confessata authentica,* wherein they themselves confessed that they were 300 horse, he marvelled at the great wonder, that a dozen or so men withstood such a huge mob. Me, he thanked, but to the sergeant-major he said: "I would have had you hanged for the commotions you made in Mścibów; but now I absolve you of blame for not letting yourselves be confounded in this circumstance; though it was due, belike, more to your commander than to your mettle. But as you arrived with good horses, you shall be the first to receive your cloth" [for uniforms].

17. Marek Matczyński was the crown equerry and a friend of Sobieski's. Piotr Mężynski was a lieutenant; Ludwik Aleksander Niezabitowski a squadron leader.

18. Heart's desire.

As the Diet in Warsaw was soon to take place, the king wrote through Father Piekarski that the Governor and his men should scoot toward the Polish border; the which he intended doing; and he had already set out from Lepel when — it seems to me 'twas the third halt for the night — an envoy from the tsar comes to him, announcing the tsar's intention to send deputies to the Diet, in view of the treaties between both nations; fearing to let them cross the border alone, lest some ill befall them from the army dissidents; he, therefore, entreats the Governor to despatch an escort abroad who would accompany them to His Majesty the king.

The Governor sends for me then and says: "My good fellow, His Highness the king wrote to me in his first as well as in subsequent letters that I should make recompense to you, whereof I myself am sensible, such a deed deserving every sort of repayment, but His Majesty the King ought rather to ponder thereon, for I am unable to requite in such a way as the king might. Neither crown property, nor tenancy can I give, it being not in my power; that wherewith I can compensate you *pro posse meo*[19] I do not begrudge. Now then with despatch, do not beg off that which may bring you honor and some gain. The tsar His Majesty sent to me asking for an escort to accompany his deputies all the way to the Diet; I would like you to undertake this, Sir, but you'll have to ride to Wiaźma" [Vyazma]. I answer: "My Benefactor, it is your office to command, mine to carry out every ordinance that you, as the steward of my blood, decree. And I am at your disposal to ride not only to Wiaźma but to Astrakhan,[20] Your Honor, My Benefactor. The Baltic journey was farther, yet by God's grace I returned safe and sound under Your Honor's fortunate guidance." He says: "Fine, I'll give you several dozen elite Cossacks and have letters of credence written; be off then, Sir, as early as you can tomorrow morning and ride in the Lord's care!" Calling then for Piwnicki, he ordered him to write the letters.

I went off to my servants and I say: "Feed the horses well, for they'll not be riding so far tomorrow, only to Moscow." Whereupon my boy says: "Won't be long now before we'll be off to Rome." Say I: "What's to be done, if our superiors will it so? Be at the ready." We're putting our things in readiness then, when up runs Wilkowski, the groom: "His Lordship, the Governor, wishes to see you." I get there and he says: "My good fellow, I've heard many entreaties here for that office; *Pan* Żerosławski and *Pan* Niegoszowski were here asking me to send them there; *Pan* Niezabitowski interceding for them. I tried not to vex the old soldiers, but told them that I had already promised it to *Pan* Pasek and that I'd earn a bad name were I to go back on my word, since the

19. Within my capabilities.
20. Astrakhan was a provincial capital at the mouth of the Volga.

king has written me twice now, asking me to do honor to his uprightness; but if he should forego it voluntarily I'll agree to it. I replied that "I am prepared to do your will, the which in holding firm, keeps me from snatching the palm myself. I can wear the mark of your respect, My Benefactor, as well as the oldest soldier." Says he: "Well and good."

He sent to Piwnicki, asking that the letter be submitted for his signature as speedily as possible, while I went off to the horses. There I found those old war horses who fell to bargaining with me; if I would renounce it, Żerosławski offers me 100 silver thalers. I consented. Off they went then to fetch the money. I reckon as it's a long journey and has to be a difficult office; I know not what advantage it may bring, while here, like manna from heaven, you take 100 thalers for doing nothing. On the other hand, I think it cannot be anything too trivial, they being so persistent in their efforts to purchase it. I tell Piwnicki about it, on going to see him. Whereupon Piwnicki: "What? You're jesting, Sir! Why that office smacks of thousands and great repute; do it not, Sir, for the Governor will be displeased if you scorn the advancement he has offered you."

I then, having made request to Piwnicki to accomplish his task with all speed, and take it to be signed, made myself scarce. They, coming with the money, ask: "Where's the master?" "I don't know; he went off with some captain or other." They search for me among the squadrons: no luck. That evening I see Piwnicki; he says "the Governor's signed it and has it in his quarters. But your rivals were with him once more, *Pan* Tetwin and Niezabitowski interceding for them; but the Governor said he had already handed over the letter to you, Sir, signed." I go to see the Governor; but only after sending a boy ahead of me to see whether they'd left so as not to be disturbed by them. I enter and he, clad now only in a caftan, asked: "Who's there?" Seeing me he says: "Where have you been keeping yourself? I sent for you, but they did not find you in." And he tells me the same as Piwnicki; and then placed those letters in my hands. One letter for crossing the border on my way to fetch the deputies *inter viscera Regni,*[21] the other one necessary abroad, which I was to conceal. Both of them I have still. The first read to this effect:

Stefan Czarniecki of Czarniec and Tykocin, Governor of Ruthenia, General of His Majesty's Army, District Supervisor of Piotrków, Kowel, and Ratyn.

I hereby make known to whomever it behooves me to inform, namely the gentlemen of the knightly estate of whichever nation and of whatever degree and distinction or office, while commending my services to my fellow gentlemen as well as to the mayors and councillors of towns, the heads of villages, and to the entire populace, that I, respecting the wishes of His Highness the tsar, am despatching an escort with a convoy of soldiers, a

21. Within the borders of Crown Poland.

cavalier from my regiment of the army, *Pan* Pasek; he from whatever spot he shall meet the aforesaid envoys of His Highness the tsar, shall conduct them by the shortest route to my regiment of the army, from whence either the same escort or another will be assigned to accompany them to their destination. In order then, for these escorts as well as the deputies to obtain food (once across the border), the customary wagon trains should be supplied, as political necessity demands, and to which I join my own authority. I declare this letter signed by my own hand and impressed with my seal.

Given in Kojdanów on the first day of February, *anno* 1662.

Stefan Czarniecki, Governor
of Ruthenia"

This letter I was ordered to conceal directly upon recrossing the frontier with the deputies, while showing the other, the which I include below; it being an insult to the hetmans and the Lithuanian people to whom the privilege belongs, according to law, of receiving and conducting Muscovite envoys as far as the Narew; the Polish escort ought to receive them only at the Narew. He arranged things then to look as if he were receiving them by chance and not purposely, having encountered them on the way. He writes then a second letter to this effect:

Stefan Czarniecki of Czarniec and Tykocin, Governor of Ruthenia, General of His Majesty's Army, District Supervisor of Piotrków, Kowel, and Ratyń.

I hereby make known to whomever it behooves me to inform, namely, the gentlemen of the knightly estate of whichever nation and of whatever degree and distinction or office, while recommending my services to my fellow gentlemen as well as to the mayors and councillors of towns, the heads of villages, and to the entire populace, that the envoys of the tsar, Afanasy Ivanovich Nesterov and Ivan Mikhailov Polikarpovich, secretary, are riding under orders to His Majesty the king on matters of urgent need; the more to speed them on their journey, I have given them an escort with a convoy of soldiers, a cavalier from the army, *Pan* Pasek. So that they may obtain food, wagon trains are to be supplied, as political necessity requires, to which I join my authority. I declare this letter signed by my own hand and impressed with my seal.

Given in Kojdanów on the twelfth day of February, *anno* 1662.

Stefan Czarniecki, Governor
of Ruthenia

In order, however, to render the hetman fitting honor, he gives me a letter for him, wherein he writes of how, meeting these envoys enroute, he assigned them an escort, releasing the other back to Szkłów; which escort in fact did not exist, nor were the envoys in Szkłów, but no matter, as long as the formality was observed. And he instructed me not to surrender that letter to him, even though I should be informed of his whereabouts on one of his estates, whether deep in Lithuania or in

Lachowicze, or anywhere else, but that I should deliver it to a district administrator or steward on one of his estates near the Narew, as long as it reached him sometime. The which letter is worded in this sense:

Your Honorable Lordship the Governor of Wilno, My Gracious Lord and Fellow Gentleman!

On the Minsk highway, I, having encountered the tsar's envoy, Afanasy Ivanovich Nestorov, did cause the escort and convoy assigned to him in Szkłów to return there. In order to speed his journey from Uryszko to His Majesty the king, I assigned him a cavalier from my regiment, *Pan* Pasek, through whom I present this my notice to Your Respected Lordship, not wishing to neglect that which is due the office of hetman and to Your Lordship's *auctoritati,* lest I not make it known, since every envoy entering *intra confinia*[22] of the Commonwealth should be brought to the attention of Your Lordship. Whether, then, the soldier assigned by me is to accompany the envoy to the indicated destination, the king himself, or Your Lordship shall assign a new escort, I leave to Your Lordship's own pleasure.

The Byelorussian lands, and the marches remaining in contact with the enemy, having been forsaken by the armies of the Grand Duchy of Lithuania, Your Lordship must needs consider how to prevent the enemy (having by now begun to grow strong) from venting his wrath. With the infantry only, and without the cavalry, I can start nothing in the field; and my endeavor to penetrate some distance into enemy territory I had to give up, for though I had wished to manifest his Majesty's might on emeny soil, I was deprived of all succour in my ready designs for the Commonwealth. Thus, then, having made this known to Your Lordship, I place myself and my service at Your Lordship's disposal.

In Kojdanów. Fraternal wishes from Your Lordship's obedient servant.

Stefan Czarniecki, Governor
of Ruthenia

It turned out that the letter written then to the hetman [Jan Paweł Sapieha] I handed to him in person, but I was already near the Narew, six or seven miles away from it. He received it graciously, answered it, treated me as a guest. (Whereof below.) Czarniecki's letter, however, I entreated him to give back to me, telling him that of these and similar occasions I keep a record so that my offspring shall have it *pro testimoniis vitae meae.*[23] He sent for his secretary at once and gave me back the letter, asking: "Will you also be keeping the reply from me?" I answered: "Yes, surely I shall, for I'm given to doing this so that my sons, if the Lord has promised me any, will see that the *florem aetatis*[24] I did not waste in idleness, but filled my part of these occasions as befits a

22. Within the boundaries.
23. As a testimony of my life.
24. Bloom of life.

nobleman. (Whereof below.) Now, I return to this situtation from which I've strayed on account of the *essentiam* of those letters.

No sooner had the Governor turned the letters over to me, but he says: "I've assigned Your Honor forty good men; be off as early as you can tomorrow, and be not tempted by any foolishness, for you'll gain more through this office than you could have in the confederacy. And is not the glory itself worth something? And what will the king say, if you show your face to him often? He'll have to remember the gratitude he owes Your Honor. Nor will I neglect to put in a word for you when — God willing — I shall arrive in Warsaw. And now to bed, Sir, but have a cup before you go! Which do you prefer, Spanish wine or good mead?" I said I preferred mead, knowing it to be excellent. "Fine," says he, "and I'll be drinking mead, too, for it's come out exceeding well." He drank to me then, I drained my cup; a second, and I finished that one too. He instructs me then: "That's the way," says he, "now tuck in a third to that Kolding dolly."[25] (Never did he allow me to forget her.) Then I bid him good night; he says: "You haven't eaten anything, old fellow, you've come after supper?" Says I, "I'll be eating at my place." I left, and Żerosławski is sitting in my quarters, a sack of thalers in front of him. On seeing him, I made as if I were in my cups, having indeed gotten a bit tipsy, for, after all, I'd put away three silver cups — more than a quartful, one of them — and the mead was to my taste. He begins to speak about the matter, but I say: "Glad to see you." He says "I've kept my word, I'm come with the money." But I say: "Pour us a drink!" He says: "Have the money counted, Your Honor." But I say: "Your health!" He tastes the mead: "Whence this mead?" Say I: "From the barrel." He says: "Is it the Governor's mead?" Say I: "Mine and yours as we're drinking it." He inquires: "Has Your Honor been given the letters?" I say: "Bottoms up! Bring on the food!" Seeing he'll get nowhere with me, he says: "Then belike the morning will be wiser." And we fell to drinking. That pot of mead so besotted him that on leaving me, he could but hang upon the shoulders of his servants. I permitted myself some as well; he did not object to this, judging me to be very fuddled.

The next day I rose early as could be, the horses were saddled. I rode off to the Governor; only now does he give me fuller instructions. The elite Cossacks also rode up. He orders them to obey me, to behave soberly, to stay out of trouble. Having taken my leave then, I mounted my horse, and there is Żerosławski panting and running right alongside me: "Turn this over to me, you gave your word: take the 100 thalers." I say: "My dear fellow, don't make me out to be a fool: I'll not be dismounting now." Says he: "You can drag more out of me." I:

25. See the year 1658,the story of the taking of the castle at Kolding from the Swedes.

"Bah, were Your Honor to cause me not only to drag you but even tear you in half, 'twould be bootless."

I set off then on the road to Smołowicze without meeting the envoys; they lodged me splendidly then in the home of a prosperous Russian. Only the master of the house is taking care of things, bustling about; the mistress you don't see; food is cooking, victuals they served plenty of, both fish and meat. There I lived four days until the envoys arrived, never once viewing the lady of the house, so do they keep their wives hidden away there, that not even the sun's light can get to her; it's a great servitude the wives suffer, and a perpetual prison. They arrived then, in fine form and splendidly: Afanasy Ivanovich Nestorov, Lord High Master of the tsar's Table, of an ancient Muscovite family; the other accompanying him, it seems, as *secretarius legationis,* Ivan Polikarpovich, a secretary, also young Mikhailo, the son of that lord of the table, a dozen or so boyars and other lesser figures, around 60 or so in all, besides the wagoners; of goods and victuals there were 40 wagonloads alone.

We greeted each other then with great courtesy. The next day an imperial banquet was to take place; that evening Mikhailo Afanasovich, the son of that lord of the table, and another boyar, came to me with a speech: *"Tsar, Osudar, Velikii Biloei i Chornyei Rusi Samoderzhtsa i Obladatel, tebe ster priatela swoigo prosit zaiutra na biluzhyne koleno i na lebedye khuzno."*[26]

I being unfamiliar with that etiquette of theirs, sulked; think I to myself, what practice is this, to go inviting someone for a KNEE and an ARSE, and I did not yet know what a beluga was. Right then, I wanted to exclaim: "Tell him to eat arse himself"; then I restrained myself. *Nemo sapiens, nisi patiens.* [27] I replied that I thank his lordship the tsar for the gracious invitation to his banquet, but being an ordinary soldier, I am loath to feed on delicacies; though I'll make my appearance, I'll find something else to eat there, and those celebrated dainties I leave to the gentlemen envoys. The interpreter having seen how I frowned on it, says: "Be not upset, Your Honor, for this is a custom of our people, just as in your country, gentlemen invite one another for boiled beef, even though hazelhens be found there too, and many other such game, so with us it is for rump of swan, though there be many dishes; and when we mention both rump of swan and knee of beluga it is to signify an illustrious banquet."

I inquired then: "What is this beluga anyway, and what is so special

26. The Tsar, Grand Monarch of White and Black Ruthenia (part of Muscovy), absolute ruler and sovereign lord, invites you, as his friend, for tomorrow for knee of beluga and rump of swan.
27. He who is not patient, is not wise.

about its knees?" He said that it's a large river fish, and that one spot near the gills has so fine a flavor, no other fish is as tasty, and the rest tastes like sturgeon; that piece being round, which they cut from the fish and bring round to the table, they call a knee. I also made inquiry about why they invite guests for a rump — why not a head, or a wing, or a breast? He said that this piece is the tastiest part of a swan. At this, I observed it would be better to invite one for a whole swan rather than the rump alone; in our country the rump of a fat capon is also rather savory, but we don't invite anyone for the rump, but in general for the capon. Said he, it's the custom.

And I was present at that banquet, to which I was once more invited with a speech, the same as the previous day's. Straightaway, they brought me the tsar's titles to be learned so that I should know how to toast the health of so great a monarch; for if, God forbid, I should make a mistake or omit any one of the titles, it would be a great affront to the tsar's name; and all that good will, in an instant, to no avail. They served heaps of food then, but 'twas tasteless and unappetizing; the fowl and the meat dishes are the most important. When they were drinking to the tsar's health, I had to read those titles from the page, because there was half a sheet of them, difficult exceedingly, and unusual; when they drank to our king's health, only the lord master of the table knew them from memory, the others all read from their sheets; for, should you make the slightest mistake in anything, then you'll have to start them all over again, even if you're at the end. They also toasted the hetmans, the commanders, and Czarniecki, they being at the time very humble. I, too, wishing to recompense kindness with kindness, drank to the health of Dolgoruky, Khovansky, Sheremetev. They were insulted; they said nothing then, to be sure, but once having taken me into their confidence, they remonstrated that "you affronted us." Quoth I: "They are just as much hetmans as ours whose health you did not forget." Said the lord of the table: "They don't deserve a dog's toasting swill to their health, for they sent men to their deaths."

They dallied in Wiaźma a week before putting themselves in readiness. Then we set off toward the border on the road to Dorohobuż, Smolensk province [in the Commonwealth]. There they sent their own horses back, while I had to look out for the horses and wagons, since their horses pulled the carts only four miles beyond the border; now you, my dear Escort, Sir, see to it there's something to harness, such being the custom. Oh, painful it was at the start, in that ravaged countryside, to try to find as many horses and carts as they had wagons; but the Lord finally came to my aid.

We set out on the Minsk road through Tołłoczyn, Jabłonica, to Oczyże, Mikołajów. By then, it was easier to get horses and carts and the further we went the easier it became; but at first I began to regret my undertaking.

The Muscovites were overjoyed to have me escort them, saying: *"Kakzhe ster khospod Bokh poblakhoslavil: peredom vodiv staryi Pas, teper bude nas voditi molodyi Pasek!*[28] My uncle, a judge in Smolensk, had always escorted them and often visited their country as an envoy; there in the capital he was familiar even to the children, everyone having *dulcem recordationem* of him.[29] Even when I told them of my misfortune, that a Muscovite almost captured me in the battle with Dolgoruky, they said: "In the capital you would have been shown every respect, both for his name and for his kind service to our people; you surely would have departed without paying ransom." But I said: "I thank you all the same, I've better to do at home."

I travelled then *magnis itineribus* at first, to escape the more speedily from these wastelands. No sooner had I come to an inhabited country, but all proceeded more easily; I had not much ado to get horses and wagons, nor did I have to look for them; the people there know their own custom. Knowing an envoy is on the way, the towns pass on the news to each other; it's obligatory to provide horses and carts. Whenever they stay in town, you have to give them food and drink until as many horses are put up as they need: each town then strove to get these guests off its hands as speedily as possible. They would ride to meet me from towns several miles away, until I'd passed them, even though I'd no mind to go there. Others I'd not even heard of, they too, came riding to me, bargaining, begging me to pass them by, to be exempt from the requisitioning; this one brought 200 zloties, that one 300, that one 100 — divers gave diversely according to their means, rich or wretched.

The Governor was in Kojdanów when I arrived, though he had taken leave of me, not expecting I would so speedily return from beyond the Dnieper, and had given me excellent intelligence of everything and *sufficientam expeditionem,*[30] having, out of certain considerations, post-dated the letters. Also he himself had not had a mind to tarry in this place; but once encamped in a good spot, he became from day to day less inclined to leave, thinking to feed the army and clean out the larders of the confederate Lithuanian gentlemen; Sapieha the

28. "How God has blessed us: old Pas used to be our guide, now young Pasek is to guide us." This is a play on words in Polish: Pasek's uncle was also named Jan Pasek. *Pas* means "belt" in Polish; *Pasek* would be a diminutive form. However, Pasek's surname does not derive from *pas,* but most likely from the name Paweł whose diminutives are Pach and Paszek; see the Introduction.)
29. A pleasant recollection.
30. Sufficient credentials.

Lithuanian hetman being also of such a mind. I sent on ahead then to the Governor, asking should I have the envoys present themselves or pass by; the envoys having themselves made request to pay Czarniecki a visit. He gave order then to stop there. The envoys then rendered him a visit, they rode in on sleighs, lying down in them as if in a bed. For such is their custom, they do not arrange the wraps for sitting up as we do, and he doesn't sit on the sleighs, but lies in feather-bedding up to his ears so that only his beard is visible; even poorer men do so: he spreads out any quilt, lays himself down, and off he drives, if only to preserve his custom.

After his audience, the Governor invited them to a camp dinner. They quaffed a good deal then and were pleased, they had ample to eat and the food was tasty. Finally, I say: "So now you see, my hetman did not invite you for a piece of arse, as you did me, yet you lacked for nothing and were pleased." Then that Polikarpovich replies: *"Kakzhe ster? Vsiudi vorona khovorit: ka, ka, ka! U vas prokhaiut na Kura: u kura bude khuzno; u nas, su, prokhaiut na khuzno: pri khuzni bude, su, kholova."*[31]

Their vodka is poór — the more smellsome, the higher the price. Not only rot-gut does he drink, whereof even the whiff is nasty, but he quaffs it down with as much gusto as if it were the greatest specialty; they even enjoy the taste, smacking their lips: *"Slazhnozhe, su, vinko khosudarskoe!"*[32] Near the capital there is one town[33] where only English reside; being a civilized people, they have all sorts of excellent liquors. When the Muscovites travel somewhere as deputies, they procure these liquors from the English, for example, various vodkas, spiced Spanish wine, which they call ROMANIA, and other wines. And thus did that lord master of the table conduct himself: he always poured his vodka from a different bottle, and mine from a different bottle. At first I understand he is drinking something better; I said nothing, only thought: "Fy, what *grubianitas!*[34] Once, we having dropped the formalities, he was pouring a drink for himself, drank it, and taking another bottle from the middle, pours one for me, I grabbed the one whereof he'd been drinking. Lunges at me he does, wants to tear it away from me, meanwhile I'd already tipped it to my mouth — vile, stinking stuff it was! Only now do I tell him: "I understood you were drinking the best yourself; but now I take you to to be a courteous fellow, as you offer others a better drink than you pour yourself." Very ashamed he was to be discovered in this, but from then on, he no longer

31. "How's that Sir? Crows say caw, caw, caw everywhere! Your people invite guests for chicken, but a chicken has a rump; our people invite guests for rump, but not far from the rump, you'll find the head too."
32. "Delicious, Sir, a royal little wine!
33. Sloboda, a settlement outside Moscow with special privileges for foreigners.
34. Boorishness.

shunned drinking such bad vodka even though ashamed before; he would call out to his boy then anytime; "*Mitiushka, davaizhe, su vinka khosudarskego!*[35] Now to gulp it down from a different bowl, now to rub his chest: "*Kakzhe ster, slazhno!*"[36] — and a taste it had that would make a goat howl if you forced it down her throat.

After our departure from the army, I travelled through the hetman's estates; the Governor having recommended to me not to create hardships there, I only sent word to the stewards everywhere that I was but passing through. But as before spirits were sent, and game, etc.

I came to Horodyszcze,[37] then Nowogródek. I was gloomy on arriving; for the townsmen, though hearing of the envoys, had sent nothing to me, while the towns behind us had sent to us early, inviting the travellers to go with them; here they said "no one can serve two masters: we have our own masters here now whom we are serving." A Lithuanian regiment had stopped there. I then sent ahead to them, requesting 150 horses for the envoys' wagons and provisions. They said "To no avail, for we already have someone here to supply." And as before no one was despatched, they not expecting I would attack a town where a mob of confederates are stopping. I, however, say to the envoys: "Gentlemen, order your men to stand by me, we're dealing with contempt here, both for my king and your tsar, if they've fed us on insolence." The envoys then: "Very well." Not only did they give the order to their men, but they themselves mounted horses.

I commanded thus: 40 elite Cossacks and my servants in front; 15 Muscovite pistoliers, the ones guarding the wagons; on both flanks, the infantry armed with muskets, and finally the Muscovite horse at the rear. I myself rode at the head of all, and the pistoliers on foot beside me. *In toto,* we were covered by 100 horse. They enter the town: no impediment. I'm halfway along the street, when two cavaliers come dashing, they've a retinue of several dozen carrying short muskets. They came to a halt then; they said nothing; we passed by them. But then groups of three and four arrive, with firearms. They lifted their caps, so did we. They standing there think I'm but passing through the town. Whereas I, taking a fancy to a place, seeing grand and respectable dwellings, suddenly come to a standstill; I show the envoy, "Gentlemen, here are your quarters: I myself stayed on the same side of the market square. They, seeing us dismount, promptly make haste to fall upon us. "But Your Honor encroaches upon our quarters then?"

35. "Mityushka, give me some royal wine."
36. "How delicious, Sir."
37. Horodyszcze is 35 kilometers to the south of Nowogródek. The route is an unlikely one; perhaps Pasek is referring to some other place on the road between Mikołajów and Nowogródek, lying to the east of Nowogródek.

I answer: "And you, Your Honor, in forbidding the townsmen, *contra iura gentium*[38] to comply with law and custom, encroach upon the authority of two Majesties, the Polish and Muscovite monarchs." He says: But a whole squadron is lodged here in this street and these are the officers' quarters where you are standing." I ask him again: "Would those be men in that squadron?" He says: "Of course, they're men." I say: "Were they devils even, I'm not afraid of them. Now cease this annoyance, at long last, for I've no dealings with you, but with a royal town, wherein you will oblige only insofar as the town fathers will lose their heads for this contempt and disobedience of his Majesty the king."

By now 300 or more of them had gathered. "But you'll not be staying here." I answer: "I'm already here." "You'll not settle in here." I say: "I've certainly no mind to make a sojourn here, for I'm on an urgent mission. But it's also certain I'll not leave here until the law has been complied with; in a word, be off, or I'll order these triggers pulled." And the Cossacks and Muscovites are holding their muskets as if on the forks,[39] and I say: "Consider now, if you have not this understanding, or else have someone teach you, what authority every deputy carries in himself, that he is a *publica persona,*[40] representing the majesties of two kingships and two monarchies: the one from whence he comes and the one whither he goes."

So they, at last, having had their say, went off. But I: "Drive their horses out!" They were chased out into the street, our own brought in; our wagons arrived, we took up quarters. Soon, a few of them come along, grab the saddles, the harnesses, the guns off the pegs.

I sent to the mayor; if he's not had the sword drawn across his neck, he'll surely not be escaping a court summons, no longer than a week he'll have, both he and the entire town, if the required horses and wagons are not provided. Not half an hour passed before the town leaders come along; they bow. I inquire which of them is the lord mayor. One points: "There he is himself." I club him directly: he fell; I caused him to be tied and put under guard [and say] "As for you, you'll come with me to Warsaw; but the rest of you go and see to it that a wagon train is supplied to me for I'm not leaving this place until it be had." And now the Muscovites: *"Oi, milenkizhe, su, pristav umieie korolevskoe i tsarskoe zderzhati velichestvo."*[41] Along came two lieutenants; who, having chatted awhile with me, say: "Trouble yourself no further,

38. Against the law of nations.
39. It means "were holding as if at the ready"; seventeenth-century muskets, being very heavy, were supported while aiming on forked rests.
40. An official person.
41. "Ay, a fine fellow, our escort, he knows how to uphold both kingly and tsarist majesty."

Your Honor; we'll order the town to give provisions, but a wagon train you'll not be getting."

Et interim I caused the wagoners to be summoned in their presence, they having driven their carts but two miles, I say to them: "Well, lads, for complying with law and custom, and for not ducking out of your obligation, nay, even going of your own accord, considering you're from a poor town, I'm relieving you, you'll not be dragged any further; having got to a large town, I'll find here the satisfaction of my needs, and you are released; return to your homes, and Godspeed." The drivers fall on their knees, thanking me, and with that, off to their horses. Hearing of this, the townsmen come running, making entreaty: "Mercy! We'll settle with money! Let them take their wagons further!" They offer 200, they offer 300 — in vain; at last, they offer 400, but by now every driver was grabbing his horses as best he could, and out of that town they fled; some even cast away the harness. I then, as if I didn't know they were gone: "Go and have the drivers wait up a bit!" They say: "They're not there anymore, except one whose horse took sick on him."

Now did the townsmen fall into a panic, they beg me to have them pursued. That I did not want to do. Those lieutenants make request to me then to release the lord mayor. I declared I would let him go the moment I shall be *in toto satisfactus* both in provisions and in wagons; but should any convenience whatsoever be denied me, he'll be sure to ride to Warsaw with me, shackled. They put forth arguments; I do the same. They say that so many wagons are not to be had here; I say that they have to be. They advise me to send to the neighboring towns so that they, too, might contribute; I say: "*Quod peto, da, Gai, non peto consilium.*"[42] They were enraged: "Pah! Your Honor's unobliging." And I say: "Pah! Your Honor's unsparing." They walked off. The townsmen they forbade to consider giving either provisions or wagons. A *shamásh*[43] came and told me this, and also that "they want to chase Your Lordship out of town, taking upon themselves this unpleasantness" — either it was kindliness on his part, or they sent him to say that in order to test me. I am not confounded; I caused the street to be blocked off with the wagons on both ends, at the market square and the entrance, wagon alongside wagon, across the entire width of the street so that no one could get through there on horseback. For provisions I do not ask, since I'm standing on the most prosperous looking street; everything must be here.

Interim, call the blacksmith — several there were on that street; I ordered him to put a pair of shackles on the mayor's legs. The Cossacks

42. Give, Gaius, what I request, advice I do not request (Martial, *Epigrammata,* 11, 300).
43. Hebrew for a servant in the synagogue, equivalent of a church sexton.

are standing on the alert. The Muscovites all in arms, none of them will budge without his long harquebus: now let them chase me out. There's plenty of beer about in our lodging, my men like to crook the elbow. I say to the innkeeper: "Is there mead anywhere nearby?" He, for the sake of his own relief, in order that less of his beer should depart: "There is, Your Honor, Sir, only I beg you not to give me away: there and there. Six boyars were lodging there. I told them to ask quietly for a pot of mead, giving money; so they did. They having emptied it, the alewife went to the cellar for a second, after her went some of my men: they sent word that there were six barrels of mead. I had them take it: "Drink up, and when you're in your cups, open fire in the streets!" Thus did we spend the whole night in revels.

The next morning, forthwith to the barns behind our stables, sheaves of rye, hay, as much as we needed, were brought. When it's clear they'll not scare us away, that I'm not begging for anything, I've plenty of everything, fattened hogs, chickens, geese have been slaughtered, along came yesterday's lieutenants finally, a few of their men with them, among whom is my acquaintance, *Pan* [Stanisław] Tryzna. We fell to dealing: "The townsmen want to come here but they're afraid; we ask in their name." I reply, "You yourselves incited them to this arrogance, now you beg for them. Let him explain that who has a mind. I, though an insignificant fellow, having understood yesterday's befogging deceit about being chased out, so too, little by little, am I now penetrating these circumstances. What I said yesterday, I repeat: My business is with the town, not with soldiers. You wish to affront not me but two monarchs, only the Lord knows if it may not be yourselves for I'll not let you chase me out of here. This much you may expect: though my men should have to fall, one upon the other, I'll not leave until my needs are filled. And should you make it difficult for me, it's no more than 100 miles to Kojdanów, and like as not the army must have slipped still nearer; I'll see who shall be feeling the squeeze here."

Whereupon the townsmen arrived; the wife of that shackled mayor, having come to plead was here since early morning, she with her children, with vodkas, and thrice pleading with tears. And so to deal with them; they promise 40 horses. "Impossible, not even 60 will do." They had then to provide 130 horses, renting them even from the soldiers, not having enough. Since they had not been prepared for us, and evening being already upon us, I did not set forth at nightfall. And so we fell to drinking to spite these arrogant people; I being born with such a character as always to return *durum contra durum*[44] even to excess, but also to treat kindness with kindness, even to my own detri-

44. Blow for blow.

ment. So then, these soldiers intervening *bonis modis,*[45] they being humbler now, unlike yesterday, and especially since Tryzna, a cavalier, was a good friend of mine and a very courteous fellow, a kinsman besides, I ordered the lord mayor divested of his bracelets, saying to him:"You know now, for the next time, how to conduct yourself in similar circumstances, and that even the soldier who is quartered with you will not act on your behalf in this strait; though he might protect you, chancing upon a blockhead of an escort, that cover would last only for awhile; afterward venegeance would fall for the abbey outlives the abbot."

We tossed back a few then, the Lithuanians came around. *Pan* Tryzna invited all his own men to come, whoever wished, and thus jollying, it even came to twanging the old sheep gut.[46] The envoy is merry, having quaffed a bit of mead beforehand, he ordered the *romania*[47] to be brought from the wagons and served. I did not mix drinks, but the Lithuanians having mixed theirs, many a one was relieved of his belt, cap, sword, moneybag.

The following morning horses were brought to the requisitioned wagons; our own horses had had a rest and were quite well fed, for whatever was needed had been brought from the granges first, the oats were brought later. Yesterday's gentlemen carousers came by, many invite us to their quarters. The colonel sent to me with a request to do him the honor of a visit, if only for an hour; but I having promised Tryzna, say to him: "My good fellow, my presence at your place is bound to cause others to reprimand my uncouthness; so saying I ought not to visit you." He implored me for a word; but I did not wish it and was not there. At parting, we all tossed down a few more "for your mettle"; they twitted my steadfastness and expressed their embarrassment saying it was all the same whether one gives cheerfully or tearfully; they presented me with hunting dogs, then we parted.

I set out then for Mosty. On leaving the town, I had my boy return to the mayor to have them send supplementary provisions for the wagoners, since I'll not release them until we reach Warsaw, or at least the Narew. Unquiet they were, especially the soldiers who had rented their horses to them. I'd not got three miles when two townsmen overtook me; to their entreaties they fell. "I'll not do it. As you acted toward me during my stay, so I toward you now; cannot be done." Off they fly to the confederate marshal, Żeromski,[48] district supervisor of

45. In a decent way.
46. To play the violin.
47. Spiced wine.
48. Kazimierz Chwalibóg Żeromski, lieutenant of W. Gosiewski's hussar squadron, was hacked to pieces later on in the same year by the Lithuanian confederates. Pasek wrongly attributes to him the title of district supervisor of Czeczera.

Opesk and Czeczera — to seek his advice and aid in this matter — a courteous man he was, dignified, of handsome bearing, medium height, and young, under forty, a beard black as pitch to the waist; more like to a grave senator than a soldier. He told them: "Aid I cannot give you, for 'tis not a mouse to play with; I know these are men of great courage; we'd not get away without bloodshed, and should it come to that, it's a hanging matter. But this piece of advice I'll give you: if you've a fat purse, run along with it; it will be your mediator." Said they, "we've 100 zloties." He replied that they'd not waste even a peek at it." They came running back to us those townsmen; oh, there were pleas, there were offers: we agreed upon 600 zloties, but they were not carrying so much. They gave me a note with the promise to deliver it in Warsaw. "Impossible." "But what can be done about it?" "It's no business of mine." Meanwhile the marshal despatches a cavalier to invite me, together with the deputies, to his quarters; he makes not the slightest mention of the townsmen in the letter, but it was written in this sense.

"My very kind *Pan* Pasek, My Lord and Friend!

Had I but received earlier the news that Your Lordship had deigned to conduct the tsar's envoy to His Majesty the king, I would have long since entreated Your Lordship to oblige me by permitting me to see the envoy and give ear to his mission, he himself having applied to me as being *in comissis*[49] of his highness the tsar. The intelligence of the Muscovite envoy and the liberated prisoners which he brought with him, having but recently reached me, I do beseech Your Lordship not to see any impediment to his rendering me a visit as he himself does exceedingly desire it. For it was none other than my *vigilantia,* with God's special guidance, that worked for the release of these prisoners now being given in exchange. Since not only my interest is at stake here but the entire army's, I do once again make request that the envoy be allowed *liberum aditum*[50] to my quarters in Wołkowysk, wherefore His Lordship *Pan* Żydowicz, a cavalier, has consented to accompany him to me in Wołkowysk.

I remain ever Your Lordship's

cordial brother and obedient servant
Kazimierz Chawalibóg Żeromski

Marshal of HM army of the GDL[51]

The letter was addressed in this way: "To My Right Honorable Lord and Friend, His Lordship *Pan* Jan Pasek, commanding cavalier of the Cossack squadron of His Excellency the Governor of Ruthenia." That he alternately addressed me as "My Lord and Friend" and in signing,

49. On a mission.
50. Free access.
51. His Majesty's . . . Grand Duchy of Lithuania.

wrote "Your Lordship's cordial brother and obedient servant" and again, addressing the outside: "To My Right Honorable Lord and Friend," treating me now as a brother, now as a friend, I disliked at once.[52] I answered, therefore, in this sense:

Most Esteemed Marshal of the armies of the Grand Duchy of Lithuania, My Lord and Brother!

On viewing how Your Lordship's letter was addressed, I was greatly confounded, understanding that Your Lordship considers me unworthy to be a brother, only a friend; then I was somewhat cheered upon reading inside, in Your Lordship's own hand, that you deign to call yourself brother. For this reason, in my reply, *non peto vindictam,* [53] supposing it to have nothing to do with Your Lordship, being but an error on the part of your secretary whom I take to be a very old man since he dredged out of his memory *hanc ideam*[54] of letter-writing and preserves it to this day; such a style was practiced in the days when one wrote "Dear Sir" even to senators; or if the man is young, it may be that formerly he served someone as chief raftsman, transporting hemp, oaken beams, and split logs to Riga; perhaps he was reminiscing while he wrote this letter, imagining it to be with some merchant he was corresponding *de anteactis.*[55]

'Twas all the vogue in the time of King Olbracht
'Twas out by King Kazimierz and that's a fact.

The which mentioned *ex occasione*[56] of Your Honor's secretary, I proceed *ad essentiam* of Your Lordship's letter. Had I been summoned a bit earlier, I would have set off from Kojdanow on a straight course, and without disturbing Your Lordship, for it would have scarcely, if at all, been out of my way. [One page of the manuscript is missing at this point. What follows is the end of Sapieha's oral reply to Czarniecki's letter, which had been given to him by Pasek.]

. . .of the Governor of Ruthenia announced to me that I would have to alter the custom, but far from doing so, I even give my approval, for I regard Your Honor as one of us, there being Paseks here in Lithuania too, and it seems, your uncle, the municipal warden of Smolensk, used to escort them; two persons with the name are now in my service and belike they are kinsmen of yours. Secondly, you're not far from the Narew; what would be the use of assigning another escort? Besides you've conducted them through the world up to now and — so

52. One could only address a townsman as "friend"; a gentryman was accorded the title of "brother." This is why Pasek felt insulted. Letters of the more wealthy gentry were written by secretaries; only the end of the letter was written in by the nobleman himself. Hence, the difference in titles.
53. I do not repay in kind.
54. This idea.
55. About bygone matters.
56. On account of.

word has reached me — *cum conservatione*[57] of your own and your commander's honor; so now, proceed with them straight to the side of his Majesty the king." I was pleased then, he did not let me go without dining, he discoursed with me, pledged the Governor's health; recalled the victories won in the past year. He asked then: "Who was that cavalier whom the court and king were detaining under suspicion?" I answered it was I. Said he: "I'd heard that that was the name and so I asked; but throughout all Lithuania you've a good reputation for the bravery you showed there." He drank then, and ordered his soldiers to drink to my health, despatching me then and with much graciousness, handing over his reply to the Governor's letter which was written in this sense:

"Your Excellency, Governor of Ruthenia,
My Esteemed Lord and Brother!

That you respect the prerogative of my office as Hetman is due, as in all your other actions, to the *indicium*[58] and courtesy of your character, for which I humbly thank you, and thus, I reiterate my former resolve, every proceeding of yours having won so much of my esteem that whatever pleases you, cannot *displicere* me. Far from wanting to remove the assigned escort, His Honor *Pan* Pasek, a cavalier of such esteemed arms, I comply with Your Lordship's will, confirming him in the function with which you entrusted him and declaring that no better escort can I myself provide, who would know how to preserve so *dextre* his own and his commander's reputation. His *modestia*[59] while guiding these men is known to me — from the contentment of the towns and hamlets — I am acquainted with his discreet conduct as well as his *generositas*,[60] wherever he has been obliged to show it: especially recently in Wołpa, where the people were rebelling *contra Maiestatem et matrem oboedientiam*[61] — the which, I assume, is already known to yourself or will be known — he not having permitted them to wrest the crown of honor either from Your Lordship or from himself. For this reason, I do not wish to drive off a good man and — as the people often exclaim — *Kyrie eleison*,[62] I wish for no amendment.

As for orphaned Byelorussia, everybody must admit the rightousness of Your Lordship's regret; no less does it touch my heart. But what is to be done when such a misfortune befalls our country? Surely, even if I'd wish it, I could not accomplish anything with my private retinue of soldiers. I acknowledge that too long has Your Lordship shielded those territories and *cum summo periculo*,[63] having such a small handful of men. For what will

57. With the preservation.
58. Sensibleness.
59. Moderation.
60. Noble station.
61. Against his Majesty and mother obedience.
62. Lord, have mercy on us.
63. With the greatest danger.

happen now, not we are to blame; whoever is the evildoer must account to God. If the enemy would at least allow us a truce so that once assembled at the Diet we might consult about this in order to plan the sooner for the defense of those territories, then there might somehow be a chance; but I doubt it.

Should this embassy intercept Your Lordship on the way through here with the army, I beg you to do me the honor of turning into my estate for a short while. I do earnestly beseech you to *conferre* with me in any event *in ulteriori tractu*[64] of our service to our bereaved fatherland; that it is deserving there can be no doubt. I commend myself to Your Lordship's habitual graciousness as your wholly devoted brother and obedient servant.

Pawel Sapieha, Governor of Wilno,
Hetman of the Grand Duchy of Lithuania

Having been thus despatched, I set out toward the Narew and not until the last days of the Carnival season [after February 15] did I make a halt in Berezyna. Only a village it was, but there was no need of a town, our wagons being filled with fine liquors, meat, game, etc. And so we passed our time merrily amid Ruthenian hooped yokes; and though but shortly acquainted, we joined in sledging parties, as of old, "seeking the whimbrel," and we in turn were visited by seekers of the whimbrel; even partners we found with whom to take a turn in a dance.[65]

On Ash Wednesday I started for the Narew. Plenty of fish the envoys had; sterlet, great sides of smoked beluga; nor was there a dearth of fresh fish, for folk everywhere carted it to us; whenever I made request for horses and carts, they brought fish too. Upon reaching the Narew, the Lithuanian horses and carts were not allowed to pull us any further; such was the law, though they had taken us but one mile; directly then, I had to look about for others. Then off I set, crossing the Narew, for Bielsko. Siemiatycze, crossing the Bug at Drohiczyn to Liw, and finally, to Warsaw. I rode on ahead from our last halt to inform the king of the envoys' arrival and make inquiry regarding their further disposition, whither and by what means to convey them.

The king no sooner saw me but recognized me at once and received me graciously; he had already had word by post from the Govenor that it was I escorting them. The king was about to leave for a session of the Diet when I entered. A goodly throng of senators and deputies were gathered in the king's chamber, both known and unknown to me. On seeing me he says: "Welcome, Sir Would-be Confederate!" Bowing I answered: "This time I'll escape such conjecture, since I'm riding from

64. On the next stage.

65. This Carnival season pastime, called a *kulig* in Polish — named after a bird, the *kulik* (in English, the whimbrel) — consisted of going out in parties of a dozen or so sleighs, riding from estate to estate in pursuit of merriment and the whimbrel. One imagines that by the twelfth stop, the sledgers most certainly saw the whimbrel.

Smolensk, not from Kielce" [a confederate area]. Says the king: "Nay, all the more can someone make accusation that you've been won over by Muscovy there." I reply: "And let him mightily accuse, but Your Royal Highness will pay me again for it." He burst into laughter and hugged my head. "Never again shall we be led to believe such a thing, were even an angel to tell us so." And then he says to the senators: "I shall return shortly; you gentlemen, meanwhile may sit down and take your ease." Ordering me to follow him, he went into the bedchamber. Then did he inquire about everything, on what business the envoys were riding. I replied that they desire peace. He asked then whether I'd not been impeded on my way by the Lithuanian confederates. And I told him about the Nowogródek incident. Says the king: "The Governor has written me about this, and I thank you for your fine bravery, which — I perceive — you are able to use in *in adversis et prosperis*[66] to preserve our authority."Summoning then the royal chamberlain [Teodor Denhof] he says: "Sir, do speak to Szeling [a royal courtier] about where to lodge the Muscovite *osudars;*[67] he himself rose, having chatted an hour or so with me, and went to the senate.

No sooner was I out of the chamber but, directly, the deputies from my Rawa and Łęczyca [a neighboring district] beset me. "Whence so familiar with the king?What's this? How now?" I told them. They then: *Gratulor, gratulor!*"[68] I left the senatorial chamber, paid a visit to Szeling, I dined in his quarters with him; the envoys *interim* had arrived in Praga. Since the inns were filled, they could not obtain lodging.[69] I entered the senate, placing myself in sight of the king, who, calling me to him, asked: "What is it?" — I tell him the envoys have arrived but are unable to find a lodging place. He caused Scypio, groom of the royal chamber, to go with me then, in order to turn some out of the inns in Praga and to remain there until further notice. And so it came to pass.

The next day the royal coach was sent after them and we were given quarters in the residence of a certain Frenchman; there we remained. But the king caused me to come every day to confer and get money for victuals. Hard-pressed for money I was not, still having a bit from Denmark, and recently the king had given me 500 gold ducats; for escorting the Muscovites I took 17,000; but as you came by it easily, you didn't watch it very carefully either. We imbibed often with the courtiers; for you're not long in Warsaw without company and acquaintances.

Mazepa had now made his apology to the king for that hoax in

66. In both adverse and favorable circumstances.
67. Old Russian word for "Sir."
68. I congratulate you, I congratulate you.
69. The Diet was in session (February to May 1662) and Warsaw was overcrowded.

Grodno and once more had come to Court. We rubbed shoulders, going about there side by side, for his accusation had done me no harm, indeed, it had brought me profit and fame, whereof even the confederates themselves were envious, and others offered their congratulations—but even so, I did often grumble angrily at him, the more so when in my cups, as ordinarily at such times one's resentments loom the largest. I, upon coming, once, to the king's antechamber, found Mazepa there too; there were but a few courtiers about; well fuddled was I on arriving there and I say to that Mazepa: "Hail, Sir Janizary!"[70] He being a boisterous fellow, retorts at once: "Hail, Sir Corporal,"[71] referring to those Germans[72] guarding me in Grodno. And, without thinking twice, I do punch his mug, jumping aside instantly. He grabs for his sword-hilt, the courtiers jump up: "Stay! Stay! The king is present on the other side of the door." None of the courtiers stood by him, for they also did not look kindly upon him, he being a bit of an imposter and, to boot, a recently ennobled Cossack. My grudge against him they knew to be justified, they respected me, for I'd come to treat them as boon fellows, and did not stint on money at any of our tavern sessions.

A commotion follows. One attendant entered the king's chamber then and says: "Your Highness, *Pan* Pasek has struck Mazepa in the mug." And the king strikes him one straight away: "Don't gabble before you're asked." The bishop was dumbfounded; seeing it was a criminal offense, he expected my life would be in danger. Stepping over to me, he says: "I'm not acquainted with Your Honor, but for God's sake I wish Your Honor would escape; it is a great crime to strike a king's courtier in the face in the royal chamber." I answer: "Your Grace does not know whereof that traitor is guilty toward me." Again the bishop: "Whatever it may be, this is not the place to lose one's temper; flee, Your Honor, as long as there is time, as the king has not yet found out." I say: "I'll not leave this chamber." Mazepa went off close to tears; it wasn't the blow had so much pained him as that the courtiers had not stood by him like a colleague. I then am explaining to the bishop the *originem praetensionis*[73] when the royal chamberlain

70. Pasek is being malicious; he uses *asavula,* a word that came into Polish via Ukrainian from the Turkish *jasaul,* denoting a cavalry officer originally. The Poles, however, downgraded the meaning to mere Field Watch.

71. The lowest rank in the Foreign Contingent of the Commonwealth Armies, that is, the infantry troops, organized on German principles (as opposed to the more distinguished cavalry troops of Polish tradition).

72. That is, German foot soldiers. These detachments were so called because they were composed of Germans from Pomerania (Pomorze) or Prussia and were commanded by a German.

73. Reason for my grudge.

emerges signaling the bishop to go in to the king, and they leave. He wagged his finger at me; I guessed that those in there already knew. They went into the king's chamber, and I to my lodgings.

The next day — a Saturday it was — I did not go to the castle; indeed, I was frightened, one views things differently upon sobering up. From afar, I make inquiries whether word has gotten to the king. I'm told the king knows of it but is not angry, what is more he dealt the page who told him about it a slap, saying: "That's for you, too, since they didn't deal it to you out there; mind what your tongue wags about." Sunday I went to the chamberlain asking whether I can present myself to the king. He informed me that the king had no mind to be angry, that he even said: "I don't wonder at him, for an insult pains more than any wound; a good thing they did not run across each other on the road somewhere. Good that Mazepa paid only with that; let him know next time not to spread false rumors." And I went; the royal couple was dining. Upon seeing me, the king exclaims: "Glory be! But you've grown snobbish: it's now the fourth day I've not laid eyes on you. I see I'll have to be sparing with your keep, then you and the envoys may present yourselves oftener in my chamber." I reply: "As it is, My Gracious King, they complain, though Your Majesty's kindness and hospitality is quite adequate; but were you to provide more subtle fare, I'd not stay long around there." Then on other matters with divers persons he discoursed.

I was content now, I'd not been frowned upon because of that Mazepa. Deputies were standing about, and soldiers aplenty. Sweets were being served at the time. And there was a small bear, or rather, to judge from his aspect, a human being, around thirteen years of age, whom Marcyjan Ogiński, while setting his bear-nets in Lithuania, had his beaters chase into the nets; they caught him alive, though with much harm to the stalkers, the bears defending him fiercely, one great she-bear especially; clearly she was his mother. No sooner had the hunters felled her, but they seized the boy forthwith. Everything about him was human, no bear-claws did he have on his hands and feet, but human nails; the only difference 'twixt him and a human being was the long hair, like a bear's, which covered his entire body even his face, only his eyes glittering. Divers opinions they put forth about him, some concluding he must have been conceived *ex semine viri cum ursa;*[74] others saying that while he was very young, the she-bear had plainly snatched the child from somewhere and raised him. He, having sucked at her dugs, took on therefore the *similitudinem animalis.*[75] Incapable of human speech or conduct was the lad, only animal.

74. Out of a man's seed and a she-bear.
75. The animal's likeness.

The queen, at that time, gave him her pear peel, having sprinkled a bit of sugar on it; he with great eagerness put it into his mouth; but tasting it, spat it into his hand and hurled this slobbery peel right between the queen's eyes. The king began to laugh mightily. The queen said something in French; the king laughed even harder. Ludwika, being an irritable woman, left the table; the king had us all drink to her fury, ordered wine, music, sent for the ladies-in-waiting, and we fell to feasting.

Only now, at this feast, did he have Mazepa summoned; he made us to shake hands, apologize: "Forgive one another from the heart, for now you are both guilty." And so we made our peace; afterward we sat down together and drained the cup, but in the next year, true to form, Mazepa departed from Poland in shame, and this was the reason:

He had a village in Volhynia next to Falibowski's estate which enticed him — why, I cannot conjecture — to pay frequent visits whenever Falibowski was absent. The house servants — particularly those who carried the *billets-doux* and were aware of these trysts — informed their master of these visits. Once, this Falibowski started off on a long journey somewhere, he bade his wife farewell, and set out. Then he took up a station along the route by which Mazepa used to come riding; along flies the servant, who always acted as emissary, with a note, and he had told his master of it. He, taking the note, read there of the pleasure to invite him to a party, while indicating His Lordship's absence, etc., etc. Returning the note to that secretary: "Ride on with it but request a reply in writing: say that Her Ladyship orders him to make haste." He did as he was bade, while his master waited for him to return with the reply, there being two miles to cover. The servant no sooner delivering the note there, but he charged off, giving his master the answer wherein is a declaration of desire to serve and a promise to show himself at once.

A while later along comes Mazepa. Upon meeting: "Hail!" "Hail!" "Where are you off to?" He told him some other destination. "Please stop in and visit." Mazepa begs off, having an urgent errand to attend to; I see Your Lordship is also on his way somewhere." "Oh, that can't be." Clap! he's collared him; "and this note, what does it mean?" Mazepa panicked; fell to pleading: "It's but the first time I'm riding there, I've never stopped before." They call over that secretary: "Was it plenty of times he was there in my absence?" His answers: "As many as the hairs on my head." They seized him then; and they ride on: "You choose to die?" Imploring not to be killed, he confessed to everything. So they sneered at him, tortured him; stripping him naked, they bound him to his own horse, after removing the saddle, his face toward the tail, buttocks toward the head; his arms they tied behind his back, his feet under the horse's belly; his Tartar horse — swift enough by nature — they crazed with their bellowing, flogging it, ripping the bridle off its head, firing several shots into the air above it. In a frenzy the horse raced off toward home. And the way was all dense undergrowth: hawthorn, hazel, wild pear, brambles; nor was it a spacious track, only the narrow trails the horse remembered, for Mazepa often went that way home; being on the lookout, one doesn't travel the public highway, you take the byways, and often you have to bend your head, holding fast the reins, you must avoid the bad spots and dense thickets, sometimes a branch will strike you on the head or rip your gown. But with buttocks toward the head of so fleet and crazed a horse, fleeing blindly from the fear and pain wherever his legs would carry him, what a comeuppance did that naked man get before coming out of those bushes, one can easily conjure. The two or three fellows riding in attendance with him, Falibowski did not release, so that none could rescue him. Collapsing in front of his own gates, frozen stiff, he calls out, "Guard!" The guard, recognizing the voice, opens: glimpsing this fearful sight, he shut them again and fled. He called out everyone in the manor-house. They take a look, they cross themselves; he swears he is their true master: they believe him not. They scarcely let him inside in time, unable to utter another word, beaten and frozen.

Falibowski, meanwhile, having ridden off to his wife — he knew now all their ways — rapped at the window through which Mazepa used to enter; it was opened and like a gracious guest he was received. But what suffering was endured here too — such circumstances are better not described — especially from those spurs he had prepared and purposely fastened here somewhere around his knees. *Sufficit* that it was a conspicuous and celebrated punishment for the immoral. Mazepa nearly expired, and having recovered, he left Poland for the very shame.

[Some doggerel verse on Mazepa is omitted here.]

So then, having inserted [in this narrative] these two eminent royal courtiers — the Cossack fled Poland; what became of the bear, whether they made a man of him, I know not, though I do know they sent him to the French for speech lessons, and he began to learn proper sounds — I return here to the subject undertaken.

I fulfilled my office then *in debita methodo* and *cum gratulatione*[76] of my brethren who, at the time, were *praesentes in publicis*.[77] The subject of the army's pay and the defense of the borders was being brought up. I visited the king often. One *obstaculum* there was, the treasury had been very depleted and no crown land was available, but I by nature being

76. In a fitting way . . . with the congratulations.
77. Present at the Diet.

not ambitious, contented myself with less. I made request then to ride home for the Easter holidays [April 9] 12 miles from Warsaw it was; told how I had made a solemn vow, while abroad, to render praise and thanks to God for his blessings in those battles. The king gave me his leave, *cum regressu,*[78] and in my place assigned Scypio, a standard-bearer and his own groom of the chamber, as escort for the Muscovites.

Upon arriving at my parents', ample rejoicing was had over those circumstances in Grodno whereof they now heard — if tardily. Kin and neighbours and good friends aplenty gathered. We were *bonae voluntatis.*[79] Having taken our ease at home, we resolved to *explere votum*[80] at Częstochowa; we went off, intending to set foot there on Ascension Day [May 18]. My mother rode, I travelled on foot, my horses, on which I was to return, being led behind me. Fierce was the heat. But on our way back, snow fell, doing great damage, as the rye then was already blossoming. On the ground, the snow came up to the horses' knees, it nipped the buds, ruined the orchards and other *fructifera,*[81] for it lay a week; so little if any profit was had from the rye; other grain, too, was considerably impaired. Much bread was ravaged in our country that year, by God and man both, a *poena peccati,*[82] whence the cost of rye rose exceedingly and our people felt the pinch of hard times.

In Częstochowa I also confessed that one sojourn, asking forgiveness *ex voto promissi matrimonii*[83] (whereof I've written above) to a certain lady, the which, not coming to pass, I had done out of a reckless impulse, or to deal plainly, for having fallen in love. To be sure, I was absolved, but I remember yet, and shall for a long time to come, the penance I was given and the rebuke I heard, and I'd be able to teach it till I die, what it means to blurt out those few little words: "I'll marry you."

On my return from Częstochowa I went to Warsaw, there finding great commotion, no accord; some wanting to disrupt the Diet, the army began to assemble outside Warsaw, declaring no one should leave before the Diet ended.[84] Informers were posted along the routes, and so the Diet closed, nearly under siege, having left the rest up to a commission, regarding the problem of control of the army and its wages. At the closing of the Diet, I too, after all, try to see that I'm given something in cash from the treasury for my pains, not having obtained the promised office, nor did I have any luck stalking one, though

78. Provided I return.
79. Of good cheer.
80. To fulfill the vow.
81. Fruit trees.
82. Punishment for ur sins.
83. For the vow of marriage I'd made.
84. Pasek must have come to Warsaw after the closing of the Diet, since it ended May 1.

several times the king told me: "Be on the look-out for yourself!" They were giving offices but I perceived my need was for bread; quite willing I was to forego *titulum* for *vitulum.* And so throughout the entire Diet I did not happen to track down any post, which is the speedier done *occasionaliter*[85] than when deliberately sought; we did talk of it, the king himself bringing it up, he said: "I'm in debt to you and, though you say nothing, when I see you it's as if you were calling into my ear; for I know that I owe you."

But my luck did not change; no money in the treasury either, for King Kazimierz, though a good master, had no luck with money, plainly 'twould not stick to him. It was resolved then to give me an order of payment in the amount of 6,000 zloties for the Lithuanian treasury, because of my carrying out a duty for the Grand Duchy of Lithuania, since the escort ought to have been a Lithuanian, not a Pole; belike they thought to pull the wool over my eyes in order to get me off their hands with the hope of that would-be contentment, the situation in the Lithuanian treasury being no different from our own; and Gosiewski himself, the under-treasurer and field hetman of Lithuania, had just returned from captivity at that time, having been held prisoner by Khovansky until Czarniecki and the army got to Lithuania; still walking about with beard and shaggy hair he was, thus he could not have been too rich, being but recently set free. I went then to him with that note; he looking at it, says: "But for God's sake, his Majesty knows I've collected no money during these years, that our treasury is without funds. You'll waste your time pursuing this design, Your Honor, for nothing's to be got from it, unless somehow after the confederacy has disbanded; for even should we have something to give, it's not like we could do so now. Pin no hopes on it, Your Honor, let the king consider something else."

I went off then and repeated his words to the king and I give back the order of payment. The king says: "Let me go to see him myself, that will make a difference." And so it came about that the under-treasurer promised to give me the money, but I had to go to the commission in Wilno. The king said to me: "To do well by a promise, they say one needs a fleet-footed horse; we wish you to go at once to the commission in order to be there at the outset, for the under-treasurer is to come across some money in cash; he has promised to count out Your Honor's share then directly. And make haste to return, so as to conduct the *osudary*[86] back again. We shall not forget to furnish you with something better *feliciori tempore.*"[87]

85. By chance.
86. Russian for "Sirs."
87. In a more favorable period.

The Diet having come to a close, I, bidding the king farewell, departed for home, from whence, after but a short respite, I set out for Wilno. On arriving I found things in confusion, for, from the very start of the commission — to which throngs of soldiers had come — no session, no assembly took place without tumult, uproar, and drawing swords. Lodgings were very hard to come by there with that great press of people; I was forced to take up quarters in an empty house, not yet built, having recently been started; only the framework of a room was standing and no door. There being robbings and assaults night and day, I had my men stand guard, a painful situation among strangers; but even in that deserted spot, I did not escape intruders, whereof below. I attended the assemblies until my despatch, and such law and order you've not seen the like! I, however, request that for which I'd come, it being a dangerous business *dantis et accipientis.*[88]

No sooner had money come in from some source or other, but he gives me the order of payment for the secretary of the treasury; having shown him the order, we count the money, he having locked himself and me into one very dark, vaulted chamber — only one tiny window it had — in the castle behind St. Kazimierz. Almost by stealth we were counting. Since he gave me *partem* in good coin, and *partem* in Riga coppers, which were thin and silver-plated, the one boy who was with me could not carry them — the others being forced to keep watch in that empty frame. Two haiduks from the guard he gave me then, and they carried the money on hand-barrows to my lodging-place. I, upon coming to the place, am told by my men that a cavalier was here who claimed these lodgings to be his and he takes offense at my halting here without consulting him; he would have driven the horses out, if the other who was with him had not led him away; he declared he would come again and ordered me to inform Your Honor when you arrive.

I had already dismissed those haiduks, then along comes this master of the house, or rather, the heir of this frame wherein I was stopping, and a company of seven, all drunken. He asks me: "And you, by whose leave and by whose command are you stopping here?" I reply: "He who permitted me to live and walk." He says: "But these are my quarters." I answer: "Then you're a poor gardener, leaving nettles and thistles to overgrow these quarters." Again he says: This is my lodging-place." I answer: "Not a commendable head of the house are you, if you've neither stove, nor windows, nor door in your house." Says he: "So why have you halted here?" I reply: "For the reason that I am come to a Tartar state, not to a people who ought to be courteous and therefore careful to set aside unoccupied quarters for a guest." Says the townsman who was lord of those unfinished premises: "Pah! Your

88. For giver and taker.

Lordship, have his honor's horses driven into the street: he makes fun of you, Your Honor." Says the heir: "Drive them out!" "Don't you do that!" (And this going on in that room among the horses.) The townsman dashes to untie the horses, but my man clubs him in the chest, he fell. To sword!

When that uproar started, one Lithuanian, having become embroiled, leapt out of that swordplay amongst the horses; I had a chesnut horse, shamefully swift — now does my chesnut strike out with his hooves. And that one fell. Two down. Among the nettles that suit passed through all the courts of appeal. We're outside — now, at each other! My boy watching my rear, two men hard by me. Somehow they beat the boy away from me: one ripped at me from behind, but not very much, and he jumped aside at once. At the same time, the townsman fell down in the nettles; he not having been hurt, in an instant my men jumped in front of him with rapiers, and he got up. He rushes straight at me, slashing with all his might; I withstood it, then having deferred, I slashed him across the pulses; nothing; onward to cut and thrust. There's my boy smiting his attendant on the noggin; down he went. His lordship attacks once more; I slice across his fingers again: the rapier drops, he takes to his heels. My boy in pursuit; again he fell in those nettles; my boy smiting him several times before I called out: "Stay!" The rest having also turned tail, I to the room, to my horses. The one who'd been clubbed had already crawled out and fled, the one my horse had struck is lying in a faint, dead I thought; I had him dragged out by the feet, when the fellow groaned. They say: "He lives! He lives! Bring him to!" He came to his senses, got up, and walked off; those out in the nettles they rounded up and brought out, scolding them, threatening.

"What's to be done here?" I think. "No way to lock myself in." About one o'clock at night, along comes a mob of 50 or 60 men. My boy calls out: "No closer, or I'll shoot; what is it you're needing?" They halted, then say: "And what have you sons of the devil mutilated people for?" My answer: "He who looks for trouble will find it easily; we're not mutilators, but our innocence was defending itself." He speaks again: "You'll not slip a leg out of here, you villains!" I answer: "Judge for yourself, who's to be called a villain; he who attacks by night, or he who stays quiet, provoking no one." Says he: "Oh, that's no matter! You'll have to spill your blood here, just as you spilled our brothers'." I reply: "If you've come for my head, belike you've brought your own along as well; if mine falls, yours, too, will surely go; now withdraw, or we'll be pulling triggers." At last one cautious fellow says: "Calm down; will you permit me alone to approach?" I say: "You may." He came in then, and asks: "Who are you and why are you come to Wilno?"

Stefan Czarniecki. Seventeenth-century oil portrait by Matthisen Brodero (d. 1666). Courtesy of the National Museum, Warsaw, Poland.

Charles X Gustavus, King of Sweden, by C. Gralle, 1650. Courtesy of the Library of the University of Warsaw.

Arwid Wittenberg, Swedish general, by the seventeenth-century engraver J. Falck. Courtesy of the Library of the University of Warsaw.

Frederick William, the Great Elector of Brandenburg, by Petr. de Jode, 1657.
Courtesy of the Library of the University of Warsaw.

Frederick III, King of Denmark, by Visscher. Seventeenth-century engraving. Courtesy of the Library of the University of Warsaw.

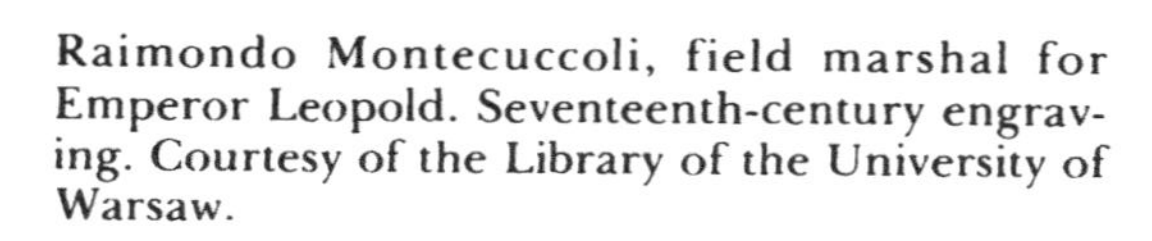

Raimondo Montecuccoli, field marshal for Emperor Leopold. Seventeenth-century engraving. Courtesy of the Library of the University of Warsaw.

Jan Kazimierz, King of Poland. Inscription beginning "nec no suecorum, etc." (but not of the Swedes, etc.) negates his claims to the Swedish throne. Engraving by Wilhelmus Hondius, 1649, from a painting by Daniel Schultz. Courtesy of the Library of the University of Warsaw.

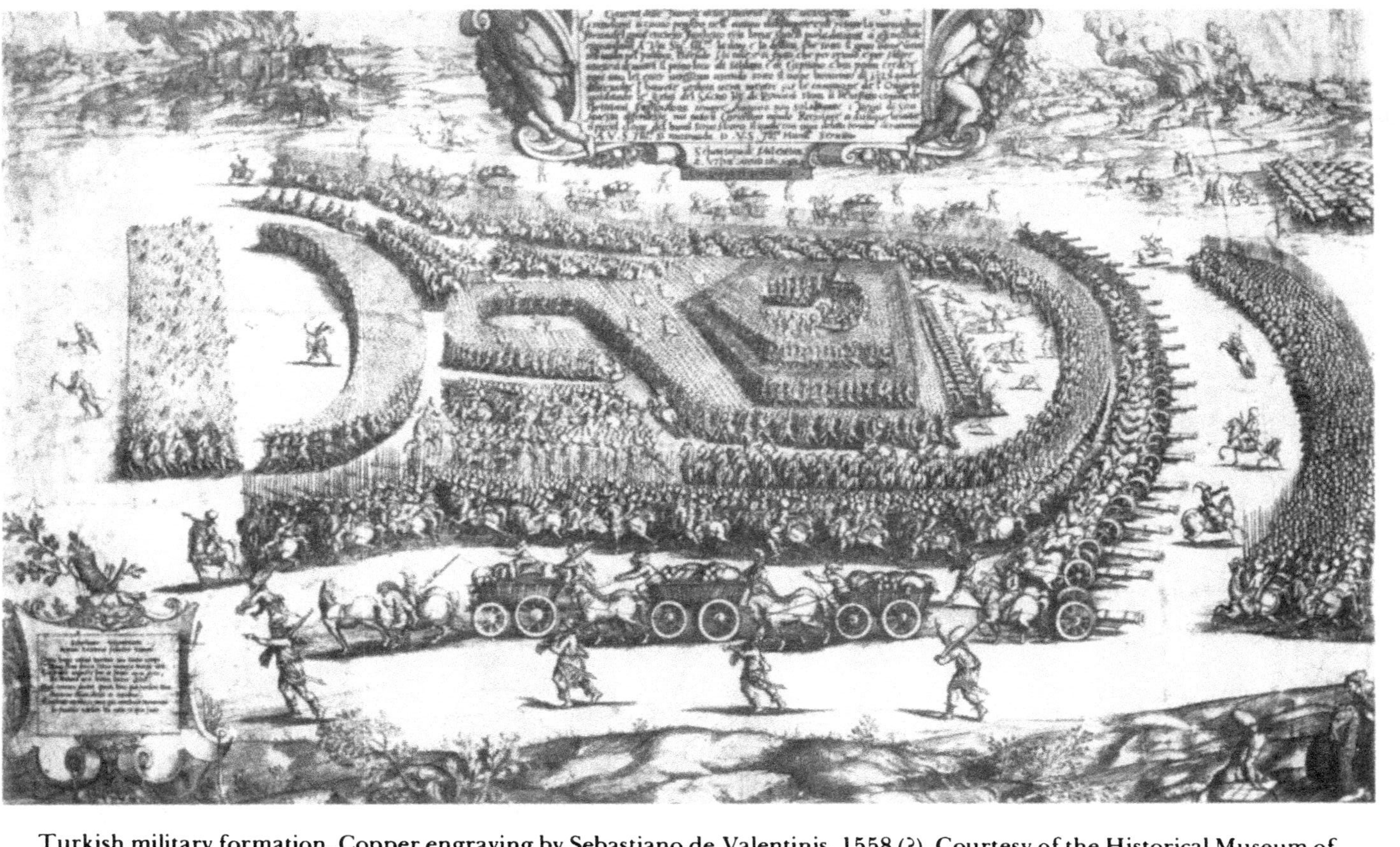

Turkish military formation. Copper engraving by Sebastiano de Valentinis, 1558 (?). Courtesy of the Historical Museum of the City of Warsaw.

Stefan Czarniecki crossing the sound in pursuit of the Swedes, seventeenth-century engraving by Corsi. Courtesy of the Historical Museum of the City of Warsaw.

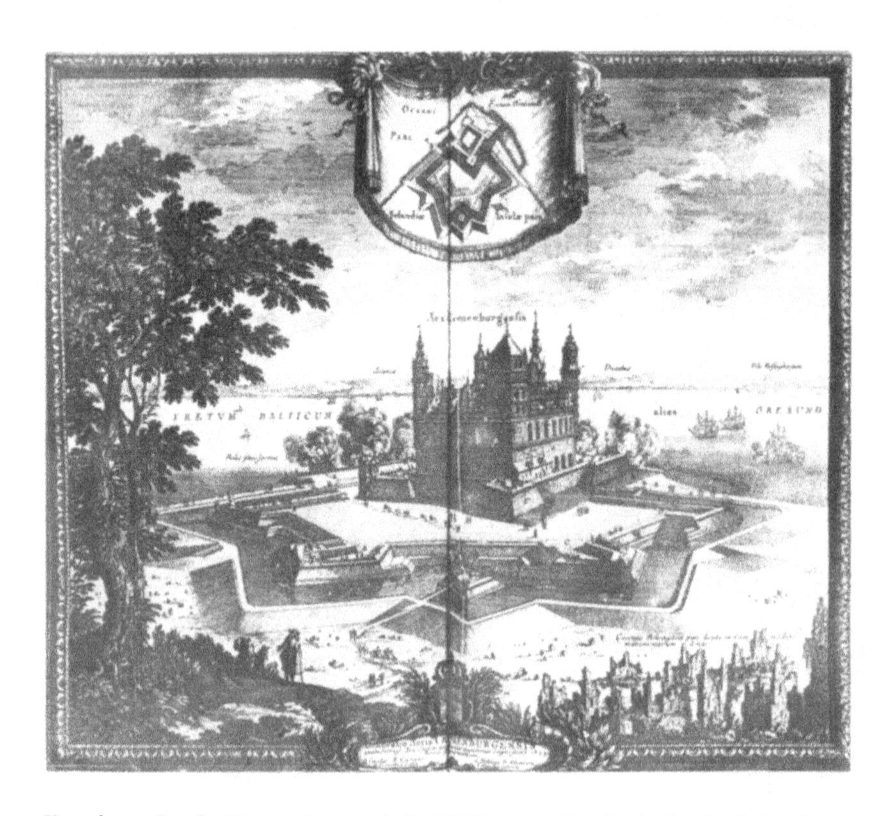

Kronborg Castle. Engraving made in 1659 appearing in Pufendorf's book *De rebus a Carolo Gustavo Sueciae Rege gestis,* Nuremberg, 1729. Courtesy of the Historical Museum of the City of Warsaw.

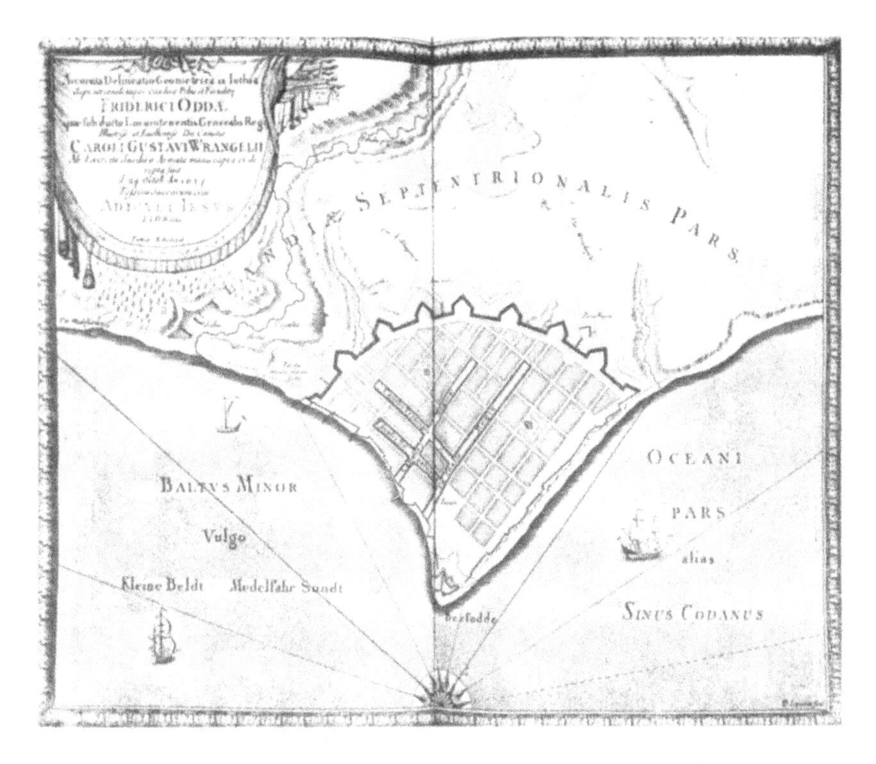

"An Accurate Geometrical Delineation of the Town and Fortress of Friederichs-Odde in North Jutland." Copper engraving by D. Lapointe from a drawing by Dahlberg in Pufendorf's *De rebus a Carlo Gustavo Sueciae Rege gestis,* Nuremberg, 1729. The map confirms Pasek's description; it also shows the Baltic meeting the Ocean just as he thought (see p. 75). Evidently Pasek did not have access to any more accurate map of the region. Courtesy of the Historical Museum of the City of Warsaw.

Styles in seventeenth-century Poland, taken from the drawings of Jan Matejko. Reproduced from Władysław Loziński, *Życie polskie w dawnych wiekach* (12th ed., Kraków: Wydawnictwo Literackie, 1958).

Zakroczym at the time of Rákóczi's invasion in 1657. In foreground, Rákóczi's troops and Cossacks and advancing Swedes. A copper engraving by I. Perelle from a drawing by Dahlberg. Courtesy of the Czartoryski Museum in Kraków.

A view of Pinćzów. Seventeenth-century engraving. Courtesy of the Historical Museum of Warsaw.

Bogusław Radziwiłł, Lithuanian magnate and Calvinist leader. Engraving by J. Falck, 1654. Courtesy of the Library of the University of Warsaw.

Haiduks in seventeenth-century Poland. Reproduced from *Polska i jej dzieje i kultura*, vol. II, by Bystroń, J. *et al.*, 1927. Courtesy of the Historical Museum of the City of Warsaw.

"Election Diet Near Warsaw," drawn and engraved by A. Pilinski. Courtesy of the Historical Museum of the City of Warsaw.

The palace at Wilanów — the terrace. Reproduced from Władysław Loziński, *Życie polskie w dawnych wiekach (12th ed. Kraków: Wydawnictwo Literackie, 1958).*

"Marysieńka" (Maria Kazimiera d'Arquien), Queen of Poland. Francesco Leone. Courtesy of the Czartoryski Museum, Krakow.

A portrait of King Jan III Sobieski surrounded by his family. Courtesy of the Museum of the City of Warsaw.

Kara Mustafa, Turkish Grand Vizier, Engraving by J. Galli (?). Courtesy of the Library of the University of Warsaw.

"Sobieski's Entry into Vienna After Victoriously Routing the Turks in 1683." Courtesy of the Historical Museum of the City of Warsaw.

King Jan III Sobieski's bedchamber in Wilanów. Reproduced from Władysław Loziński, *Życie polskie w dawnych wiekach,* (12th ed. Kraków: Wydawnictwo Literackie, 1958).

Przyiechali tedy porządkiem dobrym. pięknie Offanasy Iwanowicz Nestorow wielki Stolnik Carski, człowiek Familiey Starożytney Moskiewski; Drugi z nim niby to Secretarius Legationis. Iwan Polikarpowicz Dyak. Syn tego Stolnika młody Michayło Boiarow kilkanaście y inszych drobnieyszych czeladzi wszystkich boy coś oprocz woźnicow ludzi wozow samych z legominą y Towarami 40.

Powitaliśmy się tedy z wielką wdzięcznością nazaiutrz Bankiet Carski miał być. przyszedł do mnie wieczorem Michayło Offanasowicz syn tego Stolnika y drugi z nim Boiaryn z oracyią.

Car Ossudar Weliki Biłłoie y czornyiey Rusy. Samoderca y Obładatel tebe ster Pryiatela swoiho prosit za iutra na Biłłużyne koleno y na lebedyie Huzno.

A page from the eighteenth-century copy of Pasek's *Memoirs* now stored in the National Library in Warsaw (p. 191). It includes the transliterated formula used by the Muscovite deputies from the tsar to invite Pasek, their escort, to a banquet of beluga knee and swan's rump.

'Twould not have done to say I'd come to collect payment; nor to say who I was, so as to avoid trouble in case any of them had died there; but knowing that Dąbrowski, a colonel in the Lithuanian army, had several nephews born in Podlasie who served in different squadrons in the Polish army, I said, "I am Żebrowski, I'm here to see my uncle, *Pan* Dąbrowski; I stopped in this deserted house, being unable to find any other quarters, yet even here there is no refuge from attacks." He says to me: "But your attendants were saying, when asked, that your name is Pasek?" I reply: "That's right, for I'm *duorum cognominum;*[89] Pasek-Żebrowski." He asks: "And what is our [confederate] lord chancellor to you?" I told him "he has but the same crest, he's not kin, for he's Pasek-Gosławski,while I'm Pasek—Żebrowski." In such a strait, one had to repudiate both title and kin. He says finally: "But was it not you at the colonel's in Warsaw?" "Not I, but my relative; I was not present at the Diet in Warsaw." Says he then: "Well, we shall find you whenever we need to." I answered that: "I'll give satisfaction in any spot, but so must everyone give to me, who attacks me like a robber; for I'm not guilty of anything toward anyone, nor have I given provocation; I halted peacefully in this deserted spot; and not a copper's damage have I inflicted." He says: "I doubt if you'll have to wait 'til the morrow, for the fellow may be dead before then." I said: "Even had all of them perished on this spot, I'd fear not, for the law's on my side, *licita defensio, invasor a se ipso occiditur.*"[90] He says, "Good night." "Good night." And they went away.

To be sure, I said I was not afraid, but I had other thoughts: God forbid that one of them should die! Although they would release me, yet the procedure itself of a lawsuit, the court investigations, the cost, etc. I think how to slip away from that place, for previous court verdicts had already taught me it's easier to make your way out of a forest than to get out of prison. My experience in Kozierady came to mind, I regretting not having escaped while there was still time, trusting in my innocence; although it ended honorably, my money-bag did much groan. And I began — but very quietly — to set things in order, having invoked the Lord's help. When we were ready, we took our horses and on foot led them through those cruel nettles. And there on the edge of town were those confounded cellars — all that remained after the Muscovite burning — overgrown with nettles and thistles, so that we kept falling, either a horse, or an attendant, or myself — it being a dark night besides — into those craters; then we would rescue each other quietly, until at last we reached the open field and mounted our horses.

89. Of two names.
90. Defense is permissible, the attacker dies at his own hand.

The day was just dawning, stepping into those empty basements, and in all my years, I don't ever recall visiting so many cellars in that one night in Wilno, and in none of them, though we ransacked them thoroughly, was there a morsel of food.

I would have ridden back directly then, but Gosiewski, hetman and under-treasurer of Lithuania had ordered me to come to see him after taking the money, as he was to write to the king. I made a stop then at one butcher's shop; he was pounding beef of which there were a few sides already hanging; the horses wanted not a jot of eating, they only snorted at that stench of raw meat. I went into town alone, after changing into a *kontusz* in which I'd not been seen. I went to my cousin,[91] telling him what had happened. He too thought I should leave and he goes with me at once to the hetman to hasten my despatch. Going out we pass those people on the stairs; they noticing my absence from that abode and knowing now who I was, had come to my cousin to give an account of what happened and to make inquiry concerning me. I recognized one of them at once and I nudge my cousin: "There they are now." My cousin, as if but seeing me out in a courteous way, bade me farewell on the stairs and returned with them; I then, went off to the hetman and thanked him for his kindness; I preferred not to wait for his letter to the king, nor, having heard what happened, was he urging me, but said: "Go and God be with you, for it's a case of brigandage here."

I went from thence to the apothecary sending for my cousin, I not daring to go to his quarters lest someone recognize me. My cousin came to me then and we sat down in a quiet spot to talk. He told me they had inquired whether or not I was his kinsman. He told them: "He's my cousin." To that they reply: "Why, then, did he tell us he was of a different house?" Said my cousin: "In order to fend off your attacks, for he is here on official business, he has no time to act according to the law with you, but through me, he declares he will fight his case *in omni foro*,[92] legal or illegal; as for his charge, I can tell you he is serving with the Governor of Ruthenia, and he who wishes to do so may look for him there." They say: "But of those who got hacked up, three may not live; yet we are most pained by some verses he wrote on the wall before leaving that place, which insult our people."

My cousin replied: "Answer him line for line, and if you feel you are innocent, our armies will someday be joined, remind him of it then." So now my cousin, having recounted their speeches to me, bid me farewell. I went to my quarters but, as before, did not depart until it had grown quite dark, in order to avoid any attacks; and this time I did

91. Pasek's first cousin, the chancellor of the confederacy.

92. In every court.

not travel by the Grodno highway to Poland, as ordinarily I would have, but set out toward Uciana [to the north] turning there toward Podlasie, through which I passed safely. And as I heard later, they were lying in wait for me along the roads leading to Poland, hoping to take revenge; but the Lord did not console them, and by God's grace, those who had been wounded did recover and the matter was forgotten.

I did not go then to Warsaw, for on the way I learned that the king had gone to Lwów to sit on a commission, and my Muscovite envoys had been sent back with a different escort. I came home. Many a one reminds me of the furs I promised to buy in Wilno; all were disappointed as I had not even bought any for myself, scarcely getting away with my life, for I never expected such a vexation as those drunkards to befall me.

After my departure from Wilno, the drunkards somehow got their hands on those treasury registers, wherein I sign for the receipt of 6000 zloties. They, thinking it to be my cousin who was their chancellor and also went by the name of Jan z Gosławic, seized upon that mightily: that he had taken some kind of bribe for some sort of conspiracies and some sort of intrigues, being an army functionary. They made a strong denunciation then in the assembly, claiming to have at heart the good of the army, that "there are such people here to whom we confide our greatest secrets and clearly they are willing to sell us out; one does not take personal bribes for nothing." Fearful clamor, clanking of swords. They were asking: "Who is he? Turn him over to us yourself, we'll soon make mincemeat of him." *Ad tot instantias*[93] he had to explain what he had brought up at the assembly: "Not without reason did the chancellor take 6000 zloties from the treasury. I saw the signature in the books for his receipt of that sum." But the blockhead did not know his hand, he *simpliciter* knew the name only and the place it was written. They say to him: "Do you have proof?" "I do." Some bellow: "Smite him!" Others: "Let him give account of himself."

Kinsmen from his mother's side were panic-stricken, fearing it might be proven; but he is not upset in the least, for no evil was done, he says only: "My Lords, I know in how high a degree of Your Lordship's service I have been installed; all, *minutissima quaeque arcana,*[94] come to my attention; and I know that were I not ruled by my honesty and by that stainless fidelity wherein you have placed your fraternal trust, there is much damage I could cause. Were I to feel guilty of that which is ascribed to me, everyone will admit that I, of my own accord would write the cruellest verdict of death for myself, and I say now: if I've taken those 6000, even though committing thereby no evil, then con-

93. To so many demands.
94. Even the smallest secrets.

sider me a traitor and punish me as a traitor; only thus: let them prove it to me: I will surrender." And the other one storms: "I shall prove it; only I beg His Lordship the Under-Treasurer to have the books brought, those which I have already indicated." The under-treasurer then sent for the secretary to come and to bring the books and tell them what's what.

The spirit moved them at last, they thinking to save their kinsman after all, and themselves from being put to shame. These eminent men, local families they were, the Biernackis, Sokolnickis, Chreptowicz's, and other kin of theirs, no sooner hearing these words, but several of them at once stood beside him — the accuser — so he should conceal nothing. The register being brought, they put it into his hands: "Find it, where did you see it?" He found it directly and carries it, gloating, to the marshal. My cousin says: "Let me have that book, I beg of you," as if not knowing what was in it; after looking at it, he says: "My Lords, as I once declared, I shall gladly bear the penalty from your hands, and I do so declare now, if you can show I am guilty of what they ascribe to me; if you cannot, then let it be reciprocal, let him who accuses without proof do penance, for he who takes away my reputation takes my life. I know that in the army not many are to be found who would not know the handwriting whereby I serve Your Lordships in all official matters. There is a signature for 6000 taken; but if it was I took it and with blame, I shall bear the calumny; I place it upon your laps, My Lords."

One and another takes a look: "It's not his! Not his signature!" Now then they ask whose it is, as both first name and surname are the same, different only is the handwriting. He said that "my cousin from the Polish army received the money for such and such service on order from his Majesty the king." All those *insultus* which had begun to burst over my cousin, now turned against the informer. Now some are shouting: "Take him to court!" Others: "Strike the son of an infidel who brings such gossip to an assembly of knights!" The fellow tries to slip away, but when Sokolnicki, a lieutenant, clubs him in the back of the head, he fell down. Now do they pound him, flog him, trample him under foot, so that Żeromski, the marshal, could scarcely protect the fellow's life.

Directly from that time, they began to prepare Gosiewski's funeral, the poor devil; that being the first occasion of *suspicionis* about him, for they shouted at once: "Forsooth, My Lord Hetman, you've no money for the army, but for any order of payment from the king, you'll find it forthwith. Could you not, belike, hold back on those orders until more favorable times, but improve matters for us now? All well and good, if you had not hurt any one by that!" The hetman explained he had had to do it on account of the urgency of his Majesty's appeal, and would have had to count it out of his own purse; but these excuses carried no weight. From that time on they more and more mistrusted him and the assemblies grew more and more tumultuous. And also, more and more men of the army were giving themselves up to revels in consequence whereof one could hardly expect gravity and order, but rather roguish misdeeds, the which soon came true when they hacked up their own marshal, Kazimierz Żeromski, a very distinguished man, the Czeczera district supervisor, and later, Gosiewski, the Lithuanian field hetman and under-treasurer; having ordered him to prepare for death, they shot him *deliberatissime*[95] on but one tiny suspicion and a false witness; in these disturbances many other soldiers were put to death; for which crime, several colonels died a cruel death in Warsaw at the next Diet, drawn and quartered, namely, Niewiarowski, Jastrzębski, and others [January 3, 1665.]. Those whom they had been unable to apprehend, they sentenced to infamy.[96] My cousin, on the other hand, had to enter into the *consilium* of that brutal murder, as their counsel and chancellor. He managed to escape both death and infamy in this way:

Fleeing those who were from the other division, that is, the field hetman's, who were nabbing those cutthroats and were riding on his trail, he fled as far as the Berezyna river, frozen at that time; and in the middle of the river was an opening in the ice, which had not frozen over completely; he dismounting, smashed the ice over that opening, which was thin, with his battle-axe so that it looked as if he had fallen through the ice while escaping at night, not having perceived the dangerous opening; at the edge of the opening in the ice, he trampled the snow, as if trying to save himself, his cap he tossed on the very edge, and the cover off his pistolet he flung into the water where it thus floated, and he walked backward along the same trail, then mounting his horse, bolted from the track into the forest, with only one other man — the which forest is very dense and extends along the bank of the Berezyna; he made his way as far as Smolensk to his brother, *Pan* Piotr, who had become a subject of the Muscovite tsar — all his property won in battle by Muscovy he holds in the Smolensk region — and he did not leave until amnesty had been declared.

Those tracking him down, having come to the Berezyna and seeing that broken place, picked up the cap at the water's edge and the pistolet-cover in the water. They decided he had drowned, and returning to that noble's estate from whence he had escaped, they showed the cap, where it was better known, they told what they had seen: there were no more tracks in the snow beyond that opening; so it was

95. In cold blood.
96. A legal penalty which abrogated or limited a citizen's rights.

concluded that he'd drowned. A lament went up then in that house, but his pursuers rejoiced, saying: "*Poena peccati.*"[97] So then, when the names and surnames of those who murdered and those who were aware of the murders were published at the Diet and the news of their infamy trumpeted about, his too was included; but some deputies countered that (those who believed him dead; others, his kinsmen, who knew he was alive) saying: "Most Gracious Majesty, God has already performed the execution; why should we include him here, if he's no longer alive?" And they had it erased. And he himself directly after the Diet, left Muscovy and lived safely at home; while those condemned to infamy tossed about until the next Diet, at which all except a few were accorded a general amnesty on the recommendation of the whole Commonwealth in the Diet; for the wife of a deceased, having been left a widow, did not allow those more blameworthy, to share in the amnesty, anticipating their capture.

But when the others were thanking the king for the amnesty granted them, my cousin also appeared among those gathered, being, at the time, a deputy from Lithuania; he explained that, although *in consilio impiorum,*[98] he was obliged to be, as a duty exacted by the whole army. The king, guffawing, said: "When counseling others, you counseled badly, but you managed well enough for yourself, and so you should have, so it shall be chronicled." Not until the third Diet was this matter settled.

I return *ad statum anni huius.*[99] While the commission in Wilno held forth with carousing and brawling, another was going on in Lwów in a somewhat more orderly and decent fashion than in Lithuania, and to better effect, for by God's grace a way was found to pacify the army; they had coppers struck; silver-coppers were also struck wherein there was but 18 groschen worth of silver, but as they were valued at one zloty and given such an inscription: *Dat pretium servata salus potiorque metallo est.*[1] From that time on, the value of all silver coin and gold went up in Poland.[2]

At that time, a few Polish weathercocks did contrive to import Wallachian coppers into Poland, a lot of gold and silver coins being spent abroad on them, for which evil deed these schemers are unworthy of

97. The penalty for sin.
98. In the council of the impious.
99. To the events of this year.
1. The value which is the preservation of the common good is worth more than metal.
2. The number of coppers in a groschen (3) as well as the number of groschen in a zloty (30) remained the same; only the worth of the precious metal was diminished, as a result of which a zloty struck at that time was worth more or less 18 old groschen. From that time on, coins were differentiated. Those struck earlier were called "good," the new ones "bad."

being titled in the name of our Polish people and will be obliged to do no small accounting to God, for those Wallachian coppers caused sore impoverishment, desperation, and dreadful murders among the people.[3] Starting from Lwów, they killed each other for them at country fairs, and after the coins receded from Małopolska, they gravitated to Wielkopolska, spreading as far as the Oder river and the Baltic Sea like a plague of locusts.

The commission in Lwów, where Paweł Borzęcki, the confederate deputy marshal, a great warrior, perished *non sine suspicione veneni*[4] — according to the whispers — "for so it had to be," they said, "that candle lighting up the entire confederacy had to be extinguished so that from its brightness an even greater flame might not be kindled"; for in the whole confederacy there was none above him.

3. Wallachian coppers were struck in Suczawa and flowed into Poland in the amount of around twelve million, becoming for many the cause of economic ruin.
4. Not without suspicion of poisoning.

The Year Of Our Lord 1663

The confederacy being dissolved, the army fell into confusion; those squadrons toward whom resentment was greatest were disbanded. Who can tell where people scattered? Some men settled down and took a wife, seeing the *ingratitudinem;* others who had been good soldiers grew soft and gave themselves up to swilling — fearful it was to see. The king set off, then, *in persona sua* for parts beyond the Dnieper; but, since the confederacy, our fortune had changed, as had the hearts of our men; their ardor was no longer the same. The enemy had grown stronger, while we had accomplished nothing more worthy than besooting a few chicken coops [Pasek means castles] with cannon smoke, the which, before the confederacy, we would have devoured entirely; and we lost excellent men, returning home with nothing. And thus, discovering a considerable turn in fortune, or to speak more truly, God's grace no longer favoring our cause, we finished that year.

The Year of Our Lord 1664

There was the battle of Stawiszcze — nothing to write about, nothing to praise.[1] We, having had enough of war with the enemy, took a fancy of a sudden to try war with each other, for the reason, perchance, that in such a circumstance we might establish another confederacy, the profits from the first having now evaporated and we wishing to pack our bellies with similar riches.

Having made peace with Muscovy on wretched conditions, returning bountiful damages for the licking we gave them, we, not even touching their possessions, yet failed to recover our own, which they had taken from us before, and even increased theirs by ceding large territories;[2] thus gladly did we begin a civil war, the which is *malum supra omne malum.*[3] A Diet was convened, at which Jerzy Lubomirski, our hetman and grand marshal, was to be tried for having aspirations to the throne *post fata regnantis.*[4]

The king himself remonstrated with him first, saying: "Marshal, it has come to our knowledge that you're hoping for the Crown." He answered: "Who would not wish the best for himself? I will tell Your Majesty a story which I heard about the castellan of Wojnicz [Jan Wielopolski]. His haiduks having brought him from the royal castle, they set him in his armchair in his room, and he asked his favorite haiduk: "Andrys, what do your people say about our Diet" The haiduk answers in his way: *"Ot, milostivy Pane, koliesmo Tvoiu Pansku Milost na zamok prinesli, wsi heducy, bratia nashi khovorili tak: ot tomu by to panu korolem polskiem, shcho khozhikh pakholkov derzhyt pri sobi,*[5] For that piece of news the castellan tipped the haiduk 10 silver

1. The siege of Stawiszcze in the Ukraine lasted from July to October 1664.
2. The ceasefire with Muscovy was concluded only in 1667; the Dnieper lands together with Kiev were ceded to Muscovy.
3. The worst of all evils.
4. After the death of the ruler. In fact, Lubomirski was indicted for weakening the throne of Jan Kazimierz, by acting as a protector of the confederates, but not for aspiring to the crown.
5. "My Gracious Lord, when we carried Your Gracious Lordship to the castle, the

thalers. Consider, Your Majesty, if such a cripple, who by his own power, cannot even turn over in his own bed, is pleased to hear about himself reigning as king, so much the more am I, who still, by the grace of God, can mount a horse unaided; should someone, of his own accord, ask me to rule over them as king, I would not be much displeased. If therefore, *post fata* of Your Majesty, to whom I wish health and a long reign, such men as the castellan of Wojnicz, the castellan of Gniezno [Alexander Sielski], and the like were to announce their candidacy *ad regnandum*,[6] then I would be among them; should it be men such as the Muscovite tsar, the Swedish king, the French king, then I would be prepared to withdraw my candicacy at once."

Although the king laughed at his answer, in his heart he had already conceived a hatred to which people had incited him, especially Prażmowski, the blind archbishop of Gniezno. That traitor was the chief fomenter of this war. The which crime, being displeasing to heaven itself, brought down the wrath of God upon our country, for at the very time they began to consult about it, a terrible and huge comet appeared in the sky, the which, lasting several months, threatened the sight of men with its relentlessness, and the longer it lasted, the more it struck terror into our horrified hearts, omening unfortunate events, the which later did occur, owing to the rancor and intriguing of evil men, who in promoting their own interests, brought our country to even greater ruin than the enemy. For the truth is, that Lubomirski, seeing his lord *ultimum in linea domus regiae, domus Iagiellonicae, sine successione*,[7] seeing Queen Ludwika's embitterment and intrigues, she being by birth a French woman determined to *inducere gallicismum*[8] upon our freedom by installing a French dandy [Henri Bourbon] on the throne and seeing that even the king was being led by the nose, if he allowed the chancery office to send notices to the pre-Diet assemblies in the provinces, *proponendo novam electionem stante vita;*[9] more Frenchmen there were in Warsaw than fanned Cerberus' fires, throwing money around, carrying on intrigues — mainly nocturnal, enjoying great freedom in Warsaw and great esteem; they performed triumphal spectacles in honor of their victories, even though invented and not real; at court a Frenchman can always gain entry, while a Pole must stand nearly half the day at the door; 'tis, to be brief, a sorely exaggerated esteem.

haiduks, good fellows all, spoke thus: such a master who keeps a hundred fine lads at his side should be king of Poland."

6. For ruler.
7. The last in the line of the Jagiellonian dynasty, without a successor.
8. Impose the French form of government.
9. Proposing a new election in his lifetime.

Among their divers privileges I must mention this one: in Warsaw they were allowed to perform *in theatro publico*[10] a triumphal celebration of a victory over the German [Austrian] emperor. Upon bringing the actors to the *theatrum* along with the music and fireworks for the celebration, a mob of people gathered to view so marvelous a *spectaculum;* some came on horseback, being either on their way out of Warsaw or arriving; whoever took notice, though his affair be urgent, stayed to watch this wondrous performance. And I too was there, for I was departing from Warsaw. Having left my lodgings, I, too, stopped thus on horseback with my retainers to watch these wonders. *Circa hoc spectaculum*[11] were standing people of different rank and temper. The French performed divers scenes: now armies attacked, now the foot and horse closed ranks, now one side gave up the field to another, now Germans were taken prisoner and beheaded, now a fortress was stormed and taken — in short, such things were performed at great expense and sumptuously. No sooner had the emperor's army been routed, as it were, and the enemy defeated in the field, but they bring in the emperor bound in chains, in his imperial robes but no longer wearing the imperial crown on his head, carrying it instead in his hands and surrendering it to the French king.

We saw, of course, that the man impersonating the emperor in chains was a prominent Frenchman — he knew how to imitate his outer bearing and he stuck out his lip like the emperor. One of the Poles on horseback began to yell at the French actors: "Kill that son of a so-and-so now that you've got him; don't spare him, for if you let him go, he'll wage war after war, shed men's blood, and the world will never see peace; kill him and the French king will gain the *imperium,* he'll be emperor, and, God willing, he'll be king of Poland. But if you don't kill him, I'll kill him in the end." And if he doesn't seize his bow, insert an arrow, and now pierces Sir Emperor's side so hard that out comes the tip on the other side; he did him in. The Poles to their bows, they take after that French mob, shooting at them, even wounding the one sitting *in persona* of the king; he fell from the throne under the *theatrum* onto his crown and then fled away with the other Frenchmen.

Warsaw was in an uproar then. Those who had done the shooting rode off, each going his own way; I myself immediately made off lest I be somehow mistakenly suspect, I too having been part of that throng. Having ridden half a mile beyond Warsaw in the direction of Tarczyn, I left my bow with *Pan* Łączyński to escape suspicion, then rode on slowly, taking only my hunting piece, for I expected them to give chase. And something of the sort did happen, for Queen Ludwika, though an

10. On the public stage.
11. Around this spectacle.

imperiosus mulier,[12] to whom one could safely apply the saying coined for another monarch: *Rex erat Helisabeth, verum regina Jacobus, imperiosus mulier,*[13] shedding her haughtiness, fell at the king's feet, begging him to pursue them, to seize them. The king gave the order then, for whoever could do so, to take to the highways and bring this affair to a speedy end, only *sine effectu;* for whomever they overtook and asked, "From whence do you come riding? Was it not you who killed the emperor and wounded the French king?" [The answer was] "Not I," and they let him be.

The which query reached my ears too, only not until the following day. I stopped in to visit *Pan* Okuń; glad he was to see me; I'm telling him of this tragedy when a few dozen horse came riding into the village asking: "Was anyone riding through here from Warsaw?" They rode there, they enter the house: *"Servus." "Servus."* My host asked them to be seated. And they ask me: "From whence is Your Honor riding?" Say I: "From Warsaw." "When did Your Worship leave?" Say I: "After the death of the Christian emperor and the king of France." Did you see it happen?" "I saw it." "What sort of person was it who took the first shot at the emperor?" Say I: "Someone like Your Honor and myself." Says he, laughing: "Was it not you yourself, Your Honor?"I answer: "Bows and arrows they were using there, while I came here without a quiver." Says he: "Even were it Your Honor who did it, or whoever else, you've the Lord's forgiveness for taking up the cudgels in such a mighty outrage; his Majesty the king expresses his sympathy only in the Queens sight; in his heart he's amused by it." They then, having a hearty chortle over that converstion and making merry, drank up a barrel of my host's beer, and a second, and away they rode.

Such was the great esteem for the French under Queen Ludwika that whatsoever they could conjure up they were allowed to do. Arriving at the palace, entering the royal chambers, seldom would you see a real head of hair, but huge boxes [wigs] instead of heads, that nearly shut out the light from the windows. Some Poles, taking note of these circumstances, grumbled at the court's infatuation with this people; already ministers of state were dancing *ad Galli cantum.*[14] We with our own Polish freedom had no taste for it and made light of it all, for *ad Galli cantum non timet iste leo.*[15]

Pan Lubomirski, seeing then what was afoot, took some measures which must not have pleased everyone; though without seeking it, he himself enjoyed *magnam popularitatem* with the army and the gentry;

12. Imperious termagant.
13. Elizabeth, an imperious termagant, was king, but James queen.
14. To the cock's tune. (A play on words: *gallus* is rooster, *Gallus* is Frenchman.)
15. The lion does not fear a singing cock.

many a time, owing to some kindness of his, you could hear officers complimenting him during their carouses, as often happens, in these words: "You, O worthy Sir, ought to be king here." And he too, mindful of his own esteem and services in our country would say: "It's in your hands, my dear fellows." And there's nothing to wonder at, for *quisque suae fortunae faber;*[16] I've never read of anyone cutting himself off *ex occasione regnandi.*[17] For these reasons people were led to conjecture that he desired the great dignity of the throne; the which desire, even should he have manifested it openly by becoming a candidate, would be no cause to try him, it being common for everyone to wish this for himself, and it was not an angel we chose for the throne but a man; not a crown prince did we elect but a Polish nobleman; and in support of my sentiment I shall mention that we nominated Polanowski as a candidate, who was, at the time, but a lieutenant, formerly a cavalier with but two retainers under the command of *Pan* Lubomirski. If then, Wiśniowiecki, Polanowski could be called up for that privilege, there would be no cause for anger if Lubomirski were to be summoned in a free election. Since *spiritus ubi vult spirat,*[18] if God inclines our hearts to someone, 'tis an act of the Divine Will. But what would Envy do, wicked stepmother to the virtuous? "Shoe a horse and the frog will also lift her foot," so they say. Those fawning counselors, who forever counseled their lord badly, had hardened the king's heart towards Lubomirski.

The queen, perceiving that projects to support a Frenchman would come to nought should a Pole be elected, so much the more strenuously did she exert herself, both through her own persistent pleading and through those counselors who having shown some sympathy and good will, only desired to milk the French goat even more; others *sub praetextu* of their obliging demeanor at court had their own personal ends in view, reckoning: "Who can say whether I too shan't be called to the throne?" And the king, *flexibilis*[19] as always, went along with whatever they advised; he so believed in the advice of his blind counselor in particular, that even though the advice was the worst, it seemed as sound to him as if *ex ore Apollinis;*[20] his country might perish, but that was of no consequence, as long as it pleased him.

It was resolved then to try *Pan* Lubomirski. Witnesses are brought; because of villainous people, they're bribed to testify against him. Some deputies, being decent gentry from the provinces, looked *a fine,*[21] to the consequences of this, and defended him *potentissime* but had much

16. Each man is the maker of his own fate.
17. From the chance to rule.
18. The Spirit bloweth where it listeth.
19. Vacillating.
20. From the lips of Apollo.
21. To the final result.

ado to gain the upperhand. Tumult, great commotion in Warsaw; the entire Ukraine, as before, in rebellion; and still we do not perceive our peril. The verdict was: *infamia, exilium,* and *privatio.*[22] The *malevoli*[23] rejoiced, but our country groaned, knowing what suffering lay ahead. In the district dietines and assemblies, some praise, others condemn it; there are already rumours of another confederacy in the army; even the sky was so obscured with black clouds of misfortune, that no one could say there would be a fine spring in our country; no need for star-gazers to make clear that which the coming year would bring to our homeland, so much devastation, so much shedding of innocent blood.

22. Loss of good name, exile, and removal from offices.
23. The evil-intentioned.

The Year of Our Lord 1665

Civil war broke out *ex ratione* that *civis opressus* [Lubomirski].[1] The army went into a confederacy, choosing Ostrzycki as marshal and Borek as deputy. Forty good squadrons joined the confederacy, especially such as had a close tie to his lordship, *Pan* Lubomirski: his own, his brother's, his son's, his brother-in-law's, and several of his next of kin and good friends. Some 60 squadrons went over to the king's side. Command over these, however, was maintained by the Ruthenian Governor [Stanisław Jan Jabłonowski] in the king's stead; he set off with them from Białacerkiew toward Zasław; the confederates meanwhile set off toward Lwów, then toward Sambor, there to establish a *sedem belli.*[2] Those of us who had not joined the confederacy, were ordered to scoot off toward Lwów. Twelve thousand of the better-trained Cossacks they enlisted; while the entire Ukraine rose up in savage revolt, seeing the time was ripe. Such was the harvest of our blood we had shed for this villainous people!

We sent to the Tartar Horde, inviting them to join that war. The Khan promised to raise 100,000 at once, but later sent word "he would not do so," promising to render his services another time, but not in this war, where brother against brother has taken up the sword.

The Lithuanian army led out by the king was a good one and well-trained, but so hungry were they, so mighty their appetites, that it was as if a dozen pigsties had been opened; great brigands they were; but they also paid dearly for it at Częstochowa: in this place where people receive favors and indulgences, they received a flogging.

The provinces took different sides: some the king's, others Lubomirski's. Kraków and the castellan of Kraków, Warszycki, personally, as well as Poznań, Sandomierz, Kalisz, Sieradz, Łęczyca took up arms *pro parte* of Lubomirski. Others wanted to do the same but did not dare, owing to their close proximity to the king; but neither did the king summon them to take part in the war, for not only did he not trust

1. A citizen had been victimized.
2. Headquarters.

them, but he was confident of the forces he had. He also expected to win over to his side all those who joined Lubomirski's, and even Lubomirski himself, for so his blind counselor had promised.

[The passage omitted here is considered by Brückner and others to have come from a pen other than Pasek's.]

. . . the king led out to the field an army that was in quite good order. And I too had to present myself in their midst, though I had no mind to be a royalist; however, my squadron was part of that army, the which notwithstanding, we more ardently desired victory for the other side, seeing the insult fo Lubomirski, and in his person, to the whole nobility. For the fury against him was over nothing so much as his being *potens manu et consilio*[3] to impede the election of Conde, whom Queen Ludwika was trying *omnibus modis* to place on the throne.[4] Even the king of France himself was openly assisting, *ex ratione* that he'd be glad to see France rid of Conde, as he was very *factiosus* and *nummosus*[5] and nearly enjoyed more *popularitatem in regno Galliae*[6] than the king himself; the French king was afraid the *affectus populi*[7] might be swayed toward Conde in the event of some turn of fortune; the second reason was that with a Frenchman reigning in Poland, they could strangle the Emperor between themselves and snatch his imperial crown: so they poured money into Poland to gain their own ends.

The army then assembled in the provinces of Rawa and Mazowsze, hearing that Lubomirski was now near Krzepice, having come out of his Wrocław exile.[8] The king had quite a fine army, but alas, all his hopes collapsed after Czarniecki's death [February 16, 1665]. He had given him the field hetman's mace hoping to accomplish everything through him! How to bring Lubomirski *ad humilitatem et submissionem* – this, Czarniecki, like a great warrior, would have known how to accomplish; but to bring in Condé *per promotionem*[9] of Czarniecki — that he would never have done, for I know what he thought about that election.[10]

3. Powerful in deed and word.
4. The Prince de Condé in fact did conspire against the king and only made peace with him in 1660. The aim of French policy as reported by Pasek corresponds to the truth: the encirclement of the German states with the help of Poland. This is what Mazarin mainly had in view when he consented to the candidacy of a French prince for the throne of Poland.
5. Scheming and affluent.
6. Popularity in the kingdom of France.
7. Sympathies of the people.
8. Krzepice is a small town near Częstochowa; Lubomirski, having been condemned to exile, sojourned from December 1664 to April 1665 in Sląsk (Silesia), chiefly in Wrocław (Breslau).
9. Through the aid.
10. Not true, for Czarniecki belonged to the French party and even took money from the deputy de Lumbres.

And so his Majesty the king happily set forward with her Majesty the queen, the ladies-in-waiting, and the entire court from Warsaw for that war. And that ladies were present so befitted this dance of pursuit — for it was no war, it was a dance of pursuit — we ever chasing from place to place, but catching no one; they escaping from us yet not escaping, giving us ever more of a beating — like those Mazurians say — "Whoa! A punch I'll deal you / Whack, bang in the belly!" One gentrywoman in Sieradz province gave the king a sound scolding for this fruitless chase, they having caused her great damage, and she came to the king to complain. The king, having made some contentment in money, says to her: "Forgive me, *Pani*, so it goes in this war; we pursue that traitor and he escapes." But the gentrywoman says: "But Your Gracious King, a curious pursuit it is indeed; being able to catch up, yet not to do so; I may be an old woman, but I'd still take it upon myself today to go after him and catch him." The king, abashed, gave her something more.

We lay in camp between Rawa and Głuchów,[11] a village belonging to Sułkowski [vice-governor of Rawa]; the royal couple was stopping, however, at the Jesuit School.[12] The king grew bored in the place and said to his men: "Would there not be some noble in the vicinity whom we might visit, for I've grown weary being several weeks in this place." They recommend this one and that one, two miles away, three miles. Says the king: "But I would have him close by so that I may return for supper." One speaks up: "There is somebody, Gracious King, a courteous gentleman, *Pan* Sułkowski; he lives just beyond the camp, he will be pleased to welcome Your Majesty." The king then ordered them to make ready, and he set forth with the queen. We know nothing, we're quaffing beer, playing cards — for I too was there, *Pan* Sułkowski being a friend of my father's and myself — several officers were there too; when suddenly, in comes a servant: "Their Royal Highnesses are riding to visit you, will they disturb you?" My host jumps up: "I'll be pleased to receive His Highness, I await him with pleasure." I hear his wife saying: "Pleased are you! The devil's gotten into you! Hold on!" But we knew not what she was about. Then all of them descend, the king still a short distance off. He soon comes riding through the gate on horseback, the queen was sitting in a carriage in the rear. Sułkowska asked me: "My dear fellow, show me which one is the king, I have never met him. I know that he dresses in the German style, but I see several Germans and know not which one of them is he." I then, knowing not why she asks it, tell her: "that one on the horse between those two."

She then, approaching him, kneels, and raising her folded hands to the sky, says: "Oh just God! (the king, being about to dismount, stop-

11. Głuchów is a village a few kilometers west of Rawa.
12. In Rawa. (The building is still standing today.) Here Pasek received his education (Pollak, p. 448).

ped still) — if ever you sent divers plagues to punish evil and unjust kings, extortionists, assailants. shedders of innocent human blood, show Your justice today over our king, Jan Kazimierz. Let thunderbolts smite him from a clear sky, let the earth eat him up alive, let not the first bullet miss him, let him endure all those plagues which You sent the Pharoah, for all these wrongs, which we, his miserable people, and the whole kingdom, are suffering!" Her husband stops her mouth, the more does she scold. The king is backing toward the gate; Sułkowski dashes over to him, implores him, clutches his stirrups. "Not on your life! You've an evil-tempered spouse, Sir; I do not wish to, I do not wish to!" He rode off, coming upon the queen: "Go back, this is not the place for us." Upon reaching Rawa the king was amused, the queen in a fury: "I'd have shown her . . . this!" The king says: "That's not necessary; let the injured at least find solace in talk. But, for God's sake, have someone tell Lubomirski it's time he made it up with us, for now even the women are vexing us."

Such a bold dame she was; having given the king a piece of her mind, the next day she came to him, pleading for an audience, instructing them to announce her as the lady to whose home the king rode not wanting to descend from his horse and enter; she begs to make him obeisance. So kind-hearted was the king he caused her to be admitted at once. She explained herself by saying that "I had to act this way from sorrow over the damages done." Most of all she grieved for the birch copse she'd used as a garden close by the manor house; they cut it down to make huts for the camp. Says the king then: "Very well, My Lady, such a privilege I'll give you that in six or seven years time another copse of birch will grow back for you, and now I'll have you paid, only don't be so ill-tempered." He ordered the old woman given 2000 zloties then; she'd not have got so much for that birch brake, even selling it in Rawa at the market; barely 50 zloties she'd have gotten, for 'twas no more than a tuft. But leaving aside these things which went on during the war, I shall proceed with my subject.

When the armies had drawn close together, several thousand of the Polish crown army and the whole Lithuanian army, except for the hussars, were sent out *per modum*[13] of a strong raiding party; they clashed with Lubomirski's troops at Częstochowa [March 4, 1665]. And those Lithuanians, poor souls, when they began to offer themselves up at this place of indulgences, so ardently did they surrender themselves to their contemplations that they sweated blood, and such large votive offerings did they leave behind that they parted with everything they owned. In fine garb they had arrived at that site, on horseback they came, handsomely saddled, and they went home on foot, nearly naked,

13. In the formation.

unless one's clothes or boots were so poor his offering was not accepted. Such a pious people those Lithuanians!

But let us not speak figuratively: when Lubomirski's men swooped down upon Lithuania — and great was their appetite for them on account of Lithuania's meddling in that civil war — they gave them no chance even to form ranks, slashed them to bits, beat them to a pulp. The Lithuanians tried to escape to the cloister; the monks closed the gates, the which angered the king. But not many of them died, except in the first encounter, before their ranks were broken. Many, though, were wounded, driven away from their horses, stripped of their clothes, their armor. Others were humiliated by flogging; and so they turned the Lithuanians into infantry and sent them back to the king; the commanders, however, captains of horse and colonels, they took prisnor. One slyboots, a cavalier, Pustoszyński, [invented name] congratulating Lubomirski, says: "My Gracious Benefactor, God has given us more than we asked Him for." Lubomirski inquires: "How so?" The cavalier replies: "Well, we were always asking: *'Da pacem, Domine! Da pacem Domine!'*[14] We begged Him for one and God gave us five *Paces.*" For there were five Paces among the prisoners, all of them distinguished officers. At that time, there was Pac the chancellor, Pac the hetman, and several bishops named Pac; promoted one another's interests they did. Ensigns, drums were taken; some squadrons had handed their standards to the monks on the walls, and then bought them back the following day.

So then, after this drubbing suffered by the Lithuanians, the confederates had put us to rout; and once again they began to elude us, and we to pursue them; amid bellowing oxen and cows, sending hay stacks and wheat sheaves a-flying. They betook themselves toward Wielkopolska; we rejoiced: "Halt, thief! Now we'll drive you into a corner; now you'll surely not slip away from us, for you'll have to sail across the Baltic to Sweden; meanwhile we'll enjoy Wielkopolska's "little lambs" and cheeses![15] Scorching their trail we are, with high hopes of catching them now somewhere around the Oder or the Baltic Sea, when somehow they slip away from us. Word comes that Lubomirski with his confederates is at our rear; now do we despair of ever catching them, and we begin to deal for peace but, as before, bargaining on the run. Just like that fisherman who, fishing at sea, was unable to catch anything; bone weary, he sat down on the shore, took out his fife, and began to play very beautifully; he reckoning on his song to lure the fish up on the sand, then he'd take as many as he needed. After his respite, he threw in his net once more, for evening was near; fish had collected

14. Grant us peace, O Lord.

15. "Little lambs" *(agnuszki)* were pastry or butter molded in the shape of lambs.

there, it seems, from other places, and he dragged out fish aplenty. No sooner in the net but they began to jump as fish always do, and he, taking his stick, beats the daylights out of them, saying: "Here I played beautifully for you, but you didn't come out to dance, what are you leaping about now for, when nó one is playing for you?" Beat them and pound them he did, then stuffed them into his bag.[16] So it was with *Pan* Lubomirski and his confederates. They agreed to the treaty and called it the treaty of Palczynia.[17] Yet not trusting that pipe, seeing these were *modulamina suspecta,*[18] they withdrew, fearing a trap.

We pursued them then, as long as the weather held out; then we went off to our various positions to prepare ourselves for a better campaign to come.

16. The tale of the fisherman is the ninth tale by Babrios, a Greek writer of fairytales in the third century B.C. The Polish Renaissance writer Mikołaj Rej versified the tale in one of his *Figliki*" (no. 202).
17. November 8 the ceasefire was concluded in Palczynia. The treaty of Palczynia, despite Pasek's assertion, ended the military actions in 1665.
18. Suspicious melodies.

The Year of Our Lord 1666

Such was the *anticipative prophetia* for this year: *"Dum annus ter 6 numerabit, Marcus Alleluia cantabit, Joannes in Corpore stabit (Joannes Casimierus regnabit,* someone added later), *Polonia vae! vae! ingeminabit."*[1] And so it turned out that St. Mark's day did fall on Easter and St. John's *inter octavas Corporis Christi,*[2] and the prophecy was proven true when many a soldier as well as many a poor landowner cried out *vae!*

They called the Diet into session in order to bring about a peace, but hard it is to quench a fire when the flames have reached the roof. I went to that Diet at my own expense in order to give ear to the issues and to see what was going on. I saw enough intrigues, God Almighty! On both sides, and so cunning were they, so devious, that he'd need to write a whole book whoever wanted to describe what took place during that Diet.

In this place then, I exhort those young persons who will be reading what I've written, to make every effort, upon finishing school, to listen to and observe the sessions of the Diets. If he cannot come at his own expense, he should enter the service of some deputy or some young lordship, provided only he can be present at a few Diets; even if you're serving in the army, you should ride to the Diet several times during your winter quartering, even as I did, with your hetman or commander. For everyone ought to attend every session, and listen *diligentissime.* And when the Chamber of Deputies moves upstairs[3] where the sessions sometimes are held, and they call out: "Whoever is not a deputy, please withdraw!" One should try, as I did, to make the acquaintance of at least one of the marshals, so that in bowing to them, I

1. When the year will have three sixes, when Mark will sing "Alleluja," when John will appear on Corpus Christi (someone added later, Jan Kazimierz will be reigning) Poland will groan: woe! woe!
2. Within the octave of Corpus Christi. In fact, St. John's Day fell on the same day as Corpus Christi.
3. Usually at the end of the Diet, the Deputies went upstairs to the Senatorial Chamber, where both houses conducted sessions in the king's presence.

should, through the good offices of important people, never be ousted from the hall: for "I rode here expressly so that I might *imbibere* something *in hac palaestra;*[4] I'll reveal no secrets." The marshal would say: "Very well, I commend your noble inclination." So, while they chased the others out of the hall, I simply nodded to the marshal, while the others crammed headlong through the door, some getting a cane on the neck; then did my companions wonder: "What luck you have! I hid myself behind the stove, yet was forced to leave, while you sat through it all." They did not know I'd cajoled the marshal into it.

So *diligentissime* did I give ear then, that I had no desire even to eat. And at the close of the Diet, when the session lasted the entire night, then, too, I sat through it all. So, to everyone I'll say this: all the public meetings in the world are but a shadow in contrast to the Diets. You'll learn manners, you'll learn the law, you'll learn that which in school, as I live and breathe, you were never taught; I wish everyone might do what I did.

The Diet was in session then, throughout the whole winter,[5] at great cost and much ado, yet, as before, neither side came to any agreement, only to greater embitterment and exasperation.

On the Monday after Easter,[6] the son of the crown treasurer, *Pan* Krasiński, who married *Panna* Chodkiewicz, moved to the palace of the crown equerry, [Alexander] Lubomirski; the king was present. The queen fell very ill (she'd been sick during Lent too). Word is sent to the king that Her Majesty the queen was feeling very poorly. The king, making merry, was in his cups, he says: "Nothing will happen to her." Again they come:"Her Majesty the queen is dying." The king slaps his gentleman of the chamber in the face: "Don't tell tales when I'm making merry." A great throng of us, officers and courtiers, were standing around the king when this occurred; we saw it and we heard his words. They began to murmur among themselves: "So the king would be glad to get rid of this badger who muddles his head." And, indeed, that is how the matter stood. The king was jolly, he danced all night. Seldom was he downcast, good fortune or bad, notwithstanding; he was always the same. He called out to the treasurer's son *in haec verba:* "Host, press the officers to eat, give them a warm welcome; let them remember your feast!: Then he urged us: "Quaff some on this skinflint!" Drink we did, then, for good cheer, and danced, and made merry.

Queen Ludwika, an obstinate woman and determined to have her

4. Imbibe (something) in this school.
5. In fact the Diet lasted only six weeks in early spring — March 17 to May 4.
6. This story, according to Pollak, belongs in the year 1667 along with the news of the queen's death.

way, upon seeing that her plans for electing a Frenchman were not proceeding as she had expected, was eaten up with worry; having gone to much expense, her purse being ruined, her health impaired by worry and the strain of sitting up day and night behind a partition in the Senators' Chamber in order to see and hear how those hired mouths of hers were furthering her schemes, she took sick sometime after the fifth Sunday of Lent, barely lived through Easter Week, and then she died [May 10, 1667]. After her decease, the French lost their greatest support, while those who opposed them took heart. The advancement of Condé began to falter immediately; blind Prażmowski, and those who had promoted Condé *plenis buccis*[7] failed in their endeavor and, like the queen, were overtaken by death, and the Lord overturned their plans as His Holy Will would have it.

However, I've let my pen wander *ad eventum belli civilis;*[8] as He had from the beginning, so God, up to the end, upheld the side of the innocent. The armies went out upon the field, Lubomirski deferred to his lord, his king, but he did defend himself when sore pressed; and we pursued them when they fled from us. The armies clashed at Mątwy [Montwy]; the distance between each other was more than a mile across the ford.[9] The next day [July 13] the king had us cross to the other side. The dragoons crossed and part of the horse; Lithuania was about to cross, when suddenly a detachment from Lubomirski's army comes flying, not in ranks, not by squadrons, but higgledy-piggledy, Tartar fashion. They light upon our squadrons first, thinking us to be the Lithuanians; we close ranks with a mighty clash, men are falling from their horses in dense numbers, and suddenly they recognize one another: here's one brother, here's another, here's a son, here's a father. They let each other be. With their entire force, they lunge at our right; there the dragoons were standing and the Cossacks under Colonel Czop's command. Having held out under our fire, Lubomirski's men took to the sword, slashing and hacking, on and on. From the other side of the ford, our men are firing at them from the cannon: it did not hinder them in the least; not an hour and a half passed, before they'd cut down our men.

High-ranking officers perished, above all those excellent men, Czarniecki's commanders, such valiant cavaliers, old veterans, who, in Denmark, in the Muscovite, Cossack, and Hungarian wars accomplished such *mirabilia* and were ever invincible — all perished in this civil war; the loss of whom not only the king, but the whole army

7. Every inch of the way.
8. To the outcome of the civil war.
9. In this spot, the Noteć river widened out into a swampy area, through which ran the ford.

mourned, especially our division, having long observed their valor. And God, on account of our discords, let this befall us, he took away the flower of our brave cavaliers who had ever withstood the enemy's onslaughts.

In that battle everything was *in confuso.* We had much ado in that confusion to *discernere* who was a foe and whom to smite; we rode into each other's midst, knowing not who was who; before attacking anyone, you first asked: "Whose army are you in?" "Whose are you in?" If the adversary's then: "Let's fight!" "Go to the devil!" "Double for you!" And they let each other alone. If friend fell upon friend, they rode off after greeting one other. For it did happen that one brother might be with Lubomirski, the other with the king; the father here and the son there; no telling how to do battle. To be sure, they had signs — a kerchief tied on the left arm; but we were slow to spot this. I, too, then as they started cutting us a pretty close shave, tied something around my arm above the elbow and don't bother to keep much distance from them. They identified me from afar: "Are you ours, or not?" I raise my arm with the scarf and say: "Yours." When suddenly he says: "O, you sly-dog, you're not ours! Be off, or give yourself up to us."

When the battle was all over, a cavalier from Lubomirski's army rode up from the side, and standing there on horseback is the Cossack Colonel Czop, who takes no heed, thinking him one of his own men; the rider ambles up to him slowly; then he fired into his ear from a pistol and killed him.[10] So treacherous was that war, the clothes being the same, the style the same, God grant that its like may never again befall us in our Poland!

I recross the ford into our ranks and there's the king; some men were clustered in a circle around him, he's wringing his hands, upset. He was sincerely afflicted this time. He sent to Lubomirski to confront him in a knightly fashion, on the field in an open battle, and not furtively like a wolf. Lubomirski answered: "Not for me is it to encounter My Lord in open battle, but simply, as an offended citizen, to defend myself as best I can. Of this loss of innocent blood, which grieves me, I am not the occasion, but His Highness himself and those fine counselors who have brought us to this state of affairs in order to destroy our mother-country. But, *propter bonum Reipublicae*"[11] I agree to the treaty of Palczynia, *exclusis nonnullis;*[12] I'm willing to beg the king's pardon, though I did not anger him, and I'm prepared to do penance so long as my reputation or that of my house is not damaged.

10. Kochowski (see the year 1683) also writes of this stealthy murder of Colonel Czop by an unknown assailant.
11. For the good of the Commonwealth.
12. With some exceptions.

And so on, at this pace, as I've already said, like the Mazurian, "Whoa! A punch I'll deal you!" — again flight, again pursuit, up hill and down dale. Our villages are shuddering, our poor are weeping, our bishops and senators are urging the king to take pity on the country, seeing that we are plainly displeasing to God if luck is not with us.

Deputies were sent then; they entered into negotiations, but on the run, as before; at last, the king, in order to put an end to it, encamped near Łęgonice in the province of Rawa. There, Lubomirski's deputies rode over to our camp; conditions were set down then and signed *ab utrinque,*[13] though not without great exertions on the part of the eminent men assembled *ad hunc actum*[14] and senators and divers officials. But before describing the treaty, I'll go back a little to the subject of that unfortunate battle at Mątwy mentioned above.

The day following that unfortunate battle, I went to the royal tents. Sundry of us stand chatting, until the king came out of the tent, which they used to call his cabinet. We all made obseisance to him then, when suddenly he says to me: "If your commander, Czarniecki, were here, 'twould all be otherwise." I reply: "Gracious Lord, if God had not taken him from us, not only would this misfortune and the shedding of blood so innocent would never have befallen us Poles, nor this raising of swords to our own necks. Tears welled from the king's eyes then, just as beans release their seeds they fell, one by one; he went back inside from whence he'd come, and Father Wojnat, all ready to say Mass and in his vestments, stood waiting nearly an hour for him, before he came out. And throughout the entire Mass he said not one prayer, but knelt on his velvet pillow and sighed. He grieved for those men who had died, he had *morsum conscientiae,*[15] and besides that, the confusion and the horror of all his designs had brought discredit to his kingly authority. The king now saw that the advice of his perverse and evil counselors was responsible for the failure of his projects, which must have mortified him exceedingly, and more than all his other wars and misfortunes, this one drove him to despair, and later to abdicate. For he would say over and over: "My head will never be easy until I cover it with a monastic hood." If ever he saw one of Czarniecki's soldiers, at once he would speak of him *cum suspiriis.*[16]

[The panegyric to Czarniecki which follows is omitted here, as well as the text of the Łęgoński treaty and the general amnesty.]

After the negotiations were completed and the treaty signed, we

13. By both sides.
14. To draw up that document.
15. Pangs of conscience.
16. With sighs.

moved on from Łęgonice toward Radom, for Lubomirski was on the Vistula. We arrived at Jaroszyn the appointed place of *Pan* Lubomirski's humbling and his swearing to observe the terms of the treaty. He arrived at the camp then in the company of a few hundred cavaliers and high-ranking officers [August 8]. Only two royal squadrons of Gentlemen of the Horse attended the king, the rest of the army remained in their huts; into the royal tents, however, a large number of officers had gathered to watch this ceremony. As soon as Lubomirski, having finished his speech, entered the tent and was about to make his oath, all at once the linen tent flaps were raised so that all could view the ceremony. Afterward, the king rode off to Warsaw and *Pan* Lubomirski to Janowiec to make ready for his *exilium* abroad. However, his journey was ill-starred, for he died in Wrocław [January 31, 1667], but his passing was peaceful, he complaining of a headache only, and saying: "He who lives by his head, must die by his head." But because he had brought disorder to the Commonwealth, some mourned him, others rejoiced at his demise. Soon after, Grand Hetman [Stanislaw Rewera] Potocki also made his departure from this world; 'twas plain that Queen Ludwika, as the *primum caput*[17] of the Condé intrigues required a train for her entrance into heaven; she invited the hetmans to go with her and, shortly after, the blind counselor, her most faithful accomplice;[18] later on, many others wandered after the queen, there to give account of themselves before that fearful tribunal.

That year ended then in great misery and oppression *nobilitatis*[19] and the poor peasants. Through the amnesty people were reconciled *in perpetuum silentium;* now no one dared open his mouth over wrongs done, or resort to the law, for straightaway one was referred to the amnesty, which was supposed to cover everything. And would it not have been better to make peace without shedding so much human blood, without devastating our poor country? We could have performed brave exploits with Poland's enemies without laying our own villages to waste, and those men consumed in that war might have been around to give aid to the Commonwealth in another time of need; above all, we would not have aroused God's anger.

17. Prime leader.
18. Prażmowski did not die until 1673.
19. For the gentry.

The Year of Our Lord 1667

I went to my parents' in Węgrzynowice[1] for the whole winter, there discoursing frequently with *Pan* [Jan Albrecht] Lipski, governor of Rawa, and with *Pan* Śladkowski,[2] castellan of Sochaczew. [The Lord] had so inclined the hearts of these two gentlemen that each wished me to marry into their families. The governor had taken a liking to me after one of my speeches at the district dietine to elect the chamberlain, as well as at his own accession to the governorship, and then later at the district dietines where I presided several times; he saw I had *activitatem*[3] and was greatly fond of me. For even while still serving in the army, whenever I came to my father's and there would be an assembly, I never missed attending it; wherefore I was at least of some use to someone, and they would sometimes ask me to preside, and sometimes my services happened to please people; on this account, then, I had the respect of these gentlemen. *In anno praeterito*[4] I presided over the district dietine at the time of *Pan* Lubomirski's amnesty.

This year I also presided at the pre-Diet assembly in Rawa, which was the 7th of February, and they absolutely would have me to go to the Diet as deputy but I declined, for my father refused to pay my expenses (he also being at the dietine), and you have to make a good showing there. So the following persons went as deputies: Adam Nowomiejski, the vice-prosecutor for the Crown, and Anzelm Piekarski, the Rawa cup-bearer, to whom I gave quite enough sound instructions pertaining to the issues. These were the articles:

INSTRUCTIONS

To their Lordships, the Honorable deputies from Rawa: His Lordship *Pan* Adam Nowomiejski, vice-prosecutor for the Crown, district judge in Rawa, and His Lordship *Pan* Anzelm Piekarski, Cup-Bearer of Rawa,

1. A village near Rawa, leased by Pasek's father.
2. Piotr Śladkowski was then the Rawa standard-bearer.
3. Fortitude.
4. Last year.

unanimously elected to the six-week Diet,[5] given by the local assembly of nobles.

For the whole world it is plain to see how our entire country must grieve upon viewing with what labyrinthian difficulties it is fraught due to the exertions *malevolorum,*[6] how, in so dangerous a crisis it finds ingratitude instead of solace, having no hope of defense owing to disrupted Diets. That this exceedingly grieves His Majesty, Our Gracious King, everyone has to admit, considering under what great hardships our kind-hearted sovereign has labored in order that, after three Diets have failed, at least the fourth Diet could be brought to a successful end and he could *dextram porrigere*[7] to our faltering country; but the *adversitates* of envious fortune prevented His Majesty Our Gracious Lord from giving proof of his good will toward the country. Who will not acknowledge His Majesty's concern for the common weal, seeing how immense was his sorrow and how he labors, heedless of discomfort, tirelessly, and at considerable detriment to his health, ever mindful *boni publici,*[8] to assemble the estates of the Commonwealth for a fifth Diet, after four abortive ones. For he desires to set the Commonwealth on a firm foundation and by prior discussion, the speedier to furnish our menaced country with a means of defense. And since these efforts are an outgrowth of his kindness, we as loyal subjects commend our deputies, before all else, to express our sympathy to His Royal Highness, Our Gracious King, for the grief and weariness he has endured. We also commend them to wish him a long and successful reign and to give due thanks in the name of our entire assembly of nobles for his paternal sollicitude for the *bonum* of this land.

1. As it is through frequent, unfounded, and illegal vetoes that the Diets are dissolved and, being *cum summo Reipublicae detrimento*[9] we commend their honorable lordships, our deputies, above all to find a *modum concludendi*[10] the Diets, of limiting such vetoes by firm law so that we might once again bring a session to a successful end.

2. Further, our deputies are to beseech His Majesty the King to approve the treaty made at Łęgonice, it being the most solid foundation of domestic peace, immediately *post absoluta vota*[11] of the senators, insofar as all the conditions be ratified by the Chamber of Deputies.

3. And since we see nothing so necessary *in tanto Reipublicae passu*[12] as

5. This Diet lasted six weeks by consent of the deputies. Both deputies, Piekarski and Nowomiejski, are mentioned in the constitutions of the Diet from the year 1667 (*Volumina Legum,* IV).
6. Of malevolent men.
7. Hold out his right hand.
8. Of the public weal.
9. To the greatest damage of the Commonwealth.
10. Way of concluding.
11. After the speeches.
12. In this critical phase of the Commonwealth.

recompense for those men of the army who, *in fidem Reipublicae,*[13] have remained in service on credit, so many wages are they owed; and as the Commonwealth (especially our province) cannot manage to pay them with ordinary taxes, their lordships the deputies will propose these measures for the swift payment of the debt:

4. First, that their lordships, the colonels, squadron masters, foreign colonels and lieutenant-colonels and captains, lieutenants, and other gentlemen officers holding *bona regalia*[14] after accounting with the treasury of the Commonwealth how much pay is due them, wait for a certain period of time; and that this sum be assured for them *propter meliorem certitudinem*[15] on this same property.

5. Second, to obtain the money for so urgent a need in the Commonwealth, the honorable deputies *proponent* that the *clenodia regni*[16] be registered, notice having been given to the Chamber of Deputies, and pawned for some time.

6. Our deputies will make request to priests, bishops, abbots, curates, that they prove themselves *filii* of this land *in cuius sinu*[17] they were born, raised, decorated with considerable dignities, and since the entire commonwealth is headed for doom, that they deign to pledge a *charitativum subsidium;*[18] may they who have their revenues from nowhere else but the Commonwealth, not begrudge them to it now.

7. The taxes which those merchants who import to Poland divers goods, liquors, and other things for their own profit, as well as customs duties, sales taxes, Jewish head taxes, and other taxes collected *in fructum Reipublicae*[19] should be paid in double, since the prices of all goods rise daily.

8. Nor is the following entirely without its usefulness: although every son of this land must grieve recalling those soldiers who — God have mercy on us — perished at Mątwy, having tested their mettle many times for our country in divers battles and in the civil war, let not the officers take over their pay but surrender it for the use of the Commonwealth, especially to pay the *plebei.*[20]

9. The deputies are seriously to propose that all the money left over after the closing of the mint be turned over to paying the army.

10. It is customary to compensate a worthy endeavor with a worthy payment and a bad one with a bad payment. There being many squadrons that, despite the order from his lordship, the governor of Kraków, did not go out under *Pan* Machowski's command, it is meet that they be

13. Trusting in the Commonwealth.
14. Crown property.
15. To be the more certain.
16. Will propose (that the) crown jewels . . .
17. Sons . . . in whose womb.
18. Voluntary subsidy.
19. For the benefit of the Commonwealth.
20. Non-nobility.

deprived of their recompense; had there been an army and not such a meager number, his squadrons could have escaped such a disaster.[21]

11. Whereas in sudden need one ought to search for divers means, we do not deem it useless for their lordships the deputies to propose that money be taken *in fidem Reipublicae*[22] from various persons in return for certain securities, and they will suggest other means that would seem most expeditious.

12. So as the debts of the royal couple not be forgotten, their lordships the deputies shall communicate about them with the entire Chamber of Deputies.

13. As for the artillery, their lordships the deputies will endeavor to find a way to meet the cost.

14. Although we know that new taxes have been designed for paying off the debt to his highness the prince of Brandenburg, nevertheless, their lordships the deputies having made the correct calculations shall, insofar as it is still necessary, endeavor to see that something is done.[23]

15. Nothing is more fitting than to render thanks to his highness the prince of Courland for being patient so long. Whereas Piltyn *ab antiquo* was incorporated into the kingdom of Kurland[24] and so that we may avoid such ado as befell us with Prussia, their lordships the deputies will strive to see that the prince of Kurland, to whom it rightly belongs, shall retain it, while preserving the rights of his Majesty the king as the *supremus et directus dominus et ultimae instantiae iudex.*[25]

16. Such a man is not to be found among us who, having seen the faith and virtue of the gentlemen from Livonia, our brothers and fellow citizens, and having seen their estates laid waste and plundered, would not express his due gratitude, and we would not be *contrarii* to making strenuous efforts to see that their wishes are satisfied, our deputies having communicated with their honorable deputies.

17. The unresolved item from the Diet of 1662 having been postponed till the next Diet, the better to establish the credit of the Commonwealth with her creditors, we instruct their lordships the deputies that either the *summa proveniens*[26] — both capital and interest — be given to the Orsettis or such security as described in the postponed resolution.[27]

18. The deputies will strive to have the mint, which was closed but

21. Sebastian Machowski, a commander of the Polish army, was defeated on the 19th of December by the Cossack hetman Doroszenko at Brahiłów, and his whole division, numbering nearly 6000 men, was annihilated.
22. On the guarantee from the Commonwealth.
23. In the treaty of Welawa (September 10, 1657) the Elector Frederick Wilhelm was given Elbląg in return for 400,000 thalers. In fact, the city was never turned over to the Elector, and so he kept insisting on repayment of the money.
24. Piltyn is a town on the Winda river in Kurland; reference here is to the district of Piltyn, where the disputes between Poland and Kurland took place.
25. Sovereign lord and highest judge.
26. Corresponding amount.
27. In 1659 Wilhelm Orsetti lent delegates of the Commonwealth 553,444 Polish zloties

later reopened without the consent of the Commonwealth, closed forthwith and its dies destroyed.

19. Their lordships the deputies will support the trials of Boratyni as well as Tynf, for which the entire Commonwealth has been calling at previous Diets.[28]

20. Let the administrators of the new customs duty, as well as of the excise tax on goods, give account of their expenses, so that they too may be judged.

21. Since the estates of the Commonwealth are overburdened by the insufferable cost of materials such as cloth, as well as other things, their lordships, the deputies will suggest that his Majesty the king set the *pretia rerum*.[29]

22. The deputies will also endeavor to have that sum returned to us which was allotted to us by decree of the commission but cancelled in the treasury.

23. Let their lordships the deputies insist that those counterfeiters give an accounting of what they did with so large a sum, forging cheap coins out of good coin, since they struck as many as eight coins from one thaler; let the tax-collectors themselves give evidence that they delivered good coin to the treasury.

24. Whereas our district has not had a delivery of salt for a long time, their lordships will plead for this.

25. Their lordships the deputies will insist that foreign delegates and residents who have tarried so long in our country be sent away at once.

26. Their lordships the deputies are to insist that no private delegates should be sent *sine consensu ordinum*[30] to foreign countries.

27. Whereas our province being the most ravaged of all, owing to the continual traverses, postings, and encampments of not only his Majesty's armies but the confederate as well, their lordships the deputies will be pleading that our taxes be postponed *ad feliciora tempora*.[31]

28. Whereas *per absentiam* of the hetmans in the army, it is usual for *crescere disordo*[32] and whereas disorder brings calamities harmful to the

for payment of Tartar claims. He was to obtain the district of Knyszyń until the sum was paid back. For unknown reasons, the Diet did not ratify this. Orsetti died and his heirs claimed this amount. The Diet in 1662 postponed the matter.

28. Tytus Liwiusz Boratyni and Andrzej Tynf, as lessees of mints, were accused of embezzlement. The commission established by the Diet in 1662 did not find Boratyni guilty and signed a new contractwith him. (Tynf escaped abroad.) Accusations against Boratyni were raised again in 1666 and 1667, but the treasury court judging the case did not resolve it definitively. The case dragged on for some time. Hniłko, author of a monograph on Boratyni (*Tytus Liwiusz Boratyni*, Kraków 1923, p. 72) states, however, that no one ever heard of Boratyni "receiving any sort of penalty and the accusations died down with the passage of time until finally they ceased entirely."

29. Price of goods.

30. Without the permission of the estates.

31. Until a more favorable time.

32. Disorder to arise.

Commonwealth, their lordships the deputies will insist that their lordships the hetmans, or at least one hetman, always be present in the army *propter meliorem ordinem et disciplinam solidam.*[33]

29. Their lordships, the deputies demand that colonels, squadron masters, and other officers not absent themselves from their squadrons, *sine legali impedimento,*[34] under penalty of forfeiting their pay; since our commanders make it so irksome for us to win our pay, let them also fulfill their duties; the same for officers who miss a battle. This way we can always have squadrons *pleno numero*[35] and at full strength.

30. The deputies are to urge that our native-born nobles and our officers be allowed to serve in the foreign contingent.

31. If time allows, their lordships the deputies are to promote the *postulata et desideria*[36] of our fellow gentlemen as expressed in previous instructions, insisting that they be fulfilled. Whereas his grace the bishop of Chełm, vice-chancellor of the Crown [Andrzej Olszowski], although *ex officio suae eminentis dignitatis*[37] and his high merits in the service of the Commonwealth, deserves the favor of his Majesty the king, yet we, too, on account of his great *merita de Republica* wishing due *gratificationem,*[38] commend to their lordships our deputies that he be recompensed with a second abbey, as soon as one should become vacant, with the consent of the whole Commonwealth regardless of the law forbidding possession of several offices or government properties together by one person.

32. And also that his lordship *Pan* Alexander Załuski, the Rawa chamberlain, be suitably compensated for his villages and estates lying in the Smolensk province — Pawłowo, Szapoli, Borodyno, Putosze, Czerncowo, Radzynowo, Piotrowo, Holemszczowo — they being subject to feudal law and bequeather *post sterilem decessum*[39] of *Pan* Stanisław Kazanowski, the district supervisor of Krosinko and Przedbor, to his lordship the Chamberlain, but which are now overrun and possessed by the Muscovites.

33. Our deputies will see to it that the city of Rawa, devastated and left in ruins by the several encampments made there, be exempt from taxes and other burdens.

Their lordships the deputies will take steps to see that the wish of the priest in Budziszowice — a matter raised so many times at our district diets and included in previous instructions — that the fief purchased for a hospital and presently leased from *Pan* Piotr Śladkowski, the Rawa standard-bearer, might be granted the privilege of ecclesiastical law.

We hereby commend their lordships the deputies, obliging them *fide,*

33. For better and constant discipline.
34. Except for a lawful impediment.
35. At full count.
36. Demands and desires.
37. By reason of the eminent dignity of his office.
38. Merits in the Commonwealth (wishing due) compensation.
39. After the death without heirs.

honore et conscientia to seek the *bonum partriae*[40] so that our freedom might not be oppressed but rather embellished and to communicate in all matters with other provincial deputies.

Given in Rawa at the assembly of nobles, February 7, 1667.

Jan Chryzostom z Gosławic Pasek,
Deputy Chamberlain of Rawa, Marshal of the
Assembly of Nobles

Several weeks before this district assembly, they had conferred on me the office of deputy chamberlain, which I would not have accepted but that the governor and the crown prosecutor forced me to do so, telling me it was a step to greater honors in that province and solemnly promising as much, so long as I did not hold aloof from them; secondly, they told me that I could sooner gain a voice in the district dietine than if I were without an office.[41] Such were their kind wishes for me, they greatly desiring to support my advancement: "you'll rise at the most in three years." They sent me to the king as an envoy, to the archbishop [Wacław Leszczyński] and the bishop [Prince Florian Czartoryski] of Kujawy and I was acquiring a good reputation; now they would have employed me *ad altiora.*[42]

The governor was of a mind to marry me to Radoszowska, while *Pan* Śladkowski, then standard-bearer of Rawa, later castellan of Sochaczew, was tugging at me for his only child and heiress, *Panna* Śladkowska. She had a village called Boża Wola in the Sochaczew district, wholly debt-free, for which village her father would have given her 70,000 at a time when ducats were worth six zloties, and thalers three.[43] Each of them dampened my desire for the other's contender. Śladkowski said Radoszowska's mother was a licentious strumpet and, *consequenter,* might not she herself be one; the governor spoke of Śladkowska in terms such as: "What if she does have 70,000? The girl herself has certain *vitia et praecipue*[44] she's evil-tempered as a lizard, almost a tippler. You should be on the lookout for someone well-bred; but with her, God help you! Yet if Radoszowska isn't to your liking, I can find other matches for you, but I'll not let you wed Śladkowska." I, listening to the discourses of those two, felt as if I was hearing music played for two choirs: this one sounds beautiful and that one sounds beautiful; but my heart rather inclined to Śladowska, for I heard them say that out there on her

40. In faith, honor, and conscience (to seek the) good of the country.
41. The first to take the floor in the district dietines were the district officials.
42. For more important affairs.
43. That is, before the depreciation of coins. In 1668 a ducat was worth 9 zloties; a thaler was worth 5 zloties.
44. Faults, and in particular.

estate not only wheat grew in every field, but onions too; wherever you sow it, it'll come up; and my thirst *ad pinguem glaebam*[45] was greater than for bare cash.

Neither ever let me out of their sight; when they got hold of me, I was forced to spend three or four weeks with him who caught me. Or if I rode to my parents', there came an envoy at once from him whom I'd not visited lately; no family occasions would be celebrated without me. The governor gave away one daughter to the convent in Warsaw, to the Bernardines: he prevailed on me to give her away *ad votum in frequentia*[46] of many people of quality, as was done in Warsaw. Another daughter he gave in marriage to Grzybowski, the district supervisor of Warsaw: and I had to be there.[47] After the weddings and the receptions, he regarded me almost as kin. In Glinnik [a village in the Rawa district] during Shrovetide *Pan* Jan Potrykowski gave his stepdaughter in marriage to *Pan* Maciej Potrykowski. The groom being a relative of mine, asked me to be his best man. I went then to that wedding, not knowing that my own was being prepared. It happened this way:

Pan Śladkowski, the present castellan of Sochaczew, without saying anything to me, invites a young lady with her mother and stepfather, *Pan* Wilkowski to his estate for Shrovetide; me, Śladkowski simply asked to spend Shrovetide with him; about the young lady's presence there and his intentions he said not a word. I, of course, having promised to be at his service was obliged to consent; I think to myself: later I'll apologize to Śladkowski for not keeping my word. I went with the others to Ośow and from there to the wedding. *Pan* Śladkowski, knowing nothing of this, expected me there. He sends a letter expressly to Glinnik, begging my presence, but as before says nothing about his intention; to *accelerare* things, he had already set the date with the mother, and the priest is there, who would perform the marriage *sine bannis.*[48] In no wise would my cousins, the Chociwskis, give their consent, declaring: "Even should you be waving your sword at us, we'd not let you go, for we are kinsmen; but you shall ride off tomorrow, give us but this one day." So there was no getting away from them, if only because they'd hidden the horses and everything else; meanwhile one messenger after another comes running, and so the entire day. The same evening, a letter arrived from the lady herself, ńee Myszkowska, wherein she sets forth the whole matter candidly, declaring that "my husband is cross with me for he had intended to call you a

45. For rich soil.
46. To her vows in the presence.
47. Pasek is mistaken; the district supervisor of Warsaw, Jan Grzybowski, married Anna Lipska.
48. Without banns.

bridegroom on Ash Wednesday; now he is regretting it, since you scorn his favor." That letter fell into my cousin's hands first; they taking it, see a woman's handwriting and, the better to discover my secrets, unsealed it; Florian Chociwski, having read it, says: "Well, now we'll no longer hold you up here, for to withhold in such matters is dishonorable, it being a question of preserving friendship." So volatile was my fortune, so changeable, people were always astonished, but as usual the resolve could not have been either better or worse, only as the Lord willed it.

The next day, after thanking everyone — 'twas already afternoon — off I dashed at a fast trot, and I broke at times into a gallop, seeing it was evening. Not half a mile had I gone before swirls of snow began to come down, then it got dark. We arrived, I dismount, and here they are, just bringing in the fish supper — it's now dawn; the other guests were already sleeping, as well as the girl's stepfather, *Pan* Wilkowski. Both Śladowskis look at me crossly. I say: "Because you did not write openly in that first letter, my cousins seized the last one and did not give it back to me until I was leaving the village." Only then did they warm up a bit, recognizing at once that I'd not done it out of any malice; I'd also come with plenty of repartee and dash, whereby I brought them round, and I say: "My distinguished Lord and Lady Śladkowski, [the good] which you were to show me today will suit me just as well tomorrow; no novelty is it to wed on Ash Wednesday, especially having a priest without too many scruples, who is not afraid of the bishop." The castellan's wife (but at that time he was still standard-bearer) was about to agree, but her husband declared it impossible, and that now it would have to put off till May. "And once put off to May, 'twas blown o'er the lea,' " — plainly it was not God's will. As the same lady said later at a wedding: "Though the village was Wola Boża, 'twas not God's will."[49] When May came around, *Pan* Śladkowski was serving as deputy in Warsaw; the young lady's mother had also died, and so the undertaking was deferred. *Homo proponit, Deus disponit.*"[50]

Lubomirski died then and Hetman Potocki, the Lwów commission took place; meanwhile, my wedding having been delayed, *Pan* Jędrzej Remiszowski — espoused to a Pasek, a cousin of mine — begins to recommend to me, as kinfolk are wont to do, his own kinswoman, Remiszowska, daughter of Stanisław Remiszowski; he coaxing me to go the Kraków district, simply to get acquainted; then, should the occasion arise, to consult about further meetings. I kept it in mind; and the Lwów commission having ended, he persuaded me to go to Kraków. *Pan* Remiszowski went to Olszówka near Wodzisław to his sister's estate, while I went to visit my uncle, *Pan* Wojciech Chociwski. Upon

49. A play on words: *Wola Boża* means God's Will.
50. Man proposes, God disposes.

leaving them, having taken along my uncle and his son with me, I thought: "It won't be costing us anything to look over this widow; besides, I've another chance waiting should this not turn out, for belike no one will run off with *Panna* Sládkowska on me." We got to Olszówka *ipso die festi Beatissimae Mariae Virginis*,[51] having attended Mass in the church with the miraculous painting of Our Blessed Lady.[52] We came without music, as a sign we were not courting; but I, feeling a sincere inclination — and as our hostess began to hint of musicians — sent to Wodzisław, whence they were brought directly. And so to dance. My uncle asks me: "Well? Are you pleased with the widow?" I replied: "I feel strongly taken by her; would it be possible to talk with her this day to discover how disposed she is toward me?" My uncle answers: "To talk to her today is not the thing to do, it being the first day; as for her regard, I've already seen that she's sympathetic, for I know at once whom a woman will like, though she's not spoken a word to him. In this case you can be certain, if she pleases you, I assure you, I can see it, she won't pass you up. And you've no reason to scorn her; she's a decent woman, a good housekeeper, her house is in order and prosperous enough; the villages she holds, to be sure, are leased, but she has money and an estate that is hers for life in Smogorzów. Although it's tied up in the hands of her children's uncle on their father's side, *Pan* Jan Łącki, a quarrelsome man, but I would not worry myself about you, you will know how to deal with him. Since God has inclined your heart toward her, this is His Holy Will, and I, God granting, shall treat with her about it tomorrow." After these words, I went off to dance with her, and after the dance I sat down directly next to her. And I was enamored of her now: as she must have been fair in her youth, so she appeared to me then a young woman, and never would I have said she was so advanced in years as I later discovered: she married me at forty-six, I supposing her to be no more than thirty. Secondly, it cheered me that her last daughter, Marysia, was two years old, and so I hoped that for me God would grant yet a little boy. And so He might have, had it not been for human malice. For (such was the rumor) they fixed things so she'd not have any more offspring; various objects we used to come across in bed, I myself finding several moldy things from a coffin. From this circumstance alone I give this piece of advice to each one who reads of this *praeiudicatum*:[53] whoever marries a widow should try *ante omnia*[54] not to keep any woman, any female, in your home, but should marry them off. Our home was full of such and for us it was treachery.

51. On the very feast of the Blessed Virgin.

52. This was September 9. In nearby Pińczów was a miraculous picture of the Blessed Mother, at the monastery of the Reformation Fathers.

53. Experience.

54. Above all.

But leaving that aside, as it depends on God, I return to my suit with the widow. I address these words to her: "My Esteemed Lady, I present my compliments to you; I've stopped by at the request of His Lordship, your kinsman, only for a short while to pay my respects. And yet the food here has pleased me so much that with such food as sole recompense, I would accept service in your household until Christmas, and for a good wage, I would not refuse to stay even longer. If my service could be of any use at all to you, My Lady, I am eager to apply. For having tired of bloody games of war, I would be glad of a change to a more useful profession in my old age, that is, to learn husbandry in the service of some good housekeeper, as a farmhand, or — as they say here — herdsman. My Most Gracious, Most Esteemed Lady, if you've not a complete staff of servants and I can count myself among those in your good graces, whether you scorn or accept my desire to serve you, please reflect I will not enter into any debate over wages until I hear from Your Ladyship with what graciousness you will receive my declared proposal."

And she answers me thus: "My Esteemed Lord! 'Tis the truth that we accept servants only from the Christmas holidays. If anyone takes on a servant after St. John's,[55] he may not take his full wages except insofar as kindness bids his employer. But one should understand that this applies only to the humblest servants. When a more important one arrives, we do not contract with them until Christmas, but for a full year up to the time when they arrived. However, into such a contract I do not want to enter with Your Lordship, knowing that Your Lordship as a man of noble birth has been accustomed to live on a large wage; whereas I, being a poor gentrywoman might be unable to manage such a payment. And so I should be glad to know Your Lordship's will, what would content you, and I shall see whether I could satisfy that, and shall so declare to you tomorrow without delay."

I speak again: "Your Ladyship taunts me mightily; and not only me, but the whole knightly estate, in calling our miserable soldier's fee of 40, or at most 60, zloties a large wage, for which we are not to spare at any hour our life and blood. May Your Ladyship deign to know that were soldiers content with that wage, everyone of them, myself included, would certainly not forego it, even unto doddering old age; whereas I, in casting my soldier's life aside for the present rank and in offering Your Ladyship my cordial services, clearly expect a desirable wage, for which I do not want to bargain with Your Ladyship, but I rely on your courtesy and graciousness, whereof I do not doubt; I shall await Your Ladyship's kind declaration."

Replies she: "My Esteemed Lord, everyone, even Your Lordship, so

55. June 24, or in the second half of the year.

conducts himself when hiring a servant: you speak with him yourself, you discourse on conditions and future duties, so that he might know how to serve you and what sort of recompense to expect for his services. And so it befits me to speak with you myself of these things and declare myself — if Your Lordship is of such a mind [then it shall be today] or, for greater solemnity, tomorrow."

To which I say: "I have to acknowledge that Your Ladyship possesses not a woman's, but a knightly discernment and sense in practicing that candor, seeing the which my soul ever rejoices: in every circumstance to make known one's well-considered design by a brief word; in the second place, it is always more courteous when notice comes from the lips of the Lord himself than from chancellors;[56] the which I will look upon, no matter what it may be, as desirable news and God's will. If it be favorable, I shall give thanks; if the contrary, I shall not bear a grudge, for 'tis plain that heaven wills it no other way.

Says she to that: "It can grace no one to return sincere friendship with coarse ingratitude. Besides, my conscience would be troubled, should I, seeing Your Lordship's sincere inclination, not return a like sentiment. And if there be a good servant's constancy of mind and will, he will have a place here and a master; whereas your services, being given at my discretion, can expect special consideration.

Now did I thank her. Of what tender sentiments we spoke, plenty could be written. And later — I bade Dzięgielowski's lad, who played the violin and sang nicely, to sing:

> Let another set his hopes
> And on divers fortunes ponder
> I'll have won my triumph
> When I've made a lucky bargain.

The others guessed what is afoot from that song. Her brother came over to us: "How now, sister dear, have you come to an agreement without consulting us? Well and good, even so, praise God!" She protests that nothing of the kind, it's but the song they're singing has such a text. But they take it into their heads suddenly that "you've decided"; they pledge a toast to our health. Seeing her ring on my finger, all the more to dance then, to drink, as is customary. Now then without further ceremony we began to speak *de tempore*.[57] She said: "It can be tomorrow even, as long as it is not Friday." While I, thanking her for notice of so swift a conclusion say: "My Esteemed Lady, without the blessing of my parents I cannot change my state, this being their wish. By My Lady's leave, I am satisfied having your word, which — I

56. A chancellor used to give the deputies the king's reply in the Senate.
57. Of the date.

understand — you will deign to keep; nor am I of a mind to be inconstant, and so, finally, let us put that word to paper. In two weeks' time, I shall have ridden there and back, accomplished my parents' will, brought along a few kinsmen, and shall be bowing before you, My Lady, to beg you for the fulfillment of your promise." 'Twould not do: "let it be straight away, or not at all." Now my cousin Jędrzej enters into our council, he coaxing, imploring me not to put it off, promising to arrange everything, all the papers. How they began then, brother and sister, to belabor my brain: "But we absolutely must have it on Sunday, it ought not to be delayed longer; your parents will give you their blessing afterward too, and it shall even be more solemn when they give both of you their blessing." I was also sorry for that woman, seeing her so greatly moved, and I say: "Is it Your Ladyship's wish that it be so?" She answered: "I do wish it; the Lord knows, I don't, why the Lord has inclined my heart to you." Then I declared: "So then, let it be, for it is God's will and yours!"

On Sunday I write a letter to *Pan* Śladkowski, inviting him to the wedding and requesting musicians; meanwhile we rode off to the church in Mironice. When my Orłowski arrives there, Śladkowski goes in to his wife who was still lying abed, he tells her of this; now does she spring out of bed, dashes into the front room in her nightshirt asking: "What are you both up to there in Olszówka, Orłowski? Surely, you're telling me some dream? I don't believe it." Orłowski says: " 'Tis no dream, Your Ladyship, by this time I'm not sure if they've not gone to the church." "If that's so, then write a letter quick as you can! Run along to your master, beg him to wait until we arrive; I'll be hanged if anything will come of this." Orłowski, taking the letter, raced off; while the Śladkowskis are in a dither. "Harness the horses! Get dressed!"

Orłowski comes running; he finds us in church. I read the letter. The castellan's wife herself wrote at the bottom of the letter: "For the love of God, I beg and beseech you, hold off the marriage until I get there; it will be to your gain." I yielded myself up to God, asking: "O My God, [One] in the Holy Trinity, I beseech You, my Creator; since my coming resolve is Your blessed will, deign to inspire my heart with the Holy Spirit — to wait or not to wait." Mass ended; I say then to my future wife: "My Lady, what's to be done: wait or not?" Says she: "For God's sake, don't wait for they'll muddle things for us." We walked up to the altar then, they played *Veni Creator,* then we made our vows. We're coming back from the altar, when suddenly through the doors burst Śladkowski's musicians. "We're at Your Lordship's service." I say: "You've missed playing at the altar, but you shall make up for it at the dinner table."

We went home with the guests, and here at last come the Śladkowskis; scolding, angry, furious at me: "so that's how it is?", and "that's a gentleman's word?" and "at least you could have stayed the ceremony for us." The more I protested that their letters — both the first one and this one — came after the ceremony; 'twas vain. "Why did you not stop by our estate before riding here?" Fury. Śladkowski finally paying no heed, having quaffed a few, grew merry; he said to his wife: "Let's let him alone! 'Tis plain it was God's will, may God bless him." But *Pani* Śladkowska stayed cross, not wanting to eat, scolding, not dancing, until the next day; and we were merry all the while. And so it had to be — pleasing to God, not to men; praise and glory everlasting be His! For I'd surely have been content with that marriage, if God had given me a son by her; but he did not, and many troubles beset me on account of her children's interests, whereof below.

Mighty large harvests of every sort of wheat did I find in Olszówka, but what did it matter when grain was uselessly cheap. The lease expired, we had difficulty keeping it in the barns, a bushel went for nothing, and so that wheat only went to waste!

The week after the wedding, *Pan* Komorowski, the deputy district supervisor of Nowe Miasto, comes riding to make his last proposal of marriage, he'd nearly arrived for the wedding, he put up in Wodzisław with some friends. Now his go-between says to him: "Your Lordship, will you have meat bought for dinner?" He said: "I'll not be ordering anything for I shall eat dinner in Olszówka." A Jew says: "I'd sooner advise you to have your dinner prepared here, for Your Lordship will not be a welcome guest there." "Why not?" "For the reason that someone else is now the master, it being a week now that she's married." Komorowski then clutches his head; so then, there he supped, there he stayed the night, and the next day he and his friends departed. They sent back to each other then those rings, *symbola amicitiae:*[58] one pillow he would not give back. Afterward, we having somehow become acquainted, he congratulated me "you got what I'd taken a fancy to; and so, I'll not return that pillow, since you possess the head that slept on it." And he was ever my good friend; soon after, he married; he took a widow, *Pani* Brezinska, but such a shrew was she that he deemed himself an unfortunate man and swore to become a priest if God were to separate him from her. And so it came to pass, for soon she died, while he became a priest and died soon after, too.

There was also Queen Ludwika's funeral in Kraków[59] to which my wife and I went, and once there, we registered our lifelong estate to each other, she wanting to sign over her dowery to me *cum assistentia*[60] of her brothers; but I did not want it, saying that "I'll make my own

58. Tokens of friendship.
59. September 22, 1667. The Paseks' lifelong lease on their estate bears the same date.
60. In the presence.

fortune, so long as I have whereon to do so." People were much surprised by this, they said it was the first instance in these times that someone, taking a widow should scorn her largesse. Others praised it. During the funeral, I saw many of my kinsmen in Kraków; all were dissatisfied with my marriage for the reason that I lived so far from them.

The same year our hetmans died: Lubomirski and Potocki. The same year there was a battle at Podhajce, or to deal plainly, our army with Sobieski as hetman was besieged by both Cossacks and Tartars; but the Lord liberated our people at last.[61] The army encamped then at Otynia, there putting up a resistance that prolonged the campaign. Then there was a commission. At the first session, the Kraków gentry began to slight me, calling me a newcomer. But I, after dealing one a punch in the head, another a punch in the nose, another on the back, was left in peace and no longer called a newcomer.

61. The siege lasted from October 4 until October 19.

The Year of Our Lord 1668

I began in Olszówka — thanks be to God! — and leased Miławczyce and Biegłów[1] from *Pan* Stanisław Szembek, the deputy district supervisor of Kraków, at four thousand a year, the term in Olszówka having expired. Directly after Epiphany we brought in the wheat, and took possession — God be praised! — before mid-Lent. But these turned out to be cheap years for wheat; the property was also over-appraised, the parsley and cabbage, and even eggs, being reckoned as revenue; on this account more than two thousand were lost and I'd leased it for but two years.

I also provided a wedding for my stepdaughter, *Panna* Jadwiga Łącka, who married Samuel Dembowski, my nephew, and they lived on my estate a year. Finally, I gave them part of the dowry. My father let them have Kamień; I settled them there on their first property, while my parents I brought to my own estate.

Then came the Diet, at which the king *proposuit benevolam regni abdicationem;*[2] for his blind counselor kept wheedling — apparently guiding him to settle down in his old age, but in his heart scheming to bring a Frenchman to the throne; the king even gave tacit assent and this is why he was stepping down from the throne. But the Commonwealth was vigilant and saw to it that nothing came of this. The blind archbishop knew that *stante abdicatione*[3] the entire government of Poland would depend on him; that is why he was urging the king to abdicate, the more easily to accomplish his design, becoming the interim ruler in Poland, but as usual the Lord willed otherwise.

All the estates were imploring the king not to act in this wise. They held up to his view the *indignitatem;*[4] they set forth the *contumeliam,*[5] it being such as the country had never yet suffered from any other

1. Miławczyce i Biegłow was a small estate, 19 kilometers to the southwest of Pinczow.
2. Submitted his voluntary abdication of the crown.
3. In the event of an abdication.
4. Inappropriateness.
5. Affront.

monarch; they envisioned the *exprobrationem*[6] from peoples who, up to now, have had nought wherewith to find fault, as that we'd murdered any of our kings or driven them from the country; though several we'd had who did not make us so happy; yet we suffered each one as God gave him to us, until the time came to take him away again. When all friendly *persuasiones* had no effect, Ożga, the chamberlain from Lwów, took the floor (I was standing beside him and heard everything well). That old white head began to speak *zelose pro patria et maiestate:*[7] "Gracious King, do not embarrass us and yourself, nor this country of ours and yours, who brought you up and placed you on this throne. You were born among us into this realm, you were brought up here, and you spent your days among us; our free voices called upon you to rule over us. Do not forsake us, etc." Many were those who wept, even the king himself; at last, when all the pleading and persuading had failed, the same Ozga says, being greatly moved: "Well, Gracious King, if you do not wish to be our king, be a brother to us then." Later, some joked, snickering at his apparent slackness in letting himself be brought to this. Divers discoursed diversly on what we would call him. Not crown prince, for he was already king; but let him be *Pan* Snopkowski, *ex ratione* that he had a sheaf of wheat on his coat of arms.[8]

After the Diet, Jan Kazimierz came to Kraków, he stayed in the Krzysztofory apartments;[9] now he began to regret what he had done, but not wanting to show it, he made merry, drinking and dancing. Then he departed for France; at the start he was given a friendly reception there, but after the election of King Michał, no sooner did the news come that things were not going as France had anticipated, but they neglected the old king, and his position was not as comfortable as before. He was upset, thinking "the Poles acted out of spite toward me, electing a subject of mine king." He grieved and complained against those who had brought him to this; he recalled the speeches of his good counselors; then remorse, despair, no longer was he so good-natured as before, and, soon after, he died [December 16, 1672].

And so, there you have it, Gracious King, the *effectum* of vicious counselors, looking out for their own private interests, not your good. You filled our senatorial chairs with them, you bestowed on them the highest *subsellia,*[10] you made them our masters, these men without conscience, without God in their hearts — and where God does not

6. Rebukes.
7. Ardently for his country and the throne.
8. *Snop* is Polish for "sheaf."
9. The Krzysztofory apartments stand at the corner of the Main Square and Szczepańska St. in Kraków and were then owned by W. Wodzicki, a former royal secretary. Today the building houses a bistro, gallery, and little theater.
10. Dignities.

abide, you cannot expect them to be mindful of others, *difficile est ex animo resipiscere.*[11] Whether I die, or not, he only attends to his own interests. Though he sees he is sinning before God and the law, it makes no difference; he colors his cause, says he is doing good, says it is *Reipublicae emolumentum,*[12] says that politics requires it. But stay, you statesmen! You will see how *status caelestis* will pass judgment on *terrenos status!*[13]

As was customary, the tribunals all over Poland ceased to function and the interregnum confederacies took over. . . . The *promotores abdicationis*[14] are gleeful, hoping that now their design will be accomplished. *Director monoculus*[15] is *absolute* triumphant; he stirs the hopes of the French crown and its candidate through the newspapers; he sees the royal power in his hands; he prides himself on having become vice-king from humble vicar; he sees many around him, who are feeding at the same public trough; he has nearly accomplished everything and he rejoices. But the Lord willed otherwise.

11. It is truly hard to come to one's senses.
12. An advantage to the Commonwealth.
13. Celestial politics . . . earthly politics.
14. Promoters of abdication.
15. The one-eyed ruler.

The Year of Our Lord 1669

I was residing in Miławczyce and holding the lease on Smogorzów; my *collaterales*[1] began to show disrespect, complaining I was an *advena*[2] from another province. At first, I bore it patiently having no opportunity to avenge myself; thinking this to be common when an outsider from another province settles *inter sympatriotas*,[3] for awhile I put things off; when an opportunity came to retaliate, I did not fail to take up the challenge.

Once some relatives of my wife's on her mother's side, came to visit me, *Pan* Stanisław Szembek, the deputy district supervisor of Kraków and *Pan* Franciszek Żelecki; they brought a kinsman along, Kordowski, a frightful drunkard. I was glad to see them, but was much put out by that Kordowski, for he was constantly insulting the Mazurians [Mazovians], they're born blind, they're ne'er-do-wells, and other things. The others mightily enjoying this, went along with him too; they'd dragged him there especially to embarrass me. A calf's head being brought to the table, he said it was a Mazurian pope. Seeing the yellow pastry beneath the veal, he said they were Mazurian Communion wafers. In short, he provoked me greatly. I, seeing those insults addressed to me, say to him: "My good fellow, you should not mention the Mazurians as night approaches lest you dream of them; besides there are none here. But as I'm a neighbor of the Mazurians I must make reply to Your Lordship on their behalf."[4] Still he persists.

After supper Szembek began to dance; Żelecki says to me, "Let's go to his aid." I answer: "Fine." We're dancing then; and it's not long before they begin to do the Great Dance;[5] Kordowski then, standing in

1. Neighbors.
2. Newcomer.
3. Among another clan.
4. Rawa was united to Poland in 1462, while the Duchy of Mazovia was united to Poland in 1529 by Zygmunt I. Thus, Pasek could consider himself a neighbor of the Mazovians (or Mazurians).
5. "Great Dance" was the old name for the Polonaise. It refers here, however, to the

the line of dance began to sing: "After eating millet porridge our Mazurians/Salty beards do have, but in beer they wet them," and he repeats this ditty several times so that at last I became cross. I pick up that Żelecki in my arms like a child, he being a small chap — they think I'm doing it out of affection — and I'm carrying him past Kordowski as he sings that song, when suddenly I ram him in the chest with Zelecki; he fell on his back — a man as strong as an oak tree — he somehow hitting the bench with the back of his head, passed out. Żelecki could not stand up, for I'd knocked him against Kordowski with all my might. To sword! Only a few of their retainers were in the room, the others were already in corners, drunk, asleep; I shewed them from the room. Returning to Szembek, I rest my sword-tip upon his fat belly; he yells, "Stop, what are you blaming me for?" And those two are still on the ground. I say: "Deuce take you all! What did you come for? To confound me? Don't I see you've been trifling with me through that drunkard all day and I bore it; but I can bear it no more." The ladies jumped up: "Stay! Stay!" We let each other alone. And so to pick up *Pan* Żelecki from the floor and sober up Kordowski: pour vodka into his nose, pry his jaw apart, and then they run to fetch the barber-surgeon for he'd cut his head on the bench. Szembek and Żelecki went to bed; I fortified myself with a bit of drink and had some given to my servants. Then did my fellows play pranks on their drunken retainers, stuffing their noses with paper and lighting them, smearing their moustaches with divers stuff (for they were lying about like dead wood, in the halls, anywhere); whatever mischief they could invent they did. We apologized to each other next morning and ever since, as many times as they've visited, they always behaved toward me with respect and consideration. They were ashamed of themselves, for the incident got round to our neighbors; they could do nothing about it, and they showed me greater respect.

While living there in Milawcyzce — prices were low, the lease appraised too high — more than 2000 zloties I lost on that lease; the sole satisfaction I had from it was hunting foxes aplenty with my three greyhounds — I used no bloodhounds — three and four foxes a day I brought in .

The election of the king took place then. Announcements went out to the districts from the archbishop, urging *ordines Reipublicae*[6] to accomplish a speedy election, tendering the wish that the election be

Mazurka (which came into style during the reign of Zygmunt III). Oscar Kolberg calls the Mazurka "the great dance," for it is danced by both nobility and folk; also it is only in a Mazurka that one can sing short ditties like this one.

6. The estates of the Commonwealth.

carried off *per deputatos.*[7] But the provinces refused their assent and, indeed, ordered everyone to horse as if for war. They knew the archbishop's motives; they knew that until he died he'd not cease his French intrigues; they also knew that for this bride many fresh suitors were preparing themselves, such as the Count of St. Paul, [Prince Charles de Longueville] Prince Philip of Neuburg, and Charles of Lorraine.

The district squadrons assemble then in good order, each on his own estate, and then they set off for Warsaw. I, having married in the province of Kraków, was now serving under the standard of the Kraków district, Achacy Pisarski commanding.[8] We set off then for Wyśmierzyce, stopping there more than a week, and we set foot in Warsaw in the first days of July.[9] Then, as if spilling out of a sleeve, the district squadrons arrive, large armies, magnates' retinues, infantries; in short many and well-equipped men. Bogusław Radziwiłł himself had about eight thousand handsomely turned out men with him.[10] For the first time in Poland, we heard so-called Prussian music, which is played in front of the German heavy cavalry on bassoons.

The archbishop then was put out of countenance, he beginning to doubt in his undertaking; but ever hopeful, he does not cease his intriguing.

But when the sessions of the Diet began, divers men were of divers minds: this one'll be king, that one will, yet no one mentioned the one whom God himself had forseen. All those who sent deputies were scheming and hoping that things would turn out as they'd planned. While he, our future king, expects nothing, knowing the likelihood to be nil. The French deputies, as if cowed, work in secret, but the Neuburg and Lorraine deputies work openly. Not a word about a Polish candidate. The others are handing out money, giving it away, wining, dining, making promises; while he bestows nothing on anybody, promises nothing, requests nothing; and yet he carries off the crown.

Having sat through a few sessions and heard the embassy from the foreign deputies and listened to each deputy declaring his candidate's readiness to serve the Commonwealth, the candidate who appealed most to us was the Prince of Lorraine, *ex ratione* that he was a military man and young, and his envoy spoke these words at the end of his

7. By the deputies.
8. Achacy Pisarski later became district supervisor of Wolbrom.
9. It was June actually.
10. Bogusław Radziwiłł (1620-1669), scion of a Lithuanian magnate family, he was a famous supporter of the Swedes during the Swedish invasion; he was the head of the Lithuanian Calvinists.

peroration: *"Quotquot sunt inimici vestri, cum omnibus in hac arena certabit."*[11] *Soluta sessio ad cras.*[12]

The next day the senators rode out to the election field.[13] The field was covered with armies; different opinions are pronounced; one praising this candidate, another that. One noble from the Łęczyce district speaks up, the squadron was mounted and standing right over the assemblage. "You Condé supporters keep still, or you'll see bullets flying here." One senator answered sharply. Now did they begin to fire: commotion, uproar; the senators fled from the spot betwixt the carriages, under chairs. Straight away, some squadrons of horse rushed from the side toward the infantry, knocking them down, trampling them; the infantry's in disarray. The assembly is surrounded. Now do they begin to yell threats: "Traitors! We'll cut you down, we'll not let you out of here; to no avail do you make havoc in the Commonwealth; *constituemus*[14] other senators, we'll elect a king from our own midst as the Lord God inspires our hearts. And so the session ended in a tragic spectacle. But the officers finally collected their men; the squadrons of horse returned to the field; while the bishops and senators, half-dead, crawled out from under the chairs and carriages, and drove off to their quarters; the rest who were encamped in the election field, also went off to their tents.

The next day there was no session, for the gentlemen were recovering from the jolt, drinking extracts and infusions of hyacinth after their fright.[15] Nor did the provincial delegations come out onto the field, but stayed in camp.

The deputies from the provinces sent to the archbishop on the 16th of June[16] to ride out to the election field and open further deliberations. He replied: "I shall not ride out being unsure of my safety, nor will the other senators be riding out." Again, they sent to him, the army already assembling at the senatorial pavilion. "He who is virtuous and a senator, and who wishes to, let him ride out with us; we shall choose a king for ourselves. He who does not ride out we shall consider a traitor to the country and what sort of consequences would follow, let him conjure!" The provincial deputies then gathered an eighth of a mile from the senatorial pavilion. The senators no longer made toward the pavilion, but rode toward us. Our Kraków castellan, Warszycki, and

11. No matter how many enemies you have, he will combat all of them.
12. They adjourned the session till the next day.
13. These events occurred five days later, on June 17.
14. We'll install.
15. The Chamber of Deputies did not meet on June 18, but it was owing to a bad storm and not for the reason Pasek gives; the Senate did hold a session.
16. This should be June 19.

other senators rode over. And so, at last, to discourse on what had taken place, who favored this conduct. Warszycki, our Kraków lordship, says: "Blessed be His Name (for this was his by-word), I praise this conduct wherein Polish dignity is manifest; the king ought to be elected by the *nobilitas, non certus numerus personarum.*[17] I feel no rancor because of those bullets streaking over my head, for I know that the *malevolentia*[18] of these men, now apparent to the whole world, rankles in the heart of every nobleman; indeed, if I live long enough, I shall insist that the Diets be conducted on horseback; for otherwise, our deputies will be unable to safeguard those freedoms which our ancestors won through bloody combat." He gave examples from earlier times to show that as long as Poles acted thus, so long did our golden freedom flourish; "and now without fail we must tear ourselves from sleep, give up *pro tempore* our domestic pleasures."

At that moment the deputies from Wielkopolska break in: "What are we to do about our senators' remissness? We replied at once, sending deputies to say that "we have our own senators, we're setting off now for the senatorial pavilion and we'll counsel ourselves. The provincial deputies set off *ad locum electionis*[19] and came to a halt there. Oh! How those coaches do pour out of Warsaw — some at a trot, others at a gallop — making for the assembly with all speed (they having expected the provincial deputies to request their presence, not that they would begin without them); even the archbishop rode out then, seeing they're not bowing to him and haven't a thought to apologize for those sharp words.

They took their seats then, which were less numerous than before, for anyone who was much of a coward feigned illness, fearing another such brawl, or worse; others had genuinely taken sick from the scare, or his fat belly had got a jolt. It was said that one senator fell over a wagon shaft as he fled — all but breaking his neck, and his own haiduks had much ado to lift him off the ground and set him up on his feet. The assembled sit there as if risen from sickbeds, no one saying a word. Someone from the throng speaks out: "Your Lordships, we've not come here to sit idle; we'll not accomplish anything by looking at one another in silence. Since Our Reverend Father Prażmowski is not fulfilling the functions proper to his office, then we'll ask His Lordship the Castellan of Kraków, being the first senator in the realm, to preside; besides, it's not the Pope we're electing, we can do without a priest."

17. Nobility, not by certain individuals.
18. Malice.
19. To the election place.

Only now does the archbishop spring to his feet.[20] "Ah, My Lords, as long as I live, I shall not cease to serve my country and in particular each one of you, My Lords, in those circumstances which are proper to my office. And now let us begin felicitously; may God bless us, wherefore I have beseeched His Holy Majesty this day *cum toto clero*[21] in order that, by the grace of His Holy Spirit, He might vouchsafe to incline the hearts of all of us toward what could serve His holy glory and our country's weal, *et similia.*[22] Gentlemen, My Esteemed Lordships, name the candidate you prefer out of so many distinguished competitors, and I, your elder brother and servant, will consider the matter closed." The other senators voiced opinions *pro et contra;* and we're obstinate in our arguments. "I'm for that one." "I'm for that one." "I prefer him." "And I him." This one argued thus, that one so.

As this is going on, Wielkopolska now gives a shout: *"Vivat rex!"* Several from our delegation dash over to see whom they are cheering; they returned with the news that it was Charles of Lorraine. In Łęczyce and Kujawy they were saying, "we don't need a rich man for, upon becoming the king of Poland, he'll be rich. We don't need anyone related to other royalty, for 'tis a *periculum libertatis,*[23] but we need a *virum fortem,* a *virum bellicosum.*[24] Were Czarniecki here, he'd surely have sat on the throne; but as God took him from us, let us elect his disciple, let us elect [Alexander] Polanowski."

This is going on here; meanwhile I, *per curiositatem* dashed over to the deputies from Sandomierz, they were standing the closest to us, and what should I find but that they prefer someone *de sanguine gentis,*[25] and they're saying: "We have not far to look for a king, he's in our midst. Recalling the virtue and decency, and the many services to this country of the deceased Prince [Jeremi] Wiśniowiecki, right and fitting would it be to pay our debt of gratitude to his *posteritas.*[26] Here is Prince Michał Wiśniowiecki; why should we not elect him? Is he not from an ancient family of great princes? Is he not worthy of the crown?"

And he is sitting there among the gentry, humble as pie, wincing, saying nothing. I rush back to my own delegation and say: "Gentlemen, already several delegations are putting forth a Piast."[27] Our Kraków

20. Pasek is mistaken; Prazmowski was not present on the election field; the "*Veni Creator*" was sung by the bishop of Poznan, Wierzbowski.
21. Along with all the clergy.
22. And the like.
23. Danger to liberty.
24. A strong man, a military man.
25. Of native blood.
26. Heir.
27. The Piast kings established the first dynasty in Poland; hence, by extension, the term is used for any ruler of native Polish blood.

lordship inquires: "Who is it?" Say I: "Polanowski and Wiśniowiecki." *And meanwhile there's a roar from Sandomierz: "Vivat Piast!"* Dębicki, the chamberlain, hurls his cap into the air, yelling at the top of his voice: *"Vivat Piast! Vivat Rex Michael!"* And now our Kraków deputies too: *"Vivat Piast!"* A few of us run off to the other provincial delegations with the news, shouting *"Vivat Piast!"* Those from Łęczyce and Kujawy, thinking it's for their Polanowski, at once started shouting too; other delegations too. Returning to my own, they're now taking his arm, they're leading him to the assembly.

Our Kraków officers *negant, contradicunt,*[28] (having taken a great deal of money from others and made big promises), in particular, Pisarski and Lipski who were saying: "For God's sake, what are we doing? Have we gone mad? Wait! This cannot be." Our Kraków lordship has now withdrawn from us, the nominee being his kinsman; there he is, next to the candidate. Many other senators are coming toward us. Some protest, others remain silent. Pisarski says to me (he nonetheless held me in esteem); "My dear fellow, what think you of this situation?" I reply: "I think what God has put in my heart: *"Vivat Rex Michaę!"* Where upon, I ride out of the line and dash after Sandomierz; in all haste the squadrons with their standards follow after me, only Pisarski, slamming his cap on his head, rode off to the side.

We led Wiśniowiecki then to the assembly. Now come the *gratulationes,*[29] now was there rejoicing for men of good will, heartache for the evildoers.

The archbishop carried out the formalities proper to his office on the inauguration of the newly elected king and also the church ceremonies wherein *gratiarum actionis*[30] were offered, but with what kind of intention, what kind of zeal! Just as if you were to harness a wolf to a plough and bid him plough by force. What burst out later *in publicum,* what odd behavior toward a good king, I shall describe further on.

The next day, the king was dearer by several million; so many presents was he given: carriages, harnesses, tapestries, silver, and sundry valuable ornaments. Even the envoys of those princes who had competed for his crown gave him gifts. Enough said, that the Lord God so inclined people's hearts toward him that whoever had anything of special worth brought it to him as a gift: not only one's handsomest horse, one's best charger, but also one's best equipment, be it but a pair of pistols set in ebony or ivory.

The *nobilitas* dispersed then to their homes, no longer in squadrons

28. Do not wish it, oppose it.
29. Congratulations.
30. Prayers of thanksgiving.

but *sparsim.*[31] I, too, having passed some days with my kin in Rawa, set off for home.

The coronation took place in Kraków on the 29th of September amid a large assembly of divers people and the Coronation Diet opened at once, but *malo eventu,*[32] being dissolved by Olizar, a deputy from Kiev, which maneuvre was part of a plot.

The army was camped at Bochryn but did not attempt to engage the enemy.

Nihilominum[33] the dissolved Diet, Father Andrzej Olszowski, bishop of Chełm, was despatched to the Emperor to plead for the hand of his sister in marriage to King Michał. He obtained all readily, for the Emperor wishing it himself had even brought it up.

31. Separately.
32. Without result.
33. Notwithstanding.

The Year of Our Lord 1670

I began in Miławczyce, but being dissatisfied with that lease, after mid-Lent I moved to Smogorzów.

The royal wedding was celebrated in Częstochowa [Feb. 28] in the presence of a great many of our Poles; but the Germans made a rather foolish showing, and the bride was not dowered like an emperor's daughter.

Dwelling in Smogorzów, I went rafting for the first time.[1] Being an apprentice raftsman, I stuck with the old skippers who warned me I'd be swindled up there, being but a novice; by God's grace, however, I sold my wheat for a higher price than they, 40 zloties higher; and it came about in this way: the titular district supervisor of Ujście Solne, Piegłowski, and the Warsaw cup-bearer, Opacki, had angered some merchants who, being in cahoots, agreed together not to buy from them out of spite; I, being next in their path, was paid 150 zloties for my wheat to spite those two. *Pan* Jarlach it was who bought my wheat; the others were almost begging merchants to buy theirs; then they were paid at 110 zloties. And so, those who had threatened I'd be fleeced, were fleeced themselves.

1. Grain and timber were shipped down the Vistula to Gdańsk.

The Year of Our Lord 1671

I began in Smogorzów, but in mid-Lent I changed my residence to Skrzypiów, paying 10,000 florins to the castellan of Bełz, *Pan* Myszkowski for these properties and for Zakrzów. Smogorzów I leased for a year to *Pan* Trębicki, who had previously held Skrzypiów, he having no place to go. In the same year *Pan* Myszkowski contracted with me to lease Olszowka and Brześć, but as he could not recover these properties from the Chełmski brothers, I was obliged to wait it out in Skrzypiów for six years, though I had reckoned on them for paying off 21,000 zloties of various debts from the entailed estates; what expense and worry those estates cost me, I shall describe further on.

In Skrzypiów I prospered and with this lease I was satisfied. This year as well, I rafted to Gdańsk and sold my grain to a *Pan* Wandern, a most upright merchant.

This year the army was encamped at Trembowla; at Kalnik the Crimean Tartars took a heavy beating.[1] Afterward, the battle of Trościaniec took place. I, paying off my debts of entailment, gave 4,000 florins to *Pan* Szandorowski, a detachment commander, at the behest of his lordship, *Pan* Myszkowski, to her ladyship, *Pani* Miklaszowska, 3,000 florins, to his excellency, Prince Aleksander Ostrogski, 3,000, and 3,000 to the chamberlain of Bełz for the equipping and despatch of men to camp.

The pre-Diet regional assemblies were held in November, the Warsaw Diet *in Januario.*[2]

1. Sobieski smashed the weak Tartar forces here on October 21.
2. Pasek's mistake: the regional assemblies took place in December. The Diet lasted from January 26 to March 14, 1672.

The Year of Our Lord 1672

I resided in Skrzypiow, for my wife would never dwell in Smogorzów *ex ratione* that it was rumored to be a *locus fatalis* — its master or mistresses used to die. But I often sojourned there, and the Lord preserved me, though I was master of it for 20 years.

Summons went out for a general levy. The Turks had come out in a great force. Our army was in Batoh under the command of *Pan* Łużecki, the castellan of Podlasie. Old one-eye has not ceased his intrigues, hoping to knock another king off the throne, upon which he had been placed by God himself. In short, many and dreadful *inter viscera motus.*[1]

The Łącki family fell heir this year to Rączki; whereupon I got the children's share of the divided estate; I purchased a second from the co-heirs, and both these pieces of property I let go to my wife's daughter, Jadwiga, who was married to my nephew, Samuel Dembowski. I let them have it out of kindness, taking nothing for it, though over several years, I'd invested a great deal of money in it, not counting the bother, the comings and goings, the squabbles, brawls, duels.

Smogorzów I leased for a year to *Pani* Gołuchowska, a handsome and sensible widow; and there she married *Pan* Tomasz Olszamowski.

I departed for the army, halting at Kosina where the Kraków forces had assembled; from there we set off for Gołąb and, the king arriving there, all the provincial forces joined together in the camp.

The Turks had already taken Kamieniec [Podolski],[2] but to tell the truth they'd not really taken it, only bought it from some traitors to our country; without drawing a sword, they'd subjugated all Podolia and the Ukraine. The Lithuanian Tartars, having been trained by us, betrayed us and all of them, together with their leader, Kryczyński, went over to the Turks.[3]

1. Domestic disturbances.
2. Kamieniec Podolski on the Smotrycz river, the Commonwealth's main fortress in the south, surrendered on August 29.
3. During King Michał's reign, part of the Lithuanian Tartars emigrated to Bessarabia

After the capture of Kamieniec, the Tartars pushed deep into the country, but by the grace of God, nowhere did they have success, our army combatting them mightily in the name of our pious king; at Niemirów, at Komarno, at Kałusza they died like dogs, but most of them in the forests and swamps were slain by the peasants. Meanwhile we are halted at Gołąb with the king, it being hard to advance any further, and we join up with the regular army, since we did not trust them, seeing what *conspirationes* were afoot *contra coronatum caput,*[4] how glad they would be to see the king in jeopardy from the enemy.

As the Tartars were taking captives near Komarno, a raiding party was sent out, people being picked from the general levy, and with good mounts. We were divided into two troops. Kalinowski was given command over one, I over the other. We set out at night taking two trails. I, being well-acquainted with the tactics of a raid, set forth to Bełżyce, going by back trails and forests the whole way. This did not sit well with my gentlemen recruits, they complaining it wasn't a beaten track, your horse would stumble over a stump from time to time, a branch would cut across your face. By daybreak I stood outside of Bełżyce at the edge of a forest; to give the horses a bit of a rest we let them graze there, holding onto the reins. As dawn was breaking, I say: "Gentlemen, we must discover what is going on in the town, if we haven't perchance landed in a trap here, for you hear the dogs barking, yet no one's about. So a few horse will have to approach first, then signal to us; or if you're observed, then lure them into the field so that we can surround and attack the pursuers and obtain intelligence." No one offers to go; I'm mighty vexed and I say, "Is it thus we're going to obey orders, Gentlemen? How are we to proceed? Plainly, I've no command here, if such is the *oboedientia* I get; I'll go myself then, and you be on the alert at least, should I bring you guests." Exceeding dread there was, for such was the rumor that the Tartars were already near Bełżyce; seems they were around yesterday afternoon, but not many of them. Chociwski says: "I'll ride with Your Honor"; Sieklicki says, "And I." For they were like my own kin: one a cousin, the other a close friend. Young Stroński says: "If Your Honor is going alone, then I'll go with you, but not with anyone else." We rode off then.

We get to the town — not a sound; we ride into it — nothing budges; once again the dogs grew excited, after having been quiet for awhile. Into the houses we went, looking for people — not a soul; anyone who's alive is in the woods. We rode back out of town, and stood quietly among the farms, by now it was light; suddenly a peasant, lifting a small

and from there conducted raids on Poland.

4. Against the crowned head.

sheaf of the thatching, peeked out of a barn. Into that barn we go, calling to him, searching; no way could we find him, the barn being full of grain. Finally, I start shouting: "Peasant! Is it your doom you desire? Will you hide from the Tartars only to perish at the hands of the Christians? I need no more than to ask what is going on here for I'm from the king and in this entire town I'm unable to find a soul, and you're not showing your face, even though we've already seen you; so we've nothing else to do with you but take vengeance and set fire to you here." Now of a sudden, the peasant: "My Lord, I'm just crawling out." Out he came then. We inquire: "Were the Tartars here?" "They were here yesterday afternoon; they chased two peasants but they got away to the forest. The Tartars stopped at once on the edge, but one peasant was shot in the back from a bow, after he'd run into the forest. Towards evening, again we saw about thirty horsemen, who they were I know not, being far away."

Then I sent for my men. They came then, and we took council; meanwhile they put sheaves of grain in front of their horses. Some say, "Go on," others say, "Don't go on, go back: you'll lead us to our deaths. It's enough that we've come thus far; lead us no further." But I prevailed upon them finally to go. We ride a mile, then another, now there are *vestigia* of the Tartars, things they'd thrown away, having found something better. My men turn coward; I to cheer them say that such things were dropped by the fugitives, not the Tartars. Suddenly a gentleman rode out of the forest towards us, declaring that: "Going on but a mile, we'll seize as many Tartars as we like for they're wandering about the villages, it should be no trouble to take a captive. I was riding in the midst of them yesterday, and they dared not attack me, so encumbered they are, and their horses bone weary. I'll guide you there myself along the trails through the underbrush." Being much taken by his account, I say: "Well, Gentlemen, now we must show that God and *natura* created us men and not mushrooms; we'll outdo the others if we can write to the king that we're bringing a captive. God himself has provided this occasion whereby we can so easily win glory for ourselves; let's show that we're men." O God! What an outcry! "But are we regulars? Are we Wallachians? Are we servants?[5] We've a regular army whom we pay to fight for us. They did not send us here to get a captive, but to get intelligence, the which having gotten, let's not go any further. I've a wife and children; I'll not knock about only because someone wishes it, for I don't have to." I plead as well as I can that "we're as much men as the regulars; let us not act like Jerusalem's but like Polish

5. Inhabitants of Bessarabia and Wallachia, vassal states of the Commonwealth, which were then under Turkish rule, joined the hired troops as mercenaries and usually served in the light cavalry.

nobility; let us remember God and country; let us be ashamed of the sun that shines on us, rather than be ashamed of being men." *Surdis fabula narratur*;[6] they keep to their "we ought not, we won't go." I ask: "When you rode away from home, *qua intentione*[7] did you leave? Were you riding off to war or to a wedding?" By no means could I win them over. I swearing aloud that as long as I live, I'll never accept such a charge, that I'd rather tend pigs than lead recruits from a general levy on a raid — we turned back then from that expedition.

I had a young lad, Leśniewicz, who led my other horse for me, a great rascal; and I say to him: "Listen, my dear fellow, bid someone else take the horse, and you find a way to give us a bit of a scare." Off he rode then, assuring me he'd do it, and meanwhile I told a few trusted men that "we're going to have a little scare here of a sudden." We're arriving at the village that evening and that lad had lit a pile of hemp in a garden, the stacks, as usual in autumn, being placed close by the huts. Now it bursts into flame and they all think it's the Tartars; people scurrying about, the village in an uproar. I say: "Gentlemen, forward! this way!" But the gentlemen went the opposite way, as fast they could go in all directions. They call to me: "Commander! You better fly, Sir, for you'll lead us to our deaths, as well as endanger the army and our king, if we bring the enemy after us." I, in my usual way, say: "Bah, it's too tempting, I'll dash over to the fire, and find out what's going on." Also, those who know the cause of it say: "Let's go, let's charge; they'll not swallow us up after all." We galloped into the village then, the gentlemen made off. We turn around and went back — not a soul; we found only what the gentlemen had left behind while running off: a sack of rusks, smoked meats, cheese, cloaks, quirts, and other odds and ends. Among other things, there was a leather belt with a metal cartridge case, leather-bound; full of excellent spirits it was, nearly a half-gallon; so ashamed of this were they that no one would admit to owning it, although we showed it afterward, having tied it to a tall stick.

On the way back then, I took to thinking and I say to the others: "We acted wrongly: what if those cowards run back and alarm the army!" Someone says: "quite so, quite so! What shall we do about it?" "We'll have to send someone who will pass them all by and get there first to testify, so that should some coward say anything, he would not be believed." *Pan* Adam Sieklicki says: "Let my lad, Wilczopolski, go. He serves me on horseback; I'll order him not to spare it." In a twinkling then it was decided. We gave him those spirits to pour down his gullet and I say to him: "Don't spare the horse, my lad, for there's a lot at stake; God forbid that the army and the king should be alarmed on

6. One might as well tell a tale to a deaf man.
7. With what intention.

account of our pranks: you'd fear for your neck as well (for, being from the Lublin gentry and familiar with the place, he was there with my lad). Even if you must ride the horse into the ground, don't spare it." Being a penniless yeoman, he's somewhat reluctant to undertake it, fearing for his horse. Finally I say: "Mount mine then, and hand yours over to my lad."

So he did. He overtook them, passed them by, and what is more, while overtaking them, he gave them an even greater fright, saying: "Look at me — not even sitting on my own horse, for I lost him and had to mount another's." No sooner had he passed them all, but he slowed up, riding with the front riders; when they'd scrambled out of the woods, they had but to ride across the fields; he urged them to stay a while in the pasture, saying "our gentlemen are there in the rearguard; should it be difficult for them, we'd already see them behind us." And they, sensible that it would be a great disgrace, if they were to return without their commander and in a different troop, halted within a mile from the camp, pshaw, not even that far away. Having got their fill of scratches in those woods, banged themselves in the head, many took a week to recover, drinking potions and massaging their hides. We, however, passed the night in bivouac, and fared well, as did the horses.

So soon as morning began to dawn, we set forth at an amble collecting caps, quirts, and the like along the trail. We ride out of the forest, whereupon they, seeing us, mount their horses. I riding up to them: "Well, Gentlemen, before God and men we ought to be ashamed; we've let slip an opportunity; but for your disobedience we might have taken captives and won fame; several dozen Tartars there were, buy they got away, there being no one to surround and attack the villages; we were few, it was night, we hadn't enough men to do it alone, had there been several hundred of us, it's sure none of them would have escaped." They did not believe me straight away, saying "you deceive us." But when they caught sight of the jade which my attendant had taken from that other lad while we were in the underbrush, and that someone had run off without it, only then do they believe me, it being like a young Tartar horse and the saddle covered only with plain leather, Tartar-style. Now did they rejoice, and fell to pleading with us to say we hadn't seen any Tartars, "for we'd suffer all the blame and disgrace."

We stood in the field debating nearly an hour, leaving our attendants aside; afterward we instructed them to say they'd not seen any Tartars either. I promised them, then, to their great satisfaction, that I was not going to say anything: "You're not offending the Lord God with an untruth by saying you didn't see any Tartars; only consider how a nation is disgraced and becomes infamous if its men are without courage: in the district dietines, in general assemblies, we say plenty, we cause much commotion, but when the time comes to act, we do nothing." Moreover, I twitted them at every gathering, appearing to praise them: "These are my comrades-in-arms! We went on raids together, we were together in battles, struggled thus and so." Whoever knows the circumstances can only laugh.

We made off then for the camp, and there comes Kalinowski and his party. We joined up, he inquiring what success I'd had. I say I'd rather have been tending pigs all the while, than be in charge of such a raiding party. He says the same, and so we discoursed, riding off to one side the whole way, until we set foot in the central yard of the camp.

On our return to camp, they bid us go to the king to report. I did not wish to go, feigning illness, but Kalinowski came to me: "Go, Your Honor, for they'll think that task drained you of your strength." I say: "I don't feel inclined, I'm ashamed to go, I've nothing to say for nothing was done, nor can I lie." Says Kalinowski: "All right, I'll give the report, you were with me, commanding the other raiding party." I went with him then to the royal tents, there we found divers senators and nobles. Kalinowski then gives his report, delivers it as if under torture, he colors the account; at the end, he says that we tried with all our heart to obtain a captive, but no where could we even get at one, for those roaming Tartar bands had run back to their main camp. In fact he with his party did not cover even half the distance I did, nor did he get a whiff of a Tartar, as his men did not obey him either.

No sooner had he finished, but the mustermaster-general, Stefan Czarniecki, addresses me, "Did Your Honor take a different trail with your men?" I say: "That's correct." "Then you will have to make a separate report of your actions." The other senators said: "You certainly must do so." At last I say: "Our duty as subjects is to fulfill Your Majesty's commands, My Gracious Lord; you are now our Commander-in-Chief and dispenser of our blood which each of your loyal subjects ought voluntarily to place *in aleam fortunae*[8] and I judge myself accordingly; however, I shall not examine in what spirit or with what willingness proper in the present circumstances to Your Majesty, My Gracious Lord, who offered the sacrifice. My deeds and those of my comrades-in-arms, though the best, ought not to be praised; however, to condemn them if base, is cruel. These actions, which can be weighed *in statera iudicii,*[9] should neither be condemned, nor praised; little good it does, for *eventus acta probat.*[10] I don't know, whether it was poor eyesight that we, having come upon enemy traces, seeing fire and smoke, were unable to serve Your Royal Highness, My Gracious Lord, with one captive. The meaning of the account given by His Honor, the master of the royal hunt, my fellow officer from Podlasie is:"*Volui, sed*

8. In fortune's hands.
9. On the scale of reason.
10. The result proves the deed.

non potui."[11] Whereas if I must offend God doubly: by laziness and by untruthfulness, I prefer to confess *verius dicendo: potui, sed nolui;*[12] in the words of a great sovereign: *veni, vidi, sed non vici.*[13] In the future, should Your Gracious Majesty have need of my services for a similar expedition, I would prefer to execute that duty with 15 yeomen who are disciplined rather than a hundred or more gentlemen who are guided in military affairs by their affections. For this I do humbly beseech Your Majesty, My Gracious Lord." They look at one another then fell to laughing uproariously. Says Szczęsny [Kazimierz] Potocki, governor of Sieradz, to the king: "Such genuine praise I've not yet seen." Czarniecki, district supervisor of Kaniów and mustermaster-general, replies: "No wonder, for he's learned to wage war in the proper way." This got spread about then, the gentlemen were vexed. Old Misiowski said in front of a few: *Pan* Pasek will fare ill with us in our province for such defamation of his fellow gentrymen." And I spoke *contra:* "they behaved infamously and I'll always reproach them for it to their faces." Afterward, *Pan* Sobieski, the hetman and crown marshal, sent the king a few Tartars; but *fremebat popularitas*[14] even at that, since he was rumored to be, along with the archbishop, another malcontent. They began at once to organize a confederacy, or rather to carry through their scheme whereby all would swear *unanimi voto* to stand by the king to the death, since he enjoyed great *popularitatem* and was held in affection by all estates. For this reason, they strongly inveighed against all malcontents.

We set forth then to Lublin, and no sooner had we halted there but we talked *de modo consultationis:*[15] "What to christen it: a Mounted Diet? a Convocation Diet? a Council of War?"[16] It was resolved then that a Convocation Diet it was not, for such a Diet consists of *certum numerum personarum;*[17] nor is it an ordinary Diet, which consists of *nuntios terrestres;*[18] whereas here we had the *tota Respublica*, each man being his own deputy; so it has to be a Council of War, the Commonwealth being in a state of war. We chose as marshal, then, Stefan Czarniecki, the mustermaster-general, district supervisor of Kaniów, a man *tantae activitatis,*[19] who knows how to organize matters for the accomplish-

11. I wanted to but could not.
12. By speaking the truth: I could, but did not want to.
13. I came, I saw, but did not conquer.
14. The mass of gentry was indignant.
15. About the means of assembly.
16. The concept of a Mounted Diet was more than once put into practice in this era; it was a diet composed of all the nobility coming out in a general muster on horseback. A Convocation Diet was called during an interregnum to deal with affairs of state and prepare the election of a new king.
17. A limited number of persons.
18. Provincial deputies.
19. Of such resourcefulness.

ment of all our ends in a way that would bring no harm to the Commonwealth. God himself plainly guided men's hearts to elect someone with an eye not only on the front wheels of the cart but also on the rear, for had it been anyone else amongst those who wished the position, *infallibiliter* the confusion in the Commonwealth would have been worse than ever. For some stood firmly by the Crown, reminding us that to affront it was to strike at the foundation and cornerstone and that it must be defended *in gradu absoluto*;[20] others, however, recalled examples of the past when similar occasions occurred, having to do with but one person, and what havoc they caused in our country, how much bloodshed! It was thought that this bloodbath would result in great chaos, and Lord knows, perhaps, even ultimate doom not only for this realm alone, which is the *antemurale Christianitatis*[21] but for all of Christendom; plainly, however, the very will of God *militabat pro nobis,*[22] since we weathered it all successfully. Whereas violent men desired war and bloodshed, justifying themselves by saying that Poland cannot prosper as long as *perversa capita*[23] (who, even with a good king, will not let us enjoy our freedoms in peace) go unpunished.

So then, fortunately, Czarniecki became marshal-elect; forthwith, it was resolved that the council should be set up according to districts and that, *propter meliorem ordinem,*[24] only elected delegates shall sit in session with the marshal in order to impart a faster pace to the debates on public matters, not to waste time in speechmaking, and to make it possible for each deputy to declare in the name of his own district; we did not exclude the possibility for each noble to speak to the issue, even though not a deputy, upon asking the marshal for the floor, but he should first inform himself well from his own deputy. They met then in individual councils and elected two deputies from each district; I, too, was bade by the gentlemen from the Lelów district to serve them; and so I became a deputy with *Pan* Wojciech Giebułtowski.

We met then in the field in front of the royal tents, sitting in a large circle, and there were always a dozen or so observers on horseback around us, at times even a thousand, some sober, others drunk. The marshal opened the first session with an elegant speech. Felicitations from the king to the senate came next, *apprecando felicem eventum.*[25] The marshal replied to each one *in forma amplissima.*[26]

20. Unflinchingly in a decisive way.
21. The rampart of Christianity.
22. Was contending for us.
23. Perverse heads.
24. For better functioning.
25. With wishes for a successful outcome.
26. In the most flowery style.

The *materiae consultationis*[27] was then proposed, especially the cardinal points, that is, the defense of the country and adequate resistance to Turkish power; secondly, the king's body guard and security from the assaults and coups of malcontents. The marshal requests a motion from the circle: what to begin with. Deputies began to argue that both of them are necesssities but that *cura salutis*[28] of His Majesty the king, Our Gracious Lord, should be our main premise and that, above all, some protection for the Crown first has to be devised and then to take counsel on other matters. So beloved was our king that all agreed *unanimi voce* to the recruiting in camp of an army of 15,000 to be put directly at his disposal, and that in case of necessity the levy in mass come out at once on the field at the first royal summons — the deputies declared themselves of their own accord, and this discussion took no more than three hours.

However, *de methodo contribuendi*[29] for this expedition they could not agree for several days in the individual assemblies, for some wanted to levy taxes on fields; others on homesteads. And as collection of those taxes would not have been speedy enough to pay for that expedition, here, too, no less love for the king was shown by his subjects: whoever had money cached at home spoke up of his own accord: "I shall lend my province 50,000." "I'll lend 60." and "I, 15," etc. So, in no time they had even more than they needed. The deputies then were their own tax collectors, they delivered the sums to their commanders themselves, in return for promissory notes; which commanders the provinces had themselves elected. Others who resided nearer at hand, caused the money to be transported to camp; and thus in a flash the safety of the king was provided for.[30] All of which came about because of the genuine love of subjects for their king, who certainly needed a defense at that time, for he did not trust the other army under the hetmans.

As for resistance to Turkish might, the idea was that whatever good was done now for the king, it is a public good, *publiciter bonum*, for when we shall have a strong king, it is unlikely any fierce attacks would be stirred up against him. Then they planned the defense of the country. Finally, they passed on to the matter of bringing to trial all those who, without a cause, *consurgunt*[31] against their king. Others argue against it,

27. Agenda.
28. Precautions for the safety.
29. On the method of paying the taxes.
30. Pasek exaggerates. According to contemporary testimonies, the gentry very reluctantly voted to collect taxes for the defense of the country; the same was true at Gołąb.
31. Are rebelling.

especially the marshal: "during a terrible war one should not *irritare crabrones*[32] but rather keep silent about the offense; His Majesty, being a gracious lord, *non urget propter bonum pacis;*[33] should such an insurgent be discovered, there will be time to deal with him afterward, God willing, once this frightful Turkish conflict has been laid to rest." But oh, was it not in vain! Wasn't it the old story: "Try them!" Just let one *ex magnatibus*[34] be mentioned, they'll but cry out: "A traitor! Fit for the executioner's sword," etc. "How much longer will these traitors be upsetting us with their perfidies? King Kazimierz was not good enough for them; they did not cease tempting him until they'd brought him to eternal infamy. No sooner has God given us our present ruler — who is not a king, but a father — they dislike him at once. We ought to shake off these advisors who take so little care of us, for otherwise we shall never rest."

Now do they debate this at the Council. The deputies reply to each other *rationaliter;*[35] while those observers standing around fly off the handle at the least word; at the slightest word, swords clash, maces swing, they grab for their pistols; meanwhile, the deputies rise from their places to intercede, each for his own man, (for it was the rule that every man who rode or walked to the Council *non capiat*[36] a place except in back of his own deputies. Now it's like a storm in a kettle here; any issue, no matter how trivial, took up one and two hours. It was the same at the special councils, which met under their banners *ante sessionem;*[37] they too were carried on amid great uproar; enough said, that it was no use reproaching, or even muttering against the king: he had so captured the hearts of all, for they were saying "this is our king, our blood, *os de ossibus;*[38] it's long since we enjoyed a king of our people."

Trivial matters were discussed by the secretary of Bielsk in the Council, until the district supervisor of Środź began to speak feverishly against the malcontents, backing his argument with a letter and finally: "we must slay them all." At that moment, the secretary from Bielsk — white as a dove he was, and a great soldier, he attended every Diet as the deputy from Podlasie —exclaimed: "Your Lordship the Honorable District Supervisor will not hold out!" (for he was a deputy as well as a district supervisor). God Almighty! What a tempest breaks loose: "How's that, you son of an infidel! Won't hold out? But we shall hold out; we shan't yield, though corpse fall upon corpse. Belike you're of

32. Stir up a hornets' nest.
33. Is not demanding (it) on account of the peace.
34. Of the magnates.
35. With arguments.
36. Did not occupy.
37. Before the main session.
38. Bone of our bone.

their mind; seize him, give him a beating, send him outside the circle to our men here, we'll make a present of his head to *Pan* Sobieski." They were already slicing at him. The poor wretch jumped like a goat behind the marshal. The marshal calls out: "Infantry! Infantry!" Straightaway 600 foot are standing behind him, muskets a-quiver in their hands. The officers are saying: "When do we take up our arms?" Bishops jumped up, senators jumped up; just in time they shielded him. We deputies in the Council squeezed closer together so they'd not get at him, for they were dead set on trying to drag him out of the circle and hack him to bits. Those who were understood to be *eiusdem spiritus*[39] (there being some dissident lordships in the Council at the time), fled to their tents when the commotion began, distrusting their own justice; especially some of our commanders from Kraków.

Several times then it almost came to bloodshed, and in fact, a few days later, a tragic spectacle occurred, when a certain Firlej Broniowski arrived at Council in his cups; at first he stood behind us on horseback, that is, behind the deputies from Kraków province; he started yelling, shouting, interrupting the speeches. I thought it was someone from the Podgórze highlands until my colleagues tell me: "That man is not from our province." He began to bellow even louder, and I say to him then: "My good fellow, we don't need an overseer here. This place is for the deputies of Kraków province; either stand quietly or move along!" He took offense at me, began scolding: "I'm allowed to stand where I please." My colleagues then break in, they say to him: "You're not allowed; or don't you know the rule? Every one must stand behind the deputies of his own province. Now move along, or we'll clobber you! Or are you ashamed of your province?" Our men, who were also on horseback, amongst whom he was standing, say: "Move along, Your Honor, to your own province!" and they chased him out. He crossed over to the other side, there again setting up a clamor. And he was known to be a dissident too. Someone says to him: "Oh, oh, watch out, Your Honor, Sir, that you don't come to grief." He only grows more boisterous; then he said something against king. To sword — after him they went. He started to escape among the huts of Bielsk province; they chased him out. Finally, on the field they cruelly hacked him to pieces. We here in the Council know nothing of what is going on out there, but they drag him into our circle crying out: "Make way!" Two servants then dragged him in by the feet — one boot on, the body livid — they threw him into the center of the circle saying: "There you have the first dissident; the same will happen to the second!" We stood there with grief in our hearts and horror, looking upon that butchered body. Those who thought of themselves as dissidents were half-dead of

39. Of the same mind.

fright, with him lying there in his own blood like an ox slaughtered. So, having met for but half an hour, the marshal cut the session short; we dispersed.

Autumn's bad weather descended upon us then — ice and snow — so that a body didn't recognize his own horse upon rising in the morning; a snowfall having blanketed him. Now we held our sessions in the tents owing to the bad weather. The gentry began to depart for their homes, only we deputies and the marshal had to toil through to the end. Before the end of the Council, Castellan [Marcin] Zamoyski barely escaped being killed in the same way as Broniowski. One noble had accused him of speaking about the king thus: "more fit to carry a basket of soap around Zamość than reign as king."[40] A hairsbreadth away from hacking him to death were they, he kneeling, swearing he had not said it, folding his hands. The marshal pleaded for him: "For God's sake, Gentlemen, enough of this bloodshed now!" The king sent word: "Should he have said this, and worse even, I forgive him, and I plead for his life." They let him be.

We ended the Council of War on the 19th of November; all having signed the *acta,*[41] we bade farewell to the king. The marshal gave a speech *nomine omnium,*[42] a very eloquent piece of oratory, which eloquence few people had suspected in him; only after having been marshal at this Council did he win a reputation for being a great orator. We rode off happily then, to our separate destinations.

Upon arriving home, the 16th of November, I found the household in mourning for my dear mother, who gave up the ghost on the eve of Sts. Simon and Jude [October 27]. *"Utinam in sancta pace requiescat!"*[43] We buried her in the church of the Reformation Fathers in Stopnica.

40. Zamość was the hereditary property of the Zamoyski family.
41. Documents.
42. In the name of all.
43. May she rest in peace.

The Year of Our Lord 1673

I started out — may God grant His blessings — in Skrzypiów. Having leased Smogorzów for one year, I recovered it from *Pani* Olszamowska who married there.

Then came the Diet in Warsaw, during which Archbishop Prażmowski closed his eye in eternal slumber; though he had only one, it saw much and worked much evil. He died in Jazdów finally, from worry over being unable to carry out his French schemes.[1] Prince Czartoryski succeeded him as primate, an eminent magnate and senator, a man of great saintliness.

This winter the Turks did not leave the field, but entrenched themselves at Chocim [Khotin, Hotin], making a camp there. Our hetmans wished to do battle, having decently trained armies from Poland and Lithuania, provincial troops recruited from the peasants, excellent squadrons of Gentlemen of the Horse. The Turks would not come out to the field, the Tartars having deserted them. Our men then, in an unheard-of precedent, resolved to storm them; they went up to the trenches, encircled the camp, the infantry sapped the embankments *nemine reclamante*[2] and they collapsed in several places; not even once did the Turks fire from their artillery, though they had cannons in great quantity. Belike the Lord had blinded the pagans and taken their courage from them, since they received us so politely as we were making the assault, as if we were guests arriving, not the enemy. They stayed mobbed together in the trenches on horseback until our squadrons rode in through the breaches we'd made in the embankments; only then did they attack our men, but not long could they hold out; straightaway they began to flee to the bridge on the Dniester toward Kamieniec. There at last our men slew them. And since masses of them were pressing onto that bridge, it collapsed; now, as it sank, our men slew some, drowned others; still others they chased up a rocky pre-

1. Ujazdów, today a suburb of Warsaw, was formerly a separate community. Prażmowski died on April 15, 1673.
2. Without any opposition.

cipice, from whence they and their horses fell down upon their crowns.

Booty our men took in great abundance: harnesses, silver, sumptuous tents; in their coffers were exquisite curios, every other coffer you could reckon at 100,000; there were ornamental swords, long muskets used by the Janizaries.[3] So many camels were brought into Poland then that you could even get one for a servant's nag.

One son especially gladdened his father with his trophy. This son was a commander of the peasant recruits, and he had several camels among his spoils. Upon arriving home, he wanted to greet his father in Turkish dress: he put on a complete Turkish outfit with turban and mounted a camel; having bid his retinue stay in the village, he rode ahead to the manor. His old father is just hobbling with a cane across the barn yard to some farm, when here rides this horror through the gate. The old man started running to beat the devil, crossing himself. The son, seeing his father was terrified, runs after him, calling: "Stay, my benefactor, 'tis I, your son!" The faster did the old man fly. He fell ill, then, from the fright and, soon after, died.

Poland was flooded then with Turkish articles — beautiful embroidered things, magnificent horses, splendid quivers, and divers other curios. Miraculous was the victory God gave our nation, but what is still more miraculous about that battle: the enemy forgot how to defend itself; just as before when we stormed the Wallachian and Moldavian camps, the Turks had not come to their defense and finally did not even defend themselves, except when we forced them out of the camp. Our men received their share too: [Achacy] Pisarski, district supervisor of Wolbrom and a commander, perished along with his lieutenant; so did [Jan] Żelecki, the district supervisor of Bydgoszcz, and others. *Primo vere*[4] their army was to have gone to Lwów, and after taking it, on further into Poland. We were already begging for quarter and they willing to accept, we having no more *qui manum opponat.*[5] We asked them to leave us in peace, like the Wallachians and Moldavians, in order not to corrupt our faith.[6] "That would be impossible; the Wallachians and Moldavians surrendered of their own accord, while you have been at war with us." To be sure, they had not yet sent deputies, but through the Crimean Khan they had already begun discussions. In a word, great was the fear, great the alarm, when suddenly the Lord turned everything around, giving us a victory at Chocim. The Turks

3. Janizaries (from the Turkish *jeni-cheri*, meaning new army) comprised an elite corps recruited from Turkified Christian youth.
4. In early spring.
5. Power to resist.
6. The Wallachians and Moldavians, though Turkish subjects, were free to remain Christians.

had to lower their noses when they lost the army they considered their best; they permitted peace to be negotiated at once, being satisfied with Podole alone; it having been spread all over the kingdom that they were telling the Podole gentry: "you can't plead for such liberty as the Wallachians have, for you are unruly; but we'll disarm you, we'll turn you into tillers of the soil." Yet God willed it otherwise, He let not His holy places nor us be cast down.

That victory was won in the name of our pious king, Michał, who died directly after.[7] People were of divers minds as to how there was a *suspicio veneni*[8] in the garganey he always fancied eating. I suspect not; I write only what people were chattering about.

7. Actually, he died the day before, on November 19, 1673.
8. Suspicion of poisoning.

The Year of Our Lord 1674

I began — may God grant His blessings — in Skrzypiow. There was an *interregum;* we had the hooded tribunals. I travelled frequently to and from Radom on the matter of the Rączki estate.[1] The election of a new king took place in May[2] in Warsaw, but the assemblage was not as large as for King Michał. As before, there were many contenders and, as before, God gave us a Piast, *os de ossibus nostris.*[3] Jan Sobieski, grand hetman and marshal of Poland, became king-elect on the 19th of May, inaugurated on the 21st of that month, and today reigns happily; *utinam diutissime regnet pro gloria Dei et utilitate Reipublicae Christianae*[4] and may God multiply his tribe like that of Abraham's and may the crown never slip from the head of his successors as in the Austrian royal house.

The coronation, though, did not take place until the third year of his reign [February 2, 1676], for there followed great wars with the Turks, the Tartars, and the Cossacks, who having surrendered to the Turks, urged them into hostilities against us, wanting to destroy us with Turkish might. But so much the more did the villains ruin their own reputation and they lost the last remnant of their power, whereof I shall write below.

The Turks, regretting last year's losses of men, were very easily persuaded by the Cossacks to go to war against Poland, taking the Cossacks under their protection. They raised huge armies, young Chmielnicki remaining as a hostage in Istanbul. Mighty forces were aligned against us, but the Lord confounded them; they got in each other's way, fought one another instead, and left us in peace. The Turks

1. The provincial court and the castle court were both in Radom.
2. Actually, the election began on April 20.
3. Bone of our bone. (The Piast kings established the first dynasty in Poland; see the year 1669.)
4. Long may he reign to the glory of God and the benefit of the Commonwealth.

took the towns of Ładyżyn, Humań, and others by storm. In all the towns much blood was shed, but especially in Humań, where more than twice 100,000 Cossacks perished; but the Turks lost many men too in the assaults. And so, those who had thirsted for our blood, drank their own to the dregs.

The Year of Our Lord 1675

No sooner was I settled in Skrzypiów, but I did nothing so much as provide for takings of the veil and religious vows, as three of my stepdaughters became Bernardin nuns (the fourth having already done so in the deceased's time): Marianna, Aleksandra, Barbara, and another Marianna, the youngest. Not from any necessity or compulsion did they enter the convent (for they were comely girls with good dowries) but from a divine call. It cost me, however, a great deal of money, for the expense is greater than giving away a young lady in marriage. Whoever is not acquainted with the cost, I'd put him straight; for it's not enough to provide a dowry and settle the matter, you are always having to give money to the convent.

I also went to Gdańsk this year; I made a sale to *Pan* Wilhelm Braun.

The Turks and Tartar hordes attacked us, plundering and burning near Wiśniowiec, Podhajce, Zbaraż, inflicting much damage. Our king-elect kept the traitors at bay as best he could.

The Year of Our Lord 1676

I spent this year too in Skrzypiów. They brought King Michał's body to Kraków and the body of [Jan] Kazimierz from France; even though he had not wished to end his life with us, he came back to us after death. So, dear king, now you see how *dulcis locus patriae;*[1] you turned your back on your fatherland that bred you, cherished you always, and kept faith with you, and now your bones have yearned to return to your country, there to moulder and decay! Kraków experienced then a great and uncommon event, three Polish kings she received *inter moenia*[2] at the same time, two *simul et semel*[3] on one catafalque, a third she viewed in his majesty. Our king-elect, *Ioannes Tertius,*[4] having *in parte* driven the enemies of Poland from her borderlands, and seeing that he had merited that crown bestowed upon him by the Commonwealth, rides into Kraków on the 29th of January, received with great acclaim and rejoicing. Even those who had murmured against that election underwent such a change of heart; everyone was satisfied with his reign, seeing he was a sensible ruler, kind, militant, diligent, and fortunate; as the Lord willed it, there were no dissidents as in Michał's reign.

The funeral for both kings together took place in the castle in Kraków on the 31st of January; both coffins stood next to each other and were transported in one wagon, both bodies lay side by side on one catafalque and were given a common ceremony. King Jan III *devotissime*[5] assisted at all the ceremonies. But they were not buried in one grave; Kazimierz was placed in the chapel of his father, Zygmunt,[6] while Michał was buried in a corner chapel (which king's I know not) on the right hand side of the church as you enter.

1. Sweet is the place of one's birth.
2. Within her walls.
3. Side by side.
4. Jan III.
5. Most piously.
6. The Vaza family's chapel.

On the third day after the funeral rites, that is, the second of February, Candlemas Day, the king, His Majesty Jan III, was crowned; *quam felicissime, diutissime regnet*[7] to the glory of the Divine Majesty and the defense of the Christian Commonwealth! On February 4th the Coronation Diet opened, I being forced to spend nearly the whole time in Kraków on a matter involving some acts of violence perpetrated in Smogorzów by some Germans. I obtained *poenam colli*[8] for Chrzanowski, the captain, and Demek, the lieutenant; they were put in shackles.

Offices were distributed: the grand hetman's mace went to Prince Wiśniowiecki, the field hetman's mace to Jabłonowski, the small seal to the bishop of Warmia, the lesser baton to Sieniawski.

At Wojniłów a battle was fought with the Crimean Tartars; then our camp at Żurawno was beseiged by the Turks and Tartar hordes until our men, willing or not, were forced to treat with the enemy. We made a settlement then with the Turks: we let them have Podole and the Ukraine. But such treaties are shortlived with an enemy who is ever greedy to devour our poor fatherland.

7. May he reign long and fortunately.
8. The death penalty.

The Year of Our Lord 1677

God be praised! — I took possession of Olszówka and Brześć for seven years *per arendam*[1] in this way: I had signed a contract for those estates and counted out the money six years before. *Pan* Chełmski, the Polish master of the camp did not wish to give up the estate at that time (although an agreement had been made to that effect with his brother, Krzysztof) but only upon expiration of the contract. Those years having passed, he began to bluster and threaten me in order to frighten me out of that agreement. I arrange then with the castellan of Bełz, who was riding off to the Diet in Warsaw, to give orders for the estates to be turned over to me as soon as the *dies expirationis*[2] should come due. Before departing, he issues the order that when the time comes, his wife shall ride up there and turn the estates over to me. So it came to pass; although the gates were closed, we kept a watch on them so that when the peasants were let out to do the threshing, a few horsemen dashed up and held the gate open until we all had ridden inside. The estates were turned over to me then and the peasants. But without more ado, I return *ad cursum anni.*[3]

At that Diet, Gniński, the governor of Chełm, was appointed deputy to the Turks. A commission was sitting in Sandomierz;[4] our camp at Trembowla was prospering and led a comfortable existence, for the soldiers there were engaged in farming; they sowed, plowed, reaped hay, and in the winter they lived as comfortably as at home; everything was cheaper in the camp bazaar than in town, since they fermented beers and wines in the camp and as many wagons went to the market in the camp yard as used to go to Kazimierz.[5] Such a rule for the army is an excellent one; were it always thus, 'twould be better than roaming about Poland from pillar to post, ruining the horses.

1. On lease.
2. Date of expiration.
3. To the events of this year.
4. The commission was charged with the task of paying the army.
5. Kazimierz-on-the-Vistula was then a lively trading center, especially of the grain trade.

I pushed off for Gdansk on July 7 and arrived there on August 16.

This year my dear father died *secunda Decembris devotissime*[6] and according to the Christian reckoning on the eve of St. Barbara to whom he had great devotion. He died alert and was well prepared, for he was not in a fever, it was nearly falling asleep. I buried him in Kraków at the Carmelites' in the Piasek quarter. May God grant him eternal rest in His kingdom!

6. Most piously on December 2.

The Year of Our Lord 1678

I began — *utinam feliciter!* — in Olszówka.[1] This year no little harm befell me from this circumstance; his lordship the castellan of Bełz [Jan Myszkowski] asked me to the signing of an agreement with his lordship, *Pan* [Michał] Czerny, the district supervisor of Parnawa, concerning a decrease in payment on the lease of Kozubów, whither I went, taking along my gowns and furs, as directly from there I was to accompany *Pan* Floryjan Łącki, the lord steward of Malbork, to Kiełczyna to pay suit to *Panna* Borowska. I was given lodgings then in a tavern. The tavern burned down while we were in the manor house. My gowns went up in smoke — either that or they were stolen — a loss of at least 4000. Now that's a deed of friendship! But the Lord knows how much those deeds of friendship cost me in my life. And so I say this: the friends you help on some occasion may, it's true, offer to return the favor, but they forget easily. Rare it is that you find someone who will remember a kindness up to three years; and when you need a favor from him, either he doesn't want to do it, or, even if he does, he cannot. When a friend is needed, they'll find you; but when you need him, you'll have to search for him with a candle. There are others who will not oblige even though they could; and others to whom God did not give that ability to use their education, though they've enough of it. And so, there may be plenty of people, but one man is sometimes hard to find. *Nos numerus sumus et fruges consumere nati.*[2] And still another idler will putter around his estate, thinking of nothing else in the world, or in public life, immersed only in his domestic pleasures; he is not concerned that his name be known, he is useful to no one, he might as well be dead, if he cannot respect the *regulam vitae*[3] that we are born not only for ourselves, but as they say:

1. Would that it were felicitously!
2. We are ciphers, born but to consume bread (Horace, *Letters,* I, 1, 27).
3. Rule of life.

Whoever is with me and will lay down his life for me,
Will counsel me and if travel he must for me, he'll count not the miles,
He is a true friend of mine, him I respect:
Let him serve me these four ways, I care not for the rest.

Some of our fellow gentlemen you'll find useless in all these circumstances, but every nobleman should *de necessitate* possess at least one of these four [*qualitates*] and if he has none *ex his qualitatibus*,[4] then as the Mazurians sing: "Four little girls for a bushel of chaff." Plenty of people are there, belike, who would not give a bushel of chaff for 10 of such oafs, or they might even sell them at a price as dear as the Jews used to fetch in the camp yard of the Roman army — 30 Jews for one coin.

But having digressed, I return to my subject. Most of the year I wasted on performing favors for my friends, witnessing contracts, viewing disputed land, takings of the veil, mediating quarrels, attending weddings, funerals.

This year the Turks devastated Miedzybóż, Niemirów, Kalnik, and many other towns and villages.

4. Of these qualities.

The Year of Our Lord 1679

I began happily — God be praised! — in Olszówka. This year, by God's grace, was quiet, but a very poor harvest year, and unfruitful; as usual prices dropped, it was bad for tenants on leased estates; in some places there were epidemics.

This year the first Diet in Lithuania was held in Grodno [December 14, 1678 to April 4, 1679]. The Lithuanian gentlemen, combating our arguments, forced through a resolution to hold two Diets in Poland, one after the other, and the third in Lithuania, the journey to which is very *molestum*[1] for us, and it will be *perpetuitas*[2] now that it has come into usage. Our army, being encamped in Trembowla summer and winter, turned from soldiers into farmers; they cultivated the land — sowing, plowing — they had plenty of everything. Like home it was, only a little wife was missing.

1. Burdensome.
2. A permanent thing.

The Year of Our Lord 1680

This year also — God be praised! — I began in Olszówka. Right at the start something novel befell us; winter, having already ceased, entirely melted away and so warm did it become, so mild that the cattle went out to pasture, the buds came out, and the earth pushed forth grass, we plowed and sowed. I hesitated for a long time with the sowing; but then, seeing others had their crops already half-sown, I too began. While on outings with friends who were courting, or going to weddings, so hot was it that you could not stand your fur gown, only your summer one, as if it were *in Augusto.* By then nothing was left of winter, only passing showers. That grain sown *in Ianuario* grew so high before Easter that we even pastured the cattle in it, and so that winter the cattle used little hay, there being excellent feed in the fields.

A gentleman of the court, *Pan* Straszowski, came to me with letters from his Majesty the king, earnestly begging me to make him a present of the trained otter I had, who was such a delight that I would have given away a part of my fortune rather than her whom I loved so. The king first heard from somebody there about this otter with such and such *qualitatibus* that belonged to a squire in the province of Kraków, but my name was not known, nor did they know where to direct these pleas. So then, the crown equerry wrote to *Pan* Bełchacki — who later became vice notary in Kraków — to find out who had such an otter and what his name was.

Well, since this otter was famous throughout the province of Kraków — and, later, all over Poland too — *Pan* Bełchacki found out that she belonged to me and sent back word. The king was overjoyed and took hope, saying, "I have known *Pan* Pasek a long time; I know he will not refuse me." And off he sends *Pan* Straszowski with a letter. The crown equerry also writes — so does *Pan* Adrian Piekarski, a relative of mine and a courtier. They beg me not to deny the king this gift, as his Majesty will reward me with all his favor and esteem. After having read the letter, I wondered who could have spread the news about her there. And I asked, "Lord! What can his Majesty want with her?" The deputy said that his Majesty the king very much desires and requests it. I replied only: "I've no mind to refuse." But I was as pleased as if he had been pulling a curry-comb over my bare skin. Then I sent to the tavernkeeper, a Jew, for a sleeve of otterskin, which, when it had been brought, I laid on the table in front of him, saying, "How's that, Your Excellency, for a speedy delivery!" The man stares: "But his Majesty is asking for a live one, a pet." So then I, having had my joke, was obliged to present her, and since she was not in the house but roaming somewhere about the ponds, we took a quaff of vodka and walked out to the meadows. I started calling her nickname, which was Robak, and she came out wet from the reeds, began fawning upon me, then followed us back to the house. Straszowski was amazed and says: "By God, how could the king help loving so gentle a creature!" I answer: "My Lord, you are seeing only her gentleness and you praise it, but you shall praise even more, once you have viewed her *qualitates.*" We walked to the pond's edge, and standing on a mound, I say: "Robak! I need some fish for my guest; into the water!" The otter went; and first she brought out a small white fish; the second time I ordered her in she brought out a small pike; the third time, a pike the size of a platter, just a trifle bruised on the neck. Straszowski clutched his head: "Lord! What am I seeing?" I say then: "So you want her to fetch more? For she'll carry them out as long as I need them, and if it's a tubful she'll bring it, for her net costs her nothing." Straszowski exclaims: "Having seen this; I believe it, but if somebody had told me, I would not have believed him." Straszowski took to her exceedingly *et consensit*[1] [to watch her fetch more] seeing there would not be the least bother and besides, he would be able to tell the king about her *qualitates.*

Up to the time he left, I showed him all of her talents, which were the following: first, she slept with me in my bed, and was so tidy that not only did she never make a mess in the bedclothes but did nothing under the bed; she had one place where a potsherd had been put down for her and she used to go there to relieve herself. Second, she made such a night watch the Lord preserve anyone from setting foot near the bed! She barely let my servant pull off my boots — and then keep clear — for the racket she raised would wake the soundest sleeper. If I was drunk, and someone were to walk by the bed, she would trample on my chest, barking, until I awoke. And during the day she would sleep so, sprawling anywhere, that even if you picked her up, she'd not lift an eyelid, so trusting of man was the beast! Neither raw fish, nor raw meat would she eat; even on Fridays or a fast-day when a chicken or pigeon was stewed for her, but the parsley not added as was customary, she would not eat it. Like a dog, she understood "Stay!" and such things. If

1. And agreed.

somebody tugged at my gown and I said: "Sic'em," she would leap up with a fierce shriek, tear at his clothes, his legs, just like my dog, the only one she was fond of — Kapreol he was called, a long-haired German dog — and from whom she learned this, and other tricks too. This dog alone, being a house pet, was her friend and they went about together. Other dogs she didn't like and if one came into the house, she would cut it down to size at once, be it the tallest greyhound.

Once, *Pan* Stanisław Ożarowski came to visit me, or rather, we were simply driving together and he stopped by. I was pleased and so was my otter, not having seen me for three days; she came to me and couldn't get enough of being glad and playful. My guest had a handsome greyhound bitch with him and he says to his son: "Samuel, hold on to the greyhound so she won't devour this otter." I say, "Don't trouble yourself, Your Honor, the little creature won't let herself get hurt, though she's small." And he exclaims: "What, Sir? Are you jesting? This greyhound tangles with wolves; a fox has only to yawn once." Having had her fill of being glad to see me, the otter took notice of the hunting dog; she goes up to that greyhound, looks her in the eye, the greyhound looks back; then she circled her, sniffed at her hindleg, backed off, and went away. I think: "She won't do anything now." Well, we had begun to talk about something or other, when the otter gets up again from where she had been lying at my feet, moves quietly under the bench and falls upon the dog's hindquarters again, nipping her in the calf; the greyhound jumps toward the door, the otter after her; then toward the stove, the otter on her tail. Seeing no escape, the dog leaps onto the table, wanting to break through the window, when Ożarowski grabbed her by the leg. She broke two glasses with wine, however; and after they let her out, she did not once show herself to her master, even though he did not leave until the next day after dinner. And so, all the dogs around were afraid of her. Even traveling with me, if a dog but sniffed at her, she would screech fiercely and off the dog ran.

Traveling with her during Lent, a great convenience she was. For things being what they are, especially in our country, you arrive in a little town, you ask: "Is there any fish to buy here?" And they can't even imagine: "Now where would you be getting 'em here! We don't know of any." Then you ride along a river somewhere, or a pond, and with the otter along you need no net. You step out of the cart for a while: "Robak, hup! into the water!" and in she went and brought out whatever fish was to be had, one after the other, until there was enough. On the road, I would not pick and choose [from her catch] as I do at the pond on my estate — no sooner did she bring it, you take it, save for the frog, for she'd bring out those too, since as I've already written she was not particular, she took whatever came her way. Thus, my servants as well as myself fared well, and sometimes we even fed a guest if he was stopping at the same inn, even several guests. And they wondered: "I bade them search in this town and that town for fish but they couldn't get any; where did Your Lordship get such excellent fish?" So I told them that I got them in the water. Sometimes even on a meat day, my servants would say: "Oho, Good Sir, the fish are jumping in this pond here; let the otter go." So I went off with her — she not wishing to go with anyone else — and out she carried them; if there was a good fish, like a pike, or a large bass, I would dine on it too, not only my servants; for a good fish I'm prepared to forego the best meat dish. The irksome thing about traveling with my otter was that wherever you went, people were amazed; they mobbed us just as if we were transporting something from India; no meager audience we had, especially in Kraków, so that riding through the streets on my way out of town, I was accompanied by a throng of divers people.

Another time I was at the home of a cousin of mine, *Pan* Szczęsny Chociwski, and a priest, Father Trzebiénski, was also there; he sat down beside me at the table. My otter was lying next to me on the bench. She had eaten her fill and was sleeping, sprawled on her back, that being her favorite posture. The priest, upon sitting down, saw the otter, and thinking it a sleeve, catches it up, wanting to have a look at it; the otter, awakened, shrieks mightily, seizes his hand and bites it; the priest fainted away — half from pain, half from fright. They could scarcely revive him.

After Straszowski had seen the *qualitates* of that otter, he also had a look at my other game, such as the aviary I'd had built; it was covered with wire-netting and in it were birds *omnis generis*[2] to be found in Poland; the birds were making their nests and sitting on them in the trees planted there; not only were there birds from Poland but I had also foreign birds, and from wherever I could acquire them. Straszowski was there when the young were hatching and when they were still in the nest; he saw it all, how the birds obey me; he saw how they let themselves be stroked in their nests; he saw the partridges hatched there, leading their nestlings around, and how they came to my call like chickens at the strewing of grain.

Off to the king went Straszowski and told all he had seen. Hardly had he arrived and given his account, when the king was overcome with an impulse: "Impossible! go there once more and bring her here somehow, no matter how, so long as I have the otter." Again, letters were written, asking me what I wished in recompense for her. The crown equerry and *Pan* Piekarski both wrote, begging me: "For Lord's sake, don't refuse now; but let him have it and save yourself bother, for you'll

2. Of every kind.

have no peace so long as the king thinks of nothing, whether walking, sleeping, or eating, save that otter. For her sake, and so that nothing should stand in her way, he has already given away his beloved lynx to the governor of Malbork, and has sent his cassovary bird[3] to Jaworów[4] that the otter might be his sole delight."

Back came Straszowski and delivered the letters, telling me how obliged the king was for my promise of the otter, how eager to have her, and how he entreats me with the words: *"Qui cito dat, bis dat."*[5] There are some mighty fine promises in the letters; Straszowski tells me that the king wanted to send me a contentment in money but *Pan* Piekarski said: "Gracious king, it will be useless to send money there, for it won't be accepted; that gentleman has a gallant nature and for sure would not take it; if anything is sent, let it be something that can be received without embarrassment." Whereupon the king sent to Jaworów for two Turkish horses, very handsome horses they have there — and ordered them presented to me, richly harnessed. I said that neither money nor horses would I take, as I would be ashamed for so humble a gift to accept such *honoraria.*

I despatched my otter then to her new master; she very ungratefully accepting that despatch and her new service; whining so and yelping in her cage as they rode through the village, that I went into the house, not wanting to listen, for it made me sad. On the road, while traveling, whenever they spied some water in a flat place, where she could not hide, they would let her out into the water, several times even, to cool off and content her nature; but as before it did not help; there was squealing aplenty and uproar. Thus, she pined away and was miserable; and they brought her to the king, looking like a puffed owl. He was overjoyed to see her and says: "She has pined away but she'll come around." Whoever is asked to pet her, the otter snaps at his hand. The king says: Marysieńka, it's my turn now." The queen tries to coax him out of it, lest he get bitten; but he sits down beside the animal after they had put her on the bed, and stretches his hand out to her slowly: "I'll take it as a good sign if she doesn't bite me, and if she does, what of it, they won't be writing in the newspapers about it."[6] He stroked her

3. A cassovary is smaller than an ostrich, incapable of flight, but swift-running and pugnacious; it lives in Africa, Australia, and Asia. In the margin of the manuscript is the following note: "The cassovary is a large bird, has no feathers, but a hide like a pig's; it flies."
4. Jaworów was Jan III Sobieski's favorite residence, even before he came to the throne; he was district supervisor of Jaworów.
5. He gives twice who gives promptly.
6. The history of Polish newspapers begins in 1661 in Kraków, then moves to Warsaw. The first paper was the *Merkuriusz Polski.* It was devoted to current events with an emphasis on politics, economics, and trade, and it favored strong royal power.

then; she was friendly with him. So delighted was the king, he began to pet her all the more, then he ordered something to be brought for her to eat. And so, there he was, feeding her bit by bit, while she ate, but without appetite, lying on that rich samite. When she had been there two days, she moved more and more freely about the rooms, going wherever she pleased. They poured water into some large vessels for her and dropped in fish and crawfish: she was happy, she fetched them out. Says the king to the queen: "Marysieńka, tomorrow I'll eat no fish but what this otter will catch for me; tomorrow, we'll go to Wilanów,[7] God willing, and there we'll try her, to see if she will get acquainted with the fish."

I had written, at the time, a page of instructions on how they were to treat her; and I wrote that she was never to be tied by the collar, but alongside it by the neck, since an otter's neck is thicker than the head and she could slip right out of even the tightest collar. And so she did. They tied her by the collar with the little bells and she got away. She crawled down the stairs during the night and somehow got outside, as she had learned to do at my house when she was bored, going whither she liked, ferreting about to her heart's content among the ponds, the rivers, and coming home according to her habit. There, having gone out on some paths, she got lost, and knew not where to turn. As soon as it was morning, a dragoon spied her and, not knowing whether she was domestic or wild, struck her with his battle-axe and killed her. They get up — no otter. They call, search; dreadful confusion. They send round the city, entreating anyone who finds her to give her up and threatening anyone who dares not, when there arrives a traveling Jew from Pińczów, and a dragoon on his heels, seeking payment for the pelt. "What have you got there, Jew?" asks a gatekeeper. The Jew keeps his hand in his pocket. The gatekeeper peeks under his gown; and what does he see, but a pelt stuffed with straw. Both Jew and dragoon were seized at once and taken to the king.

The king examines the pelt, then claps one hand over his eyes, clutches his hair with the other and begins to shout: "Kill him whoever be righteous! Kill him, whoever believeth in God!" Both were thrown into the tower; it was decreed to shoot the dragoon, and he was ordered to prepare for death. But priest-confessors and bishops came to the king to plead with him and persuade him that the man did not deserve death, having sinned through ignorance. With difficulty, they managed to bring it about so that the man was ordered not to be shot but to run the gantlet through Gałecki's regiment. The regiment then stood in two rows, as was customary. It was so decreed that he should run

7. Palace residence constructed by Jan III Sobieski outside of Warsaw.

through fifteen times, resting, however, at the ends. He ran through twice — 1500 men in the regiment and each thrashes him once — the third time he fell half-way through the row, against the rules they flogged him lying on the ground. They carried him off then in a sheet, but later it was said that he never came to. Thus, a keen joy was turned into a great sorrow, for all day long the king neither ate nor spoke with anyone; and the whole court was downcast. And I was deprived of a beloved animal; far from being gladdened, they had even brought themselves chagrin.

For some time my aviary was the admiration of all around. Having started with birds, I always had excellent falcons, hawks, kestrels, hobbies, ravens; they would come to the perch, the partridges would let themselves be seized; they would circle round a hare like a saker [a large falcon]; everyone of these birds carried on his proper activity. I had one hawk, somewhat too large, but so swift he outflew every bird; clutch it he would in those fearsome talons and every bird I always retrieved from him live as could be. Throw him even the largest bird, he'd not be ashamed; he'd pursue geese, ducks, heron, kites, and ravens as well as quail, for he caught several a day. So strong was that hawk that sometimes having to do with an old hare, gripping and choking him, he would then let go, preen himself, and, after a second swoop, fly up with him, lifting him off the ground as if he were a partridge. Eight years I had him, before he died on me.

As for hunting with greyhounds, I had bred a kennel of greyhounds for myself from those of my cousin, *Pan* Stanisław Pasek of Sochaczew; whose greyhounds were both handsome and strong-bodied and at the same time so swift that never once had you need to let the pack of hounds loose on foxes or hares, only by turns, one greyhound for every hare, a different dog each time, and that hare never got away; whereas, for a wolf there was a levy in mass. And my huntsmen neighbors used to have such a saying: unhappy the beast who meets up with *Pan* Pasek, for he'll escape no more.

I was always particularly fond of training wild animals so that they grew tame; and these would not only live with the dogs but also, with the dogs, join in the chase after their wild brothers. Somebody would come to visit me and a fox would be in the yard, frolicking with the greyhounds; my guest would enter the house and a hunting dog is lying under the table with a hare seated on him. Should somebody who does not know me meet me riding to the chase, he would look, and here he'd see several handsome greyhounds, several pointers with a fox among them, here a marten, there a badger, an otter; behind my horse gambols a hare with little bells; a hawk is on the hunter's arm, a raven flies above the dogs, sometimes lighting upon a greyhound and so letting itself be borne along; then that man could only cross himself: "For God's sake! This is a wizard: every type of beast is walking there amongst the dogs. What are they seeking? Why are they not going after those in their midst?" Should a hare break into flight, they're all after him; even my trained hare, seeing the dogs dash off, he too bounds after them. But when that hare out there begins to pray, my tame one flees back to the horse, not wanting to watch. My bestiary acquired renown far and wide in Poland and people told of even more things than I have here; however, leaving my animals aside, I return *ad cursum anni.*

This year an unfortunate boundary agreement was made with the Turks concerning Podole. The army was encamped at Mikulenice. I set off for Gdańsk with two barges; nine days later I had reached Gdańsk, the current being swift and the water calm; I sold wheat to his lordship *Pan* Tynf at 160 zloties. I returned by land, and the barges arrived at the pier six weeks later.[8]

This year on the evening of October 17, the barns in Smogorzów burned down. Prices were also exessively low, and therefore I sold nothing; in Gdańsk rye did not pay either, only wheat. On this account, I suffered a loss of about 20,000 zloties reckoning lightly. The peasants *ex invidia*[9] put the blame on the overseer, as to how he was to have dropped an ember from his lamp while looking for his hog. I had him put to the rack, having taken him to court; he did not confess for he was not guilty, and those scoundrels through hatred had falsely accused him, and led me into sin, and deprived me of a good steward, for I took an aversion to him for having been in the torturer's hands and I ordered him to leave. But I regretted it later, having found out that something else had caused the damage. The fire started at the blacksmith's; at the time, a fierce wind was blowing straight toward the barn; it's likely the barn caught fire *non ab intra* but *ab extra*[10] and then it spread to the other barns, the haystacks, the corn ricks and racks. The which is God's will: *Dominus dedit, Dominus abstulit.*[11]

8. Pasek had his own dock and granary at Nowy Korczyń.
9. Out of spite.
10. Not from the inside(but) from the outside.
11. God giveth, God taketh away.

The Year of Our Lord 1681

Praise God, I began this year happily in Olszówka. In the last days of the carnival season, I married off his lordship, *Pan* Aleksander Tomicki in Kraków to a widow, her ladyship, *Pani* Makowiecka, née Głuchowska. *In Iunio,* that is, on the 21st, I fell *periculosissime* ill; I scarcely returned from death's door, but for having done so, may God's Name be praised. May the Lord in His mercy spare me another such bout! *In Augusto* I rafted to Gdańsk; by God's grace making a profitable sale and returning. Upon my return, I arranged an agreement between his lordship *Pan* Trzemeski, my cousin, and his lordship *Pan* Kiełczowski concerning Klimontów.[1]

Immediately afterward I attended the wedding of her ladyship *Pani* Tomicka, daughter of the castellan of Wieluń, to *Pan* Walewski in Pińczów. A very fine wedding it was, with great numbers of guests.

From that wedding all of us rode on to Kraków for the consecration of Father Jan Małachowski as bishop of Kraków. At the same time, the consecration of Father Konstanty Lipski as archbishop of Lwów took place there. If the ceremony for the bishop made a splendid display, then incomparably more splendid was the consecration of the archbishop and the banquets were sumptuous.

I also went to a funeral in Stopnica for the man who was a great enemy of mine *in vita,* but for the two years before his death a most constant friend, Aleksander Komornicki, a squadron-master; he died in my arms. I discharged the office of inviting the guests and my funeral oration was to everyone's liking.

This year a comet appeared *ad occidentem.*[2] Prince Dymitr, the Polish grand hetman, died.[3] The army was encamped at Trembowla; it did not take part *in opera belli*[4] this year, but lay about, eating and drinking, and we, as usual, paid for them.

1. Klimontów was a village in the region where Pasek resided.
2. In the west.
3. Dymitr Wiśniowiecki died the following year in 1682.
4. In military actions.

The Year of Our Lord 1682

Praise God, I began happily in Olszówka. The winter this year was indeed Italian, entirely without snow or freezing weather; no sleigh-riding, the rivers did not freeze. The grass was green all winter, there were leaves on the trees, and flowers; during what is usually the coldest time, people were plowing and sowing; even March was so warm, dry, and bright, it was truly unnatural. Only in April did the snow and frost come, and on the very day of Easter snow fell and in places the spring crops which had already begun to come up, especially the beans, were blighted. The second week after Easter we had so much snow and it was so cold that we could use the sleighs. But our almanac writers said nothing of this. They know the movements of stars in the sky, or rather, what's been written; belike 'twere better if he knew when his wife is writing a love letter to someone else without his knowing it; perhaps he only just found out, having been alerted, when he caught the go-between, snatched the letter out of her hand and read it.

The entry of Stanisław Myszkowski upon acceding to the title of margrave and the hereditary estate of Książ Wielki, as well as his taking of the oath, occurred *prima Decembris*;[1] but he was unfortunate, his dominion was short-lived. One must always watch and beware.

This year our armies stood idle, doing nothing. *Pan* Jabłonowski received the grand hetman's mace; *Pan* Sieniawski, the field hetman's mace.

1. Zygmunt Myszkowski had received the title from the Pope in 1601. The oath had to do with the strict observance of the law of primogeniture.

The Year of Our Lord 1683

God be praised! — I began this year in Olszówka. The year got off to a start with the wedding of his lordship the margrave with her ladyship *Panna* Bronicka; may they be merry to the end.

The Warsaw Diet followed, during which we resolved, *magno motu et deliberatione,*[1] to make an armed alliance *cum Imperio et Republica Veneta contra potentiam Ottomanicam.*[2] May God bless the pious intentions of these Christian monarchs *et totius Christianitatis!*[3] Vienna, being sorely oppressed by the Turks and the Emperor's armies unable to hold out, had retreated, for in the very first encounter the Germans were cut down, taken prisoner, and driven from the field. Vienna remained under siege; the enemy made breaches in the walls, blew up the fortifications; they brought mines right up to the city gates, so that Vienna *vix, vix spirabat,*[4] just as when a strong fellow flattens a weaker man and is choking him, then that man no longer thinks of wrenching himself from the other's grip, but only of begging for mercy. There was, to be sure, a large garrison in Vienna, and the commandant was a good soldier, General Staremberk;[5] there were cannon and gunpowder in profusion, plenty of victuals; but to what avail, when no fortress under the sun could withstand *modernas inventiones oppugnationum propria virtute.*[6] It was different, years ago, when men hurled stones and spears at each other or pounded walls with battering rams, but now they hurl grenades and fire case shot, balls fly from cannon mouths as big as buckets, and a rain of pellets pierces the body like a drill to one's very bones, through armor, through elkskin, through all *vestimenta*; they fire horrid stink balls infecting folk, killing them, nearly causing a *pestilentiam*; other destruc-

1. After much maneuvering and debate.
2. With the Empire and the Republic of Venice against the Ottoman power.
3. Pasek is mistaken. Poland made an alliance, but only with the Emperor, on April 1, 1683; the league with the Emperor, Venice, and the Pope was not established until March 5, 1684.
4. Was nearly breathing her last.
5. The spelling in the text is Pasek's. See the Index of Proper Names: Starhemberg.
6. The modern weapons of siege with bravery alone.

tive substances are sent over which poison the drinking water; and finally, just when you think you are standing safely on this earth, firmly set here by God and nature, yet know not what is going on under the ground beneath you, at that moment you, together with the place whereon you are standing, together with bastions, with mighty brick walls, are hurled into the clouds like an insect. Today, a fortress is useful only for keeping the coachman from leaving town before daylight without paying for his bed of hay at the inn, or to prevent the wolf from carrying off the sleeping mayor; but to withstand a modern-day siege, none are up to it.

So with Vienna. Whoever would gaze upon her beauty and walled strength would think that perhaps the hand of God could destroy this work but surely not human hands. Yet take a look at what *deformitatem*[7] it suffered after but two short months of siege; when *non oppressa* but *pressa* and *extremis laborans,*[8] drained of its own strength and *omni destituta succursu*[9] from the Emperor and his people, the Germans being so stunned they lost heart and knew not how to stand up to the Tartars let alone the Turks; like timber in the forest those German wretches were cut down in every encounter — Vienna then, as I say, is sustained by nothing so much as the hope of reinforcements from the Polish army, whereof Staremberk had intelligence through secret spies sent by the Emperor. By then, those poor creatures with their own bodies were filling the breaches made by powder bursts and cannon fire, while surrender, long since resolved upon, its conditions detailed, was put off from day to day. The Turks also knew that the Poles were on their way to help or rather to relieve, but they did not believe the king himself would come *in persona* or with the whole army; they assumed only a part of the army would come. They, having concluded that they need not so much fear those Polish reinforcements, began their assault slowly, without straining too hard: "If so large an army as the German could not withstand our first assault, and now dares not look us in the eye, though the capital of their country be at stake, though they stand on their own rubble — surely a small handful of the Polish army will not drive us back."

Prince Lubomirski was already there with the Emperor,[10] accompanied by those Poles who had been recruited with the Emperor's money, and they fought well, though they had also dragged along some riff-raff: any groom could become a squadron-master, a lieutenant; any servant who came on foot to enlist, they bought him a horse

7. Destruction.
8. Unconquered (but) hard-pressed . . . brought to the limit of endurance.
9. Deprived of all aid.
10. Lubomirski had arrived in June with a division of reinforcement troops.

and there he was — a gentleman, a cavalier. And the Germans flattered them, though they had a fine leader to thank. When the Polish king set off on that expedition, all his men felt their hearts soar as though they would be birds, the faster to fly across the distance. And this was a sign of future good fortune; even the king rode there in such high spirits, as if to an unmistakable and certain victory, for he summoned historians and panegyrists to accompany him, to celebrate and to describe his deeds and those of the Polish nation. Kochowski was invited to observe that war for no other reason than to pen a fitting description of the victory.[11] Even on the day [August 15] the king mounted his horse in Kraków, I heard from his own lips these words: "I pray God the Turks are still there: may Turkish horses be plentiful in Poland." So that, wondrous it seemed, upon hearing about the victory afterward, how he had spoken *profetico spiritu* of what was soon to come to pass. Some *nurmurabant* against these words at the time, saying: "For God's sake, may the Lord not punish him if he speaks so arrogantly, since *cum potenti et victrici populo res est.*"[12] But plainly he said it out of a great trust in the Lord, since it happened so.

The king was awaiting the Lithuanian army, while envoy after envoy flies from the Emperor, imploring him, for God's sake, to hasten, for Vienna will perish. At last, unable to wait any longer for the Lithuanians, the king set forth, having made solemn oaths to God, installed the queen in Kraków, and commended the safety of Ruthenia to Potocki, the castellan of Kraków.

When the king crossed the border, abundant victuals were dispensed to the army and divers comforts provided. The king proceeded, however, in forced marches, fearing lest Vienna receive *post bellum auxilium*;[13] whereupon the Turks, hearing the Polish army was soon to arrive, began a heavy assault. For the Turkish emperor [Mohammed IV]; having gained intelligence of the Alliance and fearing that defeat which, indeed, he was not spared, sent letters to the vizier [Kara Mustafa] at Vienna and a cord with the assurance that "you'll hang by this cord, if you fail to capture Vienna in these days; for you were the one who desired this war, you are also the one to answer for it, should it turn out badly." The scoundrel bribed the Janizaries,[14] plied them with spirits to make them fight bravely; he drove the slaves ahead of the Janizaries to make the initial assault, while, with that cord tied around his neck, he himself rushed about like a madman; he

11. Wespazjan Kochowski (1630-1699), a poet and historian, described the campaign in his little work *Commentarius belli adversus Turcas ad Viennam et in Hungaria anno Chr. 1683 gesti* (Cracoviae, 1684).
12. We have to do with a powerful and victorious people.
13. Help after the war was over.
14. Detachments of an elite corps of Turkified Christian youth.

goaded his troops, entreated them, by the great prophet Mohammed, to keep in mind the glory of their unvanquished nation, to consider his fate, which is to die by that halter he is wearing around his neck, if he does not take Vienna. Thus did the infidel swarm into the fire and they fell like sheaves of grain.

As the king with the army was marching from Tulln,[15] the Turks were making their heaviest attacks. Even when the Polish army came to a halt and our regiments joined the German divisions, the vizier did not order the Janizaries to cease storming, but turned on us the Spahis, the Tartars, and [Imre] Thököly's Hungarians.[16] Twice the Tartars charged us, then fell back. The vizier sends to the Tartar Khan [Murad Girey] and inquires of him: "Do you think the Polish king is here?" The Khan said: "I think he is and I see he is; for if those spear-carriers [the Polish hussars] are here, the king must be around too." The vizier says: "Take counsel and advise me what I am to do!" The Khan answered: "Take your own counsel, and I'll take mine; long ago I advised you to withdraw from Vienna, not to wait for the Poles." Off to his men he galloped from the vizier: "Allah, Allah!" And as fast as you can hurl a ball, the Tartars had gone. The Turks, too, began to weaken, and off they fled. Now slice through them, hack them, give chase! Within the city, the besieged, seeing the Turks in flight, flew at those storming the walls, and fell to slicing them; they cut down those heathen in rows; as a penance, they drove flocks of them alive into Vienna to repair the breaches in the walls and embankments.

All the Turkish cannons were left behind with the camp and all its riches. Piles of gold, droves of horses, camels, buffalo, oxen, sheep. Beautiful and luxurious tents, coffers of exotic and magnificent garb, even money they'd not stopped to gather up, for quite a bit was left in all the tents. The tents of the vizier were as spacious as the whole of walled Warsaw; these treasures were now the possession of our king; sacks of thalers lay around in large piles; the ground was strewn with rugs woven of gold and silver; a bed with its bedclothes they reckoned at scores of thousands of thalers. So secret were the little chambers in those tents that only on the third day did they find one of the vizier's concubines hidden there; another, a very elegant one, was found slain in front of the tent; it was said that the vizier himself slew her rather than let her fall into the hands of the enemy.

The other tents stood there for one week, two weeks, it being impos-

15. Tulln is separated from Vienna by the Vienna Woods; the Polish royal army crossed the Danube here.

16. Imre Thököly (1657-1705), the leader of the Hungarian insurrectionists, was appointed king of Hungary by the Sultan; after the occupation of Hungary he sought refuge in Turkey.

sible to cart them all away. And our Poles who had hauled off this booty, being ordered to march to Hungary, would, while in passage, cast them out of the wagons anywhere; if the horses got stuck in the mud they would spread a tent worth a thousand or more beneath the horses, the faster to pull the wagon out.

Our men have told us what comforts the Turks had in their tents, what tubs they had, and baths with all the fittings one could have in town, what excellent timbered wells close by, perfumed soaps heaped on ledges, vials of fragrance; even separate medicine chests with sundry balms, potions; and other articles, such as silver water jugs, pitchers, basins, knives, scimitars encrusted with rubies and diamonds, unique clocks hanging in cases, prayer beads of either sapphire or corral, and if of corral they were embedded with rubies or other precious stones; even coins lay piled in bags on the ground or had been strewn in heaps about the tent floor, they were never in caskets save in the tents of the less well-off who bound them up in a small coffer — the Turks being unwont to steal one from the other, you'll not find a thief among them. Unusual foods there were too — rice, meat, bread, flour, butter, sugar, olive oil, and others. What inconvenience could be suffered in a camp so well-provided? Where there's prosperity, there's stability, as they say. No wonder, for they are the *depopulatores totius mundi et possessores quadraginta regnorum.*[17]

Agreeable and alluring for everybody should be a war with Turkey; I do not regret risking my skin if I know that, having won, I'll have wherewith to buy bandages and bind my wounds.

Turkish horses also live in great comfort, never getting wet, never standing in the open air, only under a tent, keeping dry and handsome; they are exercised, they are covered with warm blankets, and their silken saddle cloths sewn with gold. To be short, everything you touch is precious. It is fitting that all should have a desire to go to war against Turkey; for in doing so you are serving God by combating His enemy. They are now an effeminate people, less industrious than heretofore. They are drowning in their riches and luxury, they've grown soft. They fight only with Tartar assistance and with the slaves they capture from other nations, training them for war, turning them into Janizaries and Spahis. They themselves have been unmanned and that softness will fast be their undoing; for we have the examples of what happened *per nimiam mollitiem et voluptatem*[18] to other nations that once terrified the whole world and wielded great power. We have made a good start in combating the Turk, since God has provided us with the means to destroy him and to recover from them so many kingdoms and temples.

17. The despoilers of the entire world and rulers of forty kingdoms.
18. Through excessive comfort and pleasure.

That fortunate victory occurred on the 12th of September; it elated all of Christendom,it enlivened the desperate Emperor who had yielded himself up to God's protection alone; it inspired the whole German state, and especially the Viennese, whose backs were nearest that scourge; for our nation it won eternal glory which all peoples now acknowledge. I heard it uttered by a worthy Frenchman that *"Poloni sunt genitores Germaniae."*[19] For sure it is, that another three days and Vienna would have fallen, in consequence of which all the *ditiones Imperii*[20] would have fallen as well as the other Christian countries. Wherefore our king is due thanks for not shielding himself *in persona* from this war, as Christendom greatly benefited from his zeal; in particular was it beneficial in that every young Polish lord, every Polish gentleman, in order to oblige the king, went off to that war *personaliter*, and with their armed retinues rendered our fighting forces immeasurably larger and more imposing; secondly, it confounded the enemy, inspiring in him great fear, knowing that the king himself was there *in persona*, for they considered him a fortunate warrior and had not forgotten the bloodbath he caused them at Chocim on the Dniester *in anno* 1673.

All men of the Catholic faith were gladdened by our monarch's resolve, except the Lutherans and Calvinists, for they considered that war as their own; they beseeched God to give victory to the Turks, saying it was to their advantage and siding with the oppressed Thököly and all the Protestants.

I was in Gdańsk at the time; and at all the church meetings they were praying to God for a Turkish victory. If they guessed from reading the newspapers that things were going well for Thököly, that he had strangled a few Germans somewhere on a raid, forthwith there were triumphs, forthwith *gratiarum actiones. "Och, Her Got! Och, liber Got!"*[21] They were selling pictures of Thököly in full armor, on horseback; handbills were no sooner printed but they were sung at once by the sellers. Once, I'm walking along and one fellow is singing; I'd had a few quaffs, and I ask, What he is singing about that everyone listens so keenly? They said it was news of how Thököly is winning out over the Emperor. The fellow singing, having heard me inquire, shows me the writing in German, "*Ja,Pan,* buy it, buy it!" I ask; "How much?" He answers: "A copper." I gave it to him. A throng of peasants followed me to a tavern looking for some coins. I say to one slyboots: "You'll have a zloty, my good lad, if you wipe your backside with this paper." The peasant with great relish drops down his pants and he rubbed his bare

19. Through the Poles the Germans have been reborn.
20. Lands of the Empire.
21. Prayers of thanksgiving. O lord! O dear God!

behind with those bills, then he tossed them into the Motława.[22] The Germans began to murmur, to grumble; I went off. The Catholics and those who watched the incident from the boats nearly burst their bellies laughing. However, when I was telling the Catholic townsmen, also some Dominican fathers and Jesuits, they told me: "Lucky for you, it didn't start an uproar, for Thököly gets nearly divine veneration here."

I, having been advised to buy horses at a certain trader's in Nowe Ogrody (precincts in the direction of Oliva), set out there late one Sunday afternoon when nearly everyone in Gdańsk goes out for a walk or a ride. On my way back from the trader's, it began to rain. The weather being fair when I left, I had not taken my cloak; so then, I stopped at an inn to wait out the rain. Those Sunday strollers were also running for shelter wherever they could find it, several of them slipped into the room where I was and sat down at some tables; they began to discourse about the war. I did not understand their discourse, no more than a few words here and there: later, however, the fellow I shall write about explained it to me (and there's a heavy downpour outside, water flowing in the gutters like rivers). Looking out the window, one of them says: "Ach, God grant there be streams of Catholic blood flowing in Vienna like that water." Another one says: "Our hope is in God." But one German — sitting apart from them — shrugs his shoulders, rolls his eyes to heaven, glances at me, saying nothing, only shaking his head. [The manuscript is damaged here.] I see it but do not understand why he is doing it, nor do I understand the words the others had spoken, nor do I ask him, for I do not know the fellow and do not trust him. Until once again they speak of the king in these words: "But what did that stuffed swine go there for? What business of his was it? May they both, king and emperor, hear the clank of shackles!"

Meanwhile, that one sitting apart from them could restrain himself no longer, he being a Catholic. He was German, though not from Gdańsk, from some Prussian town; a trade broker who had dealings with the merchants. He, addressing them in Polish not in German, so I would understand, utters these words: "I thought I was sitting among Christians, but I see I'm among pagans; I thought I was among men, but I see you are beasts; is it permitted to talk such crimes? May you be hanged!" And they seize their daggers; he had but a reed cane. One of them wanted either to smite him with the flat of his dagger or perhaps slash him; he parried with his cane; the other wounded him slightly. He calls out to me: "Your Honor, they're talking against the king!" I to sword, the Germans take to their heels, but 'twas a bother to run off toward Gdańsk after them.

He told me then what had been said. I say: "Come with me to the lord

22. The Motława is a tributary of the Vistula that runs through Gdansk.

mayor!" "I'll come." 'Will you give testimony?" "I will." We set off. At the time, a certain Szuman was mayor, a courteous and sensible man. On our coming there, he's not in! He'd gone off to his estate. The man went back with me to the inn. At nightfall, I again sent to the mayor's. He'd come back, but had already retired, being sore spent, without eating supper. And so, until the morrow. Baliński [the German] was to come to my lodgings in the morning and from there we'd go to the mayor; but two days went by, and a third — nothing. They'd bribed him and he was shunning me. I ask the other brokers about him. One broker, Felski, told me he is conducting his affairs in an alcove at Kępka's. I went there; finding him in, I say: "And where's your word?" He starts to squirm out of it, "I don't know them, don't know their names; how am I to accuse them without knowing who they are!" I understood the matter and I say: "They won you over, wretch, but know this: it is worse to defend such a criminal offense; it is a *crimen laesae Maiestatis*[23] as well as a great blasphemy against God." He confessed they had given him money, imploring him to keep quiet. I entreated him to tell me at least their names; for I'd have had them arrested at the magistrate's, then I'd have sent a subpoena to the city; but even that he was unwilling to do, pleading that those are young lords, influential people, "and I'm a servant here, I earn my living in Gdańsk and its precincts; I'd not be able to stay here." And so it came to nothing; my only regret was not to have gone at once to another magistrate *in absentia* of the mayor to testify while fresh, for he could not very easily have retracted his words, having once sworn testimony, though they give him the largest sum.

And so, some Christians desired a successful end to this war, others hoped we would lose. But the Lord, being with those who were *bonarum partium*,[24] gave us a fortunate victory; he strengthened the hearts of good Christians and confounded the Protestants and their protector.

After this fortunate victory, no sooner had the two monarchs, the Christian emperor Leopold and the Polish king, Jan III, ridden up to one another *ad mutuum amplexum*[25] but what was the rejoicing! what the acclaim! When the *principes Imperii*[26] came riding up, that is, the prince of Lorraine, the prince of Bavaria, the prince of Baden, and others, how graciously they welcomed the king, how gratefully they accepted his services; chroniclers will write lengthily thereof. Afterward, the king rode off to observe Vienna and its devastation, Staremberk inviting him to dine there with him. They say that as he rode through the

23. Crime to insult his Majesty.
24. On the side of the right.
25. To embrace.
26. Princes of the Empire.

city, the press of throngs was not so great to defend the town during the storming as to see the Polish king. The people, poor creatures, weeping for joy, raised their arms to heaven, called upon God to bless and reward our king, they hailed him as their savior until he had to plug his ears. In the taverns they would take no money for wine from the soldiers; for other things, too, they would take nothing; some however, being churlish, did.

The Imperial and Polish armies set off then for Hungary in pursuit of the Turks, there to attack a few of their fortresses. After passing Komorno [on the Danube], an Imperial stronghold not yet in the hands of the infidel, they captured some forts and, beyond Nowe Zamki built by the Turks, going in the direction of Strygonia, they came upon the Turkish army at Parkany, whereof our men had intelligence; yet thinking it to be a rather small contingent, recklessly did our vanguard push forward. When the Turks descended upon them there was no time even to fire; an entire regiment of dragoons under the royal sergeant at arms, Bidzieński, was put to the sword; many dragoons attached to the vanguard were also cut down. Bidzieński himself barely escaped, and over two thousand men perished — young officers, some from the gentry, and many of his own kinsmen. So quietly did it happen, so swiftly, that our main army, being beyond a hill and not far away, knew nothing.

The king with the army then comes upon those corpses: our men at once lost their spirit. The Turks dashed toward us in a sudden charge. At first our men put up some resistance, but no sooner had the Turks taken the rear of the Ruthenian governor's squadron (he was the Polish hetman) but one hussar squadron begins to flee, then another, then a third — and then the whole army was in retreat, along with the king, the hetmans, and everyone else, much to their chagrin and the glee of the Germans and so, ignominiously, for one great mile they retreated until they came up against the Imperial army. Denhoff, the governor of Pomorze — a clumsy and fat fellow — perished; Siemianowski, a lieutenant, perished; many cavaliers died, having flung away standards, lances, drums. The king's horse was near to give way beneath him, but having both of its sides tickled by the flats of swords, it did bear its master out of the fray. And thus in that Thursday's infamous flight would we have eternally blotted out the ineffable splendor of our victory at Vienna save that the Lord let us shine again in Saturday's triumph, in a victory even greater than what we had won at Vienna.

Belike pride had puffed up the hearts of our men who listened to those blandishments of fortune in the words *ab ore populi:*[27] "Our savior, our redeemer!" and we thought, like that haughty conqueror:

27. From the lips of the people.

"Quis est, qui de manibus meis eripere possit populum hunc?"[28] Before our eyes He laid low several thousand fine cavaliers so that we should recall that our lives, like the lives of those rows of corpses, are at His disposal; so that we should know the enemy is vanquished neither by great numbers nor by the strength of the army but by heavenly [powers]; so that we should understand it is neither reason nor experience but the hand of God that subdues the enemy and brings victory. On that Thursday we took a drubbing; on Friday He permitted us to be sorry for our sins and to humble ourselves before God; on Saturday God raises us up once more and gives us strength to avenge ourselves, we believing, along with the psalmist, that today's afflicted is tomorrow's beloved.[29]

The pasha of Silistria [Kara Mehmed], *victor triumphator,* having vanquished our forces by God's will and driven them from the field, now gathered up from the battlefield those discarded lances, drums, many flags, and captives and sent them to the commander-in-chief at Buda, informing him he had crushed the entire Polish army; afterward, he sent him the head of the governor of Pomorze, Denhoff, swearing it was the royal head, that it should be sent at once to the emperor, and humbly declaring that within three days the same would befall the German army, he being near to stuffing them all in a sack. The commander-in-chief was cheered by that victory; he summoned *ad recognoscentiam*[30] of that head all those who were well-acquainted with the king; divers men were of divers minds. The commander-in-chief, despatching the army he had with him to the aid of the Silistrian pasha, congratulated him on the victory, requesting him to carry on the victorious action he had commenced, and informing him on how further to proceed.

There was a bridge then over the Danube between Buda and Parkany; on Friday the Turkish army crossed over to the left side of the Danube to join the Silistrian pasha. The pasha's forces were larger than before and he now was full of hope that the Germans would not stand up to them, since the Lord had granted him such a success. Our king, though embarrassed by this ill luck, was as usual in good spirits, saying in front of the Imperial generals that it will turn out otherwise. God had sent us but a *belli vicissitudinem.*[31] And so, both sides hoped for the best.

On Saturday morning, that is, on the 9th of October, our army sallied forth to meet the enemy, the German battalions directly behind

28. Who is there who could tear that people from my hands.
29. A paraphrase of a couplet from the *Psaltery* of the Polish renaissance poet Jan Kochanowski: *"Kogo wieczór zafrasuje/ Tego rano umiluje."*
30. For the recognition.
31. A setback in the war.

us; they arrived in Parkany and stood in ranks. And at once the Turks like bees to honey came out of their camp onto the field; recklessly they charged first those squadrons that had begun the retreat on Thursday; and to fighting they fell. Now did their other formations clash with other regiments of ours. The pashas lead their men into the battle, in particular the pasha from Silistria dashes like a shot at the ranks. The battle begins. The *Caesariani,*[32] following close upon us, now mix with us and with the Turks; they cut them in half. The Turks take to their heels, some heading to the bridge, others to the fortress, to Parkany. With the other flank from the field, the Imperial army hastened after them; and now to fight with a vengeance! The fortress could not hold those who fled there, they at once obstructed the gates with their own bodies; the others ended up in the Danube. Such was the slaughter that corpse fell upon corpse; and in one attempt the fortress was taken. The Turks, giving fire from there at first, ceased soon after, not knowing at whom to shoot, so thoroughly had our troops mingled with Turks. Some, not wanting to stay around on land for our Polish sabres, plunged into the Danube; some drowned; others, swimming 'til they were spent, came back to shore, and begged for mercy. One of them, astonishingly, swam so swiftly to Strygonia, a fish could not swim faster; and that horse, so fleet a swimmer, fell again into the hands of our soldiers when they took Strygonium and — as they tell it — brought a high price: where the wolf casts his spell, there's no escape.

The Turks who had fled to the bridge, however, died an even more wretched death, killing themselves in that tumult at the bridge, this one pressing ahead of that one, while at the rear our men cutting and shooting them down — a dreadful mess. When that huge multitude squeezed onto the bridge — and those who'd been driven off and did not go under *primo instanti* were clinging to it too — so great an imbalance occurred, that the bridge burst asunder. Now did those Turkish gentlemen swim, now sink! And all those heaps drowned at Parkany the current had carried down, so clogging the Danube with men and horses that the water rose up more than a foot and spilled over the banks. Parkany, though mightily defended from cannon on the Strygonian side, was captured, the cannons were taken; and of those cannon balls some carried over and struck, others splashed into the water.

He who lost his banner on Thursday, or his drums, retrieved them now at Parkany *sine contradictione*[33] from his lordship the pasha of Silistria. Even those of our men captured alive were found there — only a few heads having been sent along with the head of the governor

32. Imperial troops.
33. Without any objection.

of Pomorze to the Turkish commander-in-chief; some fools declared it was the king's head, the governor and the king being alike in body, one as fat as the other.

Multitudes fell in that battle. Those who claimed to be victors on Thursday were the defeated on Saturday; those who were pursuers on Thursday, were fugitives on Saturday; those who had sliced off a foreign head on Thursday could not save their own from our Polish sabres on Saturday; those who had thirsted hungrily for Christian blood on Thursday, were drenched in their own on Saturday. Six pashas, finally, along with all their wealth, were captured and two killed; both the pasha of Aleppo [Alil Basha] and the pasha of Silistria, the chief commanding officer, were taken alive. The Imperial forces plundered their camp ahead of us; our men, fighting *prima fronte,*[34] raced on in pursuit of the Turks in order to avenge Thursday's chagrin and their brothers' blood; they did not even look back at the spoils. But the Germans did not reap anything like the harvest we had at Vienna, for these were troops that had been in Vienna and fled from there, leaving their treasures behind; if the Turk did carry away any of his coffers, then he lost it in Parkany along with his life.

What joy ineffable, when Our Merciful Father, having threatened us, once more cast upon us His compassionate glance and in three days restored our nation's glory, allowing us to take full vengeance for our brothers' blood, and lavishly strewing the field, the swift currents, and the limitless depths of the Danube with Turkish corpses! No novelty was God's protection of our nation, which remains in His holy care. For Christendom, how gratifying a *spectaculum* to put to the sword — till our arms dropped — both the Lord's and our own principal enemies; to delight our eyes with the death of those struck down *a vindici manu Dei,*[35] watching this one cling on to that one, another being drowned, some swimming a long way to save themselves, others sinking like stones to the very bottom, and turbans floating like flocks of ducks down the Danube; to see that haughty pasha of Silistria led by the neck by a rather unimportant cavalier to our hetman and to see the other, the pasha of Aleppo, gray as a dove, lamenting being taken into captivity in his old age, also led to the same Polish hetman, Jabłonowski. They presented many other distinguished persons to the king and the hetmans, and any common soldier presented himself in a Turkish fur-trimmed gown and turban, astride those handsome Arab horses; in a word, God granted our men good fortune enough and showed great mercy, rewarding Thursday's disgrace with so soon and distinguished a victory.

34. In the front ranks.
35. By God's avenging hand.

The Germans, on the other hand, took no captives, but killed them *crudelissime.*[36] Even after death, they dragged their corpses about; flayed them, twisted the flayed strips into straps they might use; the third day after the battle, it was already hard to see a Turk on the battlefield with his body entire; and if [any of our men] was not cautious in leading a captive, and he rode among Germans, they would seize the prisoner out of his grasp and kill him. My nephew, Stanisław Pasek, was leading a Turk, some kind of important fellow, for he was handsomely attired and riding a beautiful horse; my nephew, having disarmed the captive, was leading him along on his horse, holding only the reins, when along comes a German, rides alongside the Turk, and stabs him with a dagger. The Turk only groaned; my nephew looked back, and the Turk, mouth agape, is slipping off his horse. Having stabbed him, the German rode off at once to the side. My nephew begins to scold him: "You pig, you knave! Killed my prisoner you have, and is that permitted?" The German but laughs and says: "*Ja, Pan,* are you Poles feeding the devil?" My nephew rails at him that you're a scoundrel, not a cavalier — to kill a captive already in our hands. But the German only rides on, laughing.

What else was there to do? The Germans feel great rancor as the Turks robbed them of so much of their country, their provinces and fortresses; secondly, they are *a natura crudeles*[37] and know not how to observe knightly restraint *in victoria*; besides, the Turks routed them in every battle, the Germans never had any luck with them anywhere, no matter where they attacked; when the Turks descended upon them with their swords, they were slaughtered like cattle. Even when the grand vizier was besieging Vienna, the Germans never dared to *oppónere offensive*[38] until the Poles came, they but shielded themselves in that battle *defensive* near the fortresses. After the vizier had passed through the whole country without raising his sword, there being none to stand in his way, he first despatched the Tartars to Vienna as the *praecursores*[39] who themselves, and without the Turks, so decisively routed the Germans that nearly half of a regiment of foot was cut down; the Germans withdrew in shame across the bridges; they themselves burned those bridges on the Danube which had been built at great cost, thereby leaving to the enemy a free access to Vienna.

Those German gentlemen discovered in these and in previous battles the art of Tartar warfare and what it is to fight them. They who had

36. With exceeding cruelty.
37. Innately cruel.
38. Resist offensively.
39. Vanguard.

sneered at us before, *et toties exprobrabant*[40] for fighting with a wretched, unarmed people, with a people quick to flee, a hundred of them from one musket barrel; yet German flintlocks proved no match for Tartar sabres, huge cannons worthless. I say this: not only the cavalier who withstands a charge *pugna stataria,*[41] but also he should not be made light of who, though he quit the field for awhile, yet comes back again and does battle. The first, if he wins, is fortunate — if he loses, it is usually his life, whereas the second like a bird flies away and returns. *Fugiendo pugnat, fugiendo vincit.*[42] I, too, have contended with Tartars, and never did I see as many Tartar corpses piled up after a battle as Germans, Muscovites, and other nations; a heap of three hundred, four hundred dead Tartars and great was the victory; while the others like woodpiles you could always look at. Do battle with a German! If he overpowers me, he'll not chase me; if I overpower him, he'll not run away; but with a Tartar flight is to no avail, and pursuit is irksome — even if you do overtake him you'll not make your fortune off him. But I return to the matter from which I have digressed.

After that fortunate victory at Parkany and the taking of Strygonium, our army set off for the border across Hungary. There, having entered a mountain pass, we were sore beset by the Hungarian rebels,[43] attacking from the mountains and forests, greatly hindering our men on the march, seizing and killing our soldiers on their lookouts, raiding and pillaging our wagon trains, then escaping into the hills when the going was rough, having a safe spot *a natura locorum.*[44] Then the autumn rains came, horses died aplenty, and cartloads of those spoils from Vienna were thrown over, others preferred to burn it rather than enrich the Hungarian rebels. Enough that others should act thus: if one's wagon got stuck in the mountain pass, he'd pull out a tent, a proper Turkish tent, and he'd spread it out in front of the horses, the sooner to pull out of the mud and once the wagon was drawn out of the impasse, he'd ride off, leaving that tent worth several thousand trampled in the mud. How much pewter and brass, how many chests, leather sacks, divers Turkish curios were flung into the mud, into rivers, by whomever lost his horses!

The emperor had wished the army to go straight to Silesia, back to Poland, after a respite in Moravia; it was we who insisted on proceeding to Hungary, anticipating there was something to gain. But we ought to have begun this campaign at the beginning of summer, not winter; it

40. And so often mocked us.
41. In regular battle formation.
42. In flight he fights, in flight he conquers.
43. Fighting for Imre Thököly.
44. In an inaccessible place.

was clear that our intention was not God's will, for our designs did not turn out as we had expected. Nevertheless, on their way through Hungary, our men took Łewcza and Seczyn where there were Turkish garrisons.[45] As they were advancing on Seczyn and needing intelligence from the town by any means, they bade the Cossacks to have a try and promised them a reward. A few went off to the orchards but they were unable to capture anybody, for the people, being cautious, never went outside of the town.

The Cossacks devised this ruse: a dozen or so lay in ambush in the orchards, while two set off toward the town, keeping their eye out as they approach ever closer. No sooner were they judged in town to be within musket shot, but they were fired at, either with a harquebus or a long musket. One Cossack, though he'd not been hit, fell to the ground; the other pretended to be bringing him to, to set him on his feet, and then to loosen his clothes. Seeing this, the Turks fired a few shots at him as well, who, having half-disrobed the other one, takes to his heels without a glance backward, fleeing across the bare fields so that in town they should see him going toward the camp. The other Cossack lies there pretending to be dead (he had dressed in bright garb, in a red coat); and in no time a Turk comes along to have a look. Making his way over, halting, glancing in all directions; he suspects something in the trees — nothing there; he creeps toward him, looks him in the eyes — the Cossack had closed eyes and bared teeth — and begins to tender his services (not dressing the poor wretch, however, the Turk wanting to strip the fellow); he kneels down to undo the buttons; the Cossack grabs him by the neck. The Turk yells; they struggle with each other. The town is far from here and to rescue him from the other side of the moat impossible; now the Cossacks dash from their ambush; the Turk tries to wrench himself free, he'd be glad to let go, if only the Cossack would let him. The others jumped upon him, seized him, and took him to the king. What fine cunning and skill these Cossacks possess!

The king, having perceived from the prisoner that Seczyn, or Syczyn, with God's help could fall into our hands, he ordered the army to make ready for a siege. In the town the Turks had also prepared for their guests quite well; no sooner had our regiments advanced to the assault, but the Turks gave fire *potentissime*,[46] shooting down many of our men and some eminent commanders. But when the Turks saw that we pressed forward to the attack like hungry flies to a skinned ox, blindly, without regard for that heavy fire, they, begging for mercy, surrendered; and they were granted pardon.

45. Łewcza (Levice) is a town in Slovakia north of Esztergom; Seczyn (Szecsény) is a town and a castle not far from the Ipoly river.

46. With all their might.

In that assault they shot off the left leg of a valiant cavalier, Franciszek Lanckoroński of Brześć, district supervisor of Stopnica; so distraught by this mishap were both the king and the hetmans that they would have preferred to have never taken that fortress, nor ever seen it, and to have passed by it from afar, rather than be deprived of so worthy a knight, so indispensable to his country. But jealous fortune was disappointed in wanting to deprive our country of her much needed son! God's grace and divine protection did not allow her to triumph. His spirit and courage are the same as before; his prowess and boldness are the same, as is his stamina; and his willingness to serve his country is even greater; in short, we do whatever must be done, go wherever we are needed; we shall be there along with everyone else; we shall not flinch from appearing *in locis Tyriis.*[47] No misfortune can hurt our country's best sons, who are mercifully preserved by the Lord's protective hand; on the contrary, in attempting to ruin them, she but improves them, since they win a good name and immortal glory. May the heavens grant bounteous favors to such sons of ours as these; with the poet, let us wish: *"Vivite fortes/Fortiaque adversis opponite pectora rebus."*[48] [There follows a long ode to Pasek's great friend Lanckoroński, and to Polish knighthood in general. It has been omitted from this translation.]

After the battle at Seczyn, our men hungered for the fortresses of Proszów and Koszyce; but the weather being the greatest impediment, as winter was approaching, the army but let itself be seen at those strongholds and marched on toward the border, yet lost Modrzewski there on account of that whim, he dying in cannon fire. An old soldier he was, and tried, a cavalier who'd been a lieutenant and captain of horse, had led regiments, was used to command; but at Proszów he perished, having carelessly stood by a target mark, at which the town had aimed its cannons. For one must always take care, while approaching a fortress, not to stand in any spot where there is some mark or bush, but pass by such places as rapidly as you can, for usually the canoneers have marked them as target finders.

As the king neared the border, the Lithuanian army finally joined forces with ours; a fine and well-trained army they had, but what good was it, when it was *post bellum auxilium.*[49] For they had procrastinated in setting off on that campaign, and should the king have waited for them, as some advised, things would have turned out very badly indeed, for time would have run out; Vienna, unable to hold out any

47. In Tyrrhenian places. Here Pasek has changed *Tyria maria* (Tyhrennian Sea), meaning "dangerous sea," to "dangerous places."
48. Live O valiant men/ And bravely shoulder adversity (Horace, *Satires,* II, 2).
49. Aid after the war had been won.

longer, would have been taken, which even the Germans themselves admitted, *et consequenter,* we could not have won so favorable a victory at a fortress already in the hands of the enemy. But all turned out well in the end, I might even say, it happened according to King Jan's prophetic inspiration, a special gift of the Holy Spirit. So firm was his hope in future victory that he made for Vienna *tanta festinatione et alacritate;*[50] belike, had he but half the army he set off with, he'd not have waited longer. Besides, the Viennese, like souls in purgatory, kept watching for the *desiderabilem praesentiam,*[51] soon to arrive, any moment now; just as the fleeing sheep when the wolf's greedy fangs are about to sink into her, she, miserable creature, redoubles her effort in the hope that some hunter may arrive to save her from this terror, so too, the Emperor, bewildered and despairing of good fortune, unable to rescue his capital, not daring to look the enemy in the eye, not daring to resist, his army having lost courage, took refuge in God alone, praying and watching for the Poles, despatching envoys without cease to the king [urging] that he arrive as speedily as he can to assist in quenching this terrible conflagration, which was like to devour all of Christendom. The king, being a sensible ruler, weighed all the circumstances; and therefore wished to make all possible haste thence, knowing reinforcements are more surely effective one year before the battle than one hour after it.

The Lithuanians were sore distressed for missing so fortunate a battle. Both hetmans, [Kazimierz] Sapieha and [Jan] Ogiński, received an earful of sarcastic rebukes from the king, the which distressed them still more, yet not more than their missing the chance to show off their army in the enemy's lands, so handsomely equipped and armed at the expense of the Commonwealth. Whereas the soldiers, poor souls, on hearing our men tell how God had blessed them with so fortunate a victory, how they fell upon all that wealth and luxury in the Turkish camp, shriveled up from envy; especially heartbroken were they upon seeing with their own eyes those luxuries, the silver, the gold, the richly embroidered garments, divers ingenious things, curios, and valuable booty, and they accused the *incuriam*[52] of their commanders.

So then, our army upon leaving Hungary, traveled by way of the Spisz district towns in Podgórze; while the Lithuanians set forth toward Volhynia, there to vent their spite on Podlasie, Polesie, and Volhynia, having missed their chance with the Turks, and they gave them a good raking.

Departing from Hungary, Sieniawski, our field hetman, died, he

50. With such haste and impatience.
51. Desired presence.
52. Slackness.

having been ailing since the outset of the Vienna expedition; so holy a war he did not want to miss, on account of his innate ardor. Gladly he went, though ill most of the time, and afterward died in the service of his country and the defense of all Christendom. The hetman's mace was given then to Potocki, castellan of Kraków, son of Stanisław Potocki, who had also been hetman during the reign of Jan Kazimierz.

During the Vienna expedition, Kunicki, under orders from the Crown, invaded the Tartar lands; the king having appointed him, before departing for Vienna, hetman of the Cossacks; a nobleman he was, from Lublin. Kunicki and his Cossacks went on a spree, for the best of the Tartar hordes were gone off to Vienna. Whenever a band of Tartars put up resistance, he had time to burn and kill; his army was gathering more and more strength, for he was collecting so many of those captives who had settled there; others came of their own accord, hearing from afar of the Christian army. The Cossacks committed unbelievable mischief, sparing no one, slaying the women, tearing children asunder, doing those people the worst possible wrongs; they were saying that Kunicki had laid low three times 100,000 Tartars and went about with a bold face, having no one to fear. But as the khan was returning from Hungary, 30,000 of select Tartars, not like the other hordes, were sent to relieve them, there were also some Turks with them. Kunicki gave battle at Kilia, routed them, and carried off the spoils, returning safely across the border. But later, the Cossacks themselves killed him, pretending he had robbed them of their booty, it being no novelty for Cossacks to kill their hetman on the slightest pretext. He had not wronged them in any way but for having taken great booty, which they could not wrench from him by any other means than violence; and so the villains basely destroyed an excellent soldier, who would have given the Tartars something to worry about, he having grown so accustomed to their ways.

The Tartars, finding desolation in their land, the corpses of their wives and children, their herds of cattle stolen, mourned their misfortune.

In short, the Lord blessed Christendom everywhere at this time: in Germany, in Venice, and in Poland; for, after Kunicki, Dymidecki[53] accomplished plenty in Wallachia, fighting the Turks and Wallachians; he drove them from the field, captured Grzegorz III Duca [the Moldavian prince] and led him off to prison.

In the Turkish lands, *in contrarium,* there followed great disturbances, murmurings, and uprisings against their commanders for the unsuccessful conduct of the war and the loss of so many men, the

53. Dymidecki was a colonel of the royal troops; a brave commander, he was killed later by the Turks at Kamieniec.

blame for which the emperor sought to foist upon the vizier, causing him to be strangled *in publico foro,*[54] hoping to divert *insultum populi*[55] away from himself; but he could not avoid it and was deposed.

The year ended then with good fortune and jubilation for all Christian peoples except the Lutherans, who had asked God for a Turkish victory; Thököly, the rebel, who fought on the Turkish side so that the Lutheran provinces would aid him with money, had misled them into believing that the Turks had mounted the war in order to destroy the Roman religion and set Lutheranism in its place all over Europe. To this end, great services to petition the Lord were held, and collections taken up, which they gave to Thököly to pursue the war. At that time, when those services — very annoying to God — were being celebrated, I was in Gdańsk; but, after all, as it turned out, He did not hear them. As long as the Turks had not been repulsed at Vienna and there was still hope of their taking the city, broadsides were sung in the streets, verses recited on the boulevards, copies dropped everywhere; pictures of Thököly as defender of the faith were painted, sold dearly, and nearly everyone sought to have one in his home; in the churches *gratiarum actiones*[56] were held at the news of every Turkish success, and it made your heart sink. I'll never know, on the other hand, what sort of satisfaction they had, upon learning *de contrario rerum successu,*[57] for I was already home at the time of the victory.

The year departed then, with God's blessings, not only in the public sphere but also in my own, for my health was good the entire year, and I was favored in all my undertakings. Such years, O Gracious Lord, grant me so long as I shall live and for this one let Your Most Holy Name be praised!

54. In public view.
55. Popular discontent.
56. Prayers of thanksgiving.
57. Of the contrary outcome.

The Year of Our Lord 1684

I began in Olszówka — God be praised! This too was a fortunate year in public affairs; as for my personal ones, it was a bad bargain.[1]

This year our armies did not join forces *cum Caesarianis*,[2] since they could now survive on their own, encouraged by last year's triumph; as they say, a tamed and oft-ridden horse anyone will mount, a bold and swift one not so many; besides, the *colligati principes* had accomplished an *aversionem belli.*[3] The Venetians stood up to a *magnam partem* of the enemy's army, which out of necessity was forced to guard its shores on that side of the sea. Our king, together with the crown army, crossed the Dniester and there personally subdued those territories up and down, setting himself against the prime strength of the Turkish state, through which its *imperium potissimum floret*[4] that is, the Crimean, Nogai, Białogród, and Budziak Tartars,[5] along with the Wallachians and Moldavians, all of whom would surely have gone out to counter the Germans had it not been for this diversion. Throughout that campaign,our men engaged in *tot conflictus*[6] with them, standing up to *potentissimos impetus*[7] with great loss of their men but also of our own; they, seizing our soldiers above all on their lookouts, while mowing, or grazing the horses, which has long been the way of this people. Meanwhile, the Germans are battling the Turks as hard as ever they can;

1. Pasek had eight lawsuits on his hands.
2. With the Emperor's men.
3. Allied princes . . . diversion of the war.
4. Empire has flourished the most.
5. The Tartar hordes that inhabited the territory between the Volga and the Danube were split into independent khanates: The Nogai, who roamed the northeastern shores of the Black Sea, from the Volga to the Crimea; the Crimean, who had settled in the Crimea and immediate vicinity; the Białogród, who lived between the Crimea and the Dniester river; and the Budziak, who lived between the Prut and Dniester and Danube rivers (in what is now southern Bessarabia, the plain between the Prut, Dniester, and Danube rivers).
6. So many clashes.
7. The most powerful attacks.

twice this year they drove them from the field in the first encounter, they seized towns, fortresses — Nowe Zamki, Buda, and other places *superioris et inferioris Hungariae*[8] — long ago conquered by the Turks and now recovered. The Venetians captured many Morlaks[9] who, having revolted against the Turks, surrendered voluntarily; they took the *regnum Moreae,*[10] and many other towns in the immediate vicinity. In brief, 'tis a smooth course when two minds have but a single thought. Yet, after God's grace, our Poles are the greatest cause of this good fortune, and especially the king in resolving to go against that fearsome enemy for the sake of the whole Christian world; in leading the army *personaliter,* he bit into the enemy's strength and drove him off, while the Germans being lazier, having snatched the spent beast from its nimble pursuer, now do not let up the chase until the prey is caught, and sooner will they line their pockets than he who drove it off. [The manuscript is cut off at this spot.] 'tis unseemly in this our alliance that we began the offensive for them, aided them sincerely, they lining their pockets beside us, and now, belike shall fill them still fuller doing battle with those who *effeminate illa diuturna pace, molles et imbelles facti*[11] (it being the *status imperii Ottomanici*[12] to render them defenseless after having defeated us and to turn them into tillers of the soil or other toilers so they would not rebel). And we were left to entertain those nations who not only from time immemorial have always been warlike and insurmountable but, what is more, still are, being in continual training, *in continuo belli opere*;[13] in a word, their life is ceaseless warfare and they live from war — even were we to subdue them, there is no force whereby to grow rich off them, for they're skinny wretches. To be brief, our allies chose the better *sortem* for themselves, just as one picks for himself the tastiest piece with cinnamon and sweet-meats; but for us they left a dish seasoned with horseradish and sharp pepper. O God, grant that our teeth be not set on edge by it, for 'tis, as I perceive it, an *uva acerba*;[14] as You bestowed upon us a good beginning, by Your divine grace, vouchsafe to bless us with a good ending!

8. In the upper and lower regions of Hungary.
9. Pasek spells the name Makłak. Whom he has in mind is unclear. Czubek believes it to be the name "Morlak," denoting a Dalmatian Slavic tribe; Brückner explains that the Morlaks lived on the shores of the Adriatic Sea in what is today Dalmatia. The name "Morlak" dates from the nineteenth century.
10. The Peloponesus.
11. Have grown soft on account of the long peace and become weak and unmilitant.
12. Design of the Ottoman Empire.
13. In constant military action.
14. Bitter apple.

The Year of Our Lord 1685

I began happily — praise God! — in Olszówka. The Diet was held in Warsaw. This year prices climbed in Wielkopolska on account of the failures of spring wheat crops, sending the prices sky-high in Warsaw as well. On learning of this in May, I had a barge loaded with barley and beans and set off there alone. I raked in plenty from Wielkopolska. Only it was already late; had I been a trifle more hasty, and gotten there a week sooner, I could have taken twice as much for a bushel.

This year Stanisław, the margrave of Pińczów, died while serving as deputy for a crown tribunal in Lublin, leaving me in great embarrassment due to my lease of the margrave's estates, whereof I shall write below. Many people were glad of his death, nor did I much mourn him, he being — the Lord forgive him! — a conniver, shifty, disloyal, and a dealer in prevarications; lied he did as if he were eating the best meal of his life. And so I did not regret his passing, assuming that his successor Józef [Władysław Myszkowski], his brother, would be a man of a different sort, for he appeared stable and good-natured; but in so hoping, I was no less disappointed than that woman who kept begging God for a better master, but always got a worse.[1]

On my return from Warsaw, I began making ready for Gdańsk, being anxious to transport my wheat, the which, as it was getting very warm in the granaries, needed to be treated unremittingly; however, the water being too low, I and everyone else had to wait *ad Septembrem.* When at last the anticipated time arrived, I fell exceedingly ill on the 30th of August, a Thursday it was. And this ailment befell me on account of a carouse, I being brought to that through bad company; for I never remember ever drinking so much of my own accord, as some do whom I know; yet whenever anyone is heartily glad to see me, or I to see him, especially some beloved intimate, then 'twould be unthinkable not to observe our Polish way. So *periculose* ill did I fall then, that I did

1. According to the then well-known tale by Valerian Maximus, a certain woman, out of fear of a worse tyrant, prays for the health of the reigning tyrant; in a fairy tale by Fedrus the frogs beg for a new king. Pasek has evidently confused the two stories.

not even recognize people, being seized with a delirium. What the doctors did for me I know not; enough said that they despaired, announced I was in an exceedingly bad state and *convalescentia* impossible.

Meanwhile the water was rising; my watchman at the granary comes by, leaving word to send the peasants to load, and there I am, dead to the world. My wife bade him go to the devil; off he went, not a jot of likelihood was there that God would work those miracles which he did, nearly at that moment. Here is what happened:

While lying in a feverish sleep — having been in that delirium since the 30th of August — on the night before the seventh of September, from Thursday to Friday, that is, on the eve of the Nativity of the Blessed Virgin, I felt my shoulder shaken by something that uttered these words: "Anthony is standing over you!" I face the wall and what should I see but a monk *in habitu Minorum sancti Francisci.*[2] I stare, I say nothing; it says nothing. A candle is shining in the corner; the people serving at my bedside, worn out, had fallen asleep. It was already near daybreak when that monk shakes me. It was as if I'd been in a dream, but after that jolt I was immediately awake, had my wits about me, I now grasped that I was layed out there on account of my illness, and I fully recalled what happened, though a while before, I had been senseless. And I say to myself, they've sent some monk to me, as is ordinarily done for a sick person; when that figure says on a sudden: "Since Thursday last, I've kept watch over you: fear no more, but arise!"

What joy filled me then, and it passed through my mind that this was no ordinary priest but must be a saint. I spring up, wanting to fall at his feet, and exclaimed in a loud voice "Holy Father!" and tumbled out of bed. Everyone heard my cry, they came running with candles, then I ask: "Where did he go?" They think I'm doing it in my delirium; they say to me: "Whom are you asking about? No one was here." I say: "There was. Have you no eyes?" And then I sat down, not on the bed but on a stool. My wife says: "Summon Kazimierz!" The barber-surgeon comes, feels my pulse: "You've no fever, and it's as if you never had one." I, too, after looking at myself, and resting awhile, first knelt down to give thanks to God and St. Anthony; upon arising, I began to tell them about it. Everyone wondered at it *cum stupore*;[3] some believed that it happened, others did not. Even the surgeon himself thought that the fever had left some sort of *debilitatem mentis*[4] though he saw the fever had wholly subsided.

2. In a habit of the Bernardin brothers.
3. In astonishment.
4. Feebleness of the mind.

And so they were taken up with me until I say: "I see that you offer me congratulations and rejoice at my recovery but do not ask whether I would have a bite to eat; you've starved me enough during these days of my sickness." My wife springs up: "Straight-away! Forthwith!" and inquires what I've an appetite for. Said I: "I'll eat whatever you bring with great pleasure." They consult together what to prepare for me: this — no, that — no; until at last the surgeon says: "Perhaps, something with butter, though it's the vigil of a holy day." I inquire: "What vigil?" The Blessed Virgin's Nativity, they said. I was amazed for I did not think I had been ill for so many days, and I say: "I'll not eat anything with butter, since it's the vigil." They prepared a small pot of thick gruel. I hardly felt it go down, there was so little; I bade them cook more in a bigger pot and sprinkle it with plenty of spices. They prepared it then; while I dressed myself suitably and gave orders to take a net, go to the fish pond, catch a pike and cook it in a sweet and sour sauce. Seeing me eat and drink so heartily, and my briskness [manuscript damaged, several words missing here] as it should be, only then did they believe I was *sanus mente et corpore,*[5] whereof the surgeon had been especially doubtful.

As I was eating, my wife says: "You had wanted the wheat transported, and now your illness has prevented it." I ask: "How so?" She told me word had come that the water was high; *Pan* Rupniowski had gone down, *Pan* Jaroszowski had gone down; they chased their peasants out full speed to load up. I answer: "Then I shall ride down too." They all laughed; they thought I was jesting, but I feel hale and hearty. Having eaten my fill, I pace about the chamber; I had the steward summoned, and I bid him send the peasants out to start loading, meanwhile I have the horses got ready and harnessed. They say to me: "For heaven's sake, don't do it! Your health is more precious." I say: "Leave me alone, I know better how I feel; I trust Him who gave me life to preserve my health and guide me safely to where I intend to go."

I set forth, having bade them farewell, ordering my *necessaria*[6] carted after me. Coming out on the open field, I descended from my britzka, mount on horseback and set off at a gallop, fearing the water may drop. I found them still there, some had already put off, others were waiting for dry provisions, whoever had none ready in his storehouse. Since my own peasants would have scarcely arrived by nightfall, there being seven miles to travel after all, my neighbors loaned me theirs. I loaded up two barges then; while I had the rafts loaded without me. Very early on the day of the Blessed Virgin's Nativity, I went to the Franciscans and had a Mass said in front of St. Anthony, which I heard while last

5. Of sound mind and body.
6. Effects.

preparations were being made on the barges. I made my way back, went aboard, and put off before noon, for everyone else had already left. My own peasants came too late to be of much help, my neighbor's did all that was needed, there being enough of them. Off I set, and I overtook even those who had put off a day and a half ahead of me, in spite of my having gone little or no distance, since the chief raftsman had a poor boat and was seeking another.

We stopped in the Leniwka[7] finally, on the 23rd of September, frequent winds having slowed our course, while the rafts behind me arrived fourteen days later; the rafts, having set off from Łęka,[8] reached Gdańsk in fewer days than the barges because the winds which had been hindering the barges stopped as soon as the rafts left the pier — and they left on the 21st of September — and we were then at Toruń; that was St. Matthew's day and a mighty cold day it was, ice upon the banks, extraordinary. I got there, by God's grace, quite comfortably for my having set out on that journey so *instantanee* after my illness, and by His divine grace, my head did not even ache me, wherefore may His Most Holy Name be eternally praised and let Him not withdraw His fatherly protection from us who humbly beseech Him in every affliction and especially in sickness.

7. The Leniwka is an arm of the Vistula at the delta, running through Gdańsk.
8. Łęka is a village near Nowy Korczyń.

The Year of Our Lord 1686

Residing in Olszówka, I passed the year there — God be praised! — in good health and fortune.

This year I attended *Panna* Sieklicka's taking of the veil in Kraków, her parents, *Pan* Adam Sieklicki, my great friend, and Zofia Rabsztynska, her mother, having given her away to the religious life in the Augustinian order;[1] there, in a numerous company of many people of quality, I was invited to commemorate her vows with a speech. I did not feel much inclined to it, knowing how quick to criticize they were there, but they did not deride me, perhaps they meant only to flatter me — I know not. [Pasek's flowery oration in praise of the religious life is omitted from this translation.]

That ceremony took place on the 24th of January. There was no winter to speak of this year, we had neither snow nor frost, none of the rivers froze over; *in Februario* the land was tilled for the spring crops, flowers and grass grew, we sowed the spring rye, the cattle ate their fill of hay; Lent had no sooner begun but we sowed the barley and oats, though they could have been sown even earlier. Before Easter [April 14] all the crops had been sown and winter was over, the harvests were quite good.

Uncommon for Poland it was and *supra usum*[2] for large flocks of wild geese to roam about all summer and, which is very rare, around Kraków and Sandomierz, where they never nest. We had to drive them out of the grain lest they cause much harm. But they were another species, unlike those that always came, they seemed to be piebald about the neck; they nested with our own geese and weren't very shy, they let people approach and poke them with a stick; divers people had divers explanations.

On the 7th of August I loaded my wheat onto four barges and put off for Gdańsk; having sold it, I returned safely by land, with God's grace,

1. A convent of Augustinian nuns in Kazimierz.
2. Uncustomary.

on the 17th of September. This year I took on Madziarów *modo obligatorio.*[3]

This year his highness the king and our army went to southern Bessarabia and to Wallachia. There they clashed several times with the Tartars and other enemies. What is most noteworthy is that St. Ivan transferred his residence from Wallachia to Poland[4] *cum tota argentea supellectili*[5] accompanied by a few trusted blackrobes [orthodox monks] whereas the Emperor's army, having been blessed by God at the outset of their campaign, so too, were they this year, for twice they gave the Turks a powerful beating, they took their tents and all the luxuries of their camps, and dominated several mighty fortresses, but this was thanks to us, for after all we were restraining the Tartar might.

3. In lien.
4. The remains of St. Ivan of Suczawa were transported from Suczawa to Żółkiew; not until the Austrian partition of Poland were they returned.
5. With all his silver paraphernalia.

The Year of Our Lord 1687

I began in Olszówka, my lease having now expired, that is, the eleventh year of my tenancy. I transported my effects little by little to Madziarów, having let Smogorzów go to my step-son the year before; I released it to him *in eadem qualitate*[1] as I'd received it and kept it, seventeen years belike, that is, a good piece of land, well-cultivated, which I'd found very disfigured by the tenants; the buildings are repaired and in good shape, the orchards grafted, the forests allowed to grow, and nothing is disturbed, which is a *raritas* among stepfathers, the debts have been settled and paid off in full, which put me to much trouble and expense. The deceased *Pan* Łącki had bought that estate with a mortgage, he having insufficient funds to pay for it, and he had borrowed money from convents and left behind some security payments on the estate itself; besides, the *successores*[2] of his first wife, née Grodzicki, the Gomoleński and Lubański brothers, were suing for the dowry. Since both sides claimed the *proprietatem*[3] of this inheritance, I demanded it be formally given to whomever it legally belonged in order not to pay the same amount twice; we carried on litigations over this then; there were squabbles, executions of verdicts, forays, banishments, battles, and *consequenter* damages to be paid, wherein I lost much, and which led to other circumstances which ruined my purse. This is what it means to take a widow with children and a peck of troubles; the first husband incurs debts, leaves a mess, children, *litigia,*[4] and you waste your life on other people's affairs, and ruin your health; whatever profit you should collect for yourself, you spend on lawsuits and still you earn ingratitude instead of thanks. I put this down *pro memento;*[5] whoever is about to do as I have done, look to my advice.

All my work went for repayment of loans, lawsuits, weddings, my

1. In the same condition.
2. Heirs.
3. Ownership.
4. Lawsuits.
5. As a warning.

daughters' taking the veil, and receptions, of which there were five.[6] I reckoned the expenses added up over the years to 40,000. All that, I gave up because of one humble request from my stepson and the mediation of friends; my lifelong lease I relinquished, taking nothing in return; even the ring my wife had given me at our engagement, I gave her back, so that I'd have nothing stuck to me that was not my own. His kinsmen admitted I could have withheld Smogorzów from him had I wished.

6. Pasek exaggerates. There was one wedding, three takings of the veil; the dowries of three sisters were assured on Smogorzów, and the eldest had been dowered by her own father when she entered the convent.

The Year of Our Lord 1688

I was living in Madziarów, but — I could better say — in Lublin, suing the margrave. My wife, however, resided on the Olszówka estate, as if imprisoned, whereas the Myszkowskis would have rejoiced to see her leave; had she but wished to, they'd have dismantled the fence.[1]

There was a Diet in Grodno on the 26th of January to which I was also constrained to go regarding those resolutions voted at our district assemblies *pro parte mea militantes.*[2] I reached Grodno then on the 1st of March having endured frightful roads, lumpy from the frozen mud. Our deputies from Kraków, especially my intimates and *Pan* Lanckoroński, the district supervisor of Stopnica, are telling me: "Since you've no verdict on the margrave by default, do you wish to undermine him by other means? For the margrave was elected deputy through the connections of the constable from Sandomierz,[3] and an innocent deputy he is — never opens his mouth in public, sits there gaping like a nightjar [the manuscript is damaged in this spot] paying more mind to his cards, whereby he has ingratiated himself with the queen and the courtiers, who often filled their purses in card games with him. Said I: "To be sure! For he is an *oppressor nobilitatis et raptor substantiarum.*"[4]

The margrave, seeing me then in the Deputies' Chamber, nearly expired. His own colleagues, perceiving his confusion, say to me: "For God's sake, the margrave has need of some spirits. You will deprive us of a good deputy; the Deputies' Chamber will be unable to stand behind anything without his active participation." Meanwhile the sessions of the Diet were being obstructed by private squabbles between the Lithuanian field hetman, *Pan* Słuszka, and *Pan* Dąbrowski, the

1. Pasek, while suing the margrave, did not want to give up the lease on Olszówka, claiming a right to certain of the Myszkowski properties. He left his wife on Olzowka to make it look as if she were imprisoned by his opponent.
2. Supporting my case.
3. Stefan Bidziński, who was married to Teresa Myszkowska.
4. An oppressor of the gentry and an extortionist.

Wilno deputy.[5] I, on the *consilium* of my good friends do not go first to the Chamber of Deputies to recount my grievances (a mighty outcry was to be raised there over my case and my adherents were arming themselves to the teeth), but make my complaint to the king and win his favor. [There follows Pasek's speech to the king in which he explains how he has been victimized, his fortune and land confiscated by the margrave of Pińczów.]

The king listened *diligenter* and, when I had finished he says: "That requires an answer from Holy Scripture: *Habetis legem et prophetas.*[6] What are the tribunals, the other law courts for, except to dispense justice even to the greatest lord; however, when such a thing reaches our ears, we are most willing to see that such lawlessness is stopped."

There were then in the room a dozen or so senators and deputies. The king says to Chełmski, the Polish master of the camp, "Your Honor is a close neighbor; what is this affair about?" Chełmski answers: "I know this, My Gracious Lord, that this nobleman has always paid the required amount, and was more like an honest treasurer than a tenant. In the worst straits he could be trusted, more than the other tenants, and he would sometimes barely even keep 100 zloties for himself. When he would return from Gdańsk, they'd post word about it, they did not give him leave to enjoy his money long, people gave him the title Benefactor, they revered him for his kindness and willingness to oblige, and held him up *pro exemplo boni amici.*[7] [But] when he asked to be paid back or to have his lease extended, then they were not pleased to hear him. In short, two *potentiores*[8] persecuted this gentryman in order to despoil him of his substance, to destroy him *protractione litigiorum,*[9] in a word, to bring to ruin one who did *satis superque*[10] for their family. Much more could be said. To speak plainly, they deal with everyone badly. Your Highness knows what a clamor they raised over me, over my estates, what lawsuits they involved me in, and what expenses. Lord knows, I spent more for lawyers than I earned from Olszówka during those six years of my lease. Although, remembering

5. Józef Bogusław Słuszka, the Lithuanian field hetman, refused to grant Dąbrowski the right to sit in the Diet because he had taken him to court for making a foray on his estate. In fact, Słuszka was acting in consort with the king, who wished to remove Dąbrowski from the Chamber, he being a zealous adherent of the Sapiehas.
6. You have the law and the prophets. (Here Pasek puts into the king's mouth an inaccurate quote from St. Luke's Gospel. It should be "*Habent Moysen et prophetas, audiant illos,*" meaning "you have lower courts of apeal, why do you resort to the highest?")
7. As an example of a good friend.
8. Wealthier nobles.
9. Through protracted lawsuits.
10. Enough and more than enough.

previous matters I could twit him: *Perditio tua ex te*;[11] but as I'm a Christian, 'tis wrong for me to abuse someone for their misfortune. But this much I will say, it will turn out for him as it did for me, or worse; they'll involve him in expense, upsets, will ruin him so that [manuscript damaged here] he'll bow to them, beg for his own money, which he had gladly given them, and afterward, they'll give him whatever they please, for such is their way. In short, great *inconvenientia*[12] have occurred in connection with this estate; either it ought to be done away with or brought *ad debitam forman.*[13] As it is, this estate is useless; it being caught between the devil and the deep; the onus of law placed on the shoulders of Your Majesty's predecessors now falls to Your Highness and the Commonwealth. *Incumbit* then *subvenire oppresso,*[14] for he is one who, in Your Majesty's eyes, has been deserving of every regard in this country and is now deserving both in his own person and in his kinsmen. Here now is his nephew,[15] a cavalier from my squadron, who, taken into captivity a year and a half ago, has just returned from the Crimea three days ago, having left another cavalier in his place, the sooner to obtain ransom. And his good uncle has *in parte* bought one important Tartar from *Pan* Golyński, a lieutenant; the second Tartar, this one and no other, whom he was ordered to obtain for his freedom, is among Your Majesty's captives. This captive is here petitioning Your Majesty and I add my voice to his, for he is a good soldier and no mean cavalier; he is here outside the door."

The king says: "Call him in!" The master of the camp springs toward the door; I was ahead of him. I go out — no one in that chamber. I go to the middle chamber, for we had been in the chamber where the king sleeps, when, finally, the king's valet seizes him, embraces him and kisses him, weeping. Many deputies and divers other people clustered round him, for . . . his face had been seen there before . . . at the time, when the queen . . . sent 20,000 gold ducats of aid to the camp through him and another, a Frenchman . . . .[16] Through some folly, those gold ducats had been lost.

But enough of this digression, I return to the subject. To my nephew, I said: "Go to the king, Sir!" He went; the king, receiving him cordially, inquired with whom he was staying, how he had been cap-

11. Thou has brought evil upon thyself (Isaiah 3, 9). Chełmski means to say that it serves Pasek right for being so eager to obtain the lease on Olszówka that he forced Chełmski out. See the opening of the year 1677.
12. Irregularities.
13. Under proper control.
14. It is fitting (then) to assist the oppressed.
15. Stanisław Pasek has already been mentioned in the memoirs. He was a cavalier in Chełmski's squadron and lived for a time in Tartar captivity.
16. Ellipsis dots indicate places damaged in the manuscript.

tured. He questions him about the sultans, the dignitaries, and about other prisoners. He talked of everything.

The session was about to open then; the senators began to assemble in the Hall. Says the king to Matczyński, at that time the crown equerry: "I beg of you, Your Lordship, write out a money order and place it in the hands of *Pan* Pasek — the one who has come out of captivity — that the Tartar in Żółkiew be released *ad primam requisitionem*."[17] Turning to me he says: "It will be *curae nostrae*[18] to see that you receive recompense for the wrong done to you." Again the master of the camp speaks up: "Gracious Lord, a great uproar is brewing for this session *in ordine equestri*,[19] there being opposition to several ordinances in certain provinces and in my own district diet, a protest will be carried *in facie publica*."[20] The king answers: "We know of this, but we shall find a way to quiet them *sine maiori motu*."[21] To me he says: "Be of good cheer, Your Honor, as one who has earned a deserved esteem in this country; you will be *satisfactus*." and so, after hearing a Mass said by the Dominican who had been waiting outside the door in his vestments, he went off to the senate session.

This took place on the 15th of March. The Diet was close to dissolving; the king, *consternatus*[22] by these disagreements as well as by the fresh news that the Tartars had ravaged the Ukraine, especially his own villages, I did not dare to incur his ill-will, for sometimes even a senator was turned away from his door. And so I stood aside listening and waiting for the favorable moment; for so one must always do with one's superiors. But I kept myself within view, so that he would see me. He beckons to me with a finger, and walked off to the window. The king says then: "I spoke quite plainly of this matter with the margrave, and he *firmissime negat*[23] his guilt; he places responsibility with his uncle, that his uncle took the money, let the uncle pay." I said: "The uncle did take the money, but contracted with me on behalf of his nephews as their guardian to pay their debts whereof the contract informs." The queen speaks up: "Treat the margrave kindly, My Lord." To that I reply: "You Royal Highness, My Gracious Queen, may you deign thus to persuade him who has inflicted the injury, not the injured." She again: "A decent fellow he is." I again: "The man may be decent, but his deeds are evil." The king, making a wry face, smiled slightly at that:

17. On demand.
18. Our endeavor.
19. The Deputies' Chamber.
20. Before the estates.
21. Without a major clash.
22. Worried.
23. Firmly denies.

"Marysienka, give His Honor a jack of spades for that." With that he explained that the margrave played cards with her. The queen looked a trifle out of countenance and stepped away. As soon as she had gone away, the king says: "Leave well enough alone; let them shout him down in the Deputies' Chamber: he'll be cheaper then."

The king bade me come to him after dinner, then he got into his carriage and drove off to the Church of the Carmelites. There, he was again vexed by a Carmelite who began derisively to inveigh against him for caring less about the honor of God, for not seeking to avenge the injury done to Him, and even more to rail against the Chamber of Deputies. He discoursed on *nobilitatem:* what was noble, what was a nobleman and what was his calling, and who was a true nobleman. He cited one example: "I heard a respectable foreigner discoursing about his travels and comparing divers opinions of who surpasses whom in what: this is what he said: "In Italy I saw bishops, for it has the most bishops; in Germany I saw princes, for it has the most princes; in France I saw soldiers, for it has the best-trained army; in Poland I saw nobles, for it has the most numerous gentry. But my dear *nobilitas,* forgive me, for what I am going to tell you: your prestige has come unsettled, and that prestige of yours, which our pious ancestors earned for themselves among nations so that it was held up *pro exemplari speculo (non sine invidia)*[24] to the whole world. For such were our Poles! And he elaborated further on this, giving arguments, but mostly berated them for neglecting the honor of God. For there had recently arisen an impure sect started by Łyszczeński, whereof I shall speak below.[25]

No sooner am I come to the king in the afternoon as he had bidden, but he says: "The Chamber of Deputies would have supported you, but Tokarzewski broke up the Diet; your Mazurians would have bullied the margrave to death (for I know now who was doing the backbiting) and we would have helped from the side; now we'll have to take a different tack. I hear the Governor of Sieradz is here in the castle, he is a marshal of the court; I'll have him sent for and shall commend this matter to him that it may be judged fairly and without delay." He had me wait then, while he sent for him. The governor came. The king says to him: "My Lord Governor, here we have an *hominem iniuriatum*[26] (he pointed at me), a nobleman and a soldier long known to us, who *potentioribus oppressus, desiderant iustitiam.*[27] He has a recent complaint in the court

24. (Not without envy) as a mirror of example.
25. Kazimierz Łyszczeński was accused out of malice by his debtor, Jan Brzoska, of atheism; he was condemned by a court of the Diet to burning at the stake. The king "lightened" the sentence to beheading. He was beheaded on March 30, 1689. There was no "Łyszczeński sect." Pasek is gullibly repeating the gossip of fanatics.
26. A man who has been wronged.
27. Having been exploited by one more wealthy, awaits justice.

register;[28] therefore, I commend to Your Lordship both the man and his case as a deserving veteran of this country and I ask that he be duly recompensed." The governor says: "Gracious King, I know the man very well, from the many years we spent together both in the army and in the district diet. I am also familiar with his grievance and this matter; I would not deceive my conscience were I to judge him without reading the complaint, and the more so as the authority of Your Majesty is interceding. . . .

[Here the diary breaks off.]

28. This was a list of grievances in the Lublin court (the Kraków and Sandomierz provinces both took their cases to Lublin).

Appendixes

Key to Polish Pronunciation

This key is based on the classification and description of Polish sounds in Alexander Schenker's *Beginning Polish* (Yale University Press, 1966).

A	like a in father, but shorter
Ą	see nasal vowels
B	like b in bay
Bi	like b in imbue
C	like tz in Switzerland
Ć(Ci)	instead of tz sound, middle of tongue arches and presses against roof of mouth to soften.
Ch/H	see H/CH
Cz	like tch in switch
D	like d in width
Dz	like ds in ads
Dż	like j in jam
Dź	like ć but voiced
E	like e in let
Ę	see nasal vowels
F	like f in foe
Fi	like f in few
G	like g in gay
Gi	like g in ague
H/Ch	like ch in German *ach*
H/Chi	like h in hue but breathier
I	like ee in keep
J	like y in yet
K	like c in scar
Ki	like k in skew
L	like German *die Lampe* or French *la lampe*
Li	like English *lli* in million
Ł	like w in wet
M	like m in moot
Mi	like m in mute
N	like n in cannon
Ń(Ni)	like n in canyon, but further front and has weaker y-glide.
O	like o in low

Ó/U like o in do
P like p in spar
Pi like p in spew
R a rolled r, like Italian r.
S like s in so
Ś (Si) like German ch in *ich* but further front. (the tongue is in the position for saying h in human)
Sz like sh in show (the tongue in the position for saying r in run)
T like t in star
U (see Ó)
W like v in vest
Wi like v in view
Y midway between i in sit and e in set.
Z like z in zest
Źi same position for ś but voiced
Ż/Rz like z in azure

Nasal vowels ę and ą vary with the environment:
ę like a nasalized Polish e followed by semivowel [u̯] (which is like a w as in wow)
ą like ow in known

In final position:
ę like Polish e
ą like ow in known

Before f, w, s, sz, ś, ch, z, rz/ż, ź:
ę like nasalized e [u̯]
ą like ow in known

Before ł and l:
ę like Polish e
ą like Polish o

Before b, p:
ę like em in empathy
ą like om in dome

Before t, d, c, dz:
ę like en in entire
ą like on in don't

Before ć, dź:
ę like Polish eń
ą like Polish oń

Before k, g:
ę like ę[ŋ] (as in anchor)
ą like ą[ŋ] (as in anger)

q, x, v are not used in Polish except in foreign words and symbols.

Glossary of Seventeenth-Century State and Provincial Offices of the Commonwealth of Poland and Lithuania

Since the Grand Duchy and The Crown maintained separate but similar administrations, the offices listed here should be thought of in duplicate. This list makes no claim to exhaustiveness.

Offices are alphabetized according to key word in the title; for example, Crown Chamberlain is alphabetized under *Chamberlain*. State offices are labeled (s), provincial offices (p). Asterisks signify that the office conferred a seat in the Senate.

BISHOP(s)* A high political and ecclesiastical office; all bishops were named by the king, and all had a seat in the Senate.
CROWN CARVER(s). Honorary Court title.
CASTELLAN(p).* Second highest provincial office, after Governor. Titular only. A castellan might perhaps command the troops from his district in a general levy. The number of castellans varied with every province.
CROWN CHAMBERLAIN(s). Honorary Court title.
DISTRICT CHAMBERLAIN(p). Judged property and boundary disputes.
DISTRICT DEPUTY CHAMBERLAIN(p). Assisted the Chamberlain.
CHANCELLOR(s)* Keeper of the seal. Functioned as minister of foreign affairs, carrying on diplomatic correspondence and receiving foreign emissaries; and as minister of domestic affairs, receiving petitions to the king and speaking in the king's name at the Diet.
VICE-CHANCELLOR(s).* Assisted and replaced the Chancellor when necessary.
COURT RECORDER(p). Took notes of legal proceedings.
CROWN CUP-BEARER(s). Honorary Court title.
DISTRICT CUP-BEARER(p). Titular only.
CROWN EQUERRY(s). Honorary Court title.
GOVERNOR(p).* Highest provincial office. Led the general levy of the gentry from his province to the king; represented royal authority over the Jews; established prices; supervised weights and measures; convened local dietines.

DISTRICT JUDGE(p). Appointed by the King from candidates nominated by district dietines. (Law was uncodified in the Commonwealth and so various types of courts and judges proliferated; the district judges were the only ones appointed by the king.)

DEPUTY DISTRICT JUDGE(p). Replaced District Judge, assisted.

GRAND MARSHAL OF THE DIET(s) * Maintained order in the Senate with the help of armed constables; exercised police powers wherever the king was in residence.

DEPUTY MARSHAL OF THE DIET(s)* Maintained order in the Chamber of the Deputies; assisted or replaced the Grand Marshal in policing the king's surroundings.

MARSHAL OF THE CONFEDERACY(p). Presided over and maintained order at Confederate assemblies.

DEPUTY MARSHAL OF THE CONFEDERACY(p). Assisted or replaced the Marshal of the Confederacy.

NOTARY(p). In charge of the civil archives of the gentry in a given district.

LORD HIGH STEWARD(s). Honorary Court title.

MASTER OF THE TABLE(p). Titular only.

REFERENDARIES(s). Judged cases of peasants on Crown estates.

GRAND SECRETARY(s). Often replaced the Chancellor; always an ecclesiastic.

CROWN STANDARD-BEARER(s). Ceremonial Court title; the holder bore the royal standard.

DISTRICT STANDARD-BEARER(p). During a general levy, stood at the head of provincial or district troops, bearing the local standard.

DISTRICT SUPERVISOR(p). Honorary title conferred by the King along with a piece of crown property as a reward for public service.

LORD OF THE TREASURY(s)* The state treasurer, whose significance waned as provincial treasuries were established.

MUNICIPAL WARDEN(p). Provincial office in Lithuania; the holder had the function of protecting and overseeing the towns.

Important Historical Events of the Period 1656-1688

The seventeenth century has always been the touchy spot of Polish historiography. That century saw the once-strong Commonwealth of Poland and Lithuania sink further and further into a position of weakness, producing at the same time a compensatory rationalization that I shall call "the Polish image," which has been fervently handed down even to the present day. I am referring to the messianic role in which Poland cast itself as the "rampart of Christendom" against the "infidel East," as a nation chosen by Divine Providence to suffer the martyrdom of History's brutalities for the salvation of Western Civilization. An English political observer of the seventeenth-century Commonwealth reported: "Poland is (under God) the bullwarke of Christendome, on that side, against the insulting Turke and (his bloudhound) the Tartar."[1] Behind the compensatory rhetoric, whose pathos was so artfully exploited in the nineteenth century, lies the complicated, fascinating, and melancholy spectacle of a great power become an indefensible counterculture.

The image tended to obscure a more concrete and practical vision of the seventeenth century, and the period has been neglected by historians and literary scholars alike until as recently as the early sixties of our century, when poets, scholars, and critics rediscovered the Baroque and came to radically reassess the era.

By the time Jan Chryzostom Pasek sat down to write his *cursum vitae,* the Polish Commonwealth had already receded into the shadows of the international political arena. But it is no wonder that Pasek looked back over the half century of his life as at an epic in which he himself had taken heroic part. Great events had taken place, great battles had been fought and great victories won; but unfortunate decisions had been made too, and they had brought misery to his homeland. Grave slippages occurred in the seventeenth century in Pasek's corner of the

1. From a memorandum written by John Fowler, advocate of the fleet, in 1636. *Bulletin of the Institute of Historical Research,* vol. XLII, No.105 (May 1969) University of London, Athlone Press, p. 238.

world: central government was almost a fiction, the gentry's political power was slowly eroding, a Cossack revolt had threatened to explode the underlayer of society, territory was snatched from the flanks of the country, and despite a blaze of glory after the rescue of Vienna, prestige slid from the Polish crown.

Pasek's *Memoirs* span the reigns of three kings: Jan Kazimierz (1648-1668), Michal Korybut Wiśniowiecki (1669-1673), and Jan III Sobieski (1674-1696).

Jan Kazimierz (1648-1668). The first year of Jan Kazimierz's reign was also the first in a long series of disastrous events: the violent Cossack upheavals in the Ukraine were vigorously combated, but with tremendous losses in manpower and money. Not a decade passed before the next blow was delivered, this time from Charles Gustavus of Sweden in 1655.

At the time, owing to religious and economic differences, the gentry of the Commonwealth were at odds. The intolerant mood in the country was inclining Protestant dissenters to look for support to the Lutheran Swedes. Certain Polish magnates in the east were also hoping through Swedish help to recover their lost land, since even before the Swedish attack, Muscovy had begun to encroach upon Commonwealth territory, taking advantage of the Cossack disturbances.Hostilities had broken out in 1654 when the Cossacks recognized Muscovite sovereignty over the Ukraine. The Muscovites had advanced even as far as Grodno, but when the Swedes overran the Commonwealth, Muscovy, having no desire to see Sweden threatening her western borders, especially in Livonia, concluded a treaty with Poland.

"The Deluge," as the Swedish invasion is popularly called, inundated Wielkopolska and much of Małopolska (except for Gdańsk, Częstochowa, and Lwów). The rest of the Commonwealth was occupied by the Muscovites and the Cossacks. Charles Gustavus had designs for making Sweden the mistress of a northern empire comprising all the lands on the Baltic. Correctly advised by an embittered former vice-chancellor of Crown Poland, Hieronim Radziejowski, the Swedish monarch chose the right moment to strike, for the Commonwealth had been weakened by the Cossack upheavals in 1648.

The majority of the magnates and most of the gentry dependent upon them submitted immediately to Charles Gustavus. Those inclined to collaborate were mainly dissenters alienated by the activities of the Counter-Reformation; but even some Catholic clergy, led by certain members of the Episcopate, were to be found in the Swedish camp. The rest of the gentry felt unprepared to resist the forty thousand troops of the best army in Europe, trained and hardened in the Thirty Years' War, and besides, they assumed that the action would mean little more than a change of kings. (The pretext for the invasion had been to quench once and for all the Polish king's claim to the Swedish throne.) The rather casual stance of the gentry toward their king can be explained by their having effectively constrained the royal power. In the face of the defeatist attitude of the gentry, the Polish king, Jan Kazimierz, was forced to seek refuge in Silesia.

The vast expanse of their northern lands, to which few westerners journeyed, had tended to buffer the inhabitants of the Commonwealth from the wrenching changes and bloody conflicts that were occurring in the West, and from the persistent inroads made by the Turks in the south; but now the shock of defeat hit home. Not surprisingly, it was the lower strata of society — the petty gentry, the peasants, and the townsmen — who felt the most brutal impact of the Swedish invasion and rallied to resist what soon became clear to all as an act of common agression. Part of the army joined the civilian resistance, led by the brilliant commander Stefan Czarniecki, who conducted a foxy strategy of guerrilla warfare. Jan Kazimierz returned and the part of the army that had gone over to the Swedish side joined up with Czarniecki's forces in a unified action to drive out the invader. It is at this point that the *Memoirs* or what we possess of them, begin.

Sweden was counting on the Brandenburg Elector (promising Frederick Wilhelm Ducal Prussia, then held by him as a fief of the Polish Crown); Sweden was also counting on the Cossacks (to whom she was promising the Ukraine) and on the Prince of Transylvania, György II Rákóczi, who was to invade from the south and join forces with the Swedes. The Brandenburg Elector saw in the Commonwealth's weakness a chance to consolidate his own strength. He played a deliberately ambiguous role: as vassal of Poland, he was obliged to provide troops to the Commonwealth; but he also furnished troops to the Swedes, according to the terms of their alliance, with his own eye on the Polish throne. At the outset of the Deluge, Jan Kazimierz had officially promised Rákóczi support for his candidacy to the Polish throne and even assured him of success in return for assistance. (He promised the same to the Muscovite tsar in 1656.)

Charles Gustavus had not expected such intelligently improvised and energetic opposition as that which the lower orders demonstrated under Stefan Czarniecki and other gentry leaders. Luckily, the international situation also favored the Commonwealth's interests. Poland, by releasing Ducal Prussia to the Elector in 1657, convinced him to dissolve his alliance with Sweden. It was a high price to pay and Frederick Wilhelm gained considerably. Meanwhile, Györgi Rákóczi, who had decided to fight his way to the throne with the help of the Cossacks, was put to rout by his former friend, the Grand Marshal of

Crown Poland, Jerzy Lubomirski. Pasek gloats over this tragic campaign, mercilessly turning Rákóczi into a farcical caricature. The anecdote about his expedition to get "Polish garlic" is an obscure joke today, but it was a common one at the time. A fondness for political jokes has long been a Polish tradition.

The greatest help to the Commonwealth came from the Tartars, who paralyzed Cossack activities and smashed Rákóczi's forces. Austria honored her alliance with Poland by sending reinforcements in return for the revenues of the great salt mine at Wieliczka. Charles Gustavus rapidly withdrew to Denmark, while the Poles took over the fortresses occupied by the Swedish army, and Czarniecki's division, in which Jan Chryzostom Pasek figured, was sent to aid the Danes. The campaign against the Swedes lasted until 1660; the treaty of Oliva, signed that year, simply confirmed the status quo.

No sooner had the Swedes been driven out of the Commonwealth, but hostilities with the Muscovites flared up again because the magnates in the Ukraine were determined to recover their territories from the Cossacks, to whom Muscovy had given a guarantee of defense from Polish attacks. The combined Polish and Lithuanian armies brought off hard-won victories, but owing to Jan Kazimierz's embattlement with the Diet over fundamental reforms and the army's mutiny over their unpaid wages, the campaign against Muscovy was paralyzed at the decisive moments and victory brought no real results. By the terms of the truce that was finally concluded in 1667, the Ukraine was divided up and the Commonwealth's easternmost territories with Smolensk and Kiev were ceded to Muscovy.

After the shocking events of the forties and fifties, Jan Kazimierz earnestly sought to gain decisive influence over the Commonwealth's affairs, as did Jan III Sobieski later on. The central authority of the Commonwealth had been so curtailed on the domestic front that fragile alliances with rival magnate factions and with foreign powers provided the only arena for a royal policy. Only some magnates were won over; too many desired to see the central authority kept weak, because this allowed them to retain their wealth, power, and prestige.

During Jan Kazimierz's reign, France leaped at the opportunity to win an ally in the east who would form part of an encirclement of her rival, Austria, preventing further expansion. But France, who spent large sums of money to control the course of the Commonwealth's internal affairs, found her rivals, Austria, Russia, and Prussia, competing at the Commonwealth elections as well. During Pasek's lifetime, France, Austria, and Prussia each supported candidates to the Polish throne, but their rivalry canceled out each other's efforts, and none of their candidates succeeded at the Election Diets.

Aided by his astute and energetic French-born queen, "Ludwika Maria" (Marie-Louise Gonzaga), Jan Kazimierz attempted to strengthen monarchic power by his reform proposals to introduce a two-thirds majority vote in the Diet and to impose a regular tax levy on the gentry; he was also prepared to allow an election during his lifetime, which would in effect have secured the throne of the Commonwealth for the French candidate, de Condé. Largely owing to the queen, he also accepted aid from Louis XIV, who poured yearly subsidies into the coffers of pro-French magnates like Prażmowski, Pac, Sobieski, Sapieha, and Czarniecki.

A rival magnate faction, headed by Lubomirski and subsidized by Austria and Prussia, opposed the king's reform proposals and eventually formed a confederacy against the king and court which plunged the country into a two-year civil war (1665-1666) and ended by inflicting a bloody and costly defeat on the royal forces. The defeat of the king's plans by the pro-Hapsburg faction and the death of Marie-Louise inclined Jan Kazimierz to abdicate in 1668.

Lubomirski had been able to rally a large part of the gentry by a demogogic call to defend "Golden Freedom" from the threat of French absolutism; he also found allies among the army confederates, angry at the central authority over their unpaid wages.

Michał Wiśniowiecki (1669-1673). In a display of hostility toward foreign "intriguers" and an equally hostile gesture against the oligarchs of their own country, the gentry elected as their next king Michał Wiśniowiecki, the son of the governor of Ruthenia who had distinguished himself by winning several victories over the Cossacks in the Ukraine. The son, King Michał,was a pious incompetent, but he was unusually popular with the gentry. He allowed himself to be the passive tool of Hapsburg and Papal interests promoted by the clergy upon whom he relied entirely for advice. The interests of the Empire dictated that the Commonwealth should prevent Turkish expansion into Hapsburg dominions by involving itself in a war with the Turks and their Tartar subjects on the southern borders of the Commonwealth. This pro-Hapsburg policy angered the Turks and forced them into an agressive stance toward the Commonwealth to whom none of these involvements brought any real advantage. Instead they further depleted the treasury and brought more devastation to its territories in the southeast. The Commonwealth's internal difficulties encouraged Turkey to try a full-scale invasion in 1672. After a short siege, the chief fortress in the south, Kamieniec-Podolski, was taken, and the Turks were marching on Lwów when the Hetman (field commander) Jan Sobieski checked their advance and the Commonwealth was able to sue for peace. The disgrace of that treaty (by which Poland ceded the provinces of Podolia and Bracław and part of Kiev to Turkey and was also obliged to pay tribute) moved the gentry to raise troops with Sobieski in charge. The stunning victory of the Commonwealth forces under Sobieski at Chocim in 1673 decisively thwarted Turkey's design.

Jan III Sobieski (1674-1696). The conflict with Turkey brought to the surface a new leader in Hetman Jan Sobieski. After Chocim, Sobieski easily captured the throne, to which he was elected in 1674 after Michał's death. He delayed his coronation, however, in order to continue in his function of Grand Hetman, by which he strengthened his authority and popularity with the army and the gentry. The gentry admired him but were wary of his ambitions and his French connections. In any case, his tactic did not succeed because the international situation was unfavorable. Sobieski had sought to turn the Commonwealth's foreign policy to more advantageous goals, by seeking to recover Ducal Prussia from the Elector of Brandenburg with the aid of France, who was to persuade Turkey to restore the Commonwealth's lands; and with help from Sweden, who was to lead an armed attack against Prussia. But these plans went awry, and at home certain magnates, subsidized by Austria and Prussia, were plotting to depose Sobieski. Austria and the Papacy had a stake in seeing that the Commonwealth did not make peace with the Ottoman Empire; Austria wished to prevent a dangerous alliance which might involve her arch-enemy, France. Sobieski's unsuccessful Baltic policy marked the Commonwealth's last independent move on the international chessboard.

Since Turkey once more threatened the Commonwealth, Austria and the Papacy were urging Poland to continue the war against Turkey. The Commonwealth embarked on an exhausting campaign against the Turks, which saved the Hapsburg Empire and paved the way for Austria's invasion of Hungary, but which involved no such reciprocal aid for the Commonwealth.

To prepare for the campaign against Turkey, Sobieski tried to secure a peace treaty with Muscovy, but not until 1686 did he succeed, and when he did it was at the stiff price of renouncing all claims to the territories in the east previously ceded to Muscovy. He also formed an anti-Turkish league with Austria, the Papacy, and Venice which in the long run brought no advantage. A revolt in Hapsburg-ruled Hungary under Imre Thököly and an arms build-up in Turkey led the Emperor to make a speedy alliance with Poland. Sobieski's triumph over the Turks at Vienna in 1683 — as commander of the allied forces of the Empire, the German states, and Poland — was a brilliant flash of the old glory, but it remained an isolated gesture; it did not signal the beginning of a constructive new policy. Sobieski's further campaigns against the Turks to win back Kamieniec-Podolski in the south failed, although he did recover a sizable part of the Ukraine. In any case, he lost the precarious authority he had held over the gentry, who were impressed by single victories but unwilling to risk commitment to a monarch's long-range political designs. In this manner, the Commonwealth's destiny came to be determined by the activities of competitive factions of magnates and their relations with foreign powers.

The Military in the Commonwealth of Poland and Lithuania

In the Commonwealth as elsewhere in Europe, a determining factor of life in the seventeenth century was war, and the main concerns of the state were military and financial. To maintain an adequate defensive position against such strong adversaries on so many fronts required a very heavy military effort. Pasek's *Memoirs* tell us something of both the cost and the benefit to the individual of that effort.

How did the armed forces of the Commonwealth compare with other military powers of the seventeenth century? Unlike Austria, France, Russia, and Turkey, the Commonwealth, by the second half of seventeenth century, did not possess a large standing army of well-drilled mercenaries; it had no administrative office for conducting war, and no absolutely centralized authority to sustain a full-scale military operation of any duration or range. The reason for this should be sought in the political framework of the Commonwealth, within which it was impossible to build up an army of the size and calibre already common in Western Europe. France, for example — the strongest power in Europe — had by the 1670s a standing army of 120,000; Muscovy in 1651 had 133,000 and by the 1680s had 164,000. Turkey mobilized 150,000 in 1683. In contrast, the combined Polish and Lithuanian forces at no time numbered over 56,000 and the regular army, maintained on a fraction of the revenue from crown estates and employed to defend the southeastern borderlands of the Commonwealth against Tartar raids, was quite a modest force — never more than 25,000.

Lack of steady funds was the chief impediment to an adequate defense. Although expenses for the army made up 90 percent of the state budget, the actual figures are paltry: the total expenditure was one-thirtieth of France's, one-fifteenth of Turkey's, and one-half of Sweden's. The size, composition, and salary of the army depended on the Diet — that is, on the representatives of the gentry. Subject to change, the salary was reduced in peacetime, raised in wartime. Towns were not obliged to furnish supplies to the army. Writing of the year

1662, Pasek casts himself in the amusing role of righteous gentryman defending a town's rights against a company of soldiers in his charge.

Although the peasants were taxed to finance the army's campaigns, the gentry were exempt from furnishing supplies and billeting; more often than not, though, they supported the army without recompense when asked. (Pasek's sojourn at Strzała in 1660 is an example.) On the other hand, gentry estates were often subject to pillaging and plundering by the enemy or by dissatisfied elements of the Commonwealth's forces. By law, only crown estates were designated to feed and shelter the army.

Despite numerous attempts on the part of kings Jan Kazimierz and Jan III Sobieski to bring about reforms, such as a permanent tax for the subsidy of a permanent army, all of them failed on account of the gentry's unwillingness to jeopardize their privileges. Besides, together with the peasants, they were the mainstay of the economy as producers of wheat, and their presence was needed on the manors, which were suffering from a shortage of labor and the devastation of war.

As a result of continued decentralism and the economic crisis, the army had to operate on the principle of improvisation rather than long-term strategy. Pasek vividly illustrates such improvised planning in the battle scene at the Basia River, where the Poles used a brilliant strategem against the considerably larger Muscovite army — dressing up their camp servants as hussars and having them wait mounted behind a hill for a signal to charge out at full speed as if they were fresh reinforcements arriving. Without the funds to restore its fortresses, the Commonwealth allowed them to fall into neglect, in contrast to France and other absolutist monarchies, where new forts had been constructed and old ones modernized. Nor could the Commonwealth take proper advantage of the developing science of fortification, which increased the role of the infantry and artillery. The Commonwealth's armies still relied on the cavalry; they could not afford the very latest artillery pieces. Such glaring discrepancies make it clear that the Commonwealth was ill-prepared to meet the challenges presented by the massive power shifts in the seventeenth century. The tighter the absolute monarchies tied themselves to the twin-headed golden calf of finance and war, the looser became the threads of government in the land of 'Golden Freedom."

From the army's point of view, the irregular and delayed payment of wages, and the inadequacy of supplies and equipment, was an unjust and bitter requital for their brave service in battle and endurance of cruel hardships. The problem was eloquently aired before the senators in Grodno in 1661 by Pasek himself. The army revenged itself not only in the usual way by plunder and desertion, but also by organizing a kind of confederacy to obtain back wages and supplements (for losses of horses and arms). The confederacy meant outright refusal to obey the orders of Diet, king, hetman, and regular officers.

Military organization. The two armies of Poland and Lithuania constituted the armed forces of the Commonwealth. Although separately staffed and administered, they were organized along the same lines. To understand the complications of their structure, it is necessary to know that both armies included some troops who were responsible to the central authority (let us call them "federal troops"), some who were answerable to provincial authorities, and some who were accountable to private persons (magnates).

The core of the Commonwealth's armed forces was a permanent regular army of hired professionals, subject to the central authority. It was called the "Computable Army" because its salary was legislated by the Diet and varied according to the season and the resources of the crown treasury. In the first half of the century, it had been used mainly to defend the southern and eastern borderlands of the Commonwealth from Tartar raids, and rarely against any other adversary. After 1652, it was supplemented by troops provided by the provinces and districts and authorized by the district diets. The practice of recruiting district soldiers actually goes back to the sixteenth century, when certain regions had obtained permission to do so as an alternative to a general muster of the nobility. With time, the provinces were allowed to enlist these soldiers without agreement of the Diet. They were paid from taxes levied by the district dietines. Pasek regarded these "district soldiers" (for example, the "lads from Wielkopolska" in 1658) with some scorn.

The Computable Army was never large, but it did provide cadres of seasoned veterans, especially officers, for the formation of new, often quite large armies, recruited afresh for each military campaign. With the general reduction of the army in 1667, the Commonwealth launched the practice of keeping on as many veterans during winter as possible. This saved much time and money and enabled the government to reconstitute an army rapidly. The practice was adopted by France in the following year and subsequently by other Western European countries.

Besides the cavalry, which was allegedly recruited from the nobility and which will be discussed below, the central authority recruited two formations from the peasantry: the Drafted Infantry and the Field and Cottage Expeditionary Forces. For the Infantry, one peasant for every twenty cultivated fields from crown estates was drafted to serve in the district squadron at fixed times of the year. This was a permanent institution to ensure a minimum state of preparedness. The Field and Cottage Forces, called up by the Diet (or sometimes by a district dietine, if the force was to substitute for a general levy of the gentry), consisted of both Horse and Foot squadrons of peasants from crown, clerical, or gentry estates. The officers were usually experienced gentrymen selected by the dietines. The gentry were responsible for suitably arming, clothing, supplying, and putting up wages for their peasants. The soldiers of the Field and Cottage Forces formed the nucleus of the peasant guerrilla units who fought so successfully under Czarniecki against the Swedes in 1655. Later they formed the core of the new provincial armies, and finally they were incorporated into the Computable Army. These units were more prone to pillaging and desertion, since their rewards, if any, were minimal.

The Cossacks formed a separate federal force. Since most of them had rebelled in 1648 and fled to Muscovite-controlled territory, they were no longer on the Commonwealth's regular payroll. Those who came back, however, were connected loosely to the Commonwealth's forces and employed to fight the Turks and Tartars, while others were placed in the Computable Army. They were maintained on a small wage and deliveries of cloth.

The fifth formation of federal troops (and the country's last resort) was the General Levy of the Gentry. The king called up a General Levy several times in the second half of the seventeenth century (1655, 1657, 1672). Landed non-nobles as well as landless gentry were also obliged to serve with larger or smaller retinues according to their means.

In addition to the five formations responsible to the central authority, local authorities and even private individuals could raise troops. Provincial or district detachments of Horse and Foot, paid for out of provincial treasuries, were often sent to assist the state's armies, but their availability remained within the control of the local dietines. After six months they could be joined to the Computable Army. Castle towns raised small detachments of hired mercenaries to keep order in an emergency; other rich and sizable towns enlisted special independent detachments for such purposes. (Gdańsk and Lwów did so in 1655). The wealthiest magnates, those with many vast demesnes, were required to contribute a certain number of permanent troops for the needs of the state; usually, they were employed to protect the strongholds on these estates (for example, Zamość, where the Swedish general Wittemberg was imprisoned in 1656). Both clerical and lay magnates also kept private armies of Horse and Foot not subject to any legislation. In the second half of the century, the size of private armies decreased because of the loss of territory in the Ukraine, where until the rebellion several thousands of Cossacks had filled their ranks.

Foreign vassals also provided troops (for example, Courland and Prussia). Although Prussia was released from Polish suzerainty in 1657, the Elector was still required to supply 1500 men if asked. Finally, the king possessed a private army, the Royal Guard, limited by the Diet to 1200 Horse and Foot, which functioned as a bodyguard during military campaigns.

Both Polish and Lithuanian armies were organized into two separate contingents, the "Polish Contingent" and the 'Foreign Contingent," which allowed for a combination of Western and native tactics. The king, who was supreme commander of the combined armed forces, appointed for life two commanders-in-chief, called Grand Hetmans, and two Field Hetmans, one each for Crown Poland and Lithuania. The four hetmans, who were extremely powerful in the seventeenth century, were in charge of the four basic groups of the Commonwealth's core army. Field Hetmans were not subordinate to the Grand Hetmans even when the armies were combined. The Grand Hetman took precedence only in dignity of rank. Only the Grand Hetman of Crown Poland, however, was empowered to enter into diplomatic negotiations; he was responsible for the Commonwealth's policy toward the Tartars, Moldavia, Wallachia (present-day Rumania), Transylvania, and Turkey. Most hetmans were representatives of great magnate families (Potocki and Lubomirski, for example). Stefan Czarniecki, an exception, came from the middle gentry. Like other hetmans, he was also governor of Ruthenia, a high civilian dignity which gave him a seat in the Senate. Pasek usually refers to him as "the Governor." Before he became hetman he was called "the Commandant," a vague title applicable to different functions in different periods. In Czarniecki's case, it designated his appointment by Jan Kazimierz to lead his own division of the army, independently of the control of the hetmans. But, as Pasek says, he was virtually a third hetman. Among the other higher officers were: the Muster-Master General, who kept track of the army's numbers, the General of the Artillery, the General of the Infantry, the Quartermaster, the Surgeon-General, the Architect General, and, in the 1670s, the Master of the Watch, in charge of military discipline, and the Master of the Camp, responsible for the position and layout of the camp

The "Foreign Contingent" consisted of both Horse (the *reiters*) and Foot (the dragoons). Modeled on the Holy Roman Emperor's army, it incorporated the latest Swedish reforms — that is, it was built on the principle of small units of six soldiers grouped by threes or fours into three corporalships; five to ten corporalships composed a division headed by a colonel *(oberster)* or lieutenant-colonel *(oberster-leutenant)* with a staff of officers who were usually foreign. The rankers were mostly peasants from the Commonwealth. They were armed with muskets, sometimes with pikes. In the *Memoirs* we encounter several officers from the Foreign Contingent, for example, Colonel Tedtwin of Livonia, an officer of the dragoons at the battle of Kolding. The dragoons could function either as light cavalry or as foot soldiers. In battle they were often used as infantry. They were appreciated as an excellent firing support for the cavalry in quick maneuvres and played a large role in the Swedish wars. Their main weapon was the musket or other heavy handgun, but they sometimes carried swords, axes, and even grenades. There were many smaller units and independent dragoon companies assigned to larger units — for example, the Scottish Foot.

The "Polish Contingent" also comprised Horse and Foot, but the Horse was dominant. In both, the squadron was the basic tactical and organizational unit. The structure of the Polish cavalry still retained its feudal character; basically, it was organized like a fraternal order of fellows, equal by birth and title, each of whom brought with him a retinue of one or more men, a horse, arms if possible, and some supplies. These cavaliers, by right of their traditional privileges, could opt to form a confederacy and refuse to fight further until their demands were met.

There were two types of Polish cavaliers: the Hussars ("hussar" is a Hungarian word) and the Gentlemen of the Horse *(towarzysze pancerni)*. The Hussars were organized into heavily armored squadrons of 100 to 200, though by mid-century they were wearing only a half-suit of armor and by Sobieski's time they adopted the more flexible scale-type armor. For weapons they carried lances, sabres, and swords; during the seventies they began to use firearms. An imposing sight at any time, the Hussars in full charge were terrifying, with roaring wings mounted in long, wooden cylinders which they fastened on their backs and leopard or lynx skins thrown over their chests. The most expensive squadrons to equip, they made up only 5 to 7 percent of the army until the seventies and eighties during the wars with Turkey when their number gradually increased to as much as 22 percent of the entire army.

Most numerous were the Gentlemen of the Horse. Organized into medium-armored squadrons of 100, they wore coats of mail and carried bows, pistols, or muskets. Being a more versatile force, they were able to function well in various types of combat; they were especially useful against the Turkish and Tartar cavalry. It was to this type of cavalry formation that Pasek belonged.

Yet a third type of cavalry in the "Polish Contingent" proved very useful during the war with Russia and at the turn of the century on the southern borderlands — the light cavalry. It consisted mainly of Tartar and Wallachian troops organized into squadrons of 60 to 100. By far the least costly type, each member brought with him a horse and either no retinue or one or two men. They used bows, but more and more frequently also firearms.

The ratio between Horse and Foot in the Polish Contingent was about one to one (except in the 1650s, when great losses of men in the Cossack Wars and financial difficulties drastically reduced the numbers of foot soldiers). The small ratio, compared to Western European armies, was due to the mobile nature of the traditional enemy (the Tartars), with whom the Commonwealth Armies had most frequently to deal on the borderlands; besides, the territorial vastness of the Commonwealth and the small number of strongholds made the cavalry a necessity. The squadrons of Foot, like the dragoons in the Foreign Contingent, carried muskets, maces, swords, or axes and were accompanied by a small orchestra of drums, flutes, and fifes. They were used mostly in sieges and in the defense of fortified places.

On a limited scale, both Poland and Lithuania had their own artillery corps protected by special units of infantry and dragoons who also constructed the earthworks.

National and Social Composition. By the mid-seventeenth century both armies were mainly national in composition. In general, more Poles served in foreign armies than did foreigners in the armies of the Commonwealth. After 1660, under pressure from the gentry, foreigners were dropped from the cavalry rolls, although foreign officers remained. The number of non-Poles in the infantry diminished as well. In the seventies Sobieski "nationalized" the army completely.

The reasons for the gradual ousting of foreigners from the Commonwealth armies were financial and political. The gentry considered foreign mercenaries, whether horse or foot, too costly; they also frowned upon their absolutist views and saw them as a threat to the Old Polish way of life, especially to "Golden Freedom." After the heavy losses of the Cossack Wars, a steady flow of Moldavians, Wallachians, and Tartars entered the Commonwealth and filled the ranks of the light cavalry squadrons in the Polish Contingent. The Hussars and Gentlemen of the Horse remained almost wholly Polish. The Polish army contained the greatest number of foreigners during the Swedish Wars, when hostages from the Brandenburg and Swedish armies were incorporated into the *reiters*; Germans predominated but one also found Scots, English, Italians, and French.

By the time Pasek was enlisting, the plebeian element had come to dominate in all three types of cavalry (traditionally composed of nobility alone). The retainers of a Hussar or Gentleman of the Horse were, by and large, peasants; a few were poor gentry. As long as one served for a wage in the Polish Contingent — as an armed horseman with an officer's rank, a noble lineage, and Polish blood — he was by every right a "fellow," a "cavalier," a brother, an equal. The structure of the army mirrored the patterns of political life. Squadron councils duplicated in the field the district dietines at home — that is, they functioned as extensions of the ruling class, which explains their reluctance to admit foreign or plebeian elements. Although the nobility made up, in fact, only about 20 percent of the Polish-Lithuanian forces, their power was greatest. Only "fellow" cavaliers — that is, noblemen — sat in the squadron assemblies where they elected deputies; these deputies went before the Royal Wage Commission to demand payment of back wages, and brought the money back to the commanders, by whom it was then divided among the "fellows," who in turn were obliged to provide means to their retainers. (Often the "fellows" kept a tight purse; even the retainer's booty could become the property of his gentleman.) Besides having no voice in the squadron meetings, retainers in the Polish Contingent were sworn to absolute obedience. In the Foreign Contingent, the rank and file were even more exploited by their officers, who were often foreign. This situation, needless to say, led to frequent pillaging and harassment of the civilian population.

Magnates often functioned only as titular commanders; in practice, they designated a veteran lieutenant, who might be a gentryman or a peasant, to lead their squadron. On the other hand, the magnates were quite capable of manipulating the cavalry's dissatisfaction over unpaid wages as a political weapon against the king — by incitement to confederacy (as in 1661), or even to civil war (as did Lubomirski). The troops in the Foreign Contingent, which, except for higher officers, were mostly plebeian in character, took little part in confederacies; the officers were careerists (foreigners, Polonized townsmen, gentry), while the soldier-peasants were habituated to blind obedience.

It is understandable that Pasek, the son of an impoverished gentryman, felt entitled to castigate the magnates in his Grodno speeches and elsewhere. Unlike his fellow cavaliers, Pasek remained loyal to King Jan Kazimierz. In refusing to join the confederacy of 1661, he revealed a shrewd political instinct, suspecting, rightly, manipulation of the army's discontent by certain magnates for their own ends. Perhaps he was hoping, too, for a reward from the king for his loyalty. The Grodno speeches, not without a certain grandeur and pathos, and with even a touch of humor, expressed what the average gentryman considered a justifiable hostility to those senators, those magnates who cared more for foreign gold and foreign sights than the well-being of their homeland. Less sound, it seems, was Pasek's boundless admiration for Czarniecki. Had he lived, Pasek chose to believe, Czarniecki would have put an end to the intrigues and strife which eventually compelled Jan Kazimierz to abdicate; in reality, Czarniecki was himself receiving 12,000 francs a year from the French party. But one can look with indulgence upon Pasek's hero-worship, after his having shared so many brilliant campaigns with Czarniecki and apparently having been fully appreciated by the Polish commander.

Pasek's war stories and soldier's tales can be appreciated for more than their literary skill; they are also valued by Polish historians for their wealth of military detail. To Pasek's credit, he does not, on the whole, give a generalized overview of battles (except for small-scale clashes such as Kolding and Mątwy), but a personal, fragmentary, soldier's eye-view. The geography, the dates, the size of armies may be off, but Pasek had a sharp eye and and excellent memory for the concrete and the specific, as well as for his fellow cavaliers and for other individual squadrons, most of which has been verified.

Index of Personal Names

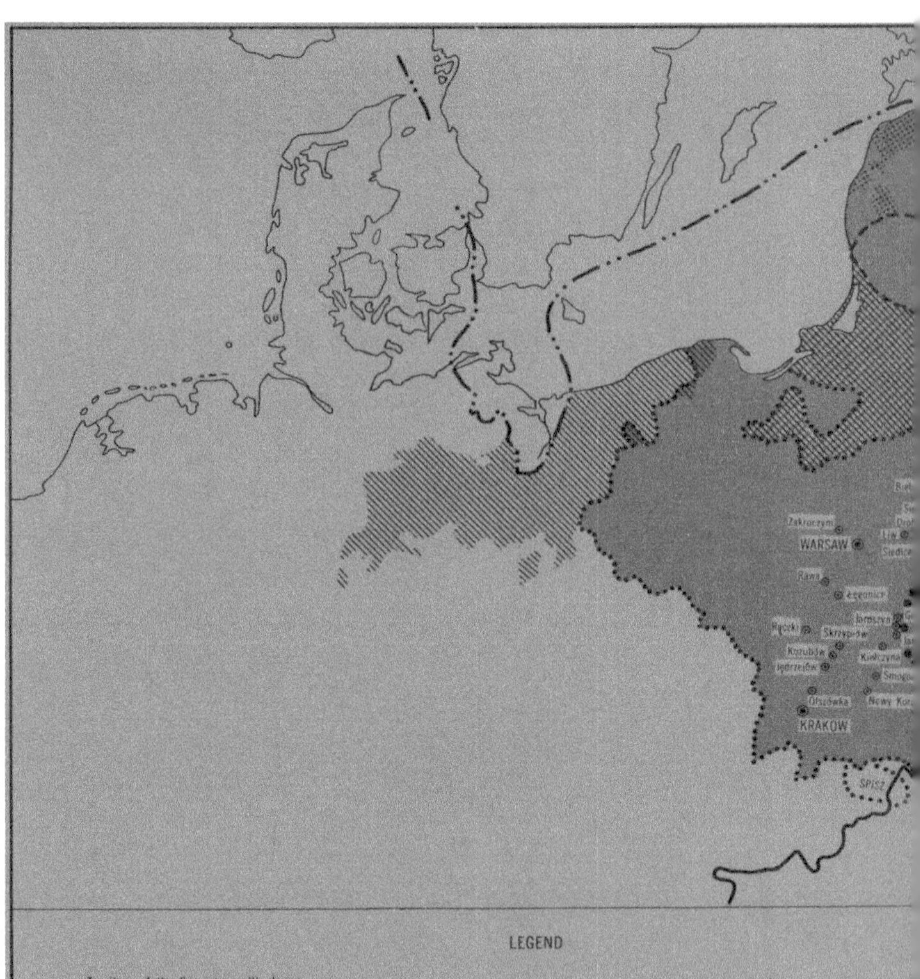

LEGEND

Territory of the Commonwealth during election of Jan Kazimierz (1648)

Crown Poland

Grand Duchy of Lithuania

Courland and Livonia

Ducal Prussia, Vassal State

Areas affected by Cossack uprising under Chmielnicki (1648-1654)

Furthest extent of Muscovite and Cossack military activity in the years 1654-1656

Boundaries of Sweden after Peace of Oliva (166

Brandenburg after 1657

Area of the Commonwealth established by the Pea in 1660, the Treaty of Andruszów in 1667, and the of Grzymułtowski in 1686. (until the first Partiti

Boundaries of Turkey after the Treaty of Buczacz in 1672

Provincial and smaller towns

Major City

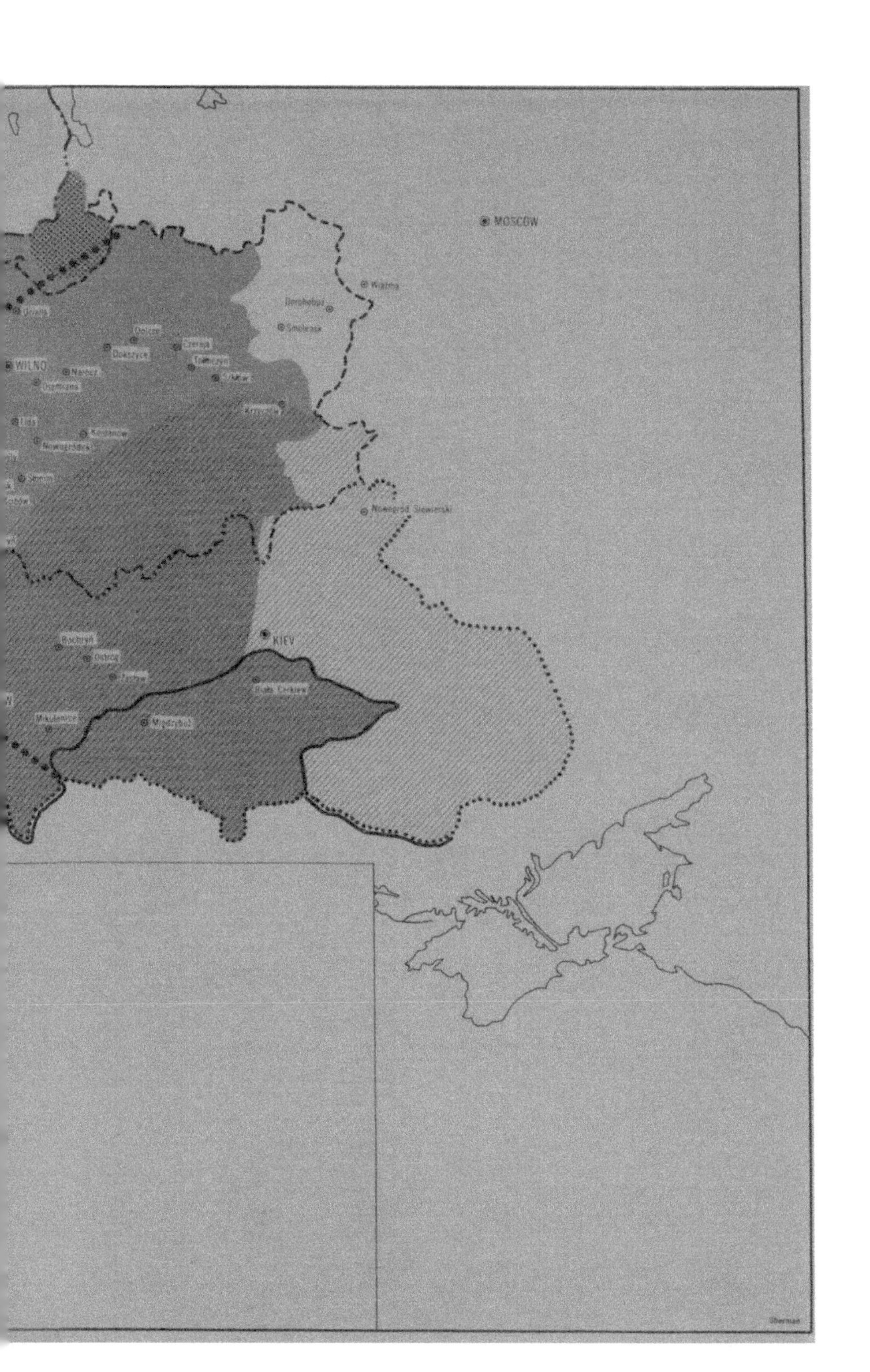
MOSCOW
Smolensk
WILNO
Lida
Nowogród Siewierski
KIEV
Ostróg

Sweden
Denmark
NORTH SEA
AARHUS
Ebeltoft 1659
Kolding 1658
Frederiks Odde 1659
COPENHAGEN
Als 1658
Fyn 1659
BALTIC SEA
GDAŃSK
MALBORK
Prussia
HAMBURG
AMSTERDAM
Oder R.
Vistula R.
Noteć R.
TORUŃ
BERLIN
Brandenburg
POZNAŃ
Gniezno 1656
Mątwy 1666
WARSAW 1656
ŁOWICZ
Warka 1656
Pilica R.
Warta R.
RADOM
WROCŁAW (BRESLAU)
Silesia
CZĘSTOCHOWA
KIELCE
PIŃCZÓW
SANDOMIERZ
PRAGUE
Vistula
KRAKÓW
Bohemia
Moravia
VIENNA 1683
Parkany 1683
Esztergom 1683
Seczyn 1683
BUDAPEST
Hungary
LEGEND
Major City
Major City and Fortress
Fortress
Fortress and Battle Site
Battle Site
Major City, Fortress and Battle Site
Modern Political Boundary
Co To the Empire
Li To the Ottoman Empire
VENICE
ADRIATIC SEA
ROME

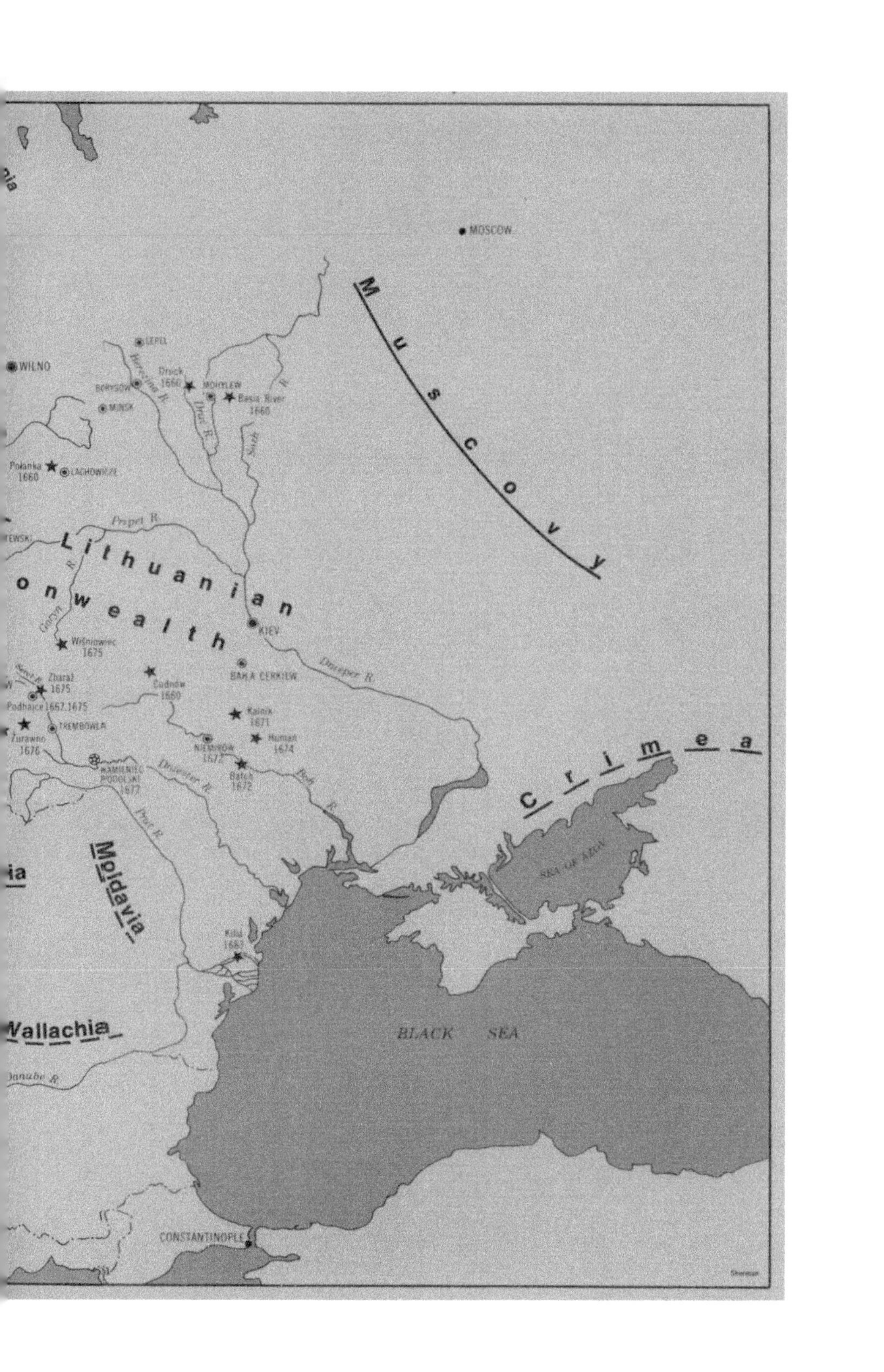

MOSCOW
Muscovy
LEPEL
WILNO
BORYSÓW
Druck 1660
MOHYLEW
Basia River 1660
MINSK
Drut R.
Połanka 1660
LACHOWICZE
Prypeć R.
Lithuanian
onwealth
KIEV
Wiśniowiec 1675
Zbaraż 1675
Cudnów 1660
BIAŁA CERKIEW
Dnieper R.
Podhajce 1667.1675
TREMBOWLA
Kalnik 1671
Humań 1674
Żurawno 1676
NIEMIRÓW 1672
Batoh 1672
Dniester R.
Bug R.
Prut R.
Moldavia
Crimea
SEA OF AZOV
Kilia 1683
Wallachia
Danube R.
BLACK SEA
CONSTANTINOPLE

Printed in the USA
CPSIA information can be obtained
at www.ICGtesting.com
LVHW041042010823
754054LV00004B/77